What Will People Say?: A Novel

Rupert Hughes

WHAT WILL PEOPLE SAY?

A NOVEL
BY
RUPERT HUGHES

ILLUSTRATED

GROSSET & DUNLAP
PUBLISHERS : - : NEW YORK

Published by arrangement with Harper & Brothers

ILLUSTRATIONS

WHAT
WILL PEOPLE SAY?

CHAPTER I

FIFTH AVENUE at flood-tide was a boiling surf of
automobiles. But at nearly every corner a policeman succeeded where King Canute had failed, and checked
the sea or let it pass with a nod or a jerk of thumb.

The young army officer just home-come from the
Philippines felt that he was in a sense a policeman himself, for he had spent his last few years keeping savage
tribes in outward peace. When he was away or asleep
the Moros rioted at will. And so the traffic-officer of this
other extreme of civilization kept these motor-Moros in
orderly array only so long as he kept them in sight.

One glare from under his vizor brought the millionaire's limousine to a sharp stop, or sent it shivering back
into position. But once the vista ahead was free of uniforms all the clutches leaped to the high; life and limb
were gaily jeopardized, and the most appalling risks run
with ecstasy.

The law of New York streets and roads forbids a car
to commit at any time a higher speed than thirty miles an
hour; and never a man that owns one but would blush
to confess it incapable of breaking that law.

As Lieutenant Forbes watched the surge of automobiles

from the superior height of a motor-bus it amused him to see how little people lose of the childhood spirit of truancy and adventure. All this grown-up, sophisticated world seemed to be run like a school, with joyous deviltry whenever and wherever the teacher's back was turned, but woe to whoso was caught; every one winking at guilt till authority detected it, then every one solemnly approving the punishment.

Mr. Forbes had not seen Fifth Avenue since the pathetic old horse-coaches were changed to the terrific motor-stages. He had not seen the Avenue since it was widened —by the simple process of slicing off the sidewalks and repairing their losses at the expense of the houses. The residences on both sides of the once so stately corridor looked to him as if a giant had drawn a huge carving-knife along the walls, lopping away all the porticos, columns, stoops, and normal approaches, and leaving the inhabitants to improvise such exits as they might.

The splendid façade of the Enslee home had suffered pitifully. He remembered how the stairway had once come down from the vestibule to the street with the sweeping gesture of a hand of welcome. Now the door was knee-deep in the basement, and the scar of the sealed-up portal was not healed above.

The barbarity of the assault along the line had not apparently relieved the choke of traffic. Or else the traffic had swollen more fiercely still, as it usually does in New York at every attempt in palliation.

As far as Forbes could see north and south the roadway was glutted from curb to curb with automobiles. And their number astonished him even less than their luxury. The designers had ceased to mimic hansoms, broughams, and victorias following invisible horses ridiculously. They had begun to create motors pure and simple, built to contain and follow and glorify their own engines.

Many of the cars were gorgeously upholstered, Aladdin's divans of comfort and speed; and some of them were decorated with vases of flowers. Their surfaces were lustrous and many-colored, sleekly tremendous. They had not yet entirely outgrown the imitation of the wooden frame, and their sides looked frail and satiny, unfit for rough usage, and sure to splinter at a shock. But he knew that they were actually built of aluminum or steel, burnished and enameled.

What he did not know was that the people in them, lolling relaxed, and apparently as soft of fiber as of skin, were not the weaklings they looked. They, too, like their cars, only affected fatigue and ineptitude, for they also were built of steel, and their splendid engines were capable of velocities and distances that would leave a gnarled peasant gasping.

This was one of the many things he was to learn.

From his swaying eery he seemed to be completely lost in a current of idle wealth. The throng, except for the chauffeurs, the policemen, and a few men whose trades evidently fetched them to this lane of pleasure—the throng was almost altogether women. And to Forbes' eye, unused to city standards, almost all the women were princesses.

At first, as his glance fell on each radiant creature, his heart would cry: "There is one I could love! I never shall forget her beauty!" And before the vow of eternal memory was finished it was forgotten for the next.

By and by the show began to pall because it would not end. As peers become commonplace at a royal court, since there is nothing else there, so beauty canceled itself here by its very multitude. For the next mile only the flamboyantly gorgeous or the flamboyantly simple beauty caught his overfed eye. And then even these were lost in the blur of a kaleidoscope twirled too fast.

There was one woman, however, that he could not forget, because he could not find out what she was like. In the slow and fitful progress up the Avenue it chanced that his stage kept close in the wake of an open landaulet.

3

The stage never fell far behind, and never quite won alongside.

A young woman was alone in the tonneau. At least, he judged that she was young, though his documents were scant. Her head was completely hidden from his view by a hat that was just exactly big enough to accomplish that work of spite.

It was a sort of inverted flower-pot of straw—one of those astonishing millinery jokes that women make triumphs of. It bore no ornament at all except a filmy white bird-of-paradise feather stuck in the center of the top and spraying out in a shape that somehow suggested an interrogation-mark.

Even a man could see that it was a beautiful plume and probably expensive. It had a sort of success of impudence, alone there, and it mocked Forbes by trailing along ahead of him, an unanswerable query.

He grew eager and more eager to see what flower-face was hidden under that overturned straw flower-pot of a hat.

Now and then, as the stage pushed forward, he would be near enough to make out the cunning architecture of the mystery's left shoulder and the curious felicity of her left arm. Seen thus detached, they fascinated him and kindled his curiosity. By and by he was swept near enough to glimpse one rounded knee crossed over the other, and one straight shin creasing a tight skirt, and a high-domed instep, and the peak of one slim shoe.

And once, when the traffic was suddenly arrested, he was close enough to be wildly tempted to bend down and snatch off that irritating hat. He would have learned at least the color of her hair, and probably she would have lifted her startled face to view like a reverted rose. He was a fearless soldier, but he was not so daring as all that. Still, he heard her voice as she gossiped to a momentary neighbor who raised his hat in a touring-car held up abeam her own.

Her voice did not especially please him; it was almost shrill, and it had the metallic glitter of the New York voice. Her words, too, were a trifle hard, and as unpoetic as possible.

"We had a rotten time," she said. "I was bored stiff. You ought to have been there."

And then she laughed a little at the malice implied. The policeman's whistle blew and the cars lurched forward. And the stage lumbered after them like a green hippopotamus. Forbes began to feel a gnawing anxiety to see what was under that paradise feather. He assumed that beauty was there, though he had learned from shocking experiences how dangerous it is to hope a woman beautiful because the back of her head is of good omen.

It became a matter of desperate necessity to overtake that will-o'-the-wisp chauffeur and observe his passenger. Great expectations seemed to be justified by the fact that nearly every policeman saluted her and smiled so pleasantly and so pleasedly that the smile lingered after she was far past.

Forbes noted, too, that the people she bowed to in other cars or on the sidewalk seemed to be important people, and yet to be proud when her hat gave a little wren-like nod in their directions.

At Fifty-first Street, in front of the affable gray Cathedral, there was a long and democratic delay while a contemptuous teamster, perched atop a huge steel girder, drove six haughty stallions across the Avenue; drove them slowly, and puffed deliberate smoke in the face of the impatient aristocracy.

Here a dismounted mounted policeman paced up and down, followed by a demure horse with kindly eyes. This officer paused to pass the time of day with the mysterious woman, and the horse put his nose into the car and accepted a caress from her little gloved hand. Again Forbes heard her voice:

"You poor old dear, I wish I had a lump of sugar."

It was to the horse that she spoke, but the officer answered:

"The sight of you, ma'am, is enough for um."

Evidently he came from where most policemen come from. The lady laughed again. She was evidently not afraid of a compliment. But the policeman was. He blushed and stammered:

"I beg your pairdon, Miss—"

He gulped the name and motioned the traffic forward. Forbes was congratulating himself that at least she was not "Mrs." Somebody, and his interest redoubled just as the young woman leaned forward to speak to her chauffeur. She had plainly seen that there was a policeless space ahead of her, for the driver put on such speed that he soon left Forbes and his stage far in the rear.

Forbes, seeing his prey escaping, made a mental note of the number of her car, "48150, N. Y. 1913."

He had read how the police traced fugitive motorists by their numerals, and he vowed to use the records for his own purposes. He must know who she was and how she looked. Meanwhile he must not forget that number—48150, N. Y. 1913—the mystic symbol on her chariot of translation.

CHAPTER II

HELPLESS to pursue her with more than his gaze, Forbes watched from his lofty perch how swiftly she fled northward. He could follow her car as it thridded the unpoliced traffic by that dwindling bird-of-paradise plume, that sphinxic riddle of a feathery question-mark.

He mused indulgently upon her as she vanished: "She breaks the law like all the rest when no one is there to stop her. She wheedles the police with a smile, but behind their backs she burns up the road."

Evidently there were narrow escapes from disaster. One or two pedestrians leaped like kangaroos to escape her wheels. Once or twice collisions with other cars were avoided by sharp swerves or abrupt stops.

The plume went very respectably across the Plaza, for policemen were there on fixed post; but, once beyond, the feather diminished into nothingness with the uncanny speed of a shooting-star.

She was gone. And now he wondered whither she sped, and why. To what tryst was she hastening at such dreadful pace, with such rash desire? He felt almost a jealousy, at least an envy, of the one who waited at the rendezvous.

And then he felt alarm for her. Already she might have met disaster. Her car might have crashed into some other—into a great steel-girder truck like that that crossed the Avenue. She might even now be lying all crumpled and shattered in a tangle of wreckage.

That taunting white question-feather might be dabbled with red. The face might be upturned to any man's

7

view and every man's horror. He was almost afraid to follow farther lest his curiosity be more than sated.

His irresolution was solved for him. The stage was turning out of Fifth Avenue, to cross over to Broadway and Riverside Drive. Forbes was not done with this lane. He rose to leave the bus. It lurched and threw him from bench to bench. He negotiated with difficulty the perilous descent, clutched the hand-rail in time to save himself from pitching head first to the street, clambered down the little stairway with ludicrous awkwardness, stepped on solid asphalt with relief, and walked south.

The press gradually thickened, and before long it was dense and viscid, as if theater audiences were debouching at every corner.

The stream was still almost entirely woman: beautiful woman at the side of beautiful woman, or treading on her high heels; chains of womankind like strings of beaded pearls, hordes of women, dressed in infinite variations of the prevailing mode. They strode or dawdled, laughing, smiling, bowing, whispering, or gazing into the windows of the shops.

The panorama of windows was nearly as beautiful as the army of women. The great show-cases, dressed with all expertness, were silently proffering wares that would tempt an empress to extravagance.

A few haberdashers displayed articles of strange gorgeousness for men—shirt-patterns and scarves, bath-robes, waistcoats that rivaled Joseph's; but mainly the bazars appealed to women or to the men who buy things for women.

The windows seemed to say: "How can you carry your beloved past my riches, or go home to her without some of my delights?" "How fine she would look in my folds!" "How well my diamonds would bedeck her hair or her bosom! If you love her, get me for her!" "It is shameful of you to pretend not to see me, or to confess to poverty! Couldn't you borrow money somewhere to buy me? Couldn't you postpone the rent or some other debt awhile? Perhaps I could be bought on credit."

Show-windows and show-women were the whole cry. The women seemed to be wearing the spoils of yesterday's pillage, and yet to yearn for to-morrow's. Women gowned like manikins from one window gazed like hungry paupers at another window's manikins.

The richness of their apparel, the frankness of their allure were almost frightful. They seemed themselves to be shop-windows offering their graces for purchase or haughtily labeling themselves "sold." Young or antique, they appeared to be setting themselves forth at their best, their one business a traffic in admiration.

"Look at me! Look at me!" they seemed to challenge, one after another. "My face is old, but so is my family." "My body is fat, but so is my husband's purse!" "I am not expensively gowned, but do I not wear my clothes well?" "I am young and beautiful and superbly garbed, and I have a rich husband." "I am only a little schoolgirl, but I am ready to be admired, and my father buys me everything I want." "I am leading a life of sin, but is not the result worth while?" "My husband is slaving down-town to pay the bills for these togs, but are you not glad that I did not wait till he could afford to dress me like this?"

Lieutenant Forbes had been so long away from a metropolis, and had lived in such rough countries, that he perhaps mistook the motives of the women of New York, and their standards, underrated their virtues. Vice may go unkempt and shabby, and a saint may take thought of her appearance. Perhaps what he rated as boldness was only the calm of innocence; what he read as a command to admire may have been only a laudable ambition to make the best of one's gifts.

But to Forbes there was an overpowering fleshliness in the display. It reminded him of the alleged festivals of Babylon, where all the women piously offered themselves

9

to every passer-by and rated their success with heaven by their prosperity with strangers.

It seemed to him that the women of other places than New York must have dressed as beautifully, but in an innocenter way. Here the women looked not so much feminine as female. They appeared to be thinking amorous thoughts. They deployed their bosoms with meaning; their very backs conveyed messages. Their clothes were not garments, but banners.

He had dwelt for years among half-clad barbarians, unashamed Igorrotes; but these women looked nakeder than those. The more studiously they were robed, the less they had on.

A cynicism unusual to his warm and woman-worshiping soul crept into Forbes' mind. He went along philosophizing:

"All these women are paid for by men. For everything that every one of these women wears some man has paid. Fathers, husbands, guardians, keepers, dead or alive, have earned the price of all this pomp.

"The men who pay for these things are not here: they are in their offices or shops or at their tasks somewhere, building, producing; or in their graves resting from their labors, while the spendthrift sex gads abroad squandering and flaunting what it has wheedled.

"What do the women give in return? They must pay something. What do they pay?"

CHAPTER III

HE brooded like a sneering Satan for a time upon the meaning of the dress-parade, and then the glory of it overpowered him again. He felt that it would be a hideous world without its luxuries. It was well, he concluded, that men should dig for gold, dive for pearls, climb for aigrets, penetrate the snows for furs, breed worms for silk, build looms, and establish shops—all in order that the she half of the world should bedeck itself.

The scarlet woman on the beast, the pink girl with the box of chocolates, the white matron, the widow in the most costly and becoming weeds—they were all more important to the world than any other of man's institutions, because they were pretty or beautiful or in some way charming—as useless, yet as lovely as music or flowers or poetry.

He was soon so overcrowded with impressions that he could not arrange them in order. He could only respond to them. The individual traits of this woman or that, swaggering afoot or reclining in her car, smote him. Every one of them was a Lorelei singing to him from her fatal cliff, and his heart turned from the next to the next like a little rudderless boat.

Each siren rescued him from the previous, but the incessant impacts upon his senses rendered him to a glow of wholesale enthusiasm. He rejoiced to be once more in New York. He began to wish to know some of these women.

It was apparent that many of them were ready enough to extend their hospitality. Numbers of them—beautiful ones, too, and lavishly adorned—had eyes like grappling-hooks. Their glances were invitations so pressingly urged that they inspired opposition. They expressed contempt in advance for a refusal. But men easily find strength to resist such invitations and such contempt.

It was not in these tavern-like hearts that Forbes would seek shelter. He wanted to find some attractive, some decently difficult woman to make friends with, make love to. He was heart-free, and impatient for companionship.

When a man is a soldier, an officer, and young, well-made and well-bred, it is improbable that he will remain long without opportunity of adventure.

The woman of the bird-of-paradise feather was buried in Forbes' mind as deeply as if a balcony full of matinée girls had collapsed upon her. Forbes fell in love at first sight a hundred and fifty times on the Avenue. Had he met any one of that cohort again under favoring auspices he might have found in her arms the response he sought. It might have brought him tragic unrest, or the sort of home comfort that makes no history.

Perhaps he did meet some of these potential sweethearts later; but if he did, he could not remember them and he did not heed them, for he was by then involved inextricably with the one he had hunted for and lost.

When he found her he did not remember her any more than the others. She impressed him as a woman of extreme fragility, yet she was to test his strength to its utmost, his endurance, his courage, his readiness for hazard.

He had won a name among brave men for caution in approaching danger, for bravery in the midst of it, and for agility in extricating himself from ambush and trap. This most delicate lady was to teach him to be reckless, foolhardy, maladroit. She would wear him out in the pursuit of happiness and disgust him with his profession, with himself and her. Under her tutelage he would run through scenes of splendor and scale the heights of excitement. He would know beauty and pleasure and intrigue and peril. He would know everything but repose, contentment, and peace. He would love her and hate her, abhor her and adore her, be her greatest friend and enemy, and she his.

At his first meeting with her he pursued her without knowing who she was and without overtaking her. And she, not knowing she was pursued, unconsciously teased him by keeping just out of his reach and denying him the glimpse of her face.

Perhaps it would have been better for both if they had never come nearer together than in that shadowy, that foreshadowing game of hide-and-seek in the full sun among the throngs.

Perhaps it was better that they should meet and endure the furnace of emotions and superb experiences in gorgeous scenes.

But, whether for better or worse, they did meet, and their souls engaged in that grapple of mutual help and harm that we call love.

The world heard much of them, as always, and inevitably misunderstood and misjudged, ignoring what justified them, not seeing that their most flippant moments were their most important and that when they seemed most to sin they were clutching at their noblest crags of attainment.

It is such fates as theirs that make the human soul cry aloud for a God to give it understanding, to give it another chance in a better world. The longing is so fierce that it sometimes becomes belief. But while we wait for that higher court it is the province of story-tellers to play at being juster judges than the popular juries are.

Meanwhile Forbes was unsuspicious of the future, and unaware of nearly everything except heart-fag and foot-weariness.

When he returned to his hotel he was a tourist who has done too much art-gallery. Fifth Avenue had been an ambulant Louvre of young mistresses, not of old masters.

WHAT WILL PEOPLE SAY?

He crept into a tub of water as hot as he could endure, and simmered there, smoking the ache out of him, and imagining himself as rich as Haroun al Raschid, instead of a poor subaltern in a hard-worked little army, with only his pay and a small sum that he had saved, mainly because he had been detailed to regions where there was almost nothing fit to buy.

The price of his room at the hotel had staggered him, but he charged it off to a well-earned holiday and pretended that he was a millionaire. He rose from the steaming pool and turned an icy shower on himself with shuddering exhilaration. His blood leaped as at a bugle-call, a reveille to life.

He heard the city shouting up to his windows, and he began to fling on his clothes. And then he realized that he knew nobody among those roaring millions. He cursed his luck and flung into his bathrobe. As he knotted the rope he felt that he might as well be a cowled and cloistered monk in a desert as his friendless self in this wilderness of luxury.

Happiness was bound to elude him as easily as that woman of the white query-plume eluded him when he in his ten-cent bus pursued her in her five-thousand-dollar landaulet. All he had of her was the back of her hat and the number of her car—N. Y. 41508. Or was it N. Y. 85140, or—what the devil was the number?

He had not brought away even that!

CHAPTER IV

NOTHING can be lonelier than a room in even a best hotel when one is lonesome and when one's window looks out upon crowds. Forbes had pitched his tent at the Knickerbocker, and his view was of Longacre Square.

The Times Building stood aloft, a huddled giraffe of a building. A fierce wind spiraled round it and played havoc with dignity. It was an ill-mannered bumpkin wind from out of town with a rural sense of humor. Women pressed forward into the gale, bending double and struggling with their tormented hats and writhing skirts. Some of the men seemed to find them an attractive spectacle till they felt their own hats caught up and kited to the level of the fourth and fifth windows.

A flock of newsboys, as brisk as sparrows, drove a hustling trade in recovering hats for men who were ashamed of bare heads as of a nakedness. The gamins darted among the street-cars and automobiles, risking their lives for dimes as sparrows for corn, and escaping death as miraculously.

At the western end of Forty-second Street stood a space of sunset like a scarlet canvas on exhibition. Then swift clouds erased it, and gusts of rain went across the town in volleys of shrapnel, clearing the streets of a mob. Everybody made for the nearest shelter.

The onset ended as quickly as it began. The stars were in the sky as suddenly as if some one had turned on an electric switch. On the pavements, black with wet and night, the reflected electric lights trickled. All the pavements had a look of patent leather.

Forbes sat in the dark room in an arm-chair and muffled his bathrobe about him, watching the electric signs working like solemn acrobats—the girl that skipped the rope, the baby that laughed and cried, the woman that danced on the wire, the skidless tire in the rain, the great sibyl face that winked and advised chewing-gum as a panacea, the kitten that tangled itself in thread, the siphons that filled the glasses—all the automatic electric voices shouting words of light.

Forbes wanted to be among the crowds again. He could not tolerate solitude. He resolved to go forth. It inspired him with pride to put on his evening clothes. While he dressed he sent his silk hat to be ironed by the hotel valet. It came back an ebon crown.

He set it on his head, tapped the top of it smartly, swaggered to the elevator, bowed to the matronly floor clerk as to a queen, went down to the main dining-room, and tried to look at least a duke. He was glad to be in full dress, for the other people were. The head waiter greeted him with respect and handed him the bill of fare with expectation.

He ordered more than he had appetite for, and tried not to blanch at the prices.

The flowers, the shaded candles, the tapestries, the china and the glass and silver, the impassioned violinist leading the sonorous orchestra, all gave him that sense of royalty from which money is most easily wooed. But the cordiality of the thing was fascinating. The whole city seemed to be attending a great reception. New York was giving a party.

And now, indeed, he was in New York again—in it, yet not of it; a poor relation at the wedding feast. He lingered at his solitary banquet like a boy sent away from the table and forced to eat by himself. His extrusion seemed to be a punishment for not being rich. But while his funds held out to burn he would pretend.

The room emptied rapidly as the hour for opera and

theater arrived. But he lingered, not knowing where to go. He pretended to be in no hurry. He had, indeed, more leisure than he enjoyed. Still he sat smoking and protracting his coffee, and haughtily playing that he was not starving for companionship.

When almost the last couple was gone he realized that he faced an evening of dismal solitude. He realized also that a number of kind-thoughted gentlemen had erected large structures for the entertainment of lonely people and had engaged numbers of gifted persons to enact stories for their diversion.

He called for his account, paid it with a large bill, and ignored the residue with a ruinous lifting of the brows as he accepted a light for his exotic cigar.

He helped to put false ideas in the hat-boy's head with the price he paid for the brief storage of his hat and coat and stick. He sauntered to the news-stand with the gracious stateliness of a czarevitch incognito, and asked the Tyson agent:

"What's a good play to see?"

The man named over the reigning successes, and some of their titles fell strangely pat with Forbes' humor:

"Romance," "The Poor Little Rich Girl," "Oh, Oh, Delphine!" "Peg o' My Heart," "The Lady of the Slipper," "The Sunshine Girl."

"They're mostly about girls," Forbes smiled.

"They mostly always are," the agent grinned. "But there's others: 'Within the Law,' 'The Argyle Case,' 'The Five Frankfurters,' 'Years of Discretion.'"

"I reckon I'd better see 'Within the Law.' I've heard a good deal abote that."

"I guess you have. It's been a sell-out for months."

"Can't I get in?"

"I'm afraid not. How many are you?"

"One."

"One? Let me see. Here's a pair ordered by a party that hasn't called for them. Could you use them both?"

"I could put my overcoat in one seat," Forbes groaned, at this added irony in his loneliness and penuriousness.

"I'd split the pair, but it's too late to sell the other one."

"I'll take both." Forbes sighed and waved a handsome five-dollar bill farewell.

The boy who twirled the squirrel-cage door told him that the theater was just down the street, and received a lavish fee for the information. Forbes was soon in the lobby, but the first act was almost finished. Rather than disturb the people already seated, he stood at the back, leaning over the rail. He thrilled instantly to the speech of the shop-girl sentenced to the penitentiary for a theft she was not guilty of, and warning the proprietor that she would amply revenge herself when she came back down the river. At the height of the outcry of militant innocence Forbes heard the susurrus of robes and turned to see a small group of later comers than himself.

At the head went something that he judged to be a woman, though all he saw was a towering head-dress, a heap of elaborately coiffed hair, a wreath of mist, an indescribably exquisite opera-cloak shimmering down to an under-cascade of satin.

This tower of fabrics went along as if it were carried on a pole, and Forbes could see no semblance of human shape or stride inside it. But he judged that it contained a personality, for it paused to listen to something another pile of fabrics said to it, and from both came a snicker—or was it only a frou-frou of garments? In any case, it angered the part of the audience adjacent. The group went down the side-aisle, up a few steps to the little space behind the box.

From where he stood Forbes could see the usher helping them lay off their wraps. They showed no anxiety to catch the remainder of the act, but stood gossiping while the frantic usher waited, not daring to reprimand them, yet dreading the noise of their incursion.

WHAT WILL PEOPLE SAY?

Forbes watched one of the clothes-horses stripped of its encumbrances.

From somewhere in the chaos two long-gloved arms came up; they were strangely shapely; they made motions like swan's necks dipping into water-lilies. A garland of fog came away, and a head on a throat appeared, a bust set upon a heap of drapery. Then the opera-cloak slipped off into the usher's hands. And now design emerged, a woman stood revealed. The head and throat were seen to be attached to a scroll of shoulders, and a figure like a column rose from the floor—strangely columnar it was, and so slender that there was merely the slightest inslope of waist, merely the slightest entasis at the hips.

In other periods only portions of the human outline have been followed by the costume. The natural lines have been broken, perverted, and caricatured by balloon sleeves, huge farthingales, or paniers like a jennet's pack-saddles, the incredible Botocudo ideal of the bustle, corsets like hour-glasses, concentric hoops about the legs, with pantalets coquetting inanely at the ankles—the almost impossible facts of fashion.

Just then the costume was hardly more of a disguise than the gold or bronze powder smeared on by those who pose as statues at the vaudevilles. Inside their outer wraps women were rather wall-papering themselves than draping their forms. It was saner so, and decenter, too, perhaps.

And yet Forbes stared at this woman as Adam must have stared at Eve when the scales were off his eyes. Even her hair was almost all her own, and it was coiled and parted with simple grace. Her head-dress was something bizarre—not a tiara of diamonds, but a black crest with a pearl or two studding it—the iridescent breast of a lyre-bird it was, though he did not know. A cord of pearls was flung around her throat. At the peak of each shoulder her gown began, but the two elements did not

19

conjoin till just in time above the breast, and just a little too late at the back.

The fabric clung lovingly to the loins, thighs, and calves, so closely that an inverted V must be cut between the ankles to make walking possible at all. There was a train of a fish-tail sort, a little twitching afterthought. And so this woman-shape came forth from a shapelessness as Aphrodite from the sea-foam.

Forbes was so startled that he felt all the chagrin of one who is caught staring at a woman just returned from the surf in a wet bathing-suit. He shifted his eyes from her. When he looked back she had vanished into the crimson cavern of the box.

The other women followed her, and the men them. They seated themselves just as the curtain fell.

And now Forbes felt at liberty to go to his own seat, found an usher to pilot him down the aisle. He bowed and murmured "Beg pardon" and "Thank you" to each of those who shoved back awkwardly and wonderingly to let him in. He felt like explaining to them that he had not just arrived, and that he really was not so foolish or so dilatory as he looked. He put his overcoat in his extra seat and studied his program.

A voice that should have reminded him of the landaulet, but did not, caught his ear and led his eyes to the box. He was not far from the late arrivals.

They were attracting a deal of attention from the audience, and paying it none. The loudness of their speech and their laughter would have shocked him in a crowd of farmers. Coming from people of evident wealth and familiarity with town customs, it astounded him.

He had not yet seen the face of the woman of whom he had seen so much else. She was talking to a man in the interior of the box. Her back was turned to the house.

It never occurred to Forbes that it might be the same back he had followed up the Avenue. How could he have told?

AND NOW DESIGN EMERGED, A WOMAN STOOD REVEALED

That back was clothed and cloaked, and even that famous left arm was sleeved. These shoulder-sheaths, not
blades, were so astoundingly bare that he felt ashamed
to look at them. Their proprietress was evidently not
ashamed to submit them for public inspection. One
might not approve her boldness, but one could hardly fail
to approve her shoulders. When she moved or shrugged
or laughed or turned to speak, their exquisite integument
creased and rippled like shaken cream.

At length the footlights went up, the curtain went up.
The three women aligned themselves in profile along the
rail as if they were seated on unseen horses. The men
were mere silhouettes in the background.

The bulk of the audience was in darkness; but the people in the boxes were illumined with a light reflected from
the scenery, and it warmed them like a dawn glowing
upon peaks of snow.

And now, at last, Forbes saw the face he had watched
for with such impatience. It did not disappoint him.
At first she gave him only the profile; but that magic
light of stage-craft was upon it, and once she turned her
head and cast a slow, vague look along the shadowy valley of the audience. She could not have seen him, but
he saw her and found her so beautiful, so bewitchingly
beautiful and desirable, that he caught his breath with a
stitch of pain, an ache of admiration.

Just a moment her eyes dreamed across the gloom, and
she turned back to watch the stage. It was like a parting
after a tryst. Then she broke the spell with a sudden
throe of laughter. The little shoplifter and blackmailer
on the stage was describing her efforts to learn the ways
of society, the technique of pouring tea and pretending
to like it. She swore, and the audience roared. Former-
ly an actor could always get a laugh by saying "damn."
Now it must be a woman that swears.

Jarred back to reasonableness by the shock of laughter,
Forbes looked again to the box to see what manner of

women this woman went with. One of them was tiny but quite perfect. She had the face of a débutante under the white hair of a matron. If her age were betrayed by her neck, the dog-collar of pearls concealed the ravage. She sat exceedingly erect and seemed to be cold and haughty till another splurge of slang from the shoplifter provoked her to a laugh that was like a child's.

The other woman laughed, too, laughed large and wide. She was beautiful, too, a Rubens ideal, drawn in liberal rotundities—cheeks, chin, throat, bust, hips. No Cubist could have painted her, for she was like a cluster of soap-bubbles. Her face was a great baby's.

The men were almost invisible, mere cut-outs in black and white.

None of them had the jaded look of boredom that Forbes supposed to be the chief characteristic of New York wealth. They were as eager and irrepressible as a box-load of children fighting over a bag of peanuts at a circus.

One of the men leaned forward and whispered something; all the women turned to hear. They forgot the play, though the situation was critical. They chattered and laughed so audibly that the audience grew restive; the people on the stage looked to be distressed.

Forbes was astonished at such bad manners from such beautiful people. He wondered how the play could go on. He had heard of actors stepping out of the picture to rebuke such disturbers of the peace. He expected such an encounter now.

Then somebody in the audience hissed. Somebody called distinctly, "Shut up!" The group turned in surprise, and received another hiss in the face. Silence and shame quieted it instanter. The women blushed like grown girls threatened with a spanking. Tremendous blushes ran all down their crimson backs.

Forbes could see that they wanted to run. A kind of pluck held them. They pretended to toss their heads with contempt, but the mob had cowed them so completely that Forbes felt sorry for them—especially for her. She was too pretty for a public humiliation.

When the curtain fell on the second act Forbes saw one of the men in the box rise and leave along the side-aisle. Forbes knew the man. His name was Ten Eyck —Murray Ten Eyck.

Forbes dreaded to repeat that voyage through the strait between knees and seat-backs; but he had seen at last a man he knew. And the man he knew knew the woman he wanted to know.

CHAPTER V

THE women he passed glared hatpins at Forbes and groaned as they rose and hunched back to let him by. They clutched at the wraps he disarranged. He rumpled one elaborate hat stuck in the back of a seat, and one silk tile that had fallen out of the wire rack he kicked under the row ahead. He had an impulse to go after it; but when he realized the postures and scrambles it would involve, it was too horrible an ordeal. He pretended not to have noticed, and pressed onward.

None was so indignant as the man who had similarly climbed out for a drink the *entr'acte* before. Forbes knew it was a drink he had gone out for the moment he passed him. Forbes was not going out for a drink, but for important information.

He apologized meekly, yet continued on his course. By the time he was in the open Ten Eyck had disappeared. He was not in the lobby, nor among the men smoking on the sidewalk or dashing across the street to one of the cafés where coffee could not be obtained. Forbes found his man at last in the smoking-room below-stairs.

He was puffing a cigarette, and met Forbes' eager glance with such blank indifference that Forbes' words of greeting stopped in his throat.

To explain his presence in the smoking-room Forbes lighted a cigar, though he knew that he could have but a few puffs of it. And it was such a good cigar! There can only be so many good cigars in the world.

The two men paced back and forth on crisscrossing paths as violently oblivious of each other as the two traditional Englishmen who were cast away on the same desert island and had never been introduced.

It was not till Murray Ten Eyck flung down his cigarette and made to leave that Forbes mustered courage enough to speak, in his Virginian voice:

"Pardon me, suh, but aren't you Mr. Mu'y Ten Eyck?"

"Yes," said Ten Eyck — simply that, and nothing more.

Forbes, nonplussed at the abrupt brevity of the answer, tried again:

"I reckon you don't remember me."

Ten Eyck showed a hint of interest. If he were a snob he blamed it on his own weaknesses.

"I seem to, but—well, I'm simply putrid at names and faces. A man pulled me out of the surf at Palm Beach last winter—I had a cramp, you know. I cut him dead two weeks later. When I knew what I had done I wished he had let me drown. So don't mind me if I don't remember you. Who are you? Did you ever save my life? Where was it we met?"

"It was in Manila. You were—"

"Oh, God bless me! You're Harvey Forbes—well, I'll be—" He reversed the prayer. "Of course it's you." He was cordial enough now as he clapped both hands on Forbes' shoulders. "But how the hell was I to know you all dolled up like this? I used to see you in uniform with cap and bronze buttons and sword and puttees. You were a lieutenant then. I dare say you're a colonel by now, what?" Forbes shook his head. "No? Well, you ought to be. You did save my life out in that God-forsaken hole. And now you're here! Well, I'll be—Let's have a drink."

"No, thank you!"

"Yes, thank you!" He hurried Forbes up the stairs, out into the street, and into a peacock-rivaling café. With one foot on the rail, one elbow on the bar, and one elbow crooked upward, they toasted each other in a hearty "How!" Then, with libations tossed inward, the old friendship was consecrated anew.

"Tell me," said Ten Eyck, "are you alone—or with somebody? Don't answer if it will incriminate you."

"No such luck," groaned Forbes. "I'm alone, a cast-away on this deserted island."

"Well, I'm the little rescuing party. How long you here for?"

"I don't know. I was ordered to Governor's Island. I don't have to report for a week, so I thought I'd have a look at New York."

"That won't take you long. There's nothing going on, and nobody in town."

Forbes remembered the crowds he had seen, and smiled. "I saw three ve'y charming ladies in that party of yours."

"Glad you like 'em. Come and meet 'em."

"Perhaps one of them is your wife. Are you ma'ied yet?"

"Not yet. Not while I have my health and strength."

"I'm right glad to hear it. I was beginning to feel afraid that you had ma'ied that wonderful one."

Ten Eyck shook his head and laughed.

"Who? Me? Me marry Persis Cabot?"

"Is that her name? Well, why not?"

"If you only knew her you wouldn't ask why. I'm not a millionaire."

"She doesn't look mercenary."

"She's not. Money is nothing to her; she doesn't know what it means; she just tosses it away. She's like a yacht. You think it costs a lot to buy, but wait till you count the upkeep. Persis is a corker. She's a fine girl to play with. But you must promise not to marry her."

"I promise."

"Fine! Come along." As they climbed the stairs Ten Eyck was saying: "I hate an obligation like poison.

Always want to pay back a mean turn or a good one. You made a devil of a hit with me, Forbesy, out in Manila there, when I was blue and sick and a million miles from home. I suppose there's nothing makes a hit with a man like calling on him when he's sick. You got your hooks on me that way, and I'm yours to boss around. I'll put you up at a lot of clubs and trot you about till you flash the S. O. S. That is, if you want that sort of thing. Maybe you want to be let alone. If you do, you can kick me out whenever I'm in the way."

Forbes denied any inclination to solitude. When they reached the head of the aisle to the box he paused. He had the Southern idea of ceremonial courtesy, and he suggested that Ten Eyck had better ask the permission of the ladies before he introduced a stranger. Forbes had the rare knack of using the word "lady" without an effect of middle class.

And he had never forgotten what Ten Eyck had said to him once: "I love the extremes of society. I can get along with the highest, and I dote on the lowest, but God, how I loathe a middle-class soul."

Ten Eyck waived Forbes' scruples, dragged him to the box, and presented him to the women and the two other men. Forbes was too much perturbed to catch a single name. Even the last name of Persis escaped both his memory and his attention.

Ten Eyck gave Forbes a glowing advertisement as a brilliant soldier and a life-saver, and offered him his own chair next to Persis.

She had answered his low bow of homage with nothing more than a wren-like nod and half a hint of a smile.

Ten Eyck threw Forbes into confusion by saying:

"You'll have to do better than that, old girl. Mr. Forbes not only rescued me from the depths, but he told me you were the most beautiful thing he ever saw on earth."

Persis smiled a little more cordially and murmured:

"That's very nice of him."

She was evidently so used to bouquets in the face that they neither offended nor excited her. But Miss—or was it Mrs?—anyway, the plump woman interposed:

"He must have been referring to me. My mirror tells me I am fatally beautiful, and God knows there's more of me than of anybody else on earth."

Forbes was in a dilemma. He had not made the comment ascribed to him, yet he could hardly deny it. Nor could he deny the plump lady's claim to the praise. He simply flushed and smiled benignly on everybody.

Fortunately, the lights sank just then, and the curtain went up with a sound like a great "Hush!" The party, having been once rebuked, fell into silence. Forbes rose to return to his own seat, but Ten Eyck, standing back of him, pressed him into his chair with powerful hands.

He stayed put. But the play no longer held him. He could think only of one thing. He was posted at the side of this creature who had fascinated him from afar and terrified him anear, and whose last name he did not yet know.

The lesson of the previous act was not long remembered by the irrepressibles. One of the men, a queer little fellow he was, whispered a comment to Persis. She laughed and answered it. The other women had to be told. They giggled. Their voices gradually rose in pitch and volume.

When the thief in the play shot the stool-pigeon with a silencered revolver a man seated below the box was overheard to say:

"I wish somebody would invent a silencer for box-parties."

Again there were almost audible stares of reproach from the audience, and quietude settled down once more like a pall. At the end of this act again Forbes rose to go, but Ten Eyck checked him again.

"What you doing after the play?"

"Nothing."

28

"Come turkey-trotting with us."

"Turkey-trotting!" Forbes gasped. "Do nice people—"

"We're not nice people," said Persis, "but we do."

"It's all we do do," said the lady of the embonpoint, whose first name by now he had gleaned as Winifred.

Forbes was surprised to hear himself speaking as if to old acquaintance. "When I was in San Francisco, six years or so ago, slumming parties were taking it up along the 'Barbary Coast.' And on my way East just now I read an editorial about its rage in New York, but I didn't believe it."

"It's awful," said the little man. "People have gone stark mad over it. The mayor ought to stop it."

"Oh, Willie, don't be a prude," said Persis. "You know it's healthier than playing bridge all day and all night."

"And much less expensive," said the white-haired one.

"It's sickening," Willie insisted. "It's unfit for a decent woman."

"Thanks!" said Persis, with a tone of zinc.

The little man made haste with an apology. "I don't mean you, my dear, of course; you dance it harmlessly enough; but—well, I don't like to see you at it, that's all."

"Your own mother is learning it," said Winifred.

"Oh, mother!" Willie gasped. "I gave her up long ago."

Ten Eyck intervened. Forbes remembered now that he was always intervening between extremists in the club quarrels in Manila.

"What difference does it make?" he said. "All dancing is impure to some people. The waltz and polka used to be considered bad enough to get you kicked out of the churches. The turkey-trot is only vulgar when vulgar people dance it, and they'd be vulgar anyway, anywhere. The trot has set people to jigging again. That's one good, wholesome thing. For several years you couldn't get people to dance at all. Now they're at it morning, noon, and night."

"The police ought to stop it, I tell you," Willie insisted, with a peevishness that was like a dash of vinegar. "I hate to see it."

"Then don't come along, my dear," Persis answered, with a glint of temper.

Forbes did not like that "my dear." It might mean nothing, but it might mean everything.

CHAPTER VI

WHEN the final curtain came down like a guillotine on the play there was a general uprising, a sort of slow panic to escape from this finished place and move on to the next event—by street-car to a welsh rabbit in a kitchenette, or by motor to a restaurant of pretense.

Everybody being in haste, everybody went slowly. Forbes retrieved his hat and overcoat after a ferocious struggle. In the lazy ooze-out of the crowd he was gradually shunted to the side of Persis, and willing enough to be there, proud to be there. He walked a little more militarily than he usually did in civilian's.

He heard people whispering with a shrillness that Persis had evidently grown accustomed to, for she could not have helped hearing, yet showed no sign. And now Forbes recaptured her last name, and it was familiar to him, little as he knew of social chronicles.

"Look! That's Persis Cabot," said one. "There's the Cabot girl you read so much about," said another. "She's got a sister who's a Countess or Marquise, or something." Then Forbes learned by roundabout the last name of Willie, and learned it with alarm from two of the sharpest whisperers:

"That's Willie Enslee with her, I suppose."

"I guess so."

"Don't see why they call that big fellow Little Willie."

"Just a joke, I guess."

"They say he's worth twenty million dollars."

"He looks it."

At any other time it would have amused Forbes im--

31

mensely to be called so far out of his name and to receive twenty million dollars by acclamation.

But now he could only busy himself with deductions: why did they assume that any man who was with Persis Cabot was sure to be Willie Enslee? Could it mean— what else could it mean?

He glanced around to take another look at Willie Enslee. Now that he knew him for what he was, the situation was intolerable. Marry this dream of beauty to that cartoon, that grotesque who came hardly to her shoulder!

His glance had showed him that the men and women they had passed were looking up and down Persis' back like appraising dry-goods merchants or plagiarizing dressmakers. When he turned his head forward he saw that the women in front were inspecting her with even more brazen curiosity. It astounded Forbes to see such well-dressed people behaving so peasantly. But Persis seemed as oblivious of their study as if they were painted heads on a fresco. Forbes, however, flushed when their eyes turned to him, because he felt that they were saying, "That must be Willie Enslee," and "Why do they call that big thing Little Willie?"

Meanwhile Little Willie himself was handing the attendant at the switchboard a punctured carriage check, with which to flash the number on the sign outside.

There was a long wait for their own car, while motor after motor slid up and slid away as soon as its number had been bawled and its cargo had detached itself from the waiting huddle.

After the close, warm theater Forbes flinched at the edged night wind coming from the river. With the caution of an athlete he turned up his collar and buttoned his overcoat over his chest. But Persis stood with throat and bosom naked to the wind, and to all those staring eyes, and never thought to gather about her even the flimsy aureole of chiffon that took the place of a scarf. And equally unafraid and unashamed stood Winifred and Mrs. Neff. (He had collected her name, too, during the conversation that flourished throughout the last act.)

At length the footman, who had howled out other people's numbers, held up a timid finger and murmured, awesomely, "Mr. Enslee?"

The limousine, whose door he opened, was by no means the handsomest of the line. Enslee was evidently rich enough to afford a shabby car. The three women bent their heads and entered with difficulty, their tight skirts sliding to their knees as they clambered in.

There was a great ado over the problem of room. Every man offered to walk or take a taxi. Ten Eyck made sure that Forbes should not be omitted. Ignoring his protests, he bundled him into one of the little extra seats and crawled in after him. The huge third man (still anonymous and taciturn) next inserted his bulk—a large cork in a small bottle.

Willie put his head in to ask:

"Where d'you want to go, Persis?"

"Trotting, of course," came from the crowded depths.

"But I don't think—"

"Then take me home and go to the devil."

"We'll trot," sighed Willie. He spoke to the chauffeur dolefully, then appeared at the door to wail helplessly:

"There seems to be no room for me."

"You're only the host," said Winifred. "Hop on behind."

"You can sit on my lap," said Ten Eyck.

And as that was the only vacant space, the big man lifted him up and set him there. The footman, reassured by the tip in his hand, grinned at the spectacle and laughed, as he closed the door: "Is you all in?"

Seven persons were packed where there was hardly space for five; but Forbes noted that they were as in-

formal and good-natured as yokels on a hay-ride. All
except Willie, and his distress was not because of the crowd.

The car had no more than left the theater when Mrs.
Neff was groaning:

"A cigarette, somebody, quick—before I faint!"

Winifred by a mighty twisting produced a concaved
golden case and snapped it open, only to gasp:

"Empty! My God, it's empty!"

Persis saved the day. "I have some. Give us a light,
Willie. There's a dear."

As usual, Willie had a counter-idea.

"But, Persis, don't you think you could wait till—"

Her only answer was, "Murray, give me a light."

Ten Eyck called out, "Right-o, milydy, if Bob will
hold our little hostlet half a mo." And he deposited Willie
in the arms of the big man while he fumbled in his waistcoat for a book of matches and passed it back into the
dark. "'Ere you are, your lydyship." He was forever
talking in some dialect or other.

But Persis gave him her cigarette and pleaded: "It's
so conspicuous holding a match to your face on Broadway. Light mine for me, Murray."

"It's highly unsanitary," said Ten Eyck; "but if you
don't mind I don't. I fancy these cigarettes of yours
would choke any self-respecting microbe to death."

Ten Eyck kindled her cigarette as delicately as he could
and handed it to her. The same service he performed
for the other eager women, and the three were soon puffing the close compartment so full of smoke that the men
felt no need of burning tobacco of their own.

When a particularly bright glare swept into the car
from the street the women made a pretense of hiding
their cigarettes; but it was an ostrich-like concealment,
and Forbes could see other women in other cabs similarly
engaged. During his absence smoking had evidently
become almost as commonplace among the women as
among the men.

Forbes, cramped of leg and choked of lung, was wondering at his presence here. It was a far cry from Manila. He had never dreamed when he showed an ordinary human interest in the melancholy Ten Eyck, fallen ill there on a jaunt around the world, that his courtesy in the wilderness would be repaid with usury in the metropolis. Nor had he learned from Ten Eyck's unobtrusive manner that he was a familiar figure in the halls of the mighty. Forbes had cast an idle crust on the waters, and lo, it returned as a frosted birthday cake!

He had come to town at noon a lonely stranger, and before midnight he was literally in the lap of beauty and chumming with wealth and aristocracy in their most intimate mood.

The sidewalks outside were packed with theater crowds till they spilled over at the curbs, and the streets were filled with all sorts of vehicles till they threatened the sidewalks. Guiding a car there was like shooting a rapids full of logs in a lumber-drive, but Enslee's man was an expert charioteer.

Suddenly they whirled off Broadway, and, describing a short curve, came to a stop. A footman opened the door, but nobody moved.

Ten Eyck said: "The problem now is how do we get out. I'm so mixed up with somebody, I don't know my own legs." Like a wise man of Gotham, he jabbed his thumb into the mixture, and asked, "Are those mine?"

"No, they are not!" said Winifred.

Willie was lowered ashore first. Bob What's-his-name bulged through next, then Ten Eyck, then Forbes. Ten Eyck dropped into the gutter the three lighted cigarettes that had been hastily pressed into his hand, and turned to help the women out.

Forbes, wondering where they were, looked up and read with difficulty a great sign in vertical electric letters, "Reisenweber's."

Willie told his chauffeur to wait, and the car drew

down the street to make room for a long queue of other cars. Ten Eyck led the flock into a narrow hall, and filled the small elevator with as many as could get in. He included Forbes with the three women, and remained behind with Willie and Bob.

Crowded into the same space were two young girls, very pretty till they spoke, and then so plebeian that their own beauty seemed to flee affrighted. The blonde seraph was chanting amid her chewing-gum:

"He says to me, 'If you was a lady you wouldn't 'a' drank with a party you never sor before,' and I come back at him, 'If you was a gempmum you'd 'a' came across with the price of a pint when you seen I was dyin' of thoist.'"

And the brunette answered: "You can't put no trust in them kind of Johns. Besides, he tangoes like he had two left feet."

Forbes was uneasy till Persis whispered, "Don't you just love them?" Then a door opened and they debarked into a crowded anteroom. While they waited for the car to descend and rise again with the rest of the party the women gave their wraps to a maid, and Forbes delivered his coat and hat and stick across a counter to a hat-boy.

When Ten Eyck, Willie, and Bob appeared and had checked their things the seven climbed a crowded staircase into an atmosphere riotous with chatter and dance-music of a peculiarly rowdy rhythm.

But they could only hear and feel the throb of it. They could not see the dancers, so thick a crowd was ahead of them.

A head waiter appeared, and, curt as he was with the rest of the mob, he was pitifully regretful at losing Mr. Enslee, who had failed to reserve a table and who would not wait.

It was disgusting to slink back down the stairs, regain the wraps and coats and hats, and make two elevator-loads again. Willie alone was cheerful.

"Now, maybe you'll go to the Plaza or some place and have a human supper."

"I'm going to have a trot and a tango if I have to hunt the town over," said Persis.

Willie gnashed his teeth, but had the car recalled, and asked her where she would go.

"Let's try the Beaux Arts," she said; and they huddled together once more.

"It's too bad we were thrown out of Reisenweber's," Winifred pouted. "I was dying to see François dance and have a dance with him."

Forbes felt well enough acquainted by now to ask: "Pardon my ignorance, but who is François?"

"Oh, he's a love of a French lad," said Winifred. "Everybody's mad over him. I used to see him in Paris dancing between the tables at the Café de Paris or the Pré-Catalan with some girl or other. Then somebody brought him over here for a musical comedy, and he's been on the crest of the wave ever since."

"They say he's getting rich dancing in theaters and restaurants and giving lessons at twenty-five per."

"Somebody was telling me he actually makes fifteen hundred to two thousand dollars a week," said Mrs. Neff.

"If I had that much, would you marry me, Persis?" said Ten Eyck.

"In a minute," said Persis. "We might earn it ourselves. You dance as well as he does, and you could practise whirling me round your neck."

"Then we're engaged," said Ten Eyck.

"It's outrageous!" said Willie. "That fellow with an income equal to five per cent. on a couple of million dollars."

"What you kicking about, Willie?" said Winifred. "You get several times as much, and you never lifted hand or foot in your life."

"But Willie's father did," said Mrs. Neff. "He killed himself working."

"Willie has it much better arranged," said Bob. "Instead of Willie working for money he has the money working for him."

"It works while he sleeps," said Winifred.

Forbes was thinking gloomily in the gloom of the car. This dancer, this mountebank, François, was earning as much in a week as the government paid him in a year, after all his training, his campaigning, his readiness to take up his residence or lay down his life wherever he was told to.

Then he compared his income with Willie Enslee's. Enslee did not even dance for his supper, yet into his banks gold rained where pennies dribbled into Forbes' meager purse. And it was not a precarious salary such as dancers and soldiers earned by their toil; it was the mere sweat from great slumbering masses of treasure.

Forbes felt no longer an exultance at falling in with these people. He felt ashamed of himself. He was no more a part of the company he kept than a gnat on an ox or a flea caught up in the ermine of a king. The air grew oppressive. He felt like a tenement waif patronized for a moment on a whim, and likely to be tossed back to his poverty at any moment. He wanted to get out before he was put out. The very luxuries that enthralled him at first were intolerable now. The perfume of the women and their flowers lost its savor. Their graces had gone. They were all elbows and knees. He suffocated as in a black hole of Calcutta.

When a footman at the Café des Beaux Arts wrenched the door open and let the cool air in, it was welcome. Forbes moved to escape. But he was kept prisoner while Bob was sent as an avant courier. He returned with the bad news that he was unable even to reach a head waiter.

The car nosed round, turned with difficulty, and went to Bustanoby's. It was the same story here.

"New York's gone mad, I tell you!" Willie raved. "And nobody is as crazy as we are. To think of us going about like a gang of beggars pleading to be taken in and allowed to dance with a lot of hoodlums and muckers. Even they won't have us."

"We'll try once more," said Persis. "The Café de Ninive."

After a brief voyage farther along Broadway the suppliant outcasts entered a great hall imposingly decorated with winged bulls and other Assyrian symbols. The huge space of the restaurant was a desert of tables untenanted save by a few dejected waiters and a few couples evidently in need of solitude.

An elevator took the determined Persis and her cohort up to another thronged vestibule.

Persis had said to Willie in the car, "If you don't get us a table here I'll never speak to you again."

With this threat as a spur Little Willie accosted a large captain of waiters, who shrugged his shoulders and indicated the crowd inside and the crowd outside. Willie fumbled in his pockets, and his hand slyly met that of the captain, who glanced into his palm, then up to heaven in gratitude, and laid aside all scruple.

Willie triumphantly beckoned Persis, who approached the captain with the pouting appeal of a lady of the court to a relenting sovereign.

"Fritz," she said, "you've got to take care of us."

"How can I refuse Mees Cabot," said Fritz. "Do you weesh to seet and watch the artists, or to seet weeth the dancers?"

"We want to dance," said Persis.

"There is one table resairve for a very great patron. You shall have it. I shall lose me my poseetion, and he will tear down the beelding; but that is better as to turn away Mees Cabot and Meester Enslee."

He whispered to a horrified captain on the other side of a silk rope. The barrier was removed, and they were within the sacred inclosure, while the baffled remnant gnashed its teeth outside.

CHAPTER VII

THE room they were in was a mass of tables compacted around a central space, where professional entertainers were displaying the latest fashions in song and dance. A pair of "Texas Tommy" dancers were finishing a wild gallopade with a climax, in which the man hurled the woman aloft as if he were playing diabolo with her, caught her on his long sticks of arms, and spun her round his neck, then let her drop head first, rescuing her from a crash by the breadth of her hair, swinging her back between his legs and across his hip. When her heels touched the floor he bent her almost double and gazed Apache murder into her eyes. Her hair fell loose on cue, and then he righted her, and they were bowing to the rapturous applause. When they retired they were panting like hunted rabbits and sweating like stevedores.

And now a somewhat haggard girl, who looked as if she had forgotten how to sleep, dashed forward in a snow-bird costume and sang a sleigh-bell song. Little bells jingled about her, and the crowd kept time by tapping wine-glasses with forks or spoons. Some kept time also with their rhythmic jaws.

The girl sang in a mock childish voice in the nasal dialect of the vaudevilles, with "yee-oo" for "you," and "tree-oo" for "true," and "lahv" for "love." The words of the song were too innocent, and not important enough to detain Persis, who felt herself drawn by the distant music of a turkey-trot in the farthest room. The warring counterpoint of the two orchestras only added to the lawless excitement of the throng. The dance was just

40

over, and the dancers were settling down to their chairs, their deserted plates and glasses. The guide led them to the only empty table, whisked off the card "Reserved," and turned them over to a waiter.

While Willie scanned the supper card Mrs. Neff lapsed into reminiscence. It was the only sign she had given thus far that she had earned her white hair by age, and not by a bleach.

"Funny how this building tells the story of the last few years," she said. "A few winters ago we thought it was amusing to go to supper at a good restaurant after the theater, have something nice to eat and drink, talk a while, and go home to bed. We thought we were very devilish, and preachers railed at the wickedness of late-supper orgies. And now the place down-stairs is deserted. Just taking late supper is like going to prayer-meeting.

"Then somebody started the cabaret. And we flocked to that. We ate the filthiest stuff and drank the rottenest wine, and didn't care so long as they had some sensational dancer or singer cavorting in the aisle. They were so close you could hear them grunt, and they looked like frights in their make-up. But we thought it was exciting, and the preachers said it was awful. But it has become so tame and stupid that it is quite respectable.

"At present we are dancing in the aisles ourselves, crowding the professional entertainers off their own floors. And now the preachers and editors are attacking this. Whatever we do is wrong, so, as my youngest boy says, 'What's the use and what's the diff?'"

"Only one thing worries me," said Winifred, as she peeled her gloves from her great arms and her tiny hands. "What will come next? Even this can't keep us interested much longer."

"The next thing," Willie snapped, "will be that we'll all go into vaudeville and do flip-flaps and the split and such things before a hired audience of reformed ballet-girls."

"I hope they play a tango next," was all Persis said. "Willie, call a waiter and ask him to ask the orchestra to play a tango."

"Wait, can't you?" he protested. "Let's get something to eat ordered first. We've got to buy champagne to hold our table; but we don't have to drink the stuff. What do you want, Persis? Winifred? Mrs. Neff, what do you want?—a little caviar to give us an appetite, what? What sort of a cocktail, eh? What sort of a cocktail, uh?"

Before an answer could be made the orchestra struck up a tune of extraordinary flippance. People began to jig in their chairs, others rose and were in the stride before they had finished the mouthfuls they were surprised with; several caught a hasty gulp of wine with the right hand while the left groped for the partner. The frenzy to dance was the strangest thing about it.

"Come on, Murray!" cried Persis. "Willie, order anything. It doesn't matter." Her voice trailed after her, for she was already backing off into the maelstrom with her arms cradled in Ten Eyck's arms.

Bob Fielding, with his usual omission of speech, swept Winifred from her chair, and she went into the stream like a ship gliding from her launching-chute. Mrs. Neff looked invitingly at Willie, but he answered the implication:

"I'll not stir till I've had food."

Forbes leaned over to explain to the marooned matron:

"I wish I could ask you to honor me; but I don't know how."

She smiled almost intolerantly and sank back with a sigh just as a huge and elderly man of capitalistic appearance skipped across the floor and bowed to her knees. She fairly bounded into his arms. The two white polls mingled their venerable locks, but their curvettings were remarkably coltish. Mrs. Neff, who had sons in college and daughters of marriageable age, was giving an amazing

.exhibition. She backed and filled like a yacht in stays; she bucked and ducked like a yacht in a squawl; she whirled like a dervish, slanting and swooping; her lithe little body draped itself closely about the capitalist's great curves; her little feet followed his big feet or retreated from them like two white mice pursued by two black cats.

At first Forbes was disgusted; the one epithet he could think of was "obscene." As he watched the mêlée he felt that he was witnessing a tribe of savages in a mating-season orgy. He had seen the Moros, the Igorrotes, the Samoans, and the Nautch girls of Chicago, and the meaning of this turmoil was the same. He knew that the dance was the invention of negroes. Its wanton barbarity was only emphasized by the fact that it was celebrated on Broadway, in the greatest city of what we are pleased to admit is the most civilized nation in the world.

He could not adjust it to his mind. In the eddies he saw women of manifest respectability, mothers and wives in the arms of their husbands, young women who were plainly what are called "nice girls," and wholesome-looking young men of deferential bearing; yet mingled with them almost inextricably, brushing against them, tripping over their feet, tangling elbows with them, were youth of precocious salacity, shop-girls of their own bodies, and repulsive veterans from the barracks of evil. And the music seemed to unite them all into one congress met with one motive: to exploit their sensual impulses over the very borders of lawlessness.

Thus Forbes, left alone with Willie Enslee, regarded the spectacle with amazement verging on horror, and thought in the terms of Jeremiah and Ezekiel denouncing Jerusalem, Moab, and Baal.

Meanwhile Willie Enslee studied the menu and gave his orders to the waiter. When the supper was commanded Enslee lifted his eyes to the dancers, shook his head hopelessly, and, reaching across the table, tapped Forbes on the arm and demanded:

WHAT WILL PEOPLE SAY?

"Look at 'em! Just look at 'em! Can you believe your own eyes, uh? Now I ask you, I ask you, if you can see how a white woman could hold herself so cheap as to mix with those muckers, and forget her self-respect so far?"

It was a weak voicing of Forbes' own repugnance, yet as soon as Willie spoke Forbes began to disagree with him. Willie was fatally established among those people with whom one hates to agree. As soon as one found Willie holding similar views, one's own views became suspect and distasteful—like food that is turned from in disgust because another's fork has touched it.

And there might have been a trace of jealousy in Forbes' immediate anger at Enslee's opinions. In any case, here he was, in the notorious haunts of society, seated in its very unholy of unholies, and gazing on its pernicious rites, and saying to his host:

"I must say I don't see anything wrong."

CHAPTER VIII

HARVEY FORBES came of a Southern stock that inherited its manners with its silver. Both were a trifle formal, yet very gracious and graceful.

The family had lost its silver in the Civil War; but the formalities and the good manners remained as heirlooms that could be neither confiscated nor sold off.

He had known something of New York as a cadet at West Point. He had seen the streets as he paraded them on one or two great occasions; he had known a few of its prominent families; but principally Southrons.

He knew that the careful people of that day would have shuddered at the thought of dancing even a minuet in public. They surrounded admission to their festivities with every possible difficulty, and conducted themselves with rigid dignity in the general eye. Even the annual event of the Charity Ball had been countenanced only for the sake of charity, and fell into disfavor because of the promiscuity of it.

In the Philippines Forbes had seen the two-step drive out the waltz; but it had not there, as here, almost ended the vogue of dancing altogether.

And now, after a few years of immunity, people were tripping again as if the plague of the dancing sickness had broken out. The epidemic had taken a new form. Grace and romance were banished for grotesque and cynical antics. The very names of the dances were atrocious—bunny-hug, Texas Tommy, grizzly bear, turkey-trot.

It was a peculiar revolution in social history that people who for so long had refused to dance in public or at all should take up the dance and lay down their exclusiveness at the same time, and with a sort of mania; and that they should be converted to these steps by a dance that had first startled the country from the vaudeville stage, and had been greeted as a disgusting exhibition even for the cheaper theaters.

By a strange insidiousness the evil rhythms had infected the general public. The oligarchy was infatuated to the point of finding any place a fit place. The aged were hobbling about. The very children were capering and refusing the more hallowed dances.

Forbes was not ready to see how quickly such things lose their wickedness as they lose their novelty and rarity. "The devil has had those tunes long enough," said John Wesley, as he turned the ribald street ballads into hymns.

But with Forbes, as with everybody, vice lost her hideous mien when her face became familiar. Like everybody else, he first endured, then pitied, then embraced. Later he would talk as Persis did and Ten Eyck; he would proclaim the turkey-trot a harmless romp, and the tango a simple walk around. Later still he would turn from them all in disgust, not because he repented, but because they were tiresome. But for the present he was smitten with revulsion. The very quality of the company had served as a proof of the evil motive.

Even though he told Willie Enslee he saw nothing wrong, he sat gasping as at a turbulent pool of iniquity.

Motherly dowagers in ball costumes bumped and caromed from the ample forms of procuresses. Young women of high degree in the arms of the scions of great houses jostled and drifted with walkers of the better streets, chorus-girls who "saved their salary," sirens from behind the counters.

As the dance swirled round and round among the gilded pillars, the same couples reeled again and again into view and out, like passengers on a merry-go-round.

Forbes watched with the eager eyes of a fisher the reappearance of Persis. It pleased him to see in her manner, and in Ten Eyck's, an entire absence of grossness; but it hurt him surprisingly to see her in such a crew and responding to the music of songs whose words, unsung but easily remembered or imagined, were all concerned with "teasing," "squeezing," "tantalizing," "hypnotizing," "honey babe," "hold me tight," "keep on a-playin'," "don't stop till I drop," and all the amorous animality of the slums.

He found himself indignant at Ten Eyck's intimacy with the wonderful girl. They clung together as closely as they could and breathe. Now they sidled, now they trotted, now twirled madly as on a pivot. Their feet seemed to be manacled together except when they dipped a knee almost to the ground and thrust the other foot far back.

Then gradually, in spite of him, the music began to invade his own feet. He felt a yearning in his ankles. The tune took on a kind of care-free swagger, a flip boastfulness. He wanted to get up and brag, too. His feeling for Ten Eyck was not of reproof, but of envy. He longed to take his place.

When at length the music ended he felt as if he had missed an opportunity that he must not miss again. He had witnessed a display of knowledge which he must make his own.

Ten Eyck brought Persis back to the table, and the other women returned, Mrs. Neff's partner nodding his head with a breathless satisfaction as he relinquished her and rejoined his own group.

The eyes of all the women were full of sated languor. They had given their youthful spirits play, and they were enjoying a refreshed fatigue.

The waiter had meanwhile set cocktails about, and deposited two silver pails full of broken ice, from which gold-necked bottles protruded. And at each place there were slices of toast covered with the black shot of caviar.

The dancers fell on the appetizers with the appetite of harvesters. Persis thrilled Forbes with a careless:

"It's too bad you don't trot, Mr. Forbes."

"He's not too old to learn," said Ten Eyck. "It's really very simple, once you get the hang of it."

And he fell into a description of the technic.

"The main thing is to keep your feet as far from each other as you can, and as close to your partner's as you can. And you've got to hold her tight. Then just step out and trot; twirl around once in a while, and once in a while do a dip. Keep your body still and dance from your hips. And—get up here a minute and I'll show you."

Forbes was embarrassed completely when Ten Eyck made him stand up and embrace him. But the people around made no more fun of them than revivalists make of a preacher and a new convert. They were proselytes to the new fanaticism. Forbes, as awkward as an overgrown school-boy, picked up a few ideas in spite of his reluctance.

He sat down flushed with confusion, but determined to retrieve himself. In a little while the music struck up once more.

"L'ave your pick in the air, the band's begun again," said Ten Eyck. "Come on, Winifred!" Bob Fielding lifted Mrs. Neff to her feet and haled her away, and Persis was left to Forbes.

"Don't you want to try it?" she said, with an irresistible simplicity.

"I'm afraid I'd disgrace you."

"You can't do that. Come along. We'll practise it here."

She was on her feet, and he could not refuse. He rose, and she came into his arms. Before he knew it they were swaying together. He had a native sense of rhythm, and he had been a famous dancer of the old dances.

He felt extremely foolish as he sidled, dragging one foot

after the other. He trod on her toes, and smote her with his knee-caps, but she only laughed.

"You're getting it! That's right. Don't be afraid!"

Her confidence and her demand gave him courage like a bugle-call. But he could not master the whirl till she said, as calmly as if she were a gymnastic instructor:

"You must lock knees with me."

Somehow and quite suddenly he got the secret of it. The music took a new meaning. With a desperate masterfulness he swept her from their back-water solitude out into the full current.

He was turkey-trotting with Persis Cabot! He wanted everybody to know it. This thought alone gave him the braggadocio necessary to success.

Perhaps he was too busy thinking of his feet, perhaps the dance really was not indecent; but certainly his thoughts of her were as chivalrous as any knight's kneeling before his queen.

And yet they were gripping one another close; they were almost one flesh; their thoughts were so harmonious that she seemed to follow even before he led. She prophesied his next impulse and coincided with it.

They moved like a single being, a four-legged—no, not a four, but a two-legged angel, for his right foot was wedded close to her left, and her left to his right.

And so they ambled with a foolish, teetering, sliding hilarity. So they spun round and round with knees clamped together. So they seesawed with thighs crossed X-wise, all intermingled and merged together. And now what had seemed odious as a spectacle was only a sane and youthful frivolity, an April response to the joy of life, the glory of motion. David dancing before the Lord could not have had a cleaner mind, though his wife, too, contemned and despised him, and for her contempt won the punishment of indignant God.

Abruptly, and all too soon, the music stopped. The dancers applauded hungrily, and the band took up the last strains again. Again Forbes caught Persis to him, and they reveled till the music repeated its final crash.

Then they stood in mutual embrace for an instant that seemed a long time to him. He ignored the other couples dispersing to their tables to resume their interrupted feasts.

He was bemused with a startled unbelief. How marvelous it was that he should be here with her! He had come to the city a stranger, forlorn with loneliness, at noonday. And at noon of night he was already embracing this wonderful one and she him, as if they were plighted lovers.

CHAPTER IX

WILLIE ENSLEE brought the dancers off their pinions and back to earth by a fretful reminder that the bouillon was chilling in the cups, and the crab-meat was scorching in the chafing-dish.

The question of drinks came up anew. Forbes was in a champagne humor; his soul seemed to be effervescent with little bubbles of joy. But Mrs. Neff wanted a Scotch highball. Winifred was taking a reduction cure in which alcohol was forbidden. Persis wanted two more cocktails. Ten Eyck was on the water-wagon in penance for a recent outbreak. Bob Fielding was one of those occasional beings who combine with total abstinence a life of the highest conviviality. Offhand, one would have said that Bob was an incessant drinker and a terrific smoker. As a matter of fact, he had never been able to endure the taste of liquor or tobacco. When he ordered mineral water, or even milk, nobody was surprised; even the waiter assumed that the big man had just sworn off once more.

Forbes experienced a sinking of the heart as each of the guests named his choice, and nobody asked for any of the waiting champagne.

Yet when Willie turned to him and said, "Mr. Forbes, you have the two bottles of *brut* all to yourself," Forbes felt compelled to shake his head in declination. He never knew who got the champagne. He wondered if the waiter smuggled it out or juggled it on the accounts. And Willie forgot to ask Forbes what he would have instead! Willie ordered for himself that most innocent of

51

beverages which masquerades ginger ale and a section of lemon peel under the ferocious name, the bloodthirsty and viking-like title of "a horse's neck." There was a lot of it in a very large glass, and Forbes noted how Willie's little hand looked like a child's as he clutched the beaker. And he guzzled it as a child mouths and mumbles a brim.

Forbes observed how variously people imbibed. There were curious differences. Some shot their glasses to their lips, jerked back their heads, snapped their tongues like triggers, and smote their throats as with a solid bullet. Some stuck their very snouts in their liquor like swine; others seemed hardly to know they were drinking as they flirted across the tops of their glasses.

Persis did not raise her eyes as she sipped her cocktail. She looked down, and her lips seemed to find other lips there. Forbes wondered whose.

There was some rapid stoking of food against the next dance. When it irrupted, Forbes, greatly as he longed to dance again with Persis, invited Winifred for decorum's sake. Winifred speedily killed the self-confidence he had gained from his first flight. His sense of rhythm was incommensurate with hers. When she foretold his next step, she foretold it wrong. He lost at once the power to act as leader, and when she usurped the post he was no better as follower.

As Forbes wrestled with her he caught glimpses of Persis dancing with Willie for partner. Little Willie's head barely reached her bare shoulder. He clutched her desperately as one who is doomed from babyhood not to be a dancer. Still he hopped ludicrously about, and almost made her ludicrous.

Forbes longed to exchange partners with Willie, for he felt that he and Winifred were equally ludicrous. They were making the heaviest of going. He gave up in despair and returned to the table.

When the music stopped there was another interlude of supper. People gulped hastily, as at a lunch-counter when the train is waiting. Forbes intended to sit out the next dance; but he found himself abandoned as on a desert island with Mrs. Neff.

"Come along, young man," she said.

"I'm afraid I don't know how."

"Then I'll teach you."

"But—"

"Don't be afraid of me. I've got a son as old as you, and I taught him."

Forbes had danced at times with elderly women, but not such a dance as this. It was uncanny to be holding in his arms the mother of a grown man, and to be whirling madly, dipping and toppling like wired puppets.

Mrs. Neff's spirit was still a girl's. Her body felt as young and lissome in his arms as a girl's. Her abandon and frivolity were of the seminary period. Now and then he had to glance down at the white hair of the hoyden to reassure himself. The music had the power of an incantation; it had bewitched her back to youth. It seemed to Forbes that this magic alone, which should turn old women back to girlhood for a time, could not be altogether accursed.

Perhaps the music had unsettled his reason, but in the logic of the moment he felt that there was a splendid value in the new fashion, which broke down at the same time the barriers of caste and the walls of old age.

It was the Saturnalia come back. The aristocrats mingled as equals with the commoners, and the old became young again for yet a few hours.

He had read so much about the cold, the haughty, and the bored-to-death society of New York, yet here he was, a young lieutenant from the frontier, and he was dancing a breakdown with one of the most important matrons in America. And she was cutting up like a hired girl at a barn-dance. Plainly the nation was still a republic.

When the music ended with a jolt Mrs. Neff clung dizzily

to him, gave him an accolade of approval with her fan, and booked him for the next dance but one. If Forbes had had social ambitions, he would have felt that he was a made man. Yet if he had had social ambitions he would probably have betrayed and so defeated them.

Mrs. Neff having granted him a reprieve of one dance, Forbes made haste to ask Persis for the next. She smiled and gave him that wren-like nod.

His heart beat with syncopation when he rose at the first note of music. How differently she nestled and fitted into his embrace. Winifred had been more than an arm-load, and gave the impression of an armor of silk and steel and strained elastic. Mrs. Neff was too slender for him, and for all her agility there was a sense of bones and muscles. But Persis was flesh in all its magic. She was not bones nor muscles nor corsets, she was a mysterious embodiment of spirit and beauty, fluid yet shapely, unresisting yet real, gentle and terrible.

By now Forbes was familiar enough with the trickeries of the steps to leave his feet to their own devices. He was a musician who knows his instrument and his art well enough to improvise: soul and fingers in such rapport that he hardly knows whether the mood compels the fingers or the fingers suggest the mood.

And the same rapport existed with Persis. They evaded collisions with the other dancers and with the gilded columns by a sort of instinct; they sidled, whirled, dipped, pranced, or pirouetted, composed strange contours of progress as if with one mind and one body.

And now the rapture of the dance was his, and he was enabled to play upon her grace and her miraculously pliant sympathy. Her brow was just at the level of his lips, and he began to wish to press his lips there. Now and then her eyelids rose slowly and she looked up into his downward gaze. They were mysterious looks she gave him. They were to her as impersonal and vague as the rapture that fills the eyes when the west is epic with sunset, or when an orchestra pours forth a chord of unusual ecstasy, or a rose is so beautiful that it inspires a kind of heavenly sorrow.

But Forbes misunderstood. He usurped to himself the tribute she was unconsciously paying to the mere beatitude of being alive and in rhythmic motion to music.

We have built up strange subtleties of perception. The most intolerable discords are those of tones that lie just next each other; the harshest of noises rise when an instrument is only a little out of tune or a voice sings a trifle off the key.

Persis had accepted Forbes at Ten Eyck's rating as a gentleman to whom she could intrust her body to embrace and carry through the complex evolutions of a dance on a floor whose very throngs made a solitude and concealment for wantonness of thought and carriage.

So intimate a union is required when two people dance that it is easy to understand why the enemies of the dance denounce it as shameless carnality. It is hard to explain to them how potently custom and minute restraints permit an innocent dalliance with the materials of passion. One can only compare it to skating over thin ice, and say that so long as one keeps on skating a tiny crust of chill permits a joyous exercise without a hint of the depths beneath. And the ice itself gives warning when the danger is too close; its tiny crackling sound is thunder in the ears.

This was Forbes' experience. A beautiful woman of exquisite breeding gave him a certain enfranchisement of her person. He could take her in his arms, and she him in hers. She would make herself one flesh with him; he could sway her this way and that, drag her forward or backward, co-exist with her breast to breast, thigh to thigh, and knee to knee. But he must not ever so slightly take advantage of her faith in him. He must not by the most delicate pressure or quirk of muscle imply anything beyond the nice conventions and romantic pretenses of the dance. Actresses make the same distinctions with stage kisses, and endure with pride before a thousand eyes what they would count a vile insult in the shadow of the wings or at a dressing-room door.

Forbes made the old mistake. Nothing venture, nothing gain, is a risky proverb. He ventured almost unconsciously, without any baseness of motive. Or, rather, he did not so much venture as relax his chivalry. He breathed too deeply of her incense, paid her the tribute of an enamored thought, constrained her with an ardor that was infinitesimally more personal than the ardor of the dance.

Somehow she understood. Instantly she was a little frightened, a little resentful. As subtle as the pressure of his arm was the resistance of her body. The spell of the dance was dissolving, the thin ice crackling. He whispered hastily:

"Forgive me!"

She simply whispered:

"All right."

And the spirit of the temple of dance was rescued and restored. He had sung a trifle sharp, and she, like a perfect accompanist, had brought him back to the key.

But even as they whirled on and hopped and skipped in the silly frivolity of the turkey-trot he was solemnly experiencing an awe of her. And now her beauty was less victorious over him than that swift pride which could rebuke so delicately, that good-sportsmanship which could so instantly accept apology.

When the music ended he mumbled:

"Will you ever dance with me again?"

She abashed him with the true forgiveness that forgets, and spoke with all cheerfulness:

"Of course! Why not?"

The incident was closed in her heart. Its influence had just begun in his.

CHAPTER X

THE turbulence of the dance increased as the respectabler people were sifted out. Hysteria is a kind of fretful fatigue, and the wearier these children of joy were, the more reckless they grew.

Willie Enslee first insinuated, then declared that he had had enough. He yawned frankly and abysmally. He urged that it was high time they were all in bed. But the women begged always for yet another dance.

"Just one little 'nother," Winifred wheedled.

Ten Eyck whispered, "About this time Winifred always begins to talk baby-talk."

She was soon calling Forbes "the li'l snojer man." Whether the wine or the dance were the chief intoxicant, a tipsiness of mood prevailed everywhere. It affected individuals individually: this one was idiotically amused, that one idiotically tearful, a third wolfishly sullen, a fourth super-royally dignified, a fifth so audacious that her befuddled companions tried to restrain her.

The thin ice was breaking through in spots, and a few of the couples were floundering in black waters.

Others were merely childish in their wickedness. They tried to be vicious, and their very effort made them only naughty.

It all reminded Forbes of certain savage debauches he had witnessed. Only the savages lacked the weapons of costume. It was curious—to a philosopher it was amusingly curious—to see how much excitement it gave some of these people to expose or behold a shoulder or a shin more than one ordinarily did. The peculiar cult that has

57

grown about the human leg, since it has been wrapped up, is surely one of the quaintest phases of human inconsistency.

But intention is the main thing, and a circus woman in trapeze costume may suggest less erotic thought than a flirt who merely gathers her opera cloak about her closely. There was no mistaking the intention of some of these dancers. It was vile, provocative, and, since it was public, it was hideous. Mobs left without rule or inspiring rulers always degenerate into excesses. The pendulum that swings too far one way is only gathering heavier and heavier impetus to the other extreme.

It happens whenever emotions are overstrained. At religious revivals and camp-meetings and crusades, no less than at revels, the aftermath is apt to be grossness. These people had danced too long. It was time to go home.

Forbes finally agreed with Willie that it was no place for decent people. He began to wish very earnestly that Persis were not there. He would rather miss the sight of her than see her watching such spectacles. He felt a deep yearning that she should be ignorant of the facets of life that were glittering here. This longing to keep another heart clean or to restore it to an earlier purity is the first blossom of real love.

The floor grew so rowdy that Forbes would no longer take Persis out upon it. He did not ask her to dance again. Even when she raised her eyebrows invitingly he pretended not to understand.

Then she spoke frankly:

"Sha'n't we have another dance? They're playing the tune that made Robert E. Lee famous."

"I'm afraid I'm too tired," he pleaded. As soon as he had spoken he felt that the pretext was insultingly inadequate addressed to a woman and coming from a soldier used to long hikes. But it was the only evasion he could imagine in his hurry. Instead of turning pale with anger, as he expected, she amazed him by her reply:

"That's very nice of you."

"Nice of me," he echoed, fatuously, "to be tired?"

"Umm-humm," she crooned.

"Why?"

"Oh, just because."

Then he understood that she had read his mind, and she became at once a sibyl of occult gifts. This ascription of extraordinary powers to ordinary people is another sign that affection is pushing common sense from his throne. Parents show it for their newborn, and what is loving but a sort of parentage by reincarnation?

Forbes thought that he wore a mask of inscrutable calm, because he was accustomed to repressing his naturally impetuous nature. He had not realized that the most eloquent form of expression is repression. It is the secret of all great actors, and enables them to publish a volume of meaning in a glance or a catch in the voice, a quirk of the lips or a twiddling of the fingers.

Forbes never dreamed that the gaucherie of his excuse showed the desperation of his mind and the strain on his feelings, and that while his lips were mumbling it his eyes were crying:

"Don't stay here any longer. You are tired. You do not belong here. I beg you to be careful of your soul and body. Both are precious. It makes a great difference to me what you see and do and are."

All this was writ so large on his whole mien that anybody might have read it. Even Winifred read it and exchanged a glance with Mrs. Neff, who read it, too. Naturally, Persis understood. The feeling surprised her in a stranger of so brief acquaintance. But she did not resent his presumption as she did Willie's equal anxiety. She rather liked Forbes for it.

. Then she saw his consternation at her miraculous powers, and she liked him better yet for a strong and simple man whose chivalry was deeper than his gallantry.

And when a man from another table came across to ask her to dance with him, she answered:

"Sorry, Jim, we're just off for home. Come along, Willie. Are you going to keep us here all night?"

Willie lost no time in huddling his flock away from the table. He fussed about them like a green collie pup.

They paused at the door for a backward look. Seen in review with sated eyes, it was a dismal spectacle. On the floor a few dancers were glued together in crass familiarity, making odious gestures of the whole body. At the disheveled tables disheveled couples were engaged in dalliance more or less maudlin. Many of the women were adding their cigarette-smoke to the haze settling over all like a gray miasma.

"Disgusting! Disgusting!" Willie sneered.

"Oh, the poor things!" sighed Mrs. Neff. "What other chance have they? At a small town dance they'd behave very carefully in the light, and stroll out into the moonlight between dances. Good Lord, I used to have my head hugged off after every waltz. I'd walk out to get a breath of air, and have my breath squeezed out of me. But these poor city couples—where can they spoon, except in a taxi going home, or on a park bench with a boozy tramp on the same bench and a policeman playing chaperon? Let 'em alone."

But she yawned as she defended them, and looked suddenly an old woman tired out. They all looked tired.

They slipped weary arms into the wraps they had flung off with such eagerness. In the elevator they leaned heavily against the walls, and they crept into the limousine as if into a bed.

Forbes said that he would walk to his hotel. It was just across the street. They bade him good night drearily and slammed the door.

He watched the car glide away, and realized that he was again alone. None of them had asked him to call, or mentioned a future meeting. Had he been tried and discarded?

CHAPTER XI

THE sky was black, and the stars dimmed by the street-lights. Stars and street-lights seemed to be weary. The electric acrobats had knocked off work, and hung lifeless upon their frames like burned-out fireworks.

A grown-up newsboy, choosing a soft tone as if afraid to waken the sleeping town, murmured confidentially: "Morn' paper? *Joinal, Woil, Hurl, Times, Sun, Tolegraf?* Paper, boss?"

Forbes bought one to enjoy the paradox of reading to-morrow's paper last night.

He entered the brightly lighted lobby of the hotel. It was deserted save by two or three scrubwomen dancing a "grizzly bear" on all fours. They looked to be grand-mothers. Perhaps their granddaughters were still danc-ing somewhere.

Once in his room, Forbes stared from his window across the slumbrous town. The very street-lamps had the dron-ing glimmer of night lights in a bedroom. The few who were abroad wore the appearance of prowlers or watch-men or hasteners home. New York was not so lively all night as he had been taught to believe.

While he peeled off his clothes he glanced at his news-paper. The chief head-lines were given, not to the epochal event of the first parliament in the new republic of China, nor to the newest audacity in the Amazonian insurrection in London, but to an open letter sent by the mayor of New York to the police commissioner of New York, calling upon him "to put an end to all these vulgar orgies" of the "vulgar, roistering, and often openly immodest" people who "indulge in lascivious dancing." The mayor announced that one o'clock in the morning was none too soon for reputable people to stop dancing. He instructed the commissioner to see to it that at that hour thereafter every dance-hall was empty, if he had to take the food and drinks from the very lips of the revelers and put them in the street.

Forbes was amazed. The great, the wicked city still had a Puritan conscience, a teacher to punish its naughtiness and send it to bed—and at an hour that many farmers and villagers would consider early for a dance to end. Forbes was startled to realize that he was included in the diatribe, and that those ferocious words were applied to Persis, too.

In all the things he had to wonder at this was not the least wonderful. He stepped into his pajamas and spread himself between his sheets, too weary to reach forth a hand and turn out the little lamp by his bed.

He had slept no more than half an hour when suddenly he wakened. The last cry of a bugle seemed to be ringing in his ears. He sat up and looked at his watch. It was the hour when for so many years the cock-a-doodle-doo of the hated reveille had dragged him from his blankets. Habit had aroused him, but he thanked the Lord that now he could roll over and go back to sleep.

He rolled over, but he could not sleep. Daylight was throbbing across the sky like the long roll of the drums. Street-cars were hammering their rails. The early-morning population was opening the city gates, and the advance-guards of the commercial armies were hurrying to their posts. The city, which he had seen at its dress-parade and at its night revels, was beginning its business day with that snap and precision, that superb zest and energy and efficiency that had made it what it was.

It was impossible for Forbes to lie abed where so much was going on. Fagged as he was, the air was electric, and he had everything to see.

He pried his heavy legs from the bed, and clenched his muscles in strenuous exercise while his tub filled with cold water. He came out of it renewed and exultant.

When he was dressed and in the hall he surprised the chambermaids at their sweeping. They were running vacuum cleaners like little lawn-mowers over the rugs.

In the breakfast-room he was quite alone. But the streets were alive, and the street-cars crowded with the humbler thousands.

He walked to Fifth Avenue. It was sparsely peopled now, and even its shops were still closed. The homes were sound asleep, save for an occasional tousled servant yawning at an area, or gathering morning papers from the sill.

He walked to Central Park. The foliage here was wide awake and all alert with the morning wind. He strolled through the Zoo; the animals were up and about—the bison and deer, the fumbling polar bears. The lions and tigers were already pacing their eternal sentry-posts; the hyenas and wolves were peering about for the loophole that must be found next time; the quizzical little raccoons were bustling to and fro, putting forth grotesque little hands.

Forbes crossed bridges and followed winding paths that led him leagues from city life, though the cliffs of the big hotels and apartment-houses were visible wherever he turned. On one arch he paused to watch a cavalcade of pupils from a riding-school. He was surprised to see them out so early. Other single equestrians came along the bridle-path, rising and falling from their park saddles in the park manner.

There were few women riding, and few of these rode sidewise. He was used to seeing women astride in the West; but here they did not wear divided skirts and sombreros; they wore smart derby hats, long-tailed coats, riding-trousers, and puttees.

Coming toward him he noted what he supposed to be

an elderly man and his son. They were dressed almost exactly alike. As they approached, he saw that the son was a daughter. The breeze blew back the skirts of her coat, and as far as garb was concerned she was as much a man as the white-mustached cavalier alongside.

He clutched the rail hard. The girl was Persis, different, yet the same. There was a quaintly attractive boyishness about her now, an unsuspected athleticism. Her hair was gathered under her hat, her throat was clasped by a white stock. Her cutaway coat was buttoned tightly over a manly bosom, and her waist was not waspish. Her legs were strong, and gripped the horse well.

He could hardly believe that the lusciously beautiful siren he had seen with bare shoulders and bosom, and clinging skirts, the night before, was this trimly buttoned-up youth in breeches and boots. Could an orchid and a hollyhock be one and the same?

He had felt sure that at this hour, and on till noon, she would be stretched out in a stupor of slumber under a silken coverlet in a dark room.

The night had been almost ended when he had left her heavy-eyed with fatigue, yet the morning was hardly begun when he saw her here with face as bright and heart as brisk as if she had fallen asleep at sunset.

Her eyes were turned full upon him when she looked up before she passed under the bridge.

A salvo of greeting leaped into Forbes' eyes, and his hand went to his hat; but before he could lift it she had lowered her eyes. She vanished from sight beneath him, without recognition.

He hurried to the other side of the bridge, to catch her glance when she turned her head. But she did not look. She was talking to the elderly man at her side. She was singing out heartily:

"Wake up, old boy, I'll beat you to the next policeman."

The old boy put spurs to his horse, and they dwindled at a gallop.

Forbes watched her till the trees at the turn in the bridle-path quenched her from his sight. The light went out of his sky with her.

She had looked at him and not remembered him! He would have known it if she had meant to snub him. He had not even that distinction. He was merely one of the starers always gazing at her.

He had held her in his arms. But then so many men had held her in their arms when she danced. Even his daring had not impressed her memory. So many men must have pressed her too daringly. It was part of the routine of her life, to rebuff men who made advances to her.

Forbes left the bridge and left the park, humbled to nausea. His cheeks were so scarlet that the conductor on the Seventh Avenue car stared at him. He could not bear to walk back to his hotel. When he reached there he went to his room, dejected. There was nothing in the town to interest him. New York was as cold and heartless as report had made it.

He realized that he was very tired. He lay down on his bed. A mercy of sleep blotted out his woes. It seemed to be only a moment later, but it was high noon when his telephone woke him. He thought it an alarm-clock, and sat up bewildered to find himself where he was and with all his clothes on.

From the telephone, when he reached it, came the voice of Ten Eyck.

"That you, Forbesy? Did I get you out of bed? Sorry! I have an invitation for you. You made a hell of a hit with Miss Cabot last night. I know it, because Little Willie is disgusted with you. Winifred says she is thinking of marrying you herself, and Mrs. Neff says you can be her third husband, if you will. Meanwhile, they want you to have tea with us somewhere, and more dancings. Wish I could ask you to take breakfast with me at the Club, but I was booked up before I met you.

5   65

Save to-morrow for me though, eh? I'll call for you this afternoon about four, eh? Right-o! 'By!"

Forbes wanted to ask a dozen questions about what Persis had said, but a click showed that Ten Eyck had hung up his receiver. Forbes clung to the wall to keep the building from falling on him.

She had not forgotten him! She had been impressed by him! It was small wonder that she had not known him this morning. Had he not thought her a young man at first? Besides, she had had only a glance of him, and he was not dressed as she had seen him first.

The main thing was that she wanted to see him again, she wanted to dance with him again. She had betrayed such a liking for him that the miserable runt of a Little Willie had been jealous.

What a splendid city New York was! How hospitable, how ready to welcome the worthy stranger to her splendid privileges!

CHAPTER XII

FORBES had planned to visit the Army and Navy Club, in which he held a membership, but now he preferred to lunch alone—yet not alone, for he was entertaining a guest.

The head waiter could not see her when Forbes presented himself at the door of the Knickerbocker café. And when he pulled out the little table to admit Forbes to a seat on the long wall-divan that encircles the room, the head waiter thought that only Forbes squeezed through and sat down. The procession of servitors brought one plate, one napkin, silver for one, ice and water for one, brown bread and toast for one; and the waiter heard but one portion ordered from the *hors d'œuvres variés*, from the *plat du jour* in the *roulante*, and from the *patisseries*.

But Forbes had a guest. She sat on the seat beside him and nibbled fascinatingly at the banquet he ordered for her.

The vivacious throng that crowds this corner room at noon paid Forbes little attention. Many would have paid him more had they understood that the ghost of Persis Cabot was nestling at his elbow, and conspiring with him to devise a still newer thing than the dancing tea or the tango luncheon—a before-breakfast one-step. In fancy he was now thridding the maze between the tables with her.

But he paid for only one luncheon. The bill, however, shocked him into a realization that he could not long afford such fodder as he had been buying for himself. He decided to get his savings deposited somewhere before they had slipped through his fingers.

WHAT WILL PEOPLE SAY?

On his way to New York he had asked advice on the important question of a bank, and had been recommended to an institution of fabulous strength. It did not pay interest on its deposits, but neither did it quiver when panics rocked the country and shook down other walls.

When Forbes computed the annual interest on his savings, the sum was almost negligible. But the thought of losing the principal in a bank-wreck was appalling. He chose safety for the hundred per cent. rather than a risky interest of four. Especially as he had heard that Wall Street was in the depths of the blues, and New York in a doldrums of uncertainty.

To Forbes, indeed, nearly everybody looked as if he had just got money from home and expected more, and the talk of hard times was ludicrous in view of these opulent mobs and these shop-windows like glimpses of Golconda. But perhaps this was but the last flare of a sunset before nightfall.

In any case, he was likely to have his funds tempted away from him, and he must hasten to push them into a stronghold. He found at the bank that there was a minimum below which an account was not welcome. His painful self-denials had enabled him just to clear that minimum with no more interval than a skilful hurdler leaves as he grazes the bar.

He felt poorer than ever for this reminder of his penury, and he almost slunk from the bank. Just outside he stumbled upon Ten Eyck, who greeted him with a surprised:

"Do you bank here?"

"I was just opening an account," Forbes answered.

"Pardon my not lifting my hat before," said Ten Eyck. "I didn't know your middle name was Crœsus."

Forbes could only shrug his shoulders with deprecation. He had no desire to pose as a man of means, and yet he had too much pride to publish his mediocrity.

"I'll call for you at four, Mr. Rothschild," said Ten Eyck. "Got a date at Sherry's here. Good-by!"

WHAT WILL PEOPLE SAY?

The afternoon promised to be unconscionably long in reaching four o'clock, and Forbes set out for another saunter down the Avenue. There was a mysterious change. It might have been that the sky had turned gray, or that the best people were not yet abroad; but the women were no longer so beautiful. He kept comparing them with one that he had learned to know since yesterday afternoon's pageant had dazzled him. Already there was a kind of fidelity to her in this unconscious disparagement of the rest of womankind.

He did not explain it so easily to himself, nor did he understand why the shop-windows had become immediately so interesting. Yesterday a spadeful of diamonds dumped upon a velvet cloth was only a spadeful of diamonds to him, and it was nothing more. It stirred in him no more desire of possession than the Metropolitan Art Gallery or the Subway. He would have been glad to own either, but the lack gave him no concern.

This afternoon, however, he kept saying: "What would she think if I gave her that crown of rubies and emeralds? Does she like sapphires, I wonder? If only I had the right to take her in there and buy her a dozen of those hats? If that astounding gown were hung upon her shoulders instead of on that wax smirker, would it be worthy of her?"

He found himself standing in front of jewelers' windows, and trying to read the prices on the little tags. He had already selected one ring as an engagement ring, when he managed by much craning to make out the price. He fell back as if a fist had reached through the glass to smite him. If he could have drawn out his bank-account twice he could not have paid for it.

He gave up looking at diamonds and solaced himself by the thought that before he bankrupted the United States Army with buying her an engagement ring, he had better get her in love with him a little.

This train of thought impelled him to pause now before the windows of haberdashers. Without being at all a fop, he had a soldier's love of splendor, and he saw nothing effeminate in the bolts of rainbow clippings which men were invited to use for shirts. He looked amorously at great squares of silk meant to be knotted into neck-scarves, of which all but a narrow inch or two would be concealed. And he saw socks that were as scandalously brilliant as spun turquoises or knitted opals.

These little splashes of color were all that the sober male of the present time permits himself to display. They were all the more enviable for that. From one window a hand seemed to reach out, not to smite, but to seize him by his overworked scarf and hale him within. He departed five dollars the poorer and one piece of silk the richer, and hurried back to his room ashamed of his vanity.

On his way thither he remembered that he was still an officer in the regular establishment, and the first thing he did on his return to his room was to compose a formal report of his arrival in New York City. He sent it to the post at Governor's Island, so that in case a war broke out unexpectedly, an anxious nation might know where to find him.

The only war on the horizon, however, was the civil conflict inside his own heart. His patriotism was under-going a severe wrench. He was expected to maintain the dignity of the government on a salary that a cabaret per-former would count beneath contempt. And for this he was to give up his liberty, his independence, and his time. For this he was to teach nincompoops to raise a gun from the ground to their round shoulders, and to keep from falling over their own feet; for this he was to plow through wildernesses, give himself to volleys of bullets or mos-quitoes to riddle, or worse yet, to live in the environs of a great city where beauty and wealth stirred a caldron of joy from which he must keep aloof.

But that was for next week. For a few days more he

was exempt; he was a free man. And she wanted to dance with him again! She would not even wait for night to fall. She would dance with him in the daylight—with tea as an excuse!

He began feverishly to robe himself for this festival. Luckily for him and his sort, men's fashions are a republic, and Forbes' well-shaped, though last year's, black morning coat, the pin his mother gave him years ago skewering the scarf he had just bought, his waistcoat with the little white edging, his heavily ironed striped trousers, and his last night's top-hat freshly pressed, clothed him as smartly as the richest fop in town. It is different with women; but a male bookkeeper can dress nearly as well, if not so variously, as a plutocrat.

Forbes had devoted such passionate attention to the proper knotting of that square of silk, that he was hardly ready when the room telephone announced that Mr. Ten Eyck was calling for Mr. Forbes.

But his pains had been so well spent that Ten Eyck, meeting him in the lobby, lifted his hat with mock servility again, and murmured:

"Oh, you millionaire! Will you deign to have a drink with a hick like me?"

Forbes pleasantly requested him not to be a damned fool, but the flattery was irresistible.

They went to the bar-room, where, under the felicitous longitude of Maxfield Parrish's fresco of "King Cole," they fortified themselves with gin rickeys, and set forth for the short walk down Broadway and across to Bustanoby's.

They had been rejected here the night before, but Ten Eyck, at Persis' request, had engaged a table by telephone.

"It's Persis' own party," he explained; "but I have sad news for you: Little Willie isn't invited. He's being punished for being so naughty last night."

"He acted as if he owned Miss Cabot," said Forbes.

"He usually does."

"But he doesn't, does he?—doesn't own her, I mean?" Forbes demanded, with an anxiety that did not escape Ten Eyck, who answered:

"Opinions differ. He'll probably get her some day, unless her old man has a change of luck."

"Her old man?"

"Yes. Papa Cabot has always lived up to every cent he could make or inherit; but he's getting mushy and losing his grip. The draught in Wall Street is too strong for him. Persis will hold on as long as she can, but Little Willie is waiting right under the peach-tree with his basket, ready for the first high wind."

"She couldn't marry him."

"Oh, couldn't she? And why not?"

"She can't love a—a—him?"

"He is an awful pill, but he's well coated. His father left him a pile of sugar a mile high, and his mother will leave him another."

"But what has that to do with love?"

"Who said anything about love? This is the era of the modern business woman."

Forbes said nothing, but looked a rebuke that led Ten Eyck to remind him:

"Remember you promised not to marry her yourself. Of course, you may be a bloated coupon-cutter, but Willie has his cut by machinery. If you put anything less than a million in the bank to-day, you'd better not take Persis too seriously. Girls like Persis are jack-pots in a big game. In fact, if you haven't got a pair of millions for openers, don't sit in. You haven't a chance."

"I don't believe you," Forbes thought, but did not say.

They reached the restaurant, and, finding that Persis had not arrived, stood on the sidewalk waiting for her. Many people were coming up in taxicabs, or private cars, or on foot. They were all in a hurry to be dancing.

WHAT WILL PEOPLE SAY?

"It's a healthier sport than sitting round watching somebody else play baseball — or Ibsen," Ten Eyck observed, answering an imaginary critic; and then he exclaimed:

"Here she is!" as a landaulet with the top lowered sped down the street. The traffic rules compelled it to go beyond and come up with the curb on its right. As it passed Forbes caught a glimpse of three hats. One of them was a man's derby, one of them had a sheaf of goura, one of them was a straw flower-pot with a white feather like a question-mark stuck in it. His heart buzzed with reminiscent anxiety. He turned quickly and noted the number of the car, "48150, N. Y. 1913." The woman he had followed up the Avenue was one of those two.

The chauffeur turned sharply, stopped, backed, and brought the landaulet around with the awkwardness of an alligator. A footman opened the door to Bob Fielding, Winifred Mather, and Persis Cabot.

The answer to the query-plume was Persis. Forbes saw a kind of mystic significance in it.

Winifred, as she put out her hand to him, turned to Persis:

"You didn't tell me our li'l snojer man was coming."

"I wasn't sure we could get him," said Persis, and gave Forbes her hand, her smile, and a cordial word. "Terribly nice of you to come."

He seized her hand to wring it with ardor, but its pressure was so lax that he refrained. His eyes, however, were so fervid that she looked away. For lack of support his hopes dropped like a flying-machine that meets a "hole in the air."

CHAPTER XIII

SHE was talking the most indifferent nothings as they went up the stairs to the dancing-room, a largish space with an encircling gallery. As usual the dancing-floor was a clearing in a thicket of tables. It was swarming already with couples engaged in the same jig as the night before.

The costumes were duller than at night, of course. Most of the men wore business suits; the women were not décolletées, and they kept on their hats.

Only Forbes noted at once that the crowd included many very young girls and mere lads. Here, too, there was a jumbled mixture of plebeian and aristocrat and all the grades between. There were girls who seemed to have been wanton in their cradles, and girls who were aureoled with an innocence that made their wildest hilarity a mere scamper of wholesome spirits.

An eccentricity of this restaurant was a searchlight stationed in the balcony. The operator swept the floor with its rays, occasionally fastening on a pair of professional dancers, and following it through the maze, whimsically changing the colors of the light to red or green or blue. For the general public the light was kept rosy.

When Forbes arrived a certain couple whirled madly off the dancing-floor straight into the midst of Persis' guests, with the havoc of a strike in a game of tenpins.

The young man's heel ground one of the buttons of Forbes' shoe deep into his instep, and the young girl's flying hand smote him in the nose. He needed all his

self-control to repress a yowl of pain and dismay. Persis
must have suffered equal battery, but she quietly straightened out the dizzy girl and smiled.

"Come right in, Alice; don't stop to knock."

The girl under whose feet the floor still eddied clung
to Persis and stared at her a second, then gasped:

"Oh, Miss Cabot, is it *you?* I must have nearly
killed you. Can you ever *ever* for*give* me?"

Persis patted her hand and turned her round to Forbes:
"You'd better ask Mr. Forbes. You gave him a lovely
black eye."

The girl acknowledged the introduction with a duck
and a prayer of wild appeal:

"Oh, Mr. Forbes, *what* a ghastly, *ghastly* shame!
Did I really hurt you? I must have simply *murdered*
you. I'm so a*shamed*. Can you ever *ever* forgive
me?"

Forbes smiled at her melodramatic agitation: "It's
nothing at all, Miss—Miss—I never liked this nose, anyway. I only wish you had hit it harder, Miss—"

"Miss Neff," Persis prompted. "You met her mother
last night."

Forbes vaguely remembered that somebody had said
something about a beautiful mother of a more beautiful
daughter; but he could not frame it into a speech, before
Persis startled the girl beyond reach of a pretty phrase,
by casually asking:

"Were you expecting to meet your mother here this
afternoon, Alice?"

"Good Lord, I should say *not!* Why?"

"I just wondered. She is to meet us here."

"When? In heaven's *name!* When?"

"She ought to be here now."

Alice thrust backward a palsied hand and, clutching the
young man she had danced with, dragged him forward.
He was shaking hands with Ten Eyck, and brought him
along.

"Stowe! Stowe!" Alice exclaimed, with a tragic fire that did not greatly alarm the young man; he was apparently used to little else from her.

"Yes, dear," he answered, with a lofty sweetness; and she cried:

"Oh, honey, what *do* you sup*pose?*"

"What, dear?"

"That awful Mother of mine is expected here any *moment!*"

The young man's majesty collapsed like an overblown balloon in one pop: "Lord!"

Tableau! Ten Eyck, seeing it, muttered, gloatingly: "Some folks gits ketched."

Alice turned eyes of reproach upon him:

"She'll *kill* us if she finds us together. Isn't there some other way out?"

"I could go down the stairs the waiters come up," said Stowe; "but how will you get home?"

"Oh, Mother will get me home all right, never fear!" said Alice. "Run for your *life*, honey. I'll have my maid call you on the 'phone later."

The young man gave her one long sad look fairly reeking with desperate kisses and embraces. Then he vanished into the crowd.

Alice must have remarked the comments in Forbes' eyes, for she turned to him:

"You mustn't misunderstand the poor boy, Mr. Forbes. Mr. Webb is as *brave* as a *lion*, but he runs away on my account. He knows that my mother will give me no rest if she finds it out."

"I understand perfectly," said Forbes. "There are times when the better a soldier is the faster he runs!"

"Mr. Forbes is a soldier," Persis explained.

"Oh, thank you, twice as much!" said Alice, "for appreciating the situation." Then she turned to Persis, and clenched her arm as if she were about to implore some unheard-of mercy: "And, Oh, Miss Cabot, will you do me one *terribly* great favor? I'll remember it to my *dying* day, if you only will."

"Of course, my dear," Persis answered, with her usual serenity. "What is it? Do you want me to tell your mother that I met you somewhere and dragged you here against your will to meet her?"

Alice's wide eyes widened to the danger-point:

"Aren't you simply *wonderful*! How on earth could you possibly have ever *ever* guessed it?"

Persis cast a sidelong glance at Forbes; it had all the effect of a wink without being so violent.

"I'm a mind-reader," she said.

Alice caught the glance but not the irony of it, and exclaimed:

"In*deed* she is, Mr. Forbes. She really *is*."

"I know she is," said Forbes, with a quiet conviction that was almost more noisy than the violent emphasis of Alice.

Persis gave Forbes another sidelong glance; this time with a meek wonderment in place of irony. Once more the man had shown a kind of awe of her. Unwittingly he was attacking her on her most defenseless wall; for a woman who is always hearing praise of her beauty or her vivacity, so hungers and thirsts after some recognition of her intellectual existence that she is usually quite helpless before a tribute to it.

Persis knew that there was no importance in her guess at what Alice was about to ask; but there was importance in the high rating Forbes gave it. The comfort she found in this homage was put to flight by Alice's nails nipping her arm.

"Before mother comes we must rehearse what we're to say. She thinks I went to one of those lectures on Current Topics. They're so very im*proving* that Mother can't bear to go herself. She sends *me* and then forgets to ask me what it was all about. So I sneaked it to-day and met Stowe."

Persis could not resist a motherly question: "Is this an ideal trysting-place, do you think?"

"Where's the harm? We couldn't go to the Park very well. Everybody's always going *by* and looking *on*."

"Why don't you receive Mr. Webb at home?"

"Oh, *why* don't I, indeed!· Mother won't allow him within a *mile* of the place. Didn't you know that?"

Persis shook her head and turned to Forbes: "Doesn't it sound old-fashioned, a young girl afraid of her parents?"

"Quite medieval," Forbes agreed.

"Oh, but you are quaint, Alice," Persis laughed. "I thought it only happened in books and plays, but here's Alice actually obeying a cruel order like that. I'd like to see my father try to boss me. I'd really enjoy it as a change."

Alice broke in: "Oh, fathers—they're different! My poor Daddelums was the sweetest thing on earth. I wrapped him round my little finger. But mother—umm, she gets her own way, I can tell you—at least she *thinks* she does. I wouldn't let *any* earthly power tear me away from my darling Stowe, but I don't dare face her down."

"I thought she always liked Mr. Webb?" Persis said.

"Oh, she did till his father's will was probated. His insurance was immense, but his debts were immenser. So poor Stowe is dumped upon the world with hardly a cent. Of course, I love him all the more; but mother has turned against him. I wouldn't mind starving with Stowe, but mother is *so* materialistic! She wants to marry me off to that dreadful old Senator Tait."

"Dreadful?" snorted Winifred, who had listened in silence. "Old? Senator Tait is neither dreadful nor old. He is a cavalier, and in the prime of his powers."

"You can have him!" snapped Alice, with a flare of temper that she regretted instantly, and the more sincerely since she knew that Winifred had long been angling vainly and desperately for the Senator. There was a bitterer sarcasm in her retort than she meant, but Winifred knew what Alice was thinking, and canceled it by meeting it frankly:

"I wish I could have him. God knows I'd prefer him to any of these half-baked whippersnappers that—"

"Winifred!" Persis murmured, subduingly; and Miss Mather subsided like a retreating thunder-storm. "The Senator is one of the—"

"I know he is, my dear," Alice broke in, in her most soothing tone. "He's far, *far* too splendid a man for a fool like me. But can't I admit how splendid he would be in the Senate Chamber without wanting him in my boudoir?"

"Alice!" gasped Persis. "Remember that there are young men present."

Forbes spoke very solemnly: "Pardon my asking, but do you really mean that Senator Tait is—is proposing for your hand?"

"So my awful mother says."

"It doesn't sound like the Senator Tait I used to know."

"You knew him well?" Persis asked, with a quick eagerness that did not quite conceal a note of surprise.

Forbes caught it, and answered somewhat icily: "I had that privilege. He and my father used to ride to the hounds together. In fact, they were together when my father's horse threw him and fell on him, and crushed him to death. Senator Tait brought the body home to my poor mother. He was very dear to us all."

Persis looked what sympathy she could for such remote suffering. And Forbes was something less of a stranger. Also he had moved one step closer to her degree.

He had appeared first under the auspices of Murray Ten Eyck, who guaranteed him as an officer in the army. He had demonstrated his own dignity and magnetism. And now his family was sponsored by an old-time friendship with Senator Tait, a very Warwick of American royalty.

CHAPTER XIV

PERSIS was not of the period or the set that thinks
much of family. In fact, the whole world and its
aristocracies have been shaken by too many earthquakes
of late to leave walls standing high enough to keep youth
from overlooking and overstepping them. Few speak of
caste nowadays except novelists, editors, and the very
old. What aristocracies we have are clubs or cliques
gathered by a community of tastes, and recruited individually.

In any case, the Persis that was willing to go out into
the byways and highways and public dancing-places would
have made no bones of granting her smiles and her hospitality to anybody that entertained her, mountebank or
mummer, tradesman or riding-master.

And yet it did Forbes no harm in her eyes to be established as of high lineage and important acquaintance. If
only now he were rich, he would be graduated quite into
the inner circle of those who were eligible to serious con-
sideration.

Unconsciously Ten Eyck gave him this diploma also,
though his motive was rather one of rebuke to Persis for
her little tang of surprise.

"You needn't raise your brows, Persis, because Forbesy
knows senators and things," he said. "He's a plutocrat,
too. I caught him depositing a million dollars in one of
our best little banks to-day."

"A million dollars!" Forbes gasped. "Is there that
much money in the world?"

Forbes had no desire to obtain the reputation of money

under false pretenses. Yet he could not delicately discuss his exact poverty. He could not decently announce: "I have only my small army pay and a few hundred dollars in the bank." It would imply that these people were interested in his financial status. Yet even the pretense by silence troubled him, till his problem was dismissed by an interruption:

"Is anybody at home?"

Mrs. Neff spoke into the stillness as if she had materialized from nothing. Nobody had noticed her approach, and every one was startled. To Forbes her sharp voice came as a rescue from incantation. And Mrs. Neff was in the mood of the most unromantic reality. She did not pause to be greeted or questioned, but went at her discourse with a flying start:

"I'm mad and I'm hungry as the devil—oh, pardon me! I didn't see my angel child. Alice, darling, how on earth did you get here? Murray, if you have a human heart in your buzzum get the waiter man to run for a sandwich and a—a—no, I'll be darned if I'll take tea, in spite of example to youngers, who never follow our good examples, anyway; make it a highball, Murray; Scotch, and quick!"

The waiter nodded in response to Ten Eyck's nod, and vanished with an excellent imitation of great speed.

"Give over, Win!" Mrs. Neff continued, prodding Miss Mather aside and wedging forward with the chair Ten Eyck surrendered to her. "What's in those sandwiches? Lettuce? Thanks! Don't all ask me at once where I've been! I'm the little lady what seen her dooty and done it. If my angel child had done hers she would be even now listening to a lecture on Current Topics, so that she could inform her awful mother, as she calls me, what the tariff talk is all about, and who Salonica is, and why the Vulgarians are fighting the Balkans. But, of course, being a modern child, she plays hookey and goes to *thés dansants* while her poor old mother works."   •

"But mother dear, I was just—"

"Don't tell it, my child! I know what you're going to say: that Persis picked you up and dragged you here by the hair, and Persis will back you up, of course, like the dear little liar she is. But I'll save you the trouble, darlings. Where is he? Is he still here or did he learn of my approach and flit?"

"He—who?" said every one, zealously, with a stare of innocence sadly overdone.

"He—who?" Mrs. Neff mocked. "He-haw! Oh, but you're a putrid lot of actors. So he has been here. Well, I mention no names, but if a certain young person whose initials are Stowe Webb wants to meet a little old lady named Trouble, let him come out from under the table."

"Mother dear, how you do run on," Alice protested. "I don't think you really need another highball."

"Another! Listen to that. Dutiful child trying to save erring mother from a drunkard's grave! And me choking with thirst since luncheon! Do you know where I've been? Yes? Then I will tell you. I've been at a committee meeting of the Vacation Savings Fund."

The waiter brought a tiny flask, a tall glass, and a siphon, and offered to mix her a potion; but she motioned him aside and arranged it to her own taste. The band struck up, and she sipped hastily as she talked:

"That's the most insulting music I ever heard, and I'm just mad enough to dance well. If nobody has any prior claim on this young soldier man, he's mine. Mr. Forbes, would you mind supporting your grandmother around the room once or twice?"

Forbes had counted on having this dance with Persis. He had wasted one important tango while Alice poured out her woes. To squander this dance on her mother was a grievous loss. There was nothing for him to do, however, but yield.

He bowed low and smiled. "Nothing would give me more pleasure."

Mrs. Neff returned his bow with an old-fashioned courtesy, as she beamed:

"Very prettily said! Old fashioned and nice. My first husband would have answered like that. Did Murray tell you that I had offered you the job of being my third husband?"

"Mother!" Alice gasped.

Forbes was exquisitely ill at ease. It is hard to parry banter of that sort from a woman. He bowed again and answered with an ambiguous smile:

"Nothing would give me more pleasure."

"Fine! Then we may as well announce our engagement. Kind friends, permit me to introduce my next husband, Mr. — Mr. — what is your first name, darling?"

"Mother!" Alice implored.

"Oh, I'm sure his first name can't be Mother. But we're missing the dance. Come along, hero mine!"

Forbes cast a farewell look of longing at Persis, who was regarding him with an amused bewilderment.

The blare of the band was as effectual as a Gabriel's trumpet opening graves. From the tables the dead came to life and took on stilts if not wings.

Big Bob Fielding and Winifred Mather set out at once in close embrace.

"Look at 'em! Look at 'em!" Ten Eyck chortled. "They're grappled like two old-time battleships on a heavy sea." Ten Eyck was the great-great-grandson of one of the first commissioned officers in the American navy, a rival even of Paul Jones. So now his comment was nautical. "Bob and Winifred remind me of the *Bonhomme Richard* and the *Serapis*. And Winifred is like old John Paul Jones: when everybody else is dead her motto is: 'I've just begun to fight.'"

But Alice could not smile. She folded her hands and sighed. "It's awful to be a widow when they play that tango."

Persis provided for her at once. "Murray, you take Alice out and dance with her."

Ten Eyck saluted. "Come on, Alice, we'll go in for the consolation stakes."

Alice protested: "But we can't leave you alone."

Persis beckoned to a lonesome-looking acquaintance at another table, and he came to her with wings outstretched. She locked pinions with him, and they were away.

Ten Eyck put his arms up like racks; Alice hung herself across them, and they romped away. As they performed it, the dance was as harmless as a game of tag.

As Persis was twirled past Forbes now and again, her eyes would meet his with a gaze of deep inquiry.

And he was thinking so earnestly of her that at some indefinitely later period he was almost surprised to find that Mrs. Neff was in his arms, and that they were footing it intricately through a restless maze. He realized, also, that he had not spoken to her yet. He cast about in his mind for a topic of conversation, as one whips a dark trout-pool, and brought up a question:

"That Vacation Savings Fund — may I ask what it is?"

"You may, indeed, young man," she answered, and talked glibly as she danced, occasionally imitating a strain of music with mocking sounds. "It's an attempt a lot of us old women have been making to teach the poor woiking goil what we can't learn ourselves; namely, to save up money—*la-de-de-da-de-da!* The poor things slave like mules and they're paid like slaves—*te-dum-te-dum!*— yet most of them never think of putting a penny by for a rainy day, or what's more important—*ta-ra-rum!*—a sunny day.

"So Willie Enslee's mother, and Mrs. Clifton Ranger, and the Atterby girls, and a gang of other busybodies got ourselves together and cooked up a scheme—*la-de-de-da-de-da!*—to encourage the girls to stay home—*ta-ra-rum!*—

84

from a few moving-picture fêtes and cut down their ice-cream-soda orgies a little, and put the pennies into a fund to be used in giving each of them—*te-dum-te-dum*—a little holiday when her chance came—*te-di-do-dee!*"

"Splendid!" said Forbes. "Did it work out?"

"Rather. We started with forty girls, and now we've got—how many do you suppose?"

"A hundred and fifty."

"Eight thousand! And they've saved fifty thousand dollars!"

"That's wonderful!" Forbes exclaimed, stopping short with amazement. Instantly they were as battered and trodden by the other dancers as a planet would be that paused in its orbit.

"Come on, or we'll be murdered!" cried Mrs. Neff, and dragged him into the current again.

Forbes looked down at her with a different feeling. This typical gadabout, light-minded, cynical little old woman with the girlish ways, was after all a big-hearted toiler in the vineyard. She did not dress as a Sister of Charity, and she did not pull a long and philanthropic face, but she was industrious in good works.

He was to learn much more of this phase of New York wealth, its enormous organizations for the relief of wretchedness, and its instant response to the human cry once it makes itself heard above the noise of the cars or the music of the band.

City people have always made a pretense of concealing their sympathetic expressions under a cynical mask. It is this mask that offends so many of the praters against cruelty, irritates them to denunciations more merciless than the lack of mercy they berate, and blinds their near-sighted eyes to the village heart that beats in every city—a huge heart made up of countless village hearts.

So Mrs. Neff, having betrayed an artless Samaritanism, made haste to resume the red domino of burlesque to hide her blushes, as children caught in a pretty action fall to capering. Her motive was not lost on Forbes when she said:

"We've got to do something to get into heaven, you know. That line about the camel and the needle's eye is always with us poor rich, though the Lord knows I'm not rich. I hope you have a lot of money, or we'll starve—unless we loot the Savings Fund."

He hardly knew what to say to this, so he danced a little harder and swept her off her feet, till she was gasping for breath and pleading:

"Stop, stop! I'm afraid I'm only an old woman after all. And I didn't want you to know."

He led her to a chair, where she sank exhausted and panting hard. By the time the dance was over and the rest had returned, she was herself again.

"My new husband is the love of a tangoist," she babbled across her highball. "If that infernal committee meeting hadn't kept me so late, I could have had more. Are you all going to the Tuesday to-night?"

They all were.

"I was to have taken Alice, but I'm going to put her to bed without any supper. I'll take Mr. Forbes instead. Will you come? Nothing would give you more pleasure. That's right. Sorry I can't accept your invitation to dinner, but I'm booked. What about the opera to-night? It's 'Tristan and Isolde' with Fremstad. Senator Tait was to have taken us, but he can't go; so Alice won't care to go. He sent me his box, and I have all those empty chairs to fill. Mr. Forbes can fill one. You can, can't you?" He nodded helplessly, and she hunted him a ticket out of a handbag as ridiculously crowded as a boy's first pocket. "It begins at a quarter to eight. I can't possibly be there before nine. You go when you want to. Who else can come?"

Persis said that she was dining at Winifred's with Willie, and added: "He hates the opera, but if I can drag him along I'll come. And if I can't I'll come anyway."

Winifred accepted for Bob. "I always think I ought to have been a grand-opera singer," she sighed, "I've got the build for it."

Ten Eyck "had a dinner-job on," but promised to drop in when he could.

Having completed her quorum, and distributed her tickets, Mrs. Neff made ready to depart by attacking her highball again. The music began before she had finished it, and Forbes rose before Persis with an old-time formula.

"May I have the honor?"

As Persis stepped into his arms, Winifred cried:

"Traitress! It's my turn with the li'l snojer man."

And Mrs. Neff caught Persis' elbow to say: "Be very circumspect or I'll sue you for alienation of the alimony."

Forbes and Persis sent back mocking smiles as they side-stepped into the carousel.

She was his again in the brief mock-marriage of the dance. His very muscles welcomed her with such exultance that he must forcibly restrain them from too ardent a clasp. The whole mood of the music was triumph, overweening boastfulness, and irresistible arrogance. It was difficult to be afraid of anything in that baronial walk-around.

But Forbes was afraid of silence. It gave imagination too loose a rein. To keep himself from loving her too well, and offending her again after she had forgiven him once, he had recourse to language, the old concealer of thought.

At first he had been too new to the steps to talk freely. Words had blurted out of him as from a beginner in a riding-school. But now there was a spirit in his feet that led him who knows how?

Forbes astonished Persis and himself by his first words:

"Don't you ever sleep, Miss Cabot?"

She threw him a startled glance. "Do I look so jaded as all that?"

He was so upset that he lost step and regained it with

awkwardness of foot and word. "No, no, it's be—because you look—you look as if you slept for—forever. I don't mean that exact—exactly, either."

"Then what do you mean, Mr. Forbes?"

"I mean: I left you this morning at about four o'clock in one costume, and I saw you at eight in another."

"At eight this morning? Oh yes, I was riding with my father. Were you riding, too? I didn't see you."

"Oh yes, you did. I stood on the bridge at daybreak. And you looked at me and cut me dead."

"Did I really? I must have been asleep."

"Far from it. Your eyes were as bright as—as—"

"This music is very reassuring, isn't it?"

"Yes; please blame the music if I grow too rash. But you really were wonderful. I thought you were a boy at first. And you ride so well! You were racing your father. How could you be so wide awake after so strenuous a night?"

"Oh, I had to get up. It is poor Dad's only chance nowadays. He's awfully busy in the Street, and he's so worried. And he needs the exercise. He won't take it unless I go along."

There was an interlude of tenderness in the music. He responded to it.

"That's very beautiful and self-sacrificing of you. But how can you keep up the pace?"

"I can't, much longer. I'm almost all in. The season is nearly over, though. If everything goes right, Dad and I will get out of town—to the other side, perhaps. Then I can sleep all the way across. If he can't go abroad, we'll be alone anyway, since everybody else will leave town. Then I can catch up on sleep."

"You must be made of iron," he said.

"Am I so heavy as all that?"

"Oh, no, no, you are—you are—" But he could not say anything without saying too much. She saved the day by a change of subject.

"And I stared right at you, and didn't know you?"

"Why should you? It was stupid of me to expect you to remember me. But I did, and—when you didn't, I was crushed."

"Of course you were," she crooned. "I always want to murder anybody who forgets me."

"Surely that can't happen often? How could any one forget You?"

It was perfectly sincere, yet it sounded like the bumptious praise of a yokel. She raised her eyelids and reproved him.

"That's pretty rough work for a West-Pointer. Rub it out and do it over again."

Again he lost the rhythm, and suffered agonies of confusion in recovering it. But the tango music put him on his feet again. How could he be humble to that uppish, vainglorious tune, that toreador pomposity?

Persis herself was like a pouter pigeon strutting and preening her high breast. All the dancers on the floor were proclaiming their grandeur, playing the peacock.

Forbes grew consequential, too, as he and Persis marched haughtily forward shoulder to shoulder, and outer hands clasped, then paused for a kick, whirled on their heels, and retraced their steps with the high knee-action of thoroughbreds winning a blue ribbon.

Then each hopped awhile on one foot, the other foot kicking between the partner's knees. Then they dipped to the floor. As he swept her back to her full height, the music turned sly and sarcastic. It gave an unreal color to his words.

"Will you pardon me one question?"

"Probably not. What is it?"

"Didn't you wear this same hat yesterday?"

Her head came up with a glare. "Isn't that a rather catty remark for a man to make?"

"Oh, I didn't mean it that way," he faltered. "It's a beautiful hat."

"No hat is beautiful two days in succession. It's unkind of you, though, to notice it, and rub it in."

"For heaven's sake, don't take it that way. I—I followed this hat of yours for miles and miles yesterday."

"You followed this hat?"

"Yes."

They danced, marched, countermarched, pirouetted, in a pink mist. And he told her in his courtly way, with his Southern fervor, how he had been captivated by the white plume, and the shoulder and arm, and the foot; how vainly he had tried to overtake her for at least a fleeting survey. He told her how keen his dismay was when she escaped him and fled north. He told her how he made a note of the number of her car. He did not tell her that he forgot it, and he did not dare to tell her that he was jealous of the unknown to whom she had hastened.

Persis could not but be pleased, though she tried to disguise her delight by saying:

"It must have been a shock to you when you saw what was really under this hat."

She had not meant to fish so outrageously for a compliment. She understood, too late, that her words gave him not only an excuse, but a compulsion to praise. Praise was not withheld.

"If you could only know how I—how you—how beautiful you—how—I wish you'd let me say it!"

"You've said it," she murmured. His confusion revealed an ardor too profound to be rebuked or resisted. She luxuriated in it, and rather sighed than smiled:

"I'm glad you like me."

It was a more girlish speech than she usually made. Unwittingly she crept a trifle closer to him, and breathed so deeply that he felt her bosom swell against him with a strangely gentle power. By immeasurably subtle degrees the barrier between them dissolved, or rather shifted until it surrounded them. They were no longer strangers. They were together within a magic inclosure.

He understood the new communion, and an impulse swept him to crush her against him. He fought it so hard that his arm quivered. She felt the battle in his muscles, and rejoiced in the duel of his two selves, both hers. She knew that she had a lover as well as a guardian in his heart.

She looked up to see what manner of man this was who had won so close to her soul in so brief a time. He looked down to see who she really was. Their eyes met and held, longer than ever before, met studiously and hospitably, as the eyes of two lonesome children that have become neighbors meet across a fence.

What she saw in his gaze gave a little added crimson to her cheeks. And then the music flared up with a fierce ecstasy that penetrated even their aloofness. He caught her close and spun with her in a frenzied rapture round and round. He shunted other dancers aside and did not know it. He was glared at, rebuked, and did not know it. The impetus of the whirl compelled a tighter, tighter clutch. Their hands gripped faster. He forgot everything in the mystic pursuit and surrender of the dance, the union and disunion of their bodies—her little feet companioning his, the satin and steel of her tense sinews, the tender duality of her breast against the rock of his, the flutter of her quick, warm breath on his throat, the sorcery of her half-averted eyes tempting his lips almost unbearably.

The light burned about them like a flaming rose. The other couples had paused and retreated, staring at them; but they did not heed their isolation. They swooped and careened and twirled till they were blurred like a spinning top, till they were exhausted and wavering in their flight.

At length he found that she was breathless, pale, squandered. She hung all her weight on his arm, and grew so heavy that it ached.

And now, when he looked down at her, he saw that the operator had inadvertently put upon them the green light. In Forbes' eyes it had a sickly, cadaverous glimmer as of death and dissolution. He did not know that she was about to swoon; but she was so gray and lifeless that he was frightened. In the green, clammy radiance she looked as if she had been buried and brought back to the daylight. She was horribly beautiful.

Just in time the music came to an abrupt end, and the *danse macabre* was done. But the floor still wheeled beneath his feet, and he staggered as he held her limp and swaying body.

She shook the dizziness from her eyes, and put away his arm, but seized it again. He supported her to the table and guided her to a seat. Then he caught up a glass and put it to her wan mouth.

Ten Eyck, who had been watching them from his place, shoved a chair against Forbes relaxing knees, and set a tall glass in his hand, saying:

"Gad, old man, you need a drink!"

Forbes took a gulp of a highball and sat staring at Persis. Ten Eyck was quietly dipping his fingers into his own glass and flicking water on Persis' face. She regained her self-control wonderingly. Her lips tried pluckily to smile, though her eyes studied Forbes with a kind of terrified anger—more at herself than at him. He met them with a gaze of adoration and dread.

As his hot brow cooled, it seemed that an icy hand passed across it.

CHAPTER XV

THE safety match that resists all other friction needs only the touch of its peculiar mate to break into flame. And many chemical compounds, including souls, change their behavior and expose their secret identities when they meet just the right—or the just the wrong—reagent.

Persis Cabot was the wonder of her world for being at the same time so cordial and so cold, so lightly amused, so extravagant, and yet apparently so immune to the follies of passion. She was thought to be incapable of losing either her head or her heart. Mrs. Neff called her "fireproof."

Willie Enslee was universally accepted as her fiancé, simply because his wealth and his family's prestige were greater than anybody's else in her circle. This made him the logical candidate. Everybody knew that he was mad about Persis in his petty way. But nobody expected Persis to fall madly in love with Willie, or to let that failure keep her from marrying him.

And now Forbes appeared from the wilderness and strange influences began to work upon her. She began to study the man with increasing interest. She resented his effect upon her, and could not resist it. He was like a sharp knife, or a loaded revolver, or the edge of a cliff, quiet and unpursuing, yet latent with danger, terrifying and therefore fascinating.

Hitherto she had played with firearms and danced along abysses and juggled daggers in many a flirtation, but always she had kept her poise and felt no danger. Now she was just a trifle startled by a feeling of insecurity.

Many men had made ferocious love to her, had tried to set up a combustion in her heart, had threatened her with violence, with murder and with suicide; and she had laughed at them, laughed them back to the sanity she had never lost.

But this man Forbes made no campaign against her. If he pressed her too hard in the dance he apologized at once. He seemed to be at her mercy, and yet she felt that he brought with him some influence stronger than both. He was like one of Homer's warriors attended by a clouded god or goddess bent on his victory or his destruction—she could not tell which. When she caught him gazing at her devouringly he looked away, yet she found herself looking away, too, and breathing a little faster.

Scores of men had embraced her as she danced with them and some of them had muttered burning love into her ear. But they left her cold. This man said little or less, and he held her almost shyly; yet she felt a strange kindling in his touch, saw in his eye a smoldering.

In this last dance with him a panic of helplessness had confounded her. He had whirled her about till she had lost all sense of floor and ceiling. She felt herself falling and spinning down the gulfs of space in a nightmare of rapture. She would have swooned had he not seen how white and lost she was and stopped short. She had felt that other people were staring and making comments.

She was afraid to dance with him again. When she had regained her self-control she made a pretext to escape out of the lateness of the hour and the necessity of dressing for dinner and the opera.

There was an almost hysterical flippancy in her chatter. In spite of the protestations of the three men, she insisted on paying the bill. It was her own party, she said. The waiter looked sad at this, but what she left on the plate tempered his despair of her sex.

She offered to drop Forbes and Ten Eyck at their destinations, and they clambered into her car with Winifred and Bob. Forbes was all too soon deposited at his hotel, where the footman and the starter hailed Persis with affectionate homage and Forbes with a new courtesy because of her. Forbes lingered at the curb to watch her away. As the landaulet sped toward Fifth Avenue all he saw of her was the fluttering white interrogation-mark.

CHAPTER XVI

FORBES was prompt at the Opera. Though it was barely half past seven, he found the foyer already swarming with a bustling mob of women swaddled in opera-cloaks, and prosperous-looking men overcoated and mufflered. Everybody was making haste. Dinners' had been gulped or skimped, and there was evident desire not to miss a note.

Forbes knew nothing of the music except a vague echo of the ridicule on which Wagner had ridden to the clouds. He was just as ignorant of the poem, and though he bought a libretto from an unpromising vocalist in the lobby, he had time only to skim the argument, and to learn with surprise that Isolde was Irish, and her royal husband, Mark, a Cornishman.

The head usher directed him up a brief flight of steps, and another attendant unlocked a door marked with the name-plate of Lindsley Tait. From the little anteroom where he hung up his hat and coat, Forbes saw as through a telescope the vast curtain and the tremendous golden arch of the proscenium; at its foot a pygmy orchestra settling into tune and making oddly pleasant discords.

When Forbes stepped to the edge of the box, he seemed to be the entire audience, another mad King of Bavaria come to witness a performance in solitude. The famous red horseshoe stretched its length a hundred yards or more on either side of him. In each of its little scallops a family of empty chairs sat facing the stage in solemn silliness. The owners were still filling chairs at dinner-tables.

96

But when Forbes took the next step forward he found a multitude. Above him he saw other horseshoes in tiers dense with faces peering downward. Below him a plain of Babel inhabited by the tops of heads, numberless pates in long windrows, the men's skulls close-cropped or bald, and their shoulders black; the women's elaborately coiffed, over an enormous acreage of bared shoulders and busts.

Suddenly all the white-gloved hands fluttered in coveys with the show and sound of innumerable agitated pigeons. Toscanini was picking his way through the orchestra to the desk.

From the opening phrase of the Vorspiel Forbes became a Wagnerian. Those first stifled moans of almost sullen desire so whelmed him that he wondered how Persis and Mrs. Neff and her guests should dare to be late and lose this precious expression. Before the opera had finished breaking his heart on its eternal wheel of anguish, he wondered that any one should care to submit to its intolerable beauty a second time.

Yet here were thousands thronging to its destroying blaze like fanatic moths—moths that paid a high price to be admitted to the lamp, and clamored to be consumed in its divine distress.

Forbes smiled at the universal lust for artistic and vicarious suffering that has made other people's pathos the most lucrative of all forms of entertainment.

The time was to come when he himself would pay dearly for the privilege of great pain; when his mind would strive futilely to dissuade his heart from clenching upon the thorn that made it bleed. Humanity has almost always preferred strong emotions at any cost, to peace however cheap.

The prelude was one long stream of bitter-sweet honey, and it affected Forbes as music had never affected him. He wondered how people could ever have ridiculed or resisted this man Wagner. He wished that Persis would come soon. He thought of her as "Persis"—or "Isolde"; he could not think of her as Miss Cabot to this music.

The first act was ended and the long intermission almost over before she arrived, with Enslee, followed immediately by Bob and Winifred, and last of all by the hostess, Mrs. Neff.

Everybody greeted Forbes with the casual informality of old friendship, except Willie Enslee, who nodded obliquely, and murmured:

"H' are yu, Mr. Ward."

Nobody corrected him, least of all Forbes, who was too much disgusted with Willie's existence there to feel any minor resentment. The three women fell to wrangling, altruistically, of course, over the two front seats. Mrs. Neff was trying to bully Persis and Winifred into occupying them. Winifred's demurrer was violent:

"If I sit there nobody can see the stage. You're such a little wisp I can see round you or through you."

Persis preferred almost anything to a disturbance, and her protest was a mere form.

Only the rising curtain brought the battle to a close. Persis dropped into a chair on the right. Winifred pushed Mrs. Neff into the other, and sat back of her. Willie annexed the chair behind Persis, Bob Fleming took that aft of Winifred, and motioned Forbes to the center chair. Then Mrs. Neff beckoned him to hunch forward into the narrow space between her and Persis.

All along the horseshoe people were just arriving or returning from visits among the boxes. There was much chatter. The orchestra might as well have been wasting its sweetness on a crowded restaurant.

Forbes pretended to be looking over the audience on his right, but he was looking at Persis. The music of the garden where Isolde awaited her Tristan, and the far-off rumorous hunting-horns of the King, her husband, were working a magic upon her. He could see its influence on her face.

She wore brighter raiment than at the theater; her head-dress was more imperious, and more jewelry glittered about her. When she breathed or moved the diamonds at her ears, her throat, and in her corsage flashed and dulled as if they had eyelids; the pearls had a veiled radiance.

She was a combination of beauty unadorned and most adorned. Despite her trappings of gem and fabric, even more of her was candidly presented than at the theater last night—or was it not a year ago? Surely he must have known her for more than a day.

Her bodice would have seemed to be shamelessly low, had it not been as high as almost any other there. This was one of those common yet amazing sessions where thousands of women of every age and class agree to display as much of their skins as the police will allow, and far more than their husbands and fathers approve.

But Forbes had not yet reached the stage where a man resents the publication of his charmer's charms. He was still hardly more than a fascinated student of Persis. He found her a most engrossing text.

She was so thoroughly alive—terribly alive all over! Wordsworth's phrase would have suited Forbes' understanding of her: she "felt her life in every limb." Her brows now moved sinuously, and now relaxed as Isolde sang of her longing and quenched the torch for a signal to her lover. One moment Persis' eyelids throbbed with excitement; the next they fell and tightened across her eyes. Accesses of emotion swelled her nostrils and made her lips waver together. Her throat arched and flexed and was restless; and her lovelily disparted bosom filled and waned.

If she sat with clasped hands, the fingers seemed to convene and commune. She was incessantly thrusting back her hair and stroking her temples, or her forearms. Her knees were always exchanging places one above the other; her feet crossed, uncrossed, and seemed unable to settle upon precedence.

If she had been a child she would have been called fidgety, but all her motions were discreet and luxurious. She was like a lotos-eater stirring in sleep and just about to open her eyes.

The second act of the opera proved to be hardly more than a prolonged duet. The rapture of it outlasted Forbes' endurance; it did not bore him, it wore him out. He grew weary of eavesdropping on these two. He was jealous to love and be loved on his own account.

The woman next him was becoming more beautiful every moment. He felt a craving to touch her—with reverence; to link arms in comradeship, and to clench hands with her when the music stormed the peaks.

An aura seemed to transpire mistily from his pores to meet the aureole that shimmered about her.

His mood was far above any thought of flirtation, or evil desire. He was too knightly at heart to dream of adventure against her sacred isolation. But he wished and wished that he knew her better; had known her longer. Unconsciously he plagiarized the sigh of Johanna Ambrosius' poem: *"Ach, hätt' ich früher dich geseh'n!"*

But Fate can play the clown as well as the tragedian, and accomplish as much by an absurd accident as by elaborate glooms.

That afternoon, when Forbes was lured into the haberdashery, he had invested in black silk hosiery, very sheer and very dear. Later he had acquired a pair of new pumps. The shoes were not too small, but their rigid edge cut his instep like a dull knife. By the time that Isolde's husband had found her in Tristan's arms, and begun to deplore his friend's treachery at great length, the pressure upon Forbes' heart relaxed enough to let his feet attract his attention. They proclaimed their discomfort acutely.

After some hesitation he resolved to slip them out of their glistening jails a moment, under cover of the darkness.

A sense of immense relief rejoiced him when he sat with his silk-stockinged feet perched on top of instead of inside of his shoes. Though he was unaware of it, he was not the only one in that box to seize the opportunity. Heaven alone knew how much empty foot-gear was scattered along the floors of that opera-house. Persis for one had vacated her slippers long ago. She always did at every opportunity.

Eventually she tucked her little left foot back of her and bent it round the leg of her chair. By and by Forbes, in shifting his position, straightened his right knee. His foot collided with a most smooth something, and paused in a kind of surprise. Primevally our feet had as much tactile intelligence as our hands, and Forbes' almost prehensile big toe pondered that tiny promontory a second; then it hastily explored the glossy surface of Persis' sole.

Silk is a facile conductor of electricity, and Persis was not divine enough to be above ticklishness. Shudders of exquisite torment ran through her before she could snatch her foot away. And before she could check the impulse she snickered aloud.

And Forbes, suddenly understanding what he had done, snickered too, and just managed to throttle down a loud guffaw.

Mrs. Neff and Winifred turned in amazement at hearing such a sound at such a time, and the women in the next box craned their necks to inflict a punitive glare. Which made it all the worse.

Persis and Forbes were suddenly backslidden almost to infancy. They were like a pair of children attacked with a fit of giggles in church. The more they wanted to be sober, the more foolish they felt. The harder they tried to smother the laughter steaming within them, the more it threatened to explode.

Persis would have taken to flight, but one of her slippers she could not find, and she could not get the other on.

She and Forbes were still stuffing their handkerchiefs into their mouths when the act ended, as the pitifully distraught Tristan permitted the infuriated Melot to thrust him through with a sword, and fell back in Kurwenal's arms.

Mrs. Neff and her faction did not join the ovation to the singers. They were too busily demanding what Persis and Forbes had found to laugh at. But neither of them would tell. It was their secret.

Willie Enslee was acutely annoyed. He had not curiosity enough to be quick to jealousy, nor intelligence enough to suspect that Persis' and Forbes' laughter might be, must be, due to some encounter.

Still, he had ideals of his own, such as they were, and his religion was to avoid attracting attention. He had liked Persis because she was of the same faith; but now she had sinned against it, and he rebuked her. She did not flare up as usual. She laughed.

She was ashamed to have been so frivolous, ashamed to have profaned the temple of art with her childishness. And so was Forbes. But when they looked into each other's eyes now they no longer stared with timorous wonderment; they smiled together in a dear and cozy intimacy. And already they owned a secret.

CHAPTER XVII

MRS. NEFF and Winifred may have had their suspicions. They were both amiable cynics, and always put the worst possible interpretation on any happening. But whatever their theories, they could never have guessed the actual reason for the contretemps, and Persis speedily changed the subject. But her feet remembered it and tingled with reminiscent little electric storms. And when she looked at Forbes she tittered like a school-girl. So she avoided his eyes.

Willie was furious at Persis' lack of dignity, and forgot his own in complaining of it.

"Cut out the soubrette spasms, for God's sake, Persis, or let us all in on the joke. If you have any comic relief for this ghastly opera let me have it. Why did you drag me here, anyway? We might have gone to Hammerstein's. It wouldn't be so bad if Caruso were singing; but Caruso knows better than to bark himself hoarse on this Wagner fella. And that Dutch tenor has got to die yet. He'll be two hours dying, and then the lady has to follow suit. Why should we sit here all that time watching people die? Why didn't we go to Bellevue Hospital and watch an amusing operation? What would you say to making a sneak just about now and—"

"I'd say, run right along, Willie, if you want to," said Persis. "*Moi, j'y suis, j'y reste!*"

"Oh, all right, I suppose I'll have to *suis* and *reste*, too. But don't mind if I snore."

Ten Eyck appeared now with apologies for his delay. And a number of callers knocked at the back door of the box and were admitted to an informal little reception, shared by the next-door neighbors, who gossiped across the rail with a charming friendliness. These latter were determined to find out what Persis had been laughing at. But she shook her head mysteriously.

Forbes heard great names bandied, and he judged that he was meeting important people, but there were no introductions, except in the case of a man and a woman who were treated with deference. To these Ten Eyck presented Forbes with flourish as an eminent military expert called home from the Philippines to help fortify New York against foreign attack.

Forbes denied this violently, but Ten Eyck winked. "Diplomatic, eh?"

When they were gone Forbes asked who they were.

"Society reporters!" said Ten Eyck. And the next day Forbes read in two of the papers a varying description of the costumes of Persis, Winifred, and Mrs. Neff, and a duplicated mention of his own name with the added information that he was "the eminent military expert called home from the Philippines to help fortify New York against foreign attack."

When he read this Forbes breathed a prayer that none of his superior officers might be addicted to the social columns.

But that was to-morrow's excitement.

The third act brought him back under the Wagnerian yoke. Tristan's castle walls ran along a cliff overlooking the ocean; in a green space under a tree the wounded knight lay eternally demanding of his devoted squire if he could not yet see the ship, the ship that was to bring Isolde to nurse him back to life.

Forbes forgot all light thoughts before the infinitely pathetic wail of the shepherd's pipe and the reiterated appeal of Tristan for "*das Schiff! das Schiff!*"

Like most men of to-day, Forbes never wept except at the theater, or at some other fiction. He had not so well since he had seen "Romeo and Juliet" played. Now again, as then, it startled him to think what a genius for love some hearts have, while others have only a talent or a taste for it. He felt a little ashamed that he had never been able to love as Romeo or Tristan loved, and yet he thanked his stars that he had been spared that fatal power.

How often we thank our stars that we have never met the very thing that waits us round the corner! Perhaps that Pharisee who stands immortally thanking the Lord that he was not as other men, found out the same afternoon how very like he was.

The thrall of the theater was so complete upon Forbes that when the sorrowful drone of the shepherd's pipe suddenly turned to joy at the sight of Isolde's ship, Forbes' heart leaped up as if he were witnessing a rescue in actual life.

The hurrying rapture of the music that described Isolde's arrival, and her haste up the cliff, sent his hopes to heaven; but when the delirious Tristan rose from his couch to his staggering feet and began to tear at the bandages about his wound, Forbes felt the stab of fear. He wanted to cry out, "Oh no! no!" He sat with lips parted in anguish, and his hand groping for support.

The left hand of Persis was reaching about in the same gesture of protest against intolerable cruelty. It met the hand of Forbes. Their fingers clutched each other in an instinct for companionship. The two souls were so intent upon the action of the scene, and so swept along by the torrential music, that they hardly knew their hands were joined.

When Tristan fell at Isolde's feet, with one poor wailing "Isolde!" and died before she could clasp him in her arms, it seemed that Forbes' heart broke. A groan escaped him; his hand clenched the hand of Persis with all its might. He heard a little gasp from her, and he thought that her heart had broken with his.

He had bitten into one of the beautiful apples of Hades, and his mouth was filled with ashes. The tears poured down his cheeks, and in his aching throat there was a lump like broken glass.

The noblest song in all music, the "love-death" of Isolde, gave the tragedy nobility; but it was the mad beauty of a grief too great for grieving over. Passion shivered in the air and seemed to come from Forbes' own soul. The harmonies kept climaxing, eternally reaching the last possible thrill, only to find that it led on to one yet higher. The melodies were crowded like the angels climbing Jacob's ladder into the clouds, where every rung seemed heaven, till it disclosed one more.

The music was a love-philter to Forbes and Persis; they could not escape it, had no thought of escape. Their hands swung in a little arc, clenched and unclenched in an utter sympathy of mind and body, in a kind of epic dance.

And then the opera was over, and Forbes began to dread the raising of the lights. He was grateful for the long ovation to the singers, since it kept the house dark till he could shake off the tears he was ashamed to dab with a handkerchief. Time was when greater soldiers than he were proud rather than ashamed of their tears, but Forbes was thankful for the gloom. He applauded and joined the cries of "Bravo!" to prolong the respite.

Mrs. Neff was sniffling as she beat her gloves together.

"Even Isolde's husband couldn't hate her—or him— for a love like that."

And Winifred, with her cheeks all blubbered, swallowed hard as she applauded.

"Why don't we have such lovers nowadays? Even I could play Isolde if I could find a Tristan."

"Permit me," said Bob Fielding. But he was referring to the opera-cloak he was holding out for her.

Willie Enslee, however, shook his head contemptuously and made no pretense of applause.

"Can you beat 'em, Mr. Lord? They're never so happy as when they're crying their make-up off. They pretend they're blue. but they've been having the time of their lives."

And Forbes hated him for saying it. Then he noted that Persis was not applauding. She was pulling off a long glove slowly and wincingly. When it was off, she looked ruefully at her left hand and nursed it in her right. She glanced to see that the others were busy with their wraps, then she held her hand out where Forbes could see it; and gave him a look of pouting reproach.

His first stare showed him only that her soft, slim fingers were almost hidden with rings. And then he saw that the flesh was all creased and bruised and marred with marks like tiny teeth. He realized that it was his fierce clench that had ground the rings and their settings into her flesh, and his heart was wrung with shame and pity.

He saw, too, that on one of the little fingers there was a thread of blood. The alert old eyes of Mrs. Neff caught the by-play of the two, and her curiosity brought her forward with a question.

"How in heaven did you hurt your finger?"

Persis answered quietly and at once:

"I caught it on the thorn of a rose. It's nothing."

Willie insisted on seeing the wound, and was frantic with excitement. He was genuinely distressed. He poured out sympathy for the pain, anxiety for the future of the wound, the necessity for sterilizing it. But it was Willie's doom to be always tactless or unwelcome, and his sympathy was an annoyance.

Forbes was compelled to silence by Persis' explanation of the accident. He must not say how sorry he was, though he had wounded her—he had wounded Persis till she bled!

CHAPTER XVIII

THERE was an atmosphere of mourning everywhere as the enormous audience issued from the exits. It had assisted at the obsequies of a tremendous love, and all the eyes were sad.

Forbes had seen it stated until he had come to believe it, that the Metropolitan Opera was supported by snobs who attended merely to show off their jewels, and that the true music-lovers were to be found in the gallery. It came upon him now that this is one of the many cheap missiles poor people of poor wit hurl at luckier folk, with no more discrimination than street Arabs show when they throw whatever they can find in the street at whoever passes by in better clothes.

Forbes was sure that most of these sad-eyed aristocrats, so lavish in their praise of the singers and the music and the conductor, had come with a musical purpose, and he wondered if some few, at least, of those in the gallery might not have climbed thither less for art's sake than to see in the flesh those people of whose goings and comings and dressings, weddings and partings, they read so greedily in the newspapers.

During the long wait for the carriage, a wealthy rabble stood in a draughty doorway waiting turns at the slowly disintegrating army of limousines and landaulets and touring-cars and taxicabs—even of obsolete broughams and coaches drawn by four-legged anachronisms.

Mrs. Neff claimed Forbes as her personal escort, and carried him off in her own chariot, which rolled up long before Enslee's.

Forbes regretted to leave Persis standing there, with throat open as usual to the night gale; but his consolation was that he could gossip about her.

Mrs. Neff's first word, of course, was of tobacco. The door was hardly slammed upon them before she had her cigarettes out.

"Give me a light, there's a dear boy. I've just time for a puff. And you light your cigar; I know you're dying for it. You can finish it in the cloak-room. You men have still a few advantages left. The one I envy you most is your right to smoke in public."

It was strange to Forbes to be proffering a light to a white-haired lady. His own mother had thought it almost an escapade to sit on a piazza with a man who was armed with a cigar. Years ago, when Forbes had come home from West Point, she had said to him after dinner:

"I reckon my boy is simply pe'ishing for a cigar. Of course a gentleman can't smoke in the drawing-room, and the odor never comes out of the curtains. But I don't mind it in the open air—much. We'll stroll in the garden. They say tobacco is good for the plants—bad for the insects."

And she took his arm and sauntered with him while he ruined the scent of the honeysuckle vines.

And Forbes had heard an anecdote, probably untrue, of the great Mrs. Astor; according to this legend, a man, hankering for a cigar, yet hesitating to suggest it, asked her casually: "What would you say if a man asked you for permission to smoke?" To which she answered, in her stately way: "I don't know. No man ever asked me." And neither did he.

But nowadays a man rarely ever murmurs the formula: "Do you object to smoke?" He is apter to say: "Do you carry your own, or will you try mine?"

The petite grande dame, Mrs. Neff, carried her own. The glow of it in the dark seemed to add one more ruby to her burdened fingers. And when she lost her light, she reached out for Forbes' cigar and rekindled her cigarette, smiling:

"Aren't we nice and clubby?"

Once her weed was prospering, she began to puff gossip:

"Isn't she a darling—Miss Cabot, I mean? Everybody is crazy over her, but Willie scares 'em all off. What a pity she's mixed up with the little bounder! Of course, she needs a lot of money, and her It of a father is nearly ready for the Old Ladies' Home; but what a shame that love and money go together so rarely! For the matter of that, though, I don't think Persis knows what love is— yet. Maybe she never will. Maybe she won't learn till it's too late. Murray Ten Eyck says you are rich. Why don't you marry Persis? What a pair you'd make! What children you'd have! They'd win a blue ribbon at any stock-breeder's show."

Forbes was much obliged to the dark for hiding his blushes. Besides, he felt it a little premature to be discussing the quality of his offspring. He made bold to ask a leading question.

"You say that Miss Cabot is mixed up hopelessly with Mr. Enslee. Do you mean that they are engaged?"

"They haven't announced it, of course, but it's generally agreed that they are. Still, I suppose that if some handsome devil came along with a million or two, he might coax her away."

"But they are not actually engaged?"

"I don't know. But it looks inevitable to me. If you've got a lot of money, ask her—and save her from Willie. She'd make a nice wife to a nice man, with a nice income. Go on and get her. Oh, Lord, here we are at Sherry's and I've got to throw my cigarette away. I'll have to sneak another in the women's room somehow."

They went through the revolving doors and into the corridor, where women in opera-cloaks were moving forward with something of the look of a spice caravan, some to the supper-rooms, and some toward the elevators to the various assembly-rooms, where various coteries were giving dances.

The ways of Mrs. Neff and Forbes parted at the elevator's upper door. His led to the large room where he passed his hat and coat across a table to be stowed in a compartment in one of the wicker wardrobes.

While he waited for Mrs. Neff, he sauntered to and fro, smoking and feeling a stranger among the men, who were just beginning to collect. Forbes noted the callowness of most of them, and felt himself a veteran among the shiny-haired blonds and glistening brunettes pulling on their white gloves, straightening their ties and trying, some of them, to find mustache enough to pull.

He could see the women they brought—girls and their mothers, or aunts or something.

After his experience at the restaurant dances, Forbes had begun to wonder if New York's aristocracy had been entirely converted to socialism, and had given over all attempt at exclusiveness. Here at last he found selection. People were here on invitation, and they were at home—*chez eux*.

If they went among the common herd, it was only as a kind of slumming excursion, a sortie of the great folk from the citadel into the town. It did not mean that the town was invited to repay the visit at the castle.

This was a dance at the castle. Everybody here seemed to belong. There were no shop-girls, no pavement-nymphs, or others of the self-supporting classes. These women had been provided for by wealthy parents. They had been provided with educations, and aseptic surroundings, and sterilized amusements, and pure food of choicest quality. Hence they all looked hale and thoroughbred. And they were not discontent. They came with the spirit of the dance.

Yet there was variety enough in the unity. Girls of intellectual type, girls of plain and old-maidish prospects, girls of prudish manner, wantons, athletes, flirts, and uncontrollables. There were good taste and bad in costume, simple little pink frocks and Sheban splendors, loud voices and soft, meek eyes and insolent. But they were all protected plants, not hothouse flowers, yet flowers from high-walled, well-tended gardens.

Inside the wall there was the pleasantest informality. Everybody seemed to call everybody else by the first name or by some nickname, and there were surprisingly many old-fashioned "Jims" and "Bills," "Kates" and "Sues." There was much hilarity, much slang, and the women seemed to use the music-hall phrases even more freely than the men.

In the dances there was a deal of boisterous romping. The turkey-trot, here called the one-step, was as vigorously performed as in the restaurants, and some of the highest born showed the most professional skill and recklessness.

While Forbes was waiting for Mrs. Neff, he saw Persis arrive with her entourage. She was like the rest, yet ever so different. In her there was the little more that meant so much. She had, of course, the advantage of his affection. Yet he could see that everybody else gave her a certain prestige, too. It was "Oh, there she is!" "Look, there's Persis!" "Hello, Persis, how darling of you to come!"

The fly in the ointment was Willie Enslee, preening himself at her side, taking all her compliments for his own, as if he were the proprietor of a prize-winning mare at a horse-show. Forbes hated himself for hating him, but could not help it. When Enslee left Persis and entered the men's coat-room, Forbes' eyes followed him balefully.

Ten Eyck happened to glance his way as he held out his hand for his coat check. He noted the glare in Forbes' eyes and followed their direction to Enslee. He was so amazed, that when the attendant put the check in his hand, he started as if some one had wakened him. Then he went to Forbes and took him by the elbow. And Forbes also started as if some one had wakened him. Ten Eyck smiled sadly:

"Is it as bad as that, already, old man?"

"Is what as bad as what already?" Forbes answered, half puzzled and half aware. Ten Eyck replied with a riddle.

"You can buy 'em for almost any price. It's the up-keep that costs."

"What the devil are you talking about?"

"Yachts."

"Yachts?"

"Yachts. Better do as I do, Forbesy: instead of trying to own and run one, cultivate the people who do; and then you can cruise without expense."

"What's that about yachts?" Willie Enslee asked, unexpectedly at his elbow. Ten Eyck answered, blandly:

"I was making the highly original remark that it's not the initial expense—"

"—But the up-keep that costs," Willie finished for him. "And that's no joke, either. Thinking of buying one, Mr. Forbes? Take my advice and don't! Gad, that ferryboat of mine costs me twenty-five or thirty thousand a year, and she's not in commission two months in the season."

Twenty-five thousand a year! The words clanged in Forbes' mind like a locomotive's warning bell. He would hardly earn so much in the next ten years. He would certainly take Enslee's advice and not buy a yacht. He was as ill-equipped for a contest with the Enslee Estates as David was for the bout with Goliath. David won, indeed; but he had only to kill the giant, not to support him in the manner he had been accustomed to.

What could Forbes offer a woman like Persis in place of a yacht? He could offer her only love. His love must be cruiser and automobile, town house and country house, home and travel. Isolde had married the king only to run away from his palace to the ruined castle of the wounded knight. Perhaps this Isolde would take warning and prefer the poor knight and his shabby castle in the first place.

As Forbes glanced down at Willie Enslee he could not feel that even the Enslee millions could suffice to make the fellow attractive. They certainly had not added a cubit to his stature. Persis could not conceivably mate herself for life to a peevish underling like him.

Plainly Forbes needed only to be brave and persistent and he would win her. Then Persis reappeared, and looked to be a prize worth fighting for, at any hazard of failure. There was a bevy of young women about her, bright clouds around a new moon. They were all jeweled to incandescence. On their fingers and wrists were rings and bracelets whose prices Forbes could guess from his inspection of shop-windows the day before. He could not give such gifts.

But he would not let anything chill him. He advanced to Persis with as much cordiality as if he had not seen her for years. Persis was too human to follow the usual New York and London custom of avoiding introductions. She presented Forbes to the galaxy with a statement that he was a famous soldier (which brought polite looks of respect), and a love of a tangoist (which evoked gushes of enthusiasm).

He had not caught a single name, and as the group dispersed, each girl took even her face from his memory as effectually as if it were a picture carried out of a room.

This did not distress him at the time, for the orchestra on the stage in the grand ballroom was busily at work.

"The music is calling us," said Forbes. "May I have the honor?"

"I wish you might," Persis sighed, "but Willie would be furious if I gave his dance away. And Mrs. Neff would snatch me baldheaded if I kidnapped her *preux chevalier.*

I'm afraid she'll expect you to pay for your ride in her car by a little honest work, won't she?"

"I'm afraid so. Of course she will," Forbes groaned, ashamed of his oversight. "But the next one I may have?"

"The next one is yours. Don't forget."

"Forget!" He cast his eyes up in a look of horror at the possibility. He hastened to Mrs. Neff, who was just simmering to a boil. She forgot her pique with the first sidewise stride. She tried to imagine herself young, and Forbes tried to imagine her Persis.

He passed Persis in the eddies again and again, and she always had some amiable wireless greeting to flash across the space. She was difficultly following the spasmodic leadership of Willie, who puffed about her like a little snubby tug conducting a graceful yacht out to sea.

When the dance was done and the inevitable encore responded to, Forbes tried to carry on a traffic of conversation with his hostess; but he had only the faintest idea of what she said or what he himself said—if anything. His mind was lackeying Persis, who knew so many people and was having so good a time. At the first squeak of the next dance Forbes abandoned Mrs. Neff like an Ariadne on a beach of chairs, and presented himself open-armed before Persis.

She slipped into his embrace as if she were mortised there. The very concord of their bodies seemed an argument for the union of their souls. They were as appropriate to each other as the melodies of a perfect duet, such a love-duet as Tristan and Isolde's.

Once more Forbes was master of Persis; she followed wherever he led. He could whirl her, dip her, sidle her, lead or pursue her; and she obeyed his will as instantly as if he were her owner. She did belong to him. How could he ever give her up? And yet at the moment the orchestra stopped he must let her go.

The end of the dance was their divorce. He transferred her into Bob Fielding's arms for a time, while he swung Winifred with as much rapture as he would have taken from trundling a bureau around. Even Winifred's surprising lightness of foot reminded Forbes of nothing more poetic than casters.

After this ordeal a strict sense of duty forced him to dance with Mrs. Neff once more. And after her with an anonymous sprig, to whom Mrs. Neff bequeathed him. This girl was as young as Alice Neff, but loud of voice, gawky, and awkward. Some day she would grow up to herself and enter into her birthright of beauty. Now she was neither chick nor pullet, but at the raw-boned, pin-feathered stage between—just out from her mother's wings. Her knees were carried so well forward that Forbes could not avoid them. He came out of the dance with both patellas bruised.

And then, at last, he was free to tango with Persis again. In the brief space of a few dances, he had held in his clasp the young-old Mrs. Neff, the super-abundant charms of Winifred, and the large-jointed frame of a young girl. When Persis was his again the contrast was astonishing. In these forms the cycle of the rose was complete; the girl was the bud still clenched in its calyx; Winifred was the flower too far expanded; Mrs. Neff the flower of yesterday with the bloom gone from the petal and the wrinkles in its place; but Persis! Persis was the rose at its exact instant of perfection.

At the close of the dance, the hour being somewhat past midnight, supper was announced. Persis seized upon one of the small tables, and stood guard over it while she despatched Forbes to round up Mrs. Neff and Willie and Bob and Winifred, and Ten Eyck and a débutante he was rushing.

Persis saw to it quite casually that Forbes sat close to her; and that was very close, since the little clique was crowded so snugly about the table, that half of those who ate had to convey the food across the elbows and knees of the others.

WHAT WILL PEOPLE SAY?

Persis sat with both elbows on the table, and raised her bouillon cup with both hands. Her elbow touched that of Forbes, and she did not draw it away. For the matter of that, all the elbows were clashing in the crowded circle.

It was now that Forbes was tempted to make his first advance. How was he to marry her if he never made love to her? How show his love except by some signal? Before all those ears he could not speak his infatuation; before all those eyes he could not seize her hand and kiss it, or kneel, or push his arm around her.

Under the table he might have held hands with her, but she kept her hands above the board. Then, as she leaned close to him to speak across him to Mrs. Neff, her foot struck lightly against his. It was gone at once, but it suggested to his mind an ancient form of flirtation that has been more honored in modern observance than in modern literature. Remembering the experience at the Opera House, he was visited with a tender temptation to renew that acquaintance of feet.

He gathered his courage together, as if he were about to step off a precipice into a fog, and pursued her foot with his. He found it, but at a touch it vanished again. Realizing that she took his silly action for an accident, he determined to see the adventure through. He sent his foot prowling after hers, found it, and raising his toe, pressed hers softly.

This time her foot was not withdrawn, and he felt that his emprise was rewarded. But a moment later, when every one's attention was attracted to another table, and the rest were discussing a prematurely fashionable costume, Persis leaned close to him and murmured:

"In the first place, how dare you? In the second place, I have on white slippers. And in the third place, you are perfectly visible from all the other tables."

And then she slipped her foot away. It was as if she had unclasped his arms from about her waist, only not so hallowed a precedent.

Forbes turned pale with shame. He felt that his deed was boorish, and now it had been properly rebuked and resented. The gentleness of the reproof made it the more galling; for it was the gentleness of authority so sure of itself that it needed no clamor of assertion. Another woman might have been, or pretended to be, furious at an insult; a flirt might have rebuked him only to encourage and tease him on; a vixen might have dug her other heel into his instep and forced her release.

But Persis was sophisticated enough not to set her protest in italics. She was probably used to such suggestions. It hurt Forbes' pride to feel that he was not the first man she had rebuffed for this. He had loved her and longed to tell her his secret secretly, and had merely apprised her that he was a blundering bumpkin. She had shamed him yet spared him open disgrace. She had made him respect her intelligence and her tact.

He gnawed his lip with remorse; but his apologies were frustrated by the return of all hands to the table. Persis chattered with the rest and nibbled a marron with an apparent relish that implied forgetfulness of what was only an incident to her.

Forbes was learning what Persis was, by all these little tests, as a general studies the enemy's strength and disposition, by trying the line at all points. If he finds the pickets always alert, his respect increases the more he is baffled.

CHAPTER XIX

AFTER the supper no time was lost in returning to the main business of the meeting. Again Willie claimed the first dance, and Forbes was deputed to Ten Eyck's débutante. The next dance, however, brought him back to Persis. He had asked for it, uneasily, and she had granted it with an amiable "Of course."

The moment they were safely lost in the vortex he began to make amends. While he was strutting his proudest through the tango, he was stammering the humblest apologies.

"Oh, don't let that worry you," she answered. "I suppose all men believe they have to do that sort of thing to entertain us. Poor fellows, you think we women expect it of you. Some of us do, I suppose; but I don't like it. And it doesn't seem quite what I had expected of you."

He got a little comfort from the thought that she had taken the trouble, at least, to form an opinion of him. But mainly he admired her for the continued good sportsmanship of her attitude. There was a kind of manliness about it, as if one gentleman should say to another:

"Pardon me, but you are trespassing on my property. It was a natural mistake, but I thought you'd like to know my boundary line."

And yet something was gone from her warmth. She danced with him, chatted, laughed. But a chill was upon her. That little bloom of tenderness that had softened her words as the down velvets the peach, had vanished. Frost had nipped the firstling of spring.

Forbes was infinitely repentant, rebuffed, but not routed. He began once more to scout along her outposts.

"That hat you wore, you remember, day before yesterday?"

"Yes."

"I told you how I followed it."

"Yes."

"My heart ran after you like a newsboy calling to you. But you didn't hear."

"I'm so sorry!"

"All of a sudden you spoke to your driver, and he put on full speed up the Avenue, as if you were in a great hurry. I had a funny idea that you might be making haste to meet some man."

"Let me see! Yes, I was. I was hurrying home to meet Willie. He is always furious when I am late."

This time the name of Enslee was like a blow in the face. It dazed Forbes with a confirmation of his worst fears. He did not realize that he thought aloud:

"I guessed right! I knew it was a man, and I was jealous."

Persis stared up at him. She smiled incredulously.

"You were jealous? But you hadn't even seen me."

"No, but I wanted to see you. I felt you in the air. And I was jealous."

His eyes were laughing into her laughing eyes. But both of them were a trifle solemn at heart. Forbes determined to learn how her affairs stood with Enslee. He could never have found the temerity to demand the information if the music had not flared with such dare-deviltry.

"Would you mind if I asked you one very personal question?" he said.

"Not if you'll look the other way when I answer it."

"Are you engaged to Willie Enslee?"

The question was so unexpected and so forthright that

it almost staggered her. She flashed one look up into his earnest eyes and laughed; but it was a cold laugh.

"You are the most amazing piece of impudence I ever met."

"You haven't answered."

"What difference could it make to you?"

"All the difference in the world. It is a matter of the utmost importance to me."

"Why?"

"Because if you are not—" The music was the most inconsequential jig, and their feet were frolic, but his voice was solemn as a prayer. "If you are not, I want to—to tell you that you have—you are—that—well, my heart is at your feet."

"Watch out, then, for I can't see my feet, and my heels are sharp."

"Won't you be serious?"

"You are the frivolous one. You've only just met me; you don't know anything about me, nor I about you, yet you talk this talk."

"I've known you long enough to know that you are—"

"Oh no, you haven't. You've only seen me with my party manners on."

"But you—you—oh, I can't talk to this music. Will you sit down a moment somewhere?"

"No, indeed. I came here to dance, and I wish you would stick to your knitting."

"You haven't answered my question. Are you engaged to that man?"

"Oh, so he is 'that man' already?"

"Are you going to marry him?"

"I'm no prophet, Mr. Forbes."

The medley broke into the ribald tune of a popular song: a woman's celebration of the generosity of her keeper whom she called "Daddy," and who always brought her gifts. The refrain was a disgustingly irresistible hilarity: "Here comes my Daddy now, Pop, oh, Pop, oh Pop!" Half the dancers shouted the refrain as they whirled.

Forbes' heart selected from the sordid lyric only its rejoicing. He selected from Persis' words only the hope they negatively implied. He began to dance in a frenzy, locking knee to knee, whipping her off her feet, and clenching her sweet body so close to him that she gasped:

"I have to breathe, you know."

"Forgive me," he murmured into the curls about her ear. "But you're a wonderful thing!"

"Am I?" she laughed, but with a sort of patient indifference.

"I'm mad about you."

"Are you?"

"I wish I dared to tell you that I love you."

"I hope you won't."

"Men are always telling you that?"

"No—not always—once or twice." She was so far away, though in his arms, that her voice seemed to come to him across a long wire.

"Did you love any of them?"

"No."

"Are you sure?"

"There's nothing I'm surer of than that."

"Does that mean that you are not engaged to Mr. Enslee?"

She laughed again.

"Not necessarily."

CHAPTER XX

FORGIVENESS and garters lose their snap when they are stretched too often. Once before Forbes had apologized to Persis for an excess of enthusiasm, and her forgiveness had brought back her cordiality with perfect elasticity. The second time there had been a slight sag.

The boundary between the impertinence of a cad and the privilege of a suitor is vague and wavering. The act that is accepted as a manifestation of devotion, a pretty caress, from the accepted lover becomes a liberty from the libertine. In his ardor Forbes had overstepped the dead-line.

There was no especial reason why the pressure of foot upon foot should be a less poetic tribute than a lingering clasp of the hands. But thinking makes it so, and when Forbes put his best foot forward, Persis resented it as a familiarity, an affront. It meant in her eyes that he held her cheap and easy. It was like her to be less angry with him than with herself. She reasoned that if a man she had just met could so speedily rate her so low, there must be some appalling fault in her manner. Her self-confidence was shaken.

But just as she had set Forbes in the category of men with whom a woman must be on her guard, he spoke of being jealous of her, and his very eyes and the flush on his cheeks shouted that he meant it.

There is, perhaps, no other tribute a woman prizes so highly as jealousy. Other tokens of esteem may be silver, gilt, or plated ware, but jealousy is the hallmark of sincerity; jealousy is at least eighteen karats fine.

The moment Forbes said he had been jealous, and by his eager questions, by their very insistent impertinence, indeed, proved that he was now jealous, he became important to Persis. The fervor of his previous actions was almost justified. Even the intrusion upon her foot was a different act.

Women usually think that love excuses almost everything, and sanctifies what were else ridiculous or disgusting. They absolve the sinner who can plead, "I was in love," more easily than the self-righteous abstainer.

Besides, there was something uncanny to Persis in Forbes' statement that he had followed her up the Avenue, and had felt a jealousy of her haste; because that had been a momentous day altogether.

She had begun it by a shopping raid. She had run across a flock of new hats, curious oddities from Paris, perched like strange birds alighted in a window. They pulled down so far on one side that they blinded one eye of the wearer, and they thrust out so far to the rear and the side that they blinded the passer-by.

As she was trying one of them on, she turned her head to speak to the rhapsodical manager. She swept the face of the saleswoman till she sneezed; and when Persis turned to apologize to the saleswoman, the manager found himself inhaling exotic goura. It was fascinating. She simply must have some of these hats.

But there had been a very polite note with her last bill, a timid plea that she pay a trifle on the venerable debt. She hardly dared increase the sum instead of diminishing it. She decided to ask her father's help. The price was beyond her own private bank-account, which was usually chaotically overdrawn, and which the bank carried along with an amused patience, because her father was one of its oldest customers.

Determined to have those hats that day or die, Persis had ridden all the way to her father's office in Broad Street to ask him to buy them. She had found him in great distress. Before she could explain her errand, he had said, with a smile that was pitifully brave:

"I needn't ask what evil motive brings you down here. It was just to tell your old father how much you love him."

"Yes, of course; you know how I worship you." She sat on the arm of his chair with a smile as alluring as a mining-stock prospectus. "Also. I thought you'd like to know that I've struck the most wonderful hats ever imported. They're marked down to almost nothing, and they're really an amazing bargain—especially when you deduct the cost of an ocean voyage, for I couldn't equal them this side of Paris."

He shook his head with a helpless finality that gave her pause. This terrified her. He had refused her something! She knew that the only things that would prevent him from giving her money were absence of funds and inability to borrow them. He explained, tenderly:

"I'm in a lot of trouble, honey. I've got to shift some of my loans to other banks, and I've got to borrow a lot more somewhere. And I don't know where. I'm sorry to tell you, but you'd better know."

She soothed him with loving terror. She told him how little she really cared for the hats; she wanted them only because everybody else had them. The hat she had on would do for a while. It had been so far in advance when she bought it that it was quite good style now—not the very latest, of course, but still good enough since he was feeling poor.

He told her that she need not worry; everything would come out all right. He was just a little pinched for the moment. But he kissed her very devoutly, and sighed and told her how beautiful she was and how dear to him.

She returned to her car, and ordered the driver home. It was a long journey up the cañon of Broadway, a plank road for miles, since a subway was burrowing underneath. She had ample time to figure out just what it meant to her to be poor. They had been pinched before. Her father was the fourth generation of wealth, and the inheritance of financial genius was wearing out in the family.

Cold flashes of fright ran through Persis as the car rumbled and swerved. Then she remembered that Willie Enslee was to call upon her that afternoon. He had said that he had something very important to say, and she had laughed inly, knowing just what he meant. He was so ridiculous in his love. But now she thought of him as a salvation. She resolved to be sensible and cut the silly romance out of her hopes. She could save her father, and have all the hats in the world. She must not keep Willie waiting. He might not wait. It was in this mood that Forbes had first seen her and her old hat from the bus.

At home she had found Willie. As she walked into the drawing-room he was pacing up and down rehearsing his proposal in whispers. He went into a blue funk at the sight of her, and she had the greatest difficulty in coaxing him to propose. Then she accepted him with proper surprise.

Willie had brought the ring—a wonderful composition by René Lalique. Fashion had changed enough to permit an engagement ring to be something besides a solitaire diamond. This poem in gold had cost him more than Forbes' salary for two years. Persis had worn it when she met Forbes that same night at the theater. She had worn it when she taught him to turkey-trot. It was the edge of that ring that had cut her finger till it bled under the fierce grip of Forbes' hand at the performance of "Tristan and Isolde."

Thoughts like this danced through Persis' mind now, while her body danced in Forbes' arms. And Forbes was talking of his jealousy!

Forbes was different from Willie in so many ways. He could be loved. She did not love him now. But he was

of the type that women love. She wondered, rather helplessly, if she were going to love him. She certainly could
never love Willie, and no woman wants to die without
loving somebody.

She would not be indiscreet, of course, or disloyal in
any important way. But— After all, she might not marry
Willie. She might marry Mr. Forbes. All things were
possible. Why not this? He would be a husband worth
having—a soldier, a gentleman, a lover, distinguished—
nobody would laugh if she went up the aisle with
him.

Luckily Forbes had money. He was surely not so rich
as Willie. But then Persis was not mercenary. She
wanted only a reasonable amount—just enough to keep
up with the procession, have a fresh hat now and then,
and some gowns and a contemporary car, and a place in
town and a place out of town, and enough to go abroad
on every summer, and South every winter, and a few
things like that. Surely Mr. Forbes must have enough
money for such a simple household.

Of course, she would not marry him, and it might
be dangerous to play with fire; but it would be pitiful
never to go near the fire. Worse, it would be pusillani-
mous. Now that she had accepted Willie, it was certain
that she was not to have love in her life unless she took
it outside.

Not all of this Cubist chaos of meditation went on during the brief remainder of the dance. But it began there,
and it was small wonder if the logic had a little rag-time
in it; as for instance:

Since Persis and Willie had agreed not to announce
their engagement just yet, this justified lying to a lot of
people; for one surely had a right to evade a question
that nobody had a right to ask. Of course, if Forbes were
really in love with Persis he had a right to ask. But if
she told him, then he would stop loving her; at least he
would stop seeing her. She knew the man. And she

didn't want him to stop seeing her. He was really very nice!

He was a box of matches. She would not strike a light. Or perhaps she might strike one; but she would let it burn only a moment, and then blow it out and not light another. Besides, she was not an official fiancée till it was announced. And Mr. Forbes danced so wonderfully—oh, Lord, it was a sad world. Yet it was very comfortable, dancing in this man's arms.

Meanwhile he was pounding at the door of her heart again:

"Are you going to ride in Central Park to-morrow—this morning?" he said.

"Yes."

"Rain or shine?"

"Yes."

"May I ride there, too?"

"It's not my park."

"That's not very encouraging."

"Isn't it? Well, haven't you been a trifle discouraging yourself?"

"I'm terribly sorry," he pleaded; and she surprised him by sighing:

"I'm rather glad."

"Glad? Why?"

"Because I had come dangerously near to feeling that you were—different."

"I am," he cried, stung by the deep significance of her light regret. "Please let me prove it. Please let me ride with you in the park?"

"I'll be with my father, you know," she answered, with a trace of relentment. "It's my only chance to visit with the poor old boy. You'd better not."

"But some day you will ride with me?"

"Maybe."

"To-morrow may I stand on the bridge and watch you go by?"

"The park is open to the public at all hours."

"Would you mind if I got a horse and rode by and said 'Good morning!'"

"Fine.   Come along.   I'll introduce you to my father."

"I'll be there!"

9

CHAPTER XXI

PERSIS had not misjudged Forbes. If she had told him then that she was another man's betrothed, he would have changed his whole attitude toward her. He would have flirted with her no more. He would have ceased to regard her with ambition or desire. She would have become again only another piece of jewelry in a shop-window—beautiful, but not for him; beautiful, but already bespoken. He was not of the covetous and burglarious type that always wants other people's property.

Equally, the romance would have ended before it began if Forbes had told Persis that he was not rich, as Ten Eyck had carelessly assumed. ·

Persis might have liked him and admired him and been great friends with him; but she would not have admitted him to the anteroom that all hearts have where those eligible to the inner soul are first admitted to wait their time.

Persis did not make a test of money any more than the rest of her set did. Many enormously wealthy strugglers were wasting coin and labor in a vain effort to bribe a smile from these really unimportant persons. Many poor artists, actors, authors, town wits, were welcomed to their boon companionship. These latter paid their way by bringing along their charm or notoriety as their contribution to the picnic. But they rarely married into the set.

In spite of all the talk of snobbery and wealth-worship, it is really very simple. People are people, and classes are merely clubs where more or less congenial neighbors coagulate, more or less haphazard. Those that cannot pay the dues drop into other clubs. Even labor-unions are run in that way.

And in classes as well as in clubs two kinds of persons are most offensive: those who try to force their way in unsolicited, and those who do not keep up their end of the expenses. The social struggler and the man who never stands treat when it comes his turn are welcome nowhere, from the slums up.

Some such thought as this came by coincidence into Forbes' mind. He realized suddenly that he was accepting a deal of hospitality and repaying none. He knew that he could do nothing to dazzle these people, but he could not endure to take their favors as charities or tips. He was wondering vaguely just what he could do when the problem was solved for him.

He was resolved not to relinquish what he had gained in Persis' esteem. He would cling to her, keep at her heels, till the chance came to prove how dear he held her.

He had dropped the question of her betrothal to Enslee, sure that it was a paradox. Now he realized that he had no further promise of meeting Persis except on horseback and with her father alongside. He put forth an antenna.

"Am I ever going to see you again?"

"I shouldn't be at all surprised," she answered, blowing neither cold nor hot.

"To-morrow?"

"Maybe."

"Where?"

"Oh, I'll probably be dancing at some tea-place or other, as usual."

"Don't you ever stop dancing?"

"Sometimes."

"Could I see you one of those times?"

"Why, yes, of course."

"When?"

"Oh, almost any time."

"Any time is no time."

"I haven't my engagement-book here. I can't remember."

He was hoping that she would ask him to call, but she failed to take the hook. He surprised himself by saying with an abrupt rashness:

"Will you take lunch with me to-morrow?"

He had a vision of a charming little hour alone with her in the solitude made by a crowd. She missed the point, and asked:

"Do you mean all of us?"

"I suppose I do. I reckon I wouldn't dare ask you alone."

"I reckon you betta hadn't," she said, mocking his accent as best she could.

"When will you-all come?"

"Oh, it would be right smart of a job to get us-all together at the same time."

He smiled at her burlesque, but persisted:

"How would you like to—to give the party and order the fodder? I'm just back from the Philippines, you know. I could get up a mess for my company, but I'm afraid I couldn't feed you people to your liking."

"Oh, nobody eats anything any more, or drinks much of anything."

"All the more reason for having what you do have right. Won't you order it for me, and tell me where to have it?"

She was tempted to seize the chance. It was a delight to her to compose a meal. It was a kind of millinery or dressmaking in its art of arrangement. She checked herself on the brink of acceptance, realizing that it would set people to talking if she conducted Forbes' entertainments for him. Even Willie, who was neither very observing nor very jealous, would raise a row at that.

"I'll tell you," she said. "Ask Mrs. Neff to be the

hostess. You're under some obligations to her, and none to me."

"May I ask her to order the luncheon, too?" said Forbes, with dwindled enthusiasm.

"Oh no; you must do that!"

"I'm afraid I don't know what to have."

"It's the simplest thing in the world. Just go to the Ritz-Carlton and ask for Fernand. Tell him I'm coming, and I said for him to take good care of you—of us. And now let's see who can come."

She strolled about with him while he made his invitations. Everybody had engagements of various sorts, but they were brittle. Mrs. Neff was flattered immeasurably, and asked if she could bring Alice along. She was afraid to leave her lest she connive with Stowe Webb at some escapade. Bob Fielding could not come so far up-town from his office, and Winifred could be present only if she were permitted to be late.

"I'm not allowed to eat anything, anyway," she moaned, "except a little dried toast and some lemon-juice; and the waiters treat me like a dog. But I'll be there if you'll protect me."

Ten Eyck had planned to run down to Piping Rock, but he would not desert Forbes in his hour of peril. Willie had an important engagement with one of the executors of his father's estate, but he quickly shifted it when he found that Persis was to be present. This made seven all told, four women and three men.

"I could get more if you want," said Persis; "but seven is lucky, and more is no fun."

"Seven is just right," said Forbes, with a little premonitory chill at the thought of the probable cost.

It was finally agreed that they were to lunch late, take a little spin round town, and then turkey-trot again in the afternoon.

Forbes was amazed at himself. Now he was to play the host, and Persis was to be at his elbow! Or should he put her opposite him, as if she were his wife? What a decoration she would be at a man's home table!

The word "home" took a new timbre in his soul. Hitherto home had meant the tall, white columns and broad lawns where his mother lived. Now it began to mean almost any place—soldiers' quarters, hotel—any place where Persis would rest awhile. Even the humming-bird has a nest to go to when its wings are tired. Some day Persis must nest, too. Her wings could not beat on forever.

CHAPTER XXII

THERE had come to be more and more room on the floor as the crowd dispersed slowly. Many of the young owls were by daylight bank-clerks and office assistants, learning their father's trades of money. They were remembering that they must be up betimes in the morning. They had been campaigning all winter on short rations of sleep. If they made up lost slumber anywhere, it was at their desks, to which nothing but a spanking cold bath could have roused them day after day.

They were glad now when their demoiselles confessed to fatigue, too, or the mothers began to mention the hour.

Even Mrs. Neff was a trifle groggy. The poor old soul was trying hard to keep from confessing how tired and sleepy she was. She kept herself young by pretending to be young, and her motto was, "A woman is just as old as she says she is." Though, for the matter of that, if her statement of her age had been correct, her eldest son must have been born before she was; and Alice would have come along when her mother was about eight years old.

Persis was growing drowsy-eyed, too, and heavy-limbed, with an almost voluptuous longing for sleep. She drooped like a flower at sunset. She ceased to smuggle her yawns as sighs, and once or twice she forgot to lift her hand to hide them.

Forbes was so infatuated that he admired even her yawns. He wanted to whisper over her round shoulder, "How pretty you are when you are a sleepy-head!" But he had been lessoned enough for one evening.

At last, however, she gave up the effort to go on dancing forever. She inquired for Willie. He was not to be seen. Ten Eyck went exploring, and found him in retirement clutching a big highball glass with his little raccoon-like fingers, and blinking his little raccoon-like eyes. He was of a surly trend in his cups, but Ten Eyck was angelically patient as he lugged him to the coat-room. Forbes was horrified at the thought of Persis under such escort; but she seemed to ignore Willie's temper, and Forbes dared not intervene.

However, as they were all waiting on the curb in the fresh auroral air, while the starter whistled up their cars, he ventured a chance to murmur to Persis:

"I beg you to go home and sleep till noon. Please don't try to get up and ride in the morning."

"I must," she answered. "It's the one duty I do."

But the note of protecting solicitude in his voice had touched her. She turned softer eyes upon him and smiled.

"We'll dance some more to-morrow afternoon. Till then, *au revoir*."

"But I am to *revoir* you in the park in a few hours?"

"So you say."

"Also at luncheon?"

"Oh yes, of course."

"Persis, are you never c-coming?" Willie Enslee hiccoughed.

"Yes, pet," she laughed, ironically, and nodded again to Forbes. Forbes winced at the endearment she gave Enslee, even though he felt it to be sarcastic. He winced again as Enslee took her white elbow in his white glove and made a fumbling effort to help her in. The white fleece she was vanished into his dark car like a moon slipping into clouds.

Ten Eyck boosted Willie in and clambered after him "as a chaperon."

Bob Fielding and Winifred tested the capacity of a taxicab, and Forbes stood ready to escort Mrs. Neff home in her own car; but she shook her head as she gaped:

"Nonsense! I'll not be so cruel. You've done enough for me. You go on back to your hotel and get to bed. But first wait—oh wait—have you a box of matches you can give me? Thanks! You've saved my life. Good night."

Forbes paused to say: "Does the chauffeur know you want to go home?"

"I should hope so, at this hour!"

Forbes closed the door with an apology and set out to walk to his hotel. It was only a few blocks away, but it seemed a hundred miles. And he yawned so ferociously that he feared for the buildings. He found the scrub-women agonizing again on their knees across the lobby floor. He was too drowsy to feel sorry for them, or to remember to leave a call for six o'clock at the desk, as he had planned.

He plucked off his clothes in a stupor, and slid straight into the abyss of sleep as he shoved his dance-weary toes down into the sheets. At five the imaginary reveille woke him for a moment. He simply came up to consciousness like a diver gulping a breath, and was underneath again at once. He dreamed that he was riding in the park and, catching sight of a saddle-horse in a tantrum, galloped forward to find that Persis was the rider. She was having a desperate battle with the frothing beast and was about to be thrown off. But Forbes, outstripping two or three mounted policemen, swept alongside and caught her from her saddle to his pommel. Her father, whose own horse was plunging, was so grateful that he presented Forbes with Persis' hand. A mounted clergyman chanced to be cantering by, and he was recruited to perform the ceremony, with the mounted policemen as bridesmaid and best man. By one of those splendid coincidences in which dreams are so fertile, a thicket of trees proved to be a pipe-organ, and began to blare a popular tune of Mr. Mendelssohn's. The noise woke Forbes, and to his unspeakable disappointment he found himself in a bachelor bed at a hotel, with Times Square furnishing a roaring offertory.

Automatically he reached for his watch, wondering if he could not have a little further nap to get back into that dream without delay.

But the dial blandly informed him that it wanted a few minutes to noon. Horror shocked him wide awake.

CHAPTER XXIII

HE leaped from his hateful couch, swearing at himself like an army teamster. He stumbled to the telephone and curtly demanded the exact time, hoping to prove his watch a liar. Back from space came the reply: "K'reck time is 'le'm fifty-eight."

His "Thanks!" had almost the effect of an oath. He slammed the innocent receiver on the hook and stood staring at the bare feet protruding from his indolent pajamas, where there should have been puttees and spurs and smartly flaring riding-breeches. He was doubly indignant with himself because he had counted upon that morning galopade. He rode like a centaur, though with the military and not the park seat, and he had expected his horsemanship to commend him to Persis.

He wondered what he should do. He reversed Sancho Panza and cursed the man that invented sleep. He formed a wild project to fling into his things, leap to horse, and hunt the park through. But he had not yet bespoken the horse, and he knew that Persis must have finished her ride hours ago, doffed her boyish togs, cold-showered her glowing body, and put on whatever finery her engagements required. She had probably spent the irretrievable hours at a committee meeting of some society for rescuing working-girls from work. And her father had probably earned or lost a million while Forbes lay annulled in a coma of stupidity.

How should he apologize? He could not wait till he saw her. The offense must be erased before it set. He must call her up instantly. He ransacked the dangling

139

telephone-tome. Her father's office was mentioned, but not his residence. Yet he must have a residence, and it must have a telephone.

Forbes banged the hook and demanded "Information," and when that mysterious dame answered from her airy throne he besought her to give him at once the number.

Information answered with a lilt as if the name of Persis were one of importance:

"I think it's a private wire; I'll see."

While Forbes waited he was interrupted, incessantly cut off, restored to the wrong number, helplessly forced into other people's personal chats, and left dangling in empty space. When at length he retrieved Information, she told him:

"Jus' z'I thought, 's a priva twire."

"Of course it's a private wire!" Forbes thundered. "I don't want to have a public conversation. What's the number?"

"'S 'gainst comp'ny rules to give numbers listed as private. Sorry."

"But this is a matter of life and death."

There was an almost audible sigh, as if she had heard that before.

"Sorry, but under no soic'mstances are we p'mitted to give numbers of parties listed private."

He insisted, pleaded, threatened; but she answered with implacable politeness. "Sorry, but—"

At length he screwed his courage to the point of calling up the office of her father. Here he learned only that Mr. Cabot had left the office, and it was contrary to orders to give his house number.

After beating his head and hands vainly for a long time against those walls that New-Yorkers have to build about themselves if they are ever to know seclusion, Forbes remembered Ten Eyck and called up his house. He was not at home, and his whereabouts were unknown.

WHAT WILL PEOPLE SAY?

A deferential, yet stately voice with the indescribable tone of a butler or a valet advised "Mr. Forbes, ah, yes," to try various clubs; "The Racquet or the Brook, possibly," or "I believe I heard him say" (the two h's were hazy) "that he was to be at the Metropolitan at one. If you could call him then, sir, I'm quite sure you'd— Not at all! Very good, sir."

Ten Eyck could give him Persis' occult number; then he could send a note and some flowers to plead for him and appease her wrath before they met at the luncheon. When they met no time must be wasted in more apologies.

But Ten Eyck was not to be found anywhere. Forbes gave up. He telephoned for "coffee and rolls and a morning paper in a powerful hurry," and stormed into his bathroom. When he came out as sparsely dressed as most of the gentlemen are in the advertising pages of the magazines, he found his breakfast on a little half-table mysteriously apported.

While he danced into his trousers his eyes were caught by head-lines on the paper folded at his plate:

"Mayor puts Lid on *Thés Dansants.*"

Forbes seized the paper, flung himself into a chair, and read with violence the dire news that the same mayor who had ordered people to quit dancing at one now ordered them not to begin dancing before dinner. He grew hot with rage, while his coffee cooled and his rolls brittled. He had found the dancing-tea a delightful institution, a joyous democracy. But, according to the scathing indictment of the mayor and the adroit wording of the reporters, the tea-dance was a home-wrecking, youth-defiling abomination, only the more dreadful because it wrought its hellish purposes in the broad daylight.

According to the newspaper account of a typical dancing-tea, it was apparent that Forbes had failed to grasp the depravity of the crowd he had been dancing with; it seemed that the women were all fat fiends pursuing immature school-girls, and the men all evil-eyed brokers whose corpulence alone was proof enough of their wickedness.

Forbes stared aghast at a wholesale condemnation that must include Mrs. Neff, Persis, Winifred, Alice, and the respectable rest. He had not yet learned that certain journalists are mere newsboys always beating out of their dreadnaught typewriters cries of "Extra! Extra! All about the turrible moider!"

Forbes was dumfounded to learn that the modern Babylon plus Nineveh, New York, could be sent to bed at one o'clock and forbidden to dance by daylight. Ordinarily nothing on earth would have mattered less to Forbes than the fate of tea-dances. But this ukase drove him further than ever from his Persis.

The curious mania for public dancing had enabled him, though come to town a stranger, to join immediately in festival relations with people to whose homes he would normally have been months in penetrating. The mayor's edict revoked this democracy, and he was once more a stranger in the city. He must meet his new-found friends formally and at long intervals, if at all. He thanked his stars that he had arranged to give the luncheon in time. He must set about ordering it at once, and he must see to it that there was no flaw in its perfection.

CHAPTER XXIV

ON his way to the Ritz-Carlton, Forbes stopped at his bank to draw some money. He decided that he would better take along a hundred dollars. It would look impressive when he paid the waiter. He realized that it would drag his bank-account below the acceptable minimum. But he set his teeth and determined to do the thing right if he bankrupted the government. He would probably need most of the rest of the hundred before the week was out. He could begin to save again when he was in his uniform again.

He drew the money, strolled to the hotel, asked for Fernand, and found him at a glass screen in a superb room that ran from street to street. A multitude of red chairs populated the floor, and the medallioned white ceiling was a huge ellipse that looked as big as the earth's orbit.

Fernand was cautiously gracious till he learned that Miss Cabot had sent Forbes to him; then he became quite paternal. Forbes slipped him a ten-dollar bill, and he listened almost tenderly as Forbes explained:

"I want to give a little luncheon—nothing elaborate, but—well, something rather nice, you know."

"Perfectly, M'sieur. And how many will there be?"

Fernand spoke English glibly, with hardly more accent than a sweetish thickness.

"We are seven," said Forbes.

"Very good, sir. Will you select what you wish, or—"

He handed Forbes the card of the day. Forbes looked at the French. He could read military memoirs and strategical works in French, but he was floored by the technical food-terms. A glimpse at the prices unnerved him further; but he asked: "What would you suggest—I'm just home from Asia. I feel a little out of it."

"If Monsieur would permit me," said Fernand, with the eagerness of a benevolent conspirator, an artist with a mission, "I will arrange it and give you a pleasant surprise or two."

Forbes swallowed a small lump of embarrassment, and was careful to ask carelessly:

"About how much would it be?"

He wanted to forestall at least one surprise.

"Oh, not a great deal," Fernand smiled, with the bedside manner of a family doctor. "Miss Cabot hates heavy food. Zhoost a little cocktel, and some *caviar d'Astrakhan* to begin; and perhaps a little broth; ah, better! she likes *purée St.-Germain*. And after, a little berd and some salade, a sweet, perhaps, or a cheese, some coffee—nothing more! Very simple is best."

This sounded so sane that Forbes began to pluck up hope. He asked:

"Does she—do they—will you give us wine of any kind?"

"Miss Cabot does not care for champagne; and Mr. Enslee—did you say he would be of the party?"

Forbes had not said it, and he flushed to think that everybody, even a head waiter, must be linking Persis' name with Enslee's. But more than ever now he must make sure not to give a shabby meal. Meanwhile he answered the question with a casual nod:

"Yes, Mr. Enslee will be here."

Fernand spoke with indulgent pity: "Mr. Enslee takes usually only a highball of the Scotch. But I think you could tempt them both with a little sherry—for the sake of the berd. I have a sherry that is delicious."

"How much delicious?" Forbes asked, trying to be flippant at his own funeral.

144

"Eight dollars the bottle. But very fine! They would all like it very much."

At the mention of a concrete price Forbes grew uneasy, and asked outright: "Could you tell me how much—about how much this luncheon is going to cost me?"

Forbes felt ashamed of discussing prices, though many a richer man, especially Enslee, would have fought all along the line and delivered an oration on the extortions of restaurateurs. But Fernand began to compute:

"Let me see; seven cocktels at twenty-five is one-seventy-five. Caviar would be one-twenty-five per person; for seven would be eight-seventy-five. The *purée St.-Germain* we shall make it special — say, about five dollars. I should recommend the *poulet de grain aux cèpes;* it is two-fifty per person. You do not really need any *légumes*, except the asparagus. Oh, this morning what asparagus! I saw it! Asparagus, yes?" Forbes nodded desperately. "That will be seven dollars more; but then you will not wish *salade*—no, you will not wish *salade*, though the endive is—no, we will not have endive. For the sweet would you wish special favors? No, it is too much; the Nesselrode pudding is nice. Miss Cabot adores the marrons — good! We might serve cheese, though it is too much. But we will have it ready. Then the coffee is special, and a liqueur, perhaps—yes? Miss Cabot likes the white mint. There will be some cigars for the gentlemen, of course—and the ladies will take their cigarettes with their coffee down the steps here, I presume. Now, let me see." He mumbled his addition a moment, then broke the news. "That makes—about fifty-four-seventy-five. Yes—ah no! we have not added the sherry—one bottle, perhaps two. So you see, Monsieur, it will come only to sixty—sixty-five dollars—roughly."

Forbes thought the word "roughly" appropriate. In his soul there was a sound like the last sough of water in an emptying bathtub. He added mentally the ten dollars he had given Fernand, and the ten dollars he must give the waiter. He wondered if he looked as sick as he felt; as sick as his hundred dollars would look. He had cherished a mad fancy for inviting everybody to dinner, the theater, and a tango supper. If his modest luncheon put him where it did, he wondered where such an evening would have left him. From this point of view he was escaping cheaply. Anyway, he had crossed the Rubicon. He was too poor to be able to afford to skimp. If he had been an Enslee Estate, he could have offered his guests toast and distilled water without being suspected of poverty.

And once committed to the course he had chosen, he would have beggared his family rather than stint his hospitality. He was a gentleman; a fool, perhaps, but a gentleman.

He gave Fernand the order to go ahead. Fernand was upset by the brevity of the time allotted him, but promised to do his best. Forbes cast his eye about for a good table. Fernand put up his hand:

"Miss Cabot has her favorite table. You shall have that, also her captain and her waiter."

Forbes remembered Persis' warning.

"But this luncheon is really in honor of Mrs. Neff," he said.

"Ah, in that case you will want her table. She prefers the opposite side, nearer the band."

Forbes, having a little while to kill, set out for a stroll round the block. It came to him suddenly that the precious hundred dollars he had drawn to make a good show would evaporate and leave almost nothing. He went to his bank and wrote a check for fifty dollars more. As he stood waiting at the paying-teller's grill he felt as if he were a forger taking money he had no right to. But the teller expressed no surprise. When Forbes returned to the Ritz-Carlton he found his guests already gathering in the lounge. Willie Enslee came in late and surly. He explained that his man had had the impudence to fall ill, and had left him to dress himself.

They had their cocktails, and then Forbes led his little flock up to the rich pasture. He had to beg pardon through a knot of people pleading vainly for tables in the circle. They were being turned off into the side rooms of mediocrity.

It gave Forbes a feeling of elation to be greeted with homage by name and led at once to his table. It made a brave showing with silver, glass, and napery already disposed, and a great bouquet of fresh lilacs in the center.

Fernand whispered to Forbes that he had taken the liberty of changing the bill of fare somewhat. The result was a surprise to those spoiled palates, and Forbes' guests were like children in their expressions of delight. Forbes was voted a gourmet, but he gave the credit to the hovering Fernand. He was honest enough still for that, though he had not the courage to admit how deep a gouge the luncheon made in his savings.

Still, he felt as he surveyed his triumph that wealth was a noble thing. If only he could give such artistic banquets every day! If only he could frequent such places and hold up his end among all these brilliant crowds! So many, many people had so much money. Thousands of them were banqueting here and in other restaurants, encouraging all the arts from architecture to salad-dressing. Why should he be denied the status of his tastes?

He attempted to grovel before Persis in apology for oversleeping. But she refused to take the offense seriously, and she congratulated him for having the courage and the honesty to confess the real excuse for absence. He told her that he was sure, from her alert and lustrous eye, that she too had overslept, but she vowed she had not, and he wondered again that such delicate beauty should be conjoined to such unfailing strength.

Save when it was interrupted by exclamations of applause for the choice of the dishes, or childish yum-yums for the exquisiteness of their preparation, the talk was all about the mayor's order closing the *thés dansants*.

"They call this a free country," Mrs. Neff grumbled, "and yet they tell us we may not dance with our tea!"

"A good thing, too!" said Enslee. "It was time somebody stepped in before the whole country went absolutely nutty over this dance business. A little more and they'd have had the waiters trotting in with soup."

"But what are we to do with our afternoons?" Winifred sighed.

"What did you do before?" said Willie.

"I don't know; but I'm sure it was stupid."

Ten Eyck, the consoler, came to the rescue. "Sigh no more, ladies! There'll be turkey-trotting in this old town when we're all trotted out to Woodlawn. Forbesy, were you ever in Yellowstone Park?"

"Yes."

"Did you see the Old Faithful geyser geyse?"

"Yes."

"Remember how she would lie quiet as a tub for an hour, and then blow off her head and explode a stream of water to the clouds, make an awful fuss for a few minutes, and then drop off to sleep again?"

"Yes."

"Well, that's reform in New York or any big town. There's wild excitement now; there'll be editorials and sermons and police raids and license-revoking for a few days. Then everything will quiet down, and in a week all the old dancing-stands will be running away as before."

Willie changed the subject with his usual abruptness. All this time he had been revealing an unexpected enthusiasm for the little purple forest of lilacs in the centerpiece. He kept pulling the nearest sprays to him and breathing their incense in.

"Do you know I simply adore lilacs," he smiled. "Up at my country place they must be glorious. My gardener writes me they have never been so good as this year. I wish I could see them."

Nobody paid much heed to his emotions until, a little later, he broke out suddenly:

"By Jove, I believe I'll take a run up in the country and see my lilacs and spend a night in real air."

"That's a fine idea," said Winifred; "we'll all go along."

"Oh no, you won't," said Willie. "The place isn't open yet. Nobody there but the gardener and his helpers."

This checked Winifred only for a moment, then she returned to the charge.

"All the more fun," she exclaimed. "Let's all go up and make a week-end of it."

"But there are no servants there, I tell you," Willie insisted.

"That's where the fun comes in," said Winifred, in love with her inspiration. "It would be a glorious lark. There's nothing to do here in town."

"We have to eat, you know," Willie reminded her, coldly; "and nobody to cook it."

"I'm a love of a cook," said Winifred. "And I've been through your kitchen up there. It's a model—electric dingblats and all sorts of things. I'll cook the meals if the rest of you will build the fires and make the beds and wash the dishes."

"Oh, Winifred, behave!" Willie sniffed.

But Winifred would not behave. She drummed up her scheme until she raised the others to a kind of amused interest in the venture. It would be a novelty at least.

"We can always cut and run at a moment's notice," Winifred explained, for a clincher. "A couple of hours in a car and we're back in town."

"But there are no servants there, I tell you," Willie reiterated. "You don't seriously expect us to go up there and do our own work?"

"Why not?" said Winifred. "It's time you learned to use your lazy hands before they drop off from neglect."

"No thank you!" Willie demurred. "If we've got to go, we'll take along some deck-hands. What do you say, Persis?"

"The only thing I like about it," said Persis, "is the absence of the servants. I can't remember a time when they haven't been standing round staring or listening through the doors. Oh, Lord, how good it would be to be out from under their thumbs for a few days!"

"We can't afford the scandal," said Willie. "Servants are the best chaperons there are. If we went up without them there'd be a sensation in the papers."

"You and your fear of the newspapers!" Winifred retorted. "They need never know."

"You can't go up to my place without some chaperon!" Willie snapped, with a pettish firmness. "I don't run a road-house, you know."

"If you've got to have a chaperon, maybe you'd take me," said Mrs. Neff.

"You!" Willie laughed cynically. "And who'll chaperon the chaperon? You'll make more mischief than anybody. Your affair with Mr. Lord—er, pardon me, Mr. Ward—is the talk of the town already."

Mrs. Neff's laugh was a mixture of ridicule at the possibility and yearning that it might not be impossible. Her comment was in the spirit of burlesque.

"But if I marry him afterward it will put a stop to the scandal."

"Mother, you are simply indecent!" her daughter piped up, with a kind of militant innocence.

The luxury of such a reproof was too dear to Mrs. Neff's unwithered heart to be neglected. She added her vote to those of Winifred and Persis.

Forbes dared not speak, but he was aglow with the vision of a few days with Persis in the country. As he crossed the continent he had seen the traces of spring everywhere; everywhere the mad incendiary had been kindling fires in tree and shrub and sward. From the train window he had watched the splendors unroll like a moving film. He had wished to leap from the car and wander with somebody—with a vague somebody. And now he had found her, and the golden opportunity tapped on the window.

Willie fenced with Winifred till the luncheon was finished. Then they retired to the lounge for coffee. Here women had the franchise for public smoking, and they puffed like small boys. Winifred renewed the battle for the picnic.

Ten Eyck had watched the contest with a grin. At last he spoke: "It's a pretty little war. Reluctant host trying to convince guests that they are not invited. Guests saying, 'We'll come anyway.' Better give in peacefully, Willie, or they'll take possession and lock you outside."

Then Willie gave in, but on the ground that Persis wanted it. He attempted a sheepish gallantry and a veiled romantic reference. He, too, had a touch of April in his frosty little heart. Forbes winced at the rivalry; but at any price he wanted to be with Persis where the spring was.

Willie, yielding to the rôle of *hôte malgré lui*, announced that since they were determined to invade his respectable ancestral home, the sooner they got it over with the better. Persis and the rest were creatures of impulse, glad to have an impulse, and they agreed to the flight as quickly as a flock of birds. What engagements they had they dismissed. Their maids could send telegrams of "regret that, owing to unexpected absence from town," etc.

Willie went to call up his gardener and have the house thrown open to the air and fresh provisions ordered in.

He had just gone when a page came to Persis with the word that her father wanted to speak to her on the telephone.

She gave a start and looked afraid as she rose. Forbes

watched her go, and his heart prayed that no bad news might await her. She was so beautiful as she moved, and so plucky. He knew that she was frightened, but she spoke to various people she passed with all the light-hearted graciousness imaginable. She came back speedily with a look of anxiety vainly resisted. She explained that her father was leaving for Chicago on the Twentieth Century, and wanted to tell her good-by. She would barely have time to reach the house before he left.

Forbes offered to accompany her home. She insisted that he should not leave his guests. Winifred and Mrs. Neff rose at once, claiming that they must also leave to make ready for the excursion.

Forbes bade them good-by rather awkwardly. He regretted the disorder of his exit as a host, but he would not forfeit this chance to be alone with Persis.

She was so distressed about her father that she forgot Willie's existence, and left no message for him. When he had finished his tempest in a telephone-booth, and conveyed his orders to his head gardener, he found Mrs. Neff and Winifred waiting for their cars. They explained Persis' flight and made arrangements for the hour and place of meeting for the journey.

CHAPTER XXV

WHEN Forbes hastened after the hastening Persis and saw how distraught she was he felt the sharp cutting-edge of sympathy. It was his first sight of her in a mood of heartache, and his own heart ached akin.

When they reached the outer door they found to their amazement that it was raining hard. Within doors there had been such luxurious peace under such glowing lights that the sun was not missed and the rain was not heard. But along the street, gusts of wind swept furious, with long javelins of rain that made the awning almost useless. Women gathered their finery about them, and men clung to their hats while they waited for their cars, and then bolted for them as they came up dripping under the guidance of dripping chauffeurs.

While Persis waited for a taxicab Forbes tried to shelter her with his body. He ventured to hope that her father's absence would not distress her.

"Oh no," she answered, bravely, "not at all. He's going on business. He told me the other day he might have to leave town for a few days—on business."

Forbes hesitated over his next words.

"I hope this won't prevent you from going up to Mr. Enslee's."

"Oh no, quite the contrary," she said. "I'd be alone at home. I'll be glad of the—the diversion. Here's the taxi. It's really not necessary for you to go with me."

For answer he took her arm and ran with her to the door the footman opened. A blast of windy rain lashed them as they crept into the car. The door slammed and they were under way, running cautiously on the skiddish pavement.

At last he was alone with her. The rain made their shelter cozier, and for all its bluster it was a spring rain. With its many-hoofed clatter it was a battalion of police clearing the way for the flower procession.

Thinking of this, Forbes said:

"I'm mighty glad you're not leaving town."

"But I am."

"With your father, I mean. You're leaving town with me, instead."

She looked him in the eye with some surprise.

"It's a good thing we put the blame for that luncheon on Mrs. Neff. It tickled her to death and—do you know that Willie really thinks you're flirting with her—or aiming at Alice? He can't tell which." She laughed deliciously. It did not grieve her to fool Willie.

The cab rocked in the wind, and the rain beat upon it with the sound of waves protesting against the rush of a yacht's prow. Forbes caught a glimpse of a street sign. It warned him that they were already passing Fiftieth Street. In a few minutes they would be at her home.

"I'm not flirting with anybody," he said. "I'm adoring you."

A little frown of bewilderment troubled the smile she gave him. She felt his hand on hers and tried to draw it away, but he held it fast.

"We're not at the opera, you know," she said. "That noise isn't the music of 'Tristan and Isolde.' That's rain."

"I know it," he answered, "and I don't want you to be Isolde. If only she had married Tristan in the first place—"

"They might have been divorced in the second place."

"Don't be—don't talk that way. I'm in deadly earnest," he pleaded, but she laughed evasively.

"That was very heady sherry you gave us to-day."

He shook his head sadly, as over the flippancy of a child, and took her hand in both of his.

"It's broad daylight, Mr. Forbes, and this is Madison Avenue."

"But nobody can see us," he answered. "Look at the rain."

"What difference does that make?" she answered, tugging at her hand. But she looked, and saw how they were closed away from the world. Sheets of water splashed and spread so thickly that they covered the windows with gray curtains.

It was as if a brief tropical flood had burst upon New York.

Somehow it did make a difference that nobody could see. It always makes a difference in us that nobody can see us.

Even Forbes felt the change in Persis. Perhaps it was only that her resistance was minutely diminished, or that one of her many fears was removed, one support gone. As a soldier he had sometime felt that slackening of morale across the space between firing-lines. It is then that the military genius orders a charge and turns the enemy's momentary weakness into a panic.

So Forbes charged Persis. In his face gathered a fierce determination. His fingers tightened upon hers, no longer caressingly, but cruelly, till they hurt. He pulled her right hand across him with his right, and thrust his left arm back of her, caught her farther shoulder in the crook of it, and drew her close till their faces almost touched, till her eyes were so close to his that they were grotesquely one.

And then he paused. He lacked the élan to seize the red flag of her lips. He paused weakly to stare at her and to beseech the kiss he might have captured.

"Kiss me!" he said.

So silly a phrase for so warm a deed. She shook her

head, and her fright was gone. She taunted him from her eyes as from an unconquered citadel.

"Kiss me!" he repeated, feeling poltroon and idiotic.

She did not upbraid him or feel any anger or any help-lessness; she just studied him, ignoring the fact that he held her body close to him in a crushing embrace. After all, that meant nothing. Almost anybody might hold her so at a dance for all the world to see. Nothing mat-tered, she thought, so long as their souls did not embrace.

But therein she was wrong, for their souls were not dancing to music. He was demanding her love, her sub-mission to his love. Their souls were debating that vital question, without speech, yet with every argument.

She enjoyed the struggle. She was striking the first of the matches. She would watch the pretty blue flame a moment before it blazed red, then she would blow it out with a little breath from the lips he demanded.

It was fascinating to see how tremendously excited he was over the privilege of touching his lips to hers. It was a quaint little act to make so much of. He was a splendid man, brave, charming, good to see, and now he was crimson and fierce-eyed and breathing hard, trem-bling with the struggle to keep from taking what was so close. She smiled at him triumphantly. She was about to puff out the flame with a whiff of sarcasm, when he said, with all the simplicity of truth:

"I couldn't take a kiss unless you gave it to me. I don't want to kiss you unless you want me to. May I?"

It was such a boyish plea that she could not be sophis-ticated in its presence. She could not answer such hunger with wit. She felt a sudden power from somewhere pressing her head forward to his lips and her heart closer to his.

She smiled tenderly with veiled eyes, and no longer held off. With a gasp of joy he understood and caught her against him. But just as their lips would have met another instinct saved her.

She had always felt a kind of sanctity about her mouth, a preciousness that must not be cheaply cast away. Among all the kisses she had given and taken there still remained this first kiss, still vestal and virgin. And that was the kiss he asked.

She turned her head swiftly, and it was her cheek that he touched. There was such a burning in the touch that the fire ran through her. Her cheeks crimsoned. She closed her eyes in a kind of sweet shame.

She was amazed to be there, huddled in his arms, with his lips preying upon her cheek. Her soul was in wild debate with itself, busy with reproaches and summons to battle against the invader. But it was like a senate without president. There was no one to give the order.

At last she opened her eyes to see again what manner of man this was that had conjured away all her pride and her wisdom and her strength. Her eyes saw that the curtain of rain was slipping from the windows. The downpour had abated. They were drawing up at her own curb.

She flung off his hands with a gasp of anger and terror. He stared at her in a daze. Then he understood.

"Forgive me!" he pleaded.

She was furious with him; but she blamed herself more, and breathed hard with rage as she straightened her hat and her hair.

An old footman was waiting at the top of the steps with an umbrella. He ran down and opened the door.

"Your father is waiting for you, miss," he said.

Forbes stepped forth into the light drizzle and helped her out.

"Good-by," he said. And again "Good-by." But she hurried up the steps. Forbes followed her with his eyes, and saw an elderly gentleman waiting for her at the door. There was a troubled look on his face. The door closed upon him as he caught Persis in his arms.

Forbes told the chauffeur to take him to his hotel, and crept back into the deserted nest of romance. The taxi-cab turned slowly round. As it passed the house again, Forbes saw another car stop at the curb. From it stepped Willie Enslee.

CHAPTER XXVI

ALL the way back to the hotel, all the while he was selecting what clothes he should take, all the while he waited for the hour of the general rendezvous to arrive Forbes was troubled by the remembrance of Willie Enslee's appearance at Persis' home.

He had apparently come in hot pursuit. On the other hand, he might have come merely to make the final arrangements for the excursion to the country. And yet Willie must be accepted as a rival. Or, rather, it was Forbes that was the rival, since Enslee's infatuation for Persis was generally known long before Forbes reached New York.

Forbes did not approve of men who went after other men's sweethearts to take them away. But Persis had told him that she had never loved any man; ergo, she had not loved Enslee—if Enslee could be called a man.

Even so, Forbes would have preferred to make love to Mr. Enslee's sweetheart somewhere else than at Mr. Enslee's home. But how was he to fight his rival except where his rival was? How rescue the imprisoned princess but by invading the ogre's castle? Physically, Enslee was hardly more than a pocket ogre, but his wealth made him a giant. It was with the Enslee Estates that Forbes must grapple. He feared that Persis might drift into their wizard power, and he wanted to save her from that life of "luxurious misery" of which he had read so much, for that life of "blissful poverty with love" of which he had read so much.

Besides, in invading Enslee's own domain he was giv-

ing Enslee every advantage. All of the splendor of Enslee's château, the armor of riches and the sword of gold,
would defend him, while Forbes would attack only with his
empty hands and the power of love. If Goliath thought
that David took an unfair advantage of him, why did not
Goliath lay aside his buckler and his bludgeon and use a
sling, too? Pebbles were plentiful enough.

Forbes reasoned at his scruples till they faced the other
way. He argued till what he would have called vicious
in other men became sincerely virtuous in his own special
instance. So men and empires, republics and religions
have always argued when they were about to try to take
something away from somebody.

As Forbes folded his togs and wished them better and
braver, he paused to laugh at what Persis had told him:
Willie believed that Forbes was flirting with Mrs. Neff for
herself or her daughter! What a blind little ape Enslee
was! Then Forbes straightened up and flushed and called
himself a double-dyed cad. He flung aside the things he
was folding and resolved not to go to Enslee's home at all.

He sank into a chair and pondered. If he did not go
he would be left alone in New York. Only a few days
remained of his little vacation. By the time Persis came
back Forbes would be at his army post, a slave of disci-
pline and the everlasting round of the same dull duties.
Persis would be angry and hurt, and she would marry
Enslee; she would live in that home with Enslee; she
would become part of the Enslee Estates, body and soul.

Forbes' gorge rose at the visions this brought to his
mind. He ripped out an oath, and flung off the withes
of such false honor. He would, he must, save Persis at
any cost. If Enslee were foolish enough to think that
Forbes was hunting Mrs. Neff or Alice, let him take the
consequences. If Enslee had not thought so, he would not
have asked Forbes to come along. To take advantage
of an enemy's weaknesses was the first rule of warfare.
To shoot from cover was the first business of a marksman.

This was not a contest in sharp-shooting at targets under strict rules, with a medal for a prize. This was a battle in rough country for the rescue of a beautiful girl.

Forbes granted himself a plenary indulgence, and resumed packing, smiling again at Willie's idea that he was a suitor for the post of third husband to Mrs. Neff.

He did not smile so well a few hours later, when Willie, with the kindliest of motives, assigned him to Mrs. Neff's automobile.

"You two sweethearts," Enslee said, with a match-maker's grin, "will want to ride together, of course. Persis and I will keep out of your way as much as we can."

Forbes was sportsman enough to credit Willie with a bull's-eye. He smothered his chagrin and helped Mrs. Neff into her car, while his two suit-cases were strapped in the trunk-rack with the family baggage.

The motor-caravan was made up of three machines. Winifred ran her own roadster, nursing the steering-wheel to her bosom, while her fat elbows harried Ten Eyck's cramped form. Bob Fielding had been unable to get away from the troubled waters of Wall Street, and Winifred had adopted Ten Eyck as his understudy.

Mrs. Neff took her four-passenger touring-car. Forbes decided after several appalling bumps that it had belonged to her first husband. Alice sat with the chauffeur, dreaming of Stowe Webb, no doubt. In the rear Mrs. Neff, in her most garrulous mood, talked nonsense through a veil whose flying ends kept snapping in Forbes' face. And when they were beyond Broadway her cigarette ashes kept sifting into his eyes.

He was as polite as possible, but his thoughts were trying to pierce the dust-wake of the great six-cylinder touring-car in which Willie Enslee led the way with Persis. All Forbes could see of her was the top of her motor-hood and the veil that fled back like a signal beseeching him to make haste and save her.

Broadway in the late afternoon was thick with the home-going armies, and it seemed to stretch as long and as crowded as the Milky Way. On through Yonkers to Dobbs Ferry and Tarrytown the journey took them, passing an occasional monument of our brief history, a tablet to mark where Rochambeau met Washington and brought France to our rescue, or a memorial to the cowboys that arrested Major André.

In Forbes' then humor no small charms of nature or legend could have caught his mind from his jealousy. Even the epic levels of the Hudson River and the Valhalla walls of the Palisades hardly impressed him. What success they had with him was mainly due to his remembrance of seeing them first from the train that brought him to New York a few days, or a few eons, ago. He was full then of ambitions to shine as a soldier in an enlarged camp. Now his treasons and stratagems were concerned with a love-campaign whose spoils was Persis Cabot.

There was a pause by agreement for dinner at a roadhouse—"their last civilized meal," as Ten Eyck mournfully prophesied, "before they entered the Purgatory of Winifred's cooking at Willie's boarding-house."

When the task of fretting out a dinner was finished they got under way, pushing north again.

Eventually the pilot-car, or, rather, its guiding cloud of dust, swept off to the east, turning its back on the Hudson and plunging into the heart of Westchester County, an ocean of hills like green billows, and valleys like their troughs; peaceful castles set on high places, and pleasant villages dispersed in low; the homely roominess of farms, and now and then a huddle of crowded rookeries, where Italian peasants had set up a congenial little slums along some ugly waste.

Everything took on a wistfulness in the evening air, which the sunset was tincturing like claret poured into water. Forbes was aching to be with Persis, and he hoped that she was wistful to be with him. The moon had loitered with torch half aglow in the wings of the sky until the sun was gone, and then its lamp was raised, and it entered its own scene. In the houses lights began to pink the dark with the trite but irresistible appeal of Christmas-card transparencies.

Forbes lost all sense of direction in the winding roads, and even Mrs. Neff's chatter yielded to the brow-caressing dusk. The swift progress of the car gave no suggestion of wheels, but rather of a flying keel on a smooth stream.

Finally the searchlights of Enslee's machine turned sharp at right angles. A beautiful granite bridge leaped into view as suddenly as if the great god Wotan had builded it with a word. At the farther side of the bridge stood a lodge-keeper's home, whose architecture seemed to shift the scene instantly to the France of the first Francis.

"Here we are!" Mrs. Neff cried. "And I'm half frozen. I hope the gardener has aired the rooms and put dry sheets on the beds, or I'm in for lumbago."

"Mother, you're just death to romance!" Alice protested. She had doubtless been thinking of Stowe Webb.

The car glided across the bridge, and the moon-whipped stream reveling below it, then proceded through a granite gateway with a portcullis suspended like a social guillotine. And then the sense of privacy began. The very moon seemed to become a part of the Enslee Estates.

The motors tilted backward as the hill rose; and Mrs. Neff's rheumatic car groaned and worried a spiraling road up and up through masses of anonymous shrubs pouring forth incense, through spaces of moon-swept hillside and thickets of somber velours. Then there was a glimpse of the radiant geometry of moon-washed roofs. A turn or two more, and the wheels were swishing into the graveled court of a stately mansion.

The door under the porte-cochère was open, and in its embrasure stood a leanish man and his fattish wife, hospitable as innkeepers, the warm light streaming back of them like peering children.

Enslee's voice came out of the silence:

"That you, Prout? H'are you, Martha?" And then, with characteristic originality, "Well, we got here."

To which Prout responded with equal importance:

"So you did, sir."

He and his wife had been working like mad since Enslee telephoned, trying to turn themselves into a troop of servants, whisking shrouds from table and piano and chairs, and mopping a cloth of dust from every surface. They were as respectful now as Philemon and Baucis welcoming Jupiter, and as apologetic as if the palace were their own unworthy cot.

"I've got a pack of Indians with me, Prout," said Enslee. "I didn't want 'em, but they would come, and now we've got to make the best of it. Don't let 'em trample your flower-beds. And if anybody breaks a flower-stem we'll have him or her shot at sunrise."

Martha giggled into her fat palm.

"Oh, 'e will 'ave 'is joke; 'e will so. And isn't this Miss Cabot? Of course it is."

Forbes, seated in the rear car, heard again that assumption of Persis and Enslee as a couple.

The cars rolled up to the door in turn. The women as they got out piled their wraps on Martha till she completely disappeared, except for a pair of clutching hands, and a voice from the depths.

The chauffeurs made off down the road to the distant garage, with instructions to stay there after one of them should have come back for Winifred's roadster.

The gardener, apologizing for his awkwardness in the office of a butler, led the little troop into the great living-room, where a big fire blazed, splashing walls and floors with banners of red and yellow.

Prout explained that he had been unable to start either the hot-water furnace that heated the house or the dynamo that lighted it. And, being short-handed like, and took with a stroke of sciatiky from the onseasonable cold of the backward spring, he had found time to make fires only in the master's room, his mother's room, and one other. The caretaker, who had kept a fire going all winter for the sake of the water-pipes, had let it go out at the first warm weather and gone for a visit to his wife's mother.

"That's what we get for coming up before the place has been set to rights," Willie grumbled. "I suppose you girls will have to draw lots for my room."

"Me for the nursery," said Winifred. "It's the sunniest place in the house, and—"

"You're not going to try to sleep on one of those children's beds?" Willie gasped.

"No, nor on two of them," said Winifred; "but there's a glorious window-seat a mile wide."

Willie's self-sacrifice was of the parsimonious sort that made acceptance impossible. None of the women would deprive him of his bed. Mrs. Neff was assigned to Willie's mother's room, and Alice and Persis to those on either side. Forbes and Ten Eyck were exiled to the southwest wing.

Prout and Martha could not believe that Mr. Enslee had come without the retinue of servants that ordinarily preceded his august appearance. In fact, the adventure was as unlike Enslee as it was uncongenial to him. He could not and would not see the fun of it.

Martha and Prout offered their service, but Winifred would not let them mar the perfection of her Swiss Family Robinson. She overawed Willie and drove the old couple back to their own cottage.

When they had retired with prophecies of disaster and evil the would-be gipsies felt relieved of all the encumbrances of civilization. Winifred called it a return to nature. For the time being, however, the chief emotion was one of blissful weariness. Host and guests had kept themselves keyed up all season, like instruments in a concert, and now that the tension was released they seemed to collapse upon themselves.

In front of the great fireplace was a divan almost as big as a life-boat, and cushioned into such a cloud as the gods rested on. Winifred and Mrs. Neff and Alice were lolling on it, and Murray Ten Eyck sat on the edge. Back of it was the usual living-room table with a pile or two of books and magazines.

Persis paused for a moment, looking over the books to select something to take up to her room. She pushed them about with indifference.

"Last year's novels!" she smiled. "As thrilling as last year's birds' nests."

She turned up an illustrated society weekly of a former spring. The frontispiece held her a moment, and she shook her head.

"And last year's reputations. Here's a big portrait of Mrs. Richard Lanthorpe and her two children." She read the caption aloud: "'Prominent young matron who is just opening her Newport villa. Though a devoted mother to her charming little daughters, Mrs. Lanthorpe is also well known as a skilful whip.'"

"Good Lord!" said Winifred, reaching out her hand. "Let me see the cat. A whip, eh? You could drive a coach and four through her reputation now."

Mrs. Neff took the paper from her hand. "Her husband got the kiddies. Pretty little tikes, too."

"She sold 'em for the Newport villa," said Alice, looking over her mother's shoulder. Mrs. Neff turned on her with a glare of amazement.

"Where do you children pick up such things?"

"I'm not children," said Alice, "and the papers were full of it."

"Mrs. Dicky was up here last spring for a week-end with her husband," said Willie. "And so was the other man. What's his name? Later I heard that people had been talking a lot even then, but I never suspected anything till later."

"You never would, Willie," said Mrs. Neff. She stared at the picture. "She's really very good-looking, and she wasn't a bad sort altogether. I wonder which one of us will be gone next winter?"

"You, probably," Willie snickered, and the others laughed lazily. But Mrs. Neff bristled.

"I don't see why you have to laugh. Am I too old to misbehave?"

"Far from it, darling!" said Willie. "You're just at the dangerous age. I—er—I don't mean exactly that, either."

Mrs. Neff turned a page hastily. "Here's a picture of Deborah Reeve in her coming-out gown."

"She came out so far and so fast she went right back," said Ten Eyck, and explained to Forbes: "Hesitated between her riding-master and her mother's chauffeur, and finally ran off with the first officer of her father's yacht. She was a born democrat."

"Here's a snapshot of Mrs. Tom Corliss at the Meadowbrook Steeplechase. Look, that's 'Pup' Mowat standing with her. Good Lord, he was hanging round her a year ago, and people are just beginning to notice. Haven't they been clever? A whole year under the rose and right under the public's nose."

"Tom Corliss will be finding it out before long," said Winifred.

"Oh no," said Willie, "I've discovered that the husband is always the last to find out." And he tossed his head in careless pride at the novelty of his pronouncement.

"Isn't Willie the observing little thing?" said Winifred. The others exchanged glances of contemptuous amusement while their host looked wise.

Persis strolled round to the divan, took Murray by the ear, and hoisted him from his place.

"No, thanks, Murray," she said. "I couldn't think of taking your seat." And dropped into it.

"What are we going to do for amusement to-night?" said Willie. "Who wants to play auction?"

"Hush!" said Mrs. Neff.

"Shall we have some music, then?" A general declination. "Some singing? A dance?"

They refused even that, and he grew desperate.

"Charades?"

"Shut up!" came from the crowd.

"I don't want to be entertained," said Persis. "I'm never so miserable as when I'm being entertained."

Everybody approved. Just to be let alone was a luxury.

Willie ventured a last retort: "Anybody want a drink?"

Everybody wanted a drink. Willie went to a side-wall and groped for a button, pushed it and held it, then resumed his place before the fire. After a time he pushed it again.

"Where is everybody?" he snapped. Then the truth dawned on him again. "Good Lord, we're marooned!"

Winifred chuckled at the situation. "You'll have to be your own barkeep, Willie. Go rustle us what you can find."

"But everything would be in the cellar," he answered. "If there's anything here at all, which I doubt. And the key is in town. Couldn't trust Prout with it. Fine old gardener—give his life to save a peony—but he's death on liquor. I couldn't trust him to order in drinkables—besides, I forgot."

There were groans of horror.

"'Water, water, everywhere,'" said Ten Eyck, "'and not a drop to drink.'"

"It's bad enough having no servants to wait on us," Mrs. Neff pondered, "but who's to do our thinking for us? Which 'll we die of first? thirst or starvation?"

"We'll get in a supply from the village to-morrow,"
said Willie, handsomely.

"To-morrow never comes," said Winifred.

For lack of artificial stimulus the momentary enthusiasm lapsed again. Nobody cared even to read. The
fireplace was books enough.

Forbes and Ten Eyck stood at either end of the mantel,
mere supporting statuary, their heads in shadow. Willie
teetered at the center of the hearth, toasting his coat-
tails.

The four women occupied the divan, sketched out bril-
liantly against the dark like a group portrait of Sargent's.
The light worked over their images as a painter works,
making and illuminating shadows, touching a strand of
hair or a cheek-bone with a high light, modeling with a
streak of red some lifted muscle, then brushing it off again.

The poses of the women were as various as their bodies
and souls. At one corner Mrs. Neff sat erect among the
cushions in a sleepy stateliness. Winifred filled the other
corner like another heap of cushions, hardly moving except
to flick her cigarette ashes on the floor to the acute distress of Willie's neat soul. Alice drooped with arched
spine in a young girl's slump, and clung to a hand of Persis', doubtless wishing it were Stowe Webb's. Persis sat
cross-legged, a smoking Sultana, her chin on the back of
one hand, one elbow on one knee.

From his coign of shadow Forbes watched them. Vague
reverie held them all. The very shadows seemed to
breathe unevenly in restless meditation. The fire-logs
alone conversed aloud in mysterious whispers, with
crackling epigrams.

Forbes wondered at the group, so real and so unreal.
He wondered what they were thinking of, each in her
castle of self, each with her yearnings backward and forward. Winifred was wishing her lover there, perhaps,
and that her slim and gracile soul were not mislodged in
so determinedly fat a body; Mrs. Neff was wishing, per-

haps, that her gray hair and her calendar of years did not
so thwart the young, romantic girl that housed in her
body, and must sleep alone, perhaps, forever. Suddenly
Forbes wished that he had not smiled so ruthlessly at the
thought of her expecting to be courted. Her longings
were pitiful, perhaps, but not ridiculous.

It was easy to guess at Alice's thoughts. She was wishing to be not so young and curbed by authority. She
was years older than Juliet had been when she went to
the church with Romeo and threw him the ladder and preceded him to the tomb; yet Alice's well-matured desires
were smiled away and patronized as childish.

And Persis: what were the thoughts that burned
within her soul and twitched at her fingers, or tugged at
her eyebrows, shook her eyelids, or tightened her lips?
Was she thinking of Forbes as he was thinking of
her?

Suddenly her drooping bosom expanded with a great
breath, her lips parted, her eyes widened, her hand rose.
She was about to speak. What would she say?

She yawned. Her hand automatically came up for
politeness' sake, but lingered to pat her straining lips
as if in approval. Her eyes blurred and fairly writhed.
All the muscles of her divine beauty were contorted.
She was not so much yawning as yawned. She was enjoying it, too, and as it ended she sighed over it as over
a sweetmeat. The musing goddess had been suddenly
restored to humanity with a thump.

Her comfortable sigh was echoed and her yawn outdone
by Winifred, who moaned:

"I'm so damned sleepy I'll turn in here if the rest of
you will get off the bed."

Then Alice yawned and wriggled, and Mrs. Neff gaped
with a slight restraint and staggered to her feet.

"I'm on my way. I'd be bored to death if I weren't
so excited over the wonderful sleep I'm to have. I hope
I don't wake up for a week."

"I hope you don't," said Willie, thrusting out his arms in an all-embracing oscitation.

There was an epidemic of yawns, and they staggered to the console table where a long row of candles waited. Ten Eyck lighted them and distributed them, and the line moved on like a drunken torchlight procession, helped and hindered one another up, and sang out faint "Good nights" as they dispersed in the upper hall.

Doors were closed, only to be flung open with wails of distress. Martha and Prout had lugged all the trunks and suit-cases and handbags to the wrong rooms.

The three men were compelled to act as porters. Willie was furious and full of "I told you so's"; but Ten Eyck impersonated the transfer-men he had met, and had a different dialect for every room.

Forbes went timidly into the exquisite apartment where Persis was ensconced. It was a shrine to him, and he averted his eyes from the carved and lace-adorned altar of her bed.

But Ten Eyck turned back to pound on the door and put in his palm, whining:

"Don't forget the poor baggage-smasher, lady."

Persis opened the door a trifle and gave him a twenty-five-cent piece. She held out another for Forbes, and he took it with a foolish rapture.

Ten Eyck bit his coin and touched his hat, with a husky murmur of:

"'Ch obliged, mum! 'Ch obliged!"

Forbes kept his for a lucky piece—the first keepsake he had had from her.

CHAPTER XXVII

IF Persis and the others were rejoicing in their emancipation from formalities too familiar, Forbes was glad that he had escaped them for the reverse reason. Hospitality had been dispensed on a lavish scale at his own home in the South before his father's death, but the servants there were negroes, slaves, or descendants of slaves, and he knew just the right mixture of affection and tyranny to administer to them. But where servile white foreigners, with their curious humilities and pomposities, bowed heads and elevated eyebrows, he had not learned just how much to demand and how much to concede.

He was glad that there was no valet to unpack his things, for he was afraid that his secret wardrobe might not pass such experienced inspection. He laid out his own pajamas, brushes, and clean things against the morning.

Ten Eyck, who shared the same bathroom with Forbes, came in to borrow a match for his pipe, noted Forbes' industry, and quoted one of the few classics that he still read—Rabelais: "Panurge had it right when he said, 'I am never so well served as when I am my own valet.'"

"Is this your first experience as your own man?" said Forbes.

"I should say not!" Ten Eyck snorted, with a cloud of smoke. "I've roughed it as rough as any rough-neck going, Forbesy."

Forbes, from the experience of a campaigner, a wilderness hiker, lifted an eyebrow of patronizing incredulity. Ten Eyck retorted:

"You needn't grin. I don't mean any of this roughing
de luxe. I had the real thing. I quarreled with the
governor once. I was hitting it up pretty hard, and he
gave me a call. I told him I didn't need his dirty money;
I could earn my own, and I swore I'd never ask him for
a cent. I lit out for the Wild and Woolly. What I took
with me went fast. I couldn't get a job I'd look at; and
by the time I was ready to look at any job I could get,
nobody would look at me. Finally they took me on as
unskilled labor in the construction camp of a railroad. I
slept in cattle-cars, or on the ground, or in wooden bunks
with Swedes and Finns, and Huns and coons, and other
swine in the adjoining styes. I fought 'em, too, when I
had to. Later I waited on the table in a cheap hashery.

"God knows where I'd have ended if my dear old dad
hadn't got so homesick he put the Pinkertons on my trail.
And when he found me he apologized and begged me
to come back. And I very graciously accepted. I had
had all the poverty I needed for a lifetime. Hereafter,
Forbesy, I'm for the nap on the velvet and the plush
on the peach. I tell you, Forbesy, we millionaires may
have our little troubles, but we escape the worst of 'em,
eh John D.?"

"I wish you'd cut out that talk about my being a
millionaire," Forbes broke in, impatiently.

"Millionaire is a newspaper term," Ten Eyck explained,
"for anybody who is worth more than a few thousand
dollars."

"But I'm not worth anything and never shall be,"
Forbes confessed. "I'm not rich at all. I've nothing
but a few hundred dollars and my picayune salary."

Ten Eyck took the great denial without emotion.
"Then I congratulate you on being one of the poor but
honest, instead of the criminal rich."

"I'm poor, but I'm not honest," Forbes said; "I'm
obtaining courtesy under false pretenses."

"Rot!" said Ten Eyck. "Money couldn't buy what

you're getting, and the lack of it couldn't lose what you've gained. They like you. You belong. That's all there is to it."

"I wonder."

"Of course that's all. What does anybody here care how much you've got or haven't got, so long as you're congenial and aren't proposing to marry anybody."

Forbes lifted his head with a quick, startled movement that did not escape Ten Eyck, who pretended to misunderstand.

"Of course, if you really are after Mrs. Neff or the little Neffkin, there might be a call for a show-down of bank-books."

"I'd be just as much obliged if you people would drop that joke about my courting Mrs. Neff," Forbes grumbled. Ten Eyck was patient; his voice fell to a deep and earnest tone:

"What I say goes along the line, Forbesy. You were good to me when I was sick in Manila. Don't you go and get sick here. You told me what I mustn't eat and drink and wear out there, and I want to warn you against the dangers of this place. There's a tropics right here, too, with deadly miasmas and mosquitoes that buzz strange things and sting you full of delirious fevers. Don't fall in love too far, Forbesy. I like you mighty well and—naming no names—I like her mighty well, but don't get false notions in your head, and don't put false notions in hers."

"About my money, you mean?"

"Umm-humm."

"You think that money would make a difference to her?"

"Hah!" Ten Eyck snorted. "Would water make any difference to a fish?"

"But if she loved—"

"My boy, you can keep a mighty sweet canary in a mighty little cage, and it will sing away like mad and be very fond of you; but you can't keep a bird of paradise there—or a sea-gull—can you?"

"I reckon not," said Forbes.

"It isn't the fault of the bird of paradise, either, is it?"

Forbes shook his head and sighed: "It's the fault of the man that puts it in the cage."

"Well, maybe he means well. He may be crazy about the bird, just crazy to keep it near him, but—he can't. That's all, he can't. It'll beat itself to death or break loose."

"Unless he lets it go," said Forbes.

"That's it! You understand me, don't you, old man?"

"I get you, Steve."

"And you won't feel too hard about it, will you? There's a lot of other birds besides the big ones. There's nothing cozier than a little canary—is there?"

"I reckon not," said Forbes, dismally.

"And there's a lot of them to be had. And some of them are very pretty."

They sat and smoked a long while. Then Ten Eyck yawned, and gripped Forbes' shoulder hard and went out, pausing to look at him sadly. For his good night he dropped into a cockney quotation: "'Wot I meanter s'y, Pip, is: allus the best o' friends?'"

He ended with a querying inflection, and Forbes echoed it with a period:

"Allus the best o' friends."

He sat smoking his cigar till it was gone. Then he made ready for bed, blew out the candle, raised the curtain, and paused to stare blankly into the dark mass of a green hill or a great cloud, whichever it was, piled up against a sky sprinkled over with a powder of little stars. Among them was one planet whose name he did not know. As he watched, it moved with imperceptible stealth out of his sight behind the hill.

He gave up Persis as completely as he gave up the

planet. A few days ago he did not know her name. A few days more and she would have slipped from his sky.

He was so tired, so full of the need of sleep, that despair was only another kind of night, black but blessed, without ecstasy, but void of torment.

CHAPTER XXVIII

THE only dream that Forbes knew that night—or remembered, at least—was a dream of his latest garrison, and the same bugle humming like the single nagging morning fly that frets a sleeper awake. It was warily intoning its old "I can't get 'em up, I can't get 'em up, I can't get 'em up in the morning."

He leaped from his bed, and was astonished to find himself standing in a strange room with an open window facing an unknown landscape. He screwed his fists into his eyes boyishly before he realized his whereabouts.

At night he had seen his room in vast shadows clouded about a meek candle. The window had shown him only a blur of gloom against a sky of star-dust.

Now he found himself in a sumptuously furnished chamber, whose window framed a scene of royally ordered beauty—a great lawn as level and almost as spacious as a parade-ground, and bordered with a marble balustrade that seemed to run on forever regardless of expense. Marble statues and bronzes and fountains were here and there. And up a noble hill a stairway, as beautiful as a sea-gull's wings, soared to a parked space where a little marble temple sheltered an image which he judged to be Cupid's.

Beyond the big hill reared aloft a primeval forest which the sunrise wind was shaking. The tips of the topmost trees were crimsoned, as if roses had bloomed at last on pines. The climbing sun had just reached them, its rays climbing down the hill as itself climbed the east.

Forbes crept back to bed, but only to reproach himself

with sloth. He could not afford to miss a sunrise such as this would be. There would be occasions enough for sleep; but he was going to leave the Enslee Eden this very day forever. The flaming sword of gold would keep him from re-entering the Paradise he had got into as a boy crawls under a circus tent.

He flung himself from the alien linen and mahogany, and, hastening into the bathroom, stepped into the tub, drew the circular curtain around him quietly not to waken his neighbor, Ten Eyck, and turned the little wheels marked "shower" and "needle" and "cold," and received the responding rains. There was no question that they were cold.

But the reaction was a jubilee in every artery, and he dressed with eagerness for whatever the day might bring. He opened his door softly and went down the twilight of the stairway like an escaping thief. The servantless tenants had neglected to bolt and chain the outside door. He swung it back and stepped out.

He glanced with admiring awe at the dew-pebbled lawn, the colonnades, and the cloisters, but hastened to the eastern side to watch the day breaking over the sky-lines of Westchester. The scene was Alpine with the Alps removed, and the green herds of foothills left. Across a marble-walled pool stood a family of birches, and held the red sun prisoner in a web of green leaves and white boughs. The light that shot through them played upon shrubs and trees and walks arranged according to the highest canons of the landscaping art, taking nature's scenario and dramatizing it.

One imperial group of lilac-trees seemed to hold torches up for the sun to kindle. They blazed with purple flame.

Forbes thought: "Those are the lilacs Enslee loves and owns. This is Enslee's heaven. That is Enslee's sun. And she is Enslee's, too." Then, with all the bravery and optimism the dawn could lavish, he felt: "Well, she be-

longs here; I don't. She needs these things. I can't
get 'em for her. So it's good-by, Persis, and no harm
done."

He was sure that Enslee would never know of the kiss
he had stolen from Enslee's property. And he was sure
that Enslee would never miss a certain lilac cluster whose
grace and color especially caught Forbes' fancy. He
plucked it. Just as it snapped in his hand and flung a
fragrant dew upon his face he heard another slight sound
above. He glanced up.

The vision he saw smote him with beauty like a thunderbolt, and knocked him Saul-wise backward off the high
horse of jaunty resolution into a new religion.

At an upper window, a few paces from where Forbes
stood, Persis leaned out like another blessed damosel looking downward at the sun. It kindled her eyes as it
kindled the lilacs, and she frowned a little against it.
She did not see Forbes as her drowsy gaze swept the hills.
She was not there, however, to adore the dawn. It had
troubled her sleep, and she wanted to shut it out. Her
hands were tugging drowsily at one of the blinds, but it
was held by a catch in the wall. She must lean far out
to release it.

The very homeliness of her motive and the act made
her the more appealing to Forbes. A creamy nightcap of
lace and bow-knots was all askew on her tousled hair, and
a long loop of it slid down into her bosom as she bent far
forward. She had not paused even to throw on a shawl,
and her nightgown was so vaporous a drapery that it
hardly mattered where it clung or lapsed.

Forbes blushed for her, but gazed entranced while she
fumbled at the lock till it yielded. Then she reached out
for the other shutter and stared forth into the sun, stared
between her white arms, outstretched like the wings of
an angel at a window in the sky.

Now Forbes knew that he loved her irretrievably. He
would storm the clouds to win her. He could afford a

home with a pair of shutters, and she could close them against the sun and be as snug as a cuckoo in a clock.

After all, she was no bird of paradise, no sea-gull. She was just a fascinating sleepy-head pouting at the morning for interfering with her dreams.

He was so resolved upon winning her that he counted her already his, and, with a gesture like throwing up his cap, flung the lilacs he held straight at her. They missed her, but they caught her eye, and she followed them down to where he darted to catch them for another cast.

When he looked up again the blinds were shut. He was alone in the world, his lilacs and his heart barred out and rejected. She had retreated to Enslee's stronghold and shuttered herself in.

Forbes turned away to exile in a world of gloom. He heard a little sound above, and whirled quickly. The shutters were opening again. He saw her eyes. She was frowning fiercely; but that was because of the sharp sun, for her lips were smiling and she was whispering something.

He hurried to the spot beneath her window. He saw that her hair had been stuffed back into her nightcap. She was muffled to the ears in a heavy bathrobe, so shapeless and opaque that its big sleeves hid her very hands. But she smiled through like an Eskimo angel. And she was whispering in Eskimese.

He could not understand her, and she could not hear his whisper. They were afraid to waken the house with louder talk. So he beckoned to her to come down. She shook her head. He insisted with ardent gesticulation at the beauty of the scene. She shook her head so violently that her cap fell off. She clutched at it, and her hair fell all about her. He caught the cap as it drifted down like a tired butterfly. She brushed her hair back and pleaded for the cap. He shook his head and tossed her the lilacs. She refused to take them, and put out her hands for the cap. He beckoned her again to come down, and she frowned ferociously. Then, at length, she smiled and nodded and turned away.

He waited, afraid to walk because the gravel crunched alarmingly. He could see the gardener's cottage down the hill, and he was glad that no one was stirring there; not a thread of smoke spun from the chimney.

After he had waited for a tiny eternity he heard her snap her fingers, and looked up to find her fully dressed, all kempt and shiny-faced and precise. She held out beseeching palms for her cap, but he pocketed it and commanded her to descend. She left the window with a look of angry amusement, and he knew that she was yielding to his orders.

It was his first command, and she had obeyed it.

CHAPTER XXIX

FOR convincing the human heart there is no argument like a parable or analogy, and there is no more worthless proof to the mind. So long as Persis could be called a bird of paradise, too rich for a canary cage, or a sea-gull, too wild, or a planet unattainable, Forbes admitted that his hopes of winning her and keeping her were foolish. He gave her up. So much for the metaphors. But when he saw her at the window in the daylight, and saw, not a sea-gull nor a planet, but just a pretty, drowsy girl with rumpled hair, he tossed aside all the arguments by parable and analogy, as candle-ends unfit for sunshine. She was only a woman, and he was all of a man, and this was America, and, by George Washington, he would have her to wife!

He would begin the day right with a wholesome morning smack. He tiptoed along the grass around to the door, and met her in the living-room. And as soon as he met her he set his arms about her. But she was almost sullen as she pushed him away.

"I won't have it!" she said, with a harshness that shocked him. "It's too early in the morning. And I don't like it. And I don't want gossip set going. And you must be doubly circumspect."

He fell back, baffled, and dropped his eyes in discontent. He saw that her little high boots were sprawling open. He smiled at the homely touch again.

"If you're so circumspect," he said, "you'd better button your shoes."

"I forgot to bring up a button-hook," she laughed, "and

when I bent over with a hairpin I got so sleepy that I nearly fell back in bed."

"Permit me," he urged.

"No, thank you!"

"You can't walk with 'em falling off like that," he insisted. "A hairpin, please."

She took one from her hair, and he dropped to one knee. He could not seem to find the right position to work from. After hunching about from position to position he said:

"I reckon your feet are put on the wrong way."

"Thanks."

"For being buttoned, I mean."

"My maid buttons them every morning."

"Tell me how on earth she gets at your foot?"

"No, thanks. I'll button them myself."

"Oh no, you won't. How do the shoe clerks manage it?"

She set her foot on the rung of a chair, and he went at his task with all awkwardness. Her feet were small, yet the shoes were as tight as could be, and she winced as the buttons ground or bit. But she choked back the little cries of pain that rose to her lips.

"Get away," she said; "you're killing me."

But he would not surrender the privilege. He took her foot on his knee and wrought with all care. The hairpin was soon a twisted wreck, and he must have another, and another.

When the lowest buttons were done she checked him. "That's enough! I'd rather my shoes fell off than my hair. And that reminds me: where is my cap?"

"In my pocket next my heart."

"Give it to me, please."

"I'm going to keep it."

"By what right?"

"Conquest and possession."

"What if somebody should see you with it?"

"Nobody shall."

"Somebody always does. Nobody would believe it fell out of a window!"

"It fell straight into my heart."

She gave him up with a shrug. "Good Lord, you men! I don't suppose there's any coffee? I'm so used to having it in bed before I get up that I'm faint."

"I could make you some, if I knew where the coffee was, and the coffee-pot, and if there were any fire."

"Let's look into the kitchen."

She knew the way, and led him into a great food-studio—a place to delight a chef with its equipment and an artist with its coppers.

But the range was as cold as its white-glazed chimney. They cast about for fuel, and found that Prout had fetched kindling and coal the afternoon before.

Forbes soon had a fire snapping under one lid, and Persis hunted through cupboards and closets till she discovered a coffee-pot, evidently belonging to the servants' dining-room, and a canister half full of coffee.

"I haven't the faintest idea how much of that goes in, have you?" she said, helplessly. He nodded and made the measurements deftly.

"Where did you learn so much?" she asked, with a primeval woman's first wonder at a cave-man's first blaze and first cookery.

"A soldier ought to be able to build a fire and make a cup of coffee, oughtn't he?"

"Oh," she shrugged, "I always forget that you're a soldier. I've never seen you in uniform. You never tell me anything about yourself. I always think of you as just one of us loafers."

"It's mighty pleasant to be building a fire for you— for just us," he maundered.

"It is fine, isn't it?" she chuckled, with glistening eyes. "Rather reversing the usual, though, for idiotic woman to stand by while strong man boils the coffee—or are you baking it? I might be getting the dishes."

"I'd be willing to do this every morning—for you—for us," he ventured, his heart thumping at its own dauntlessness.

She evaded the implied proposal as she ransacked a cabinet. "I fancy it would rather lose its charm in time. As a regular thing, I like to see breakfast brought up on a tray by a nice-looking maid."

She brought out a perilous, double arm-load of cups and saucers, and a sugar-bowl.

"This is the service china, I suppose. You could drive nails with it."

He stared at her with idolatry. She was so variously beautiful; at the theater, the opera, the luncheon, here in a country kitchen—everywhere somebody else, and everybody of her beautiful. His hands went out to seize her again, but she tumbled the crockery cracklingly on the table and waved a cup at him. "Stand back, or I'll brain you with this. There's no cream. I suppose even the cows aren't up yet. And I can't find any butter—or any bread—just these tinned biscuits."

They sat at the kitchen table. The coffee was not good, really; but she found it amusing, and he thought it was ambrosia—Mars and Venus at breakfast in an Olympian dining-room. He told her something of the sort, and implied once more that he longed to make the arrangement permanent.

"I wish you'd quit proposing before breakfast," she said. "I feel very material in the morning, anyway, and I'm having a bully time. I'm feeling far too sensible to listen to any nonsense about the simple life. I can enjoy a bit of rough road as well as anybody. I can turn in and work or do without, or dress in rags—anything for a picnic—for a while. But as a regular thing—ugh! To get breakfast once in somebody's else kitchen at an ungodly hour with a captivating stranger—glorious! But to get up every morning—every every morning, rain or shine, cold or hot, sleepy or sick or blue—no, thank you!"

"You think the rich are happier than the poor?"

"Of course they are. That's why everybody wants to be rich."

"But the rich aren't contented."

"Oh, contented! Nobody's contented except the blind, and hopeless invalids. Contentment is a question of being a sport. There's a lot of good losers that will grin if they have to walk home in the rain from the races, and there are a lot of what they call 'bum sports' that throw their winnings on the ground because the odds weren't longer. But don't tell me that there's any special joy in being poor. If I had to be poor, I suppose I'd put the best face I could on it. That happens to be my nature. It's the good sports making the best of poverty that cause so much talk; but all the poor and middlers that I've met have hated it and envied the rich.

"You see, the rich can buy everything the poor have, but the poor can buy hardly anything the rich have. Sometimes my father goes out in the field on his farm and tosses hay, or beds down the horses, or chops dead trees. Sometimes he likes to have just a bowl of milk and some crackers for his supper. But when he wants something else he can have it—at least, he always has been able to—up to now."

A little shiver agitated her like a flaw of wind running along a calm lake.

"It's cold and damp in here," she said. "Let's get out in the sunshine and quit talking poverty. We're neither of us poor—yet."

She rose and moved out to the kitchen porch, and, round the house, up a sweep of stairs to the main terrace.

"Look," she cried, "isn't it wonderful? Isn't it worth while? It costs thousands of dollars just to make that lawn smooth, and thousands more for the marble balustrades, and the fountains are a fortune, and the sunken garden—the poor can't have a glimpse of it! They don't know it exists. Even Mr. Enslee's cook hardly knows it's here; he doesn't permit any of the servants except the house staff to come out front. Isn't it a shame? But don't you love it? Isn't it heavenly under your feet? My eyes fly over it like birds. It's splendid to have tea out here in the summer, and wear long sweeping gowns and picture-hats, and have delicious things brought to you on the finest of china. Oh, I never was meant for a poor man's daughter. Even if I feed the chickens or pat the cattle, I like to do it as Marie Antoinette did at the Petit Trianon just for a contrast—an *hors d'œuvre*."

Forbes thought of the bird of paradise and the sea-gull again, and he doubted the value of his cage again. They sauntered across the lawn and up the stairs. He took her arm to help her, but she shook her head.

"Please! Now, tell me all about yourself."

"There's nothing to tell."

"There must be. I've a right to hear it. Think of it, you've kissed me once, and I didn't fight. I let you. Good Lord, I nearly kissed you!" His arms rushed toward her; but she frowned. "Don't make me go back. I was saying, you've kissed me, and we've had a terrible escapade in a strange kitchen, and I hardly know your first name. So you're a soldier." He nodded. "West Point?" He nodded. "Did you ever get in a real fight?" He nodded. "Where?"

"Cuba. Philippines."

"You were in the Spanish War? Really! I didn't know you were so old."

"I wasn't so old then. I'm very ancient now."

She mused aloud: "They say a husband should be ten years older than his wife."

The implication enraptured him. It showed that she was at least toying with the thought. "Then there's no hope for me. I'm far too old for you."

"But I'm very ancient," she said. "I ought to have been married years ago."

"I'm sorry I kept you waiting so long. There's no need for further delay."

"Are you proposing again? The man's a regular phonograph with only one old broken record! So you've been in battles and battles. Were you afraid?"

"Afterward. I suppose it's because I'm slow and stupid: but I don't usually get scared till the trouble's over. Then I'm sick as a dog and as frightened as a girl."

"That's something like me. Only I get terribly scared of little things that don't count. A mouse or a spider or anything crawly—ugh! is that a caterpillar?"

She shrank back against him in a palsy of repugnance at about an inch of moving fuzz on a rhododendron. He held her with one hand, and with the other broke off the twig and cast the vermin into space. She put his arm away, and said:

"You are brave!"

"St. George and the dragon," he smiled.

"In those battles of yours," she resumed, "were you ever by any chance wounded or killed or anything?"

"I was never killed entirely," he answered, "but I stopped a few bits of lead."

She shuddered and caught his arm with a rush of sympathy none the less fierce for being belated.

"Wounded! You were wounded?"

He put his hand on hers where it lay on his sleeve. "Yes, you blessed thing. Does it make any difference to you?"

She drew her hand away gently. "I hate to think of —of anybody getting hurt. Did it hurt—to be wounded?"

"Afterward. I didn't notice it much at the time— except when I was shot in the mouth."

"Good Lord, how?"

"I was yelling something to my sergeant, and a bullet

went right in and out here." He put his finger on his cheek.

"Great heavens! I thought it was a dimple. I rather liked it."

"Then I'm glad I got it."

She writhed with pain for his sake.

"Did it hurt—hideously?"

"Not half as much as the two pellets I got in my side. They probed for them till I made them stop, partly because I wasn't enjoying it and partly because probing kills more than cartridges."

"How did they get them out, then?"

"They didn't."

She stared at him wild-eyed.

"You don't mean to say that you're standing there with a couple of bullets in you? Why, you're positively uncanny."

"I'm sorry, if it disturbs you."

"Oh, please! You're wonderful. But aren't you afraid they'll kill you—turn green or something?"

"They're neatly surrounded by now with aseptic sacs, the surgeon tells me. I'd forgotten all about them till you reminded me."

"And they never pain you?"

"The only wound I'm suffering now is from the arrow of this sharp-shooter."

They were standing in the little temple, between them a little marble rascal with a bow and arrow. Persis put her hand to her heart. He mistook the gesture and asked, with sudden zest:

"He didn't hit you, too, did he?"

"I was thinking of you," she murmured, staring at him with wet eyes. "Wounded and bleeding, your flesh all torn, and the surgeons gouging in the wounds. Oh!"

She toppled backward and sank on a marble bench before he could help her. He stared at her in bewildered unbelief. He understood that she was nearly aswoon because he had suffered once.

"Why, God bless your wonderful sweet soul!" he gasped, and would have knelt and clasped his arms around her. But even in the swimming of her senses her prudence was on guard, and his indiscretion restored her to herself like a dash of water.

"I beg you to be careful," she said. "You are perfectly visible from the house."

"But nobody's awake. The blinds are closed."

"There are always eyes behind blinds."

"Then let them see me tell you how much I—"

"Not here!" she gasped. "Don't tell me that here."

"Why not?"

"Do you really want to know?"

"Yes."

"Mr. Enslee built this little temple to this little Cupid to propose to me in."

"And did he?" Forbes asked, in a voice that rattled. "Did he propose to you?"

"Regularly."

CHAPTER XXX

SHE studied Forbes closely and laughed aloud at the almost nausea he plainly felt.

"I thought that would shock the nonsense out of you," she triumphed. "Now let's be sensible while the sun shines, and get better acquainted. Tell me more about you, and I'll tell you some awful things about me."

She sauntered on in an arch and riant humor. He resented it, and yet he followed her, hating this mood of hers, yet finding her more precious as he found her more difficult. If he had known women better he would have guessed, or "reckoned," that her very effort to make herself difficult was a proof that she was not really so difficult as she would have him believe. The one who takes such joy in being pursued is not entirely unwilling to be caught.

She quizzed him about his life, his home, his earlier loves. She demanded descriptions of every sweetheart he had cherished, from the first chub of infancy to the girl he left behind in Manila; and she said she hated them all impartially.

She told him of her life: endowed with every material comfort, yet with a vague unhappiness for something or somebody—"perhaps it was for you," she added, but spoke teasingly. She had had nurses and governesses and maids from her first day on earth. She had been to school in France, and traveled round the world; she had been presented at the courts of England and Italy, Germany and Russia; had visited at castles and châteaux. Her sister was in England. She had married a title and was unhappy; but for the matter of that, so were the wives of most of the stanch Americans she knew, rich and poor.

Persis had had flirtations of cosmopolitan variety. Her ambition was to go on skimming the cream off of life. She had given up the hope of ever loving, at least with abandonment. There was too much else in the world. She had been so thoroughly and incessantly schooled in self-control that she doubted if even her heart could forget the rules of conduct. She did not want love to make the fool of her it had made of so many of her friends, and of the people she read about in newspapers and books.

She never took much enjoyment in adventures, anyway, she said, because her imagination was always busy with the appearance of her acts. She found herself considering: "How will this look? What gossip will that start?" She hated herself for the cold, calculating instinct; but she could not rid herself of it.

"This very minute," she admitted, "my fun is half spoiled by thinking of what those people down there in the house will say if they learn that I've been up here with you? Nothing could be more harmless than a stroll before breakfast in a highly illuminated forest, but they'd talk and—well, I'd rather they wouldn't."

She led the protesting Forbes homeward again, down the long flight of steps. The most he could exact was the promise of another walk together—sometime when it could be arranged without attracting attention or detracting from the duties toward the host and his other guests.

As they started across the lawn, whose dew the risen sun had pretty well imbibed, they met the gardener. Prout was yawning, and when he took off his hat he looked sleepy enough to fall over into it.

"You folks been up all night?" he asked, with a drowsy surliness.

Persis shook her head and smiled. "It's you that have overslept."

He changed the subject abruptly. "I just been build-in' a fire for Miss Mather."

"Good Lord, is she awake?" Persis gasped.

"Well," said Prout, "as to that, she's not wot you'd exackly call awake, but she's up an' doin' in the kitchin."

While the gardener shuffled away to play valet to his flowers, Persis stood irresolute.

"I hope Winifred hasn't seen us," she said. "The kitchen and the nursery are both to the east. We'll take a chance. You go on into the kitchen and help her, and I'll telephone down from my room. *Au 'voir!*"

She opened the outer door ever so slightly and oozed through the slit as narrowly as Bernhardt used to when she had murdered Scarpia. Forbes dawdled a few moments, then went into the kitchen.

He found Winifred playing the part of cook with a vengeance. Her hair was disheveled, her sleeves rolled back, and her face smudged from her smudgy fingers. She had assumed a cook's prerogative of wrath. The moment she saw Forbes she began with a savage, "Oh, it's you! And who's been littering up my clean kitchen?"

"I took the liberty of making myself a little coffee," said Forbes.

"There are two cups."

"I made two cups," said Forbes; and she was too busy to notice the evasion.

"Then, since you've had your breakfast," she snapped, "you can help me get something for the rest. You'd better put this on."

Like another Omphale, she fastened a womanish apron on Hercules, and set him at uncongenial tasks, retrieving butter, milk, salt, and eggs.

After a time there was a buzz, and a little hopper fell in a box on the wall. Winifred went to the house tele-phone and called out:

"Well! H'lo, Perse, what you doing awake so early? Insomnia? No, I will not send your breakfast up on a tray! You can come down and get it. My little snojer man is helping me."

She hung up the ear-piece and turned to Forbes with her broad smile.

"A cook has no chance to entertain her gempman friends. The minute I get a policeman in here somebody rings."

She kept him wretchedly ill at ease by more of the same banter, which he hardly knew how to take. And she seized his arm with a gesture of culinary coquetry just as Persis sauntered in. Forbes was horrified to note a look of anger in Persis' eyes. He should have been flattered. She greeted Winifred, and also Forbes, with a discreet "Good morning!"

"Good get-busy!" Winifred growled.

"What can I do?" said Persis, helplessly.

"For one thing, you can rout the other loafers out of bed."

"How?"

"Use the telephone. Tell 'em the house is on fire."

While Forbes fetched and carried at Winifred's beck and call, Persis rang up the various rooms and conveyed Winifred's orders. But her gentle voice carried no conviction, and Winifred took her place at the instrument and howled in her best cook lingo:

"Get up and come down, or I'll quit you cold and lave you to starve. It's scrambled eggs and bacon the marnin', and no goods exchanged."

She went back to the range, only to be called to the telephone again. Mrs. Neff was imploring a brief respite. Water boiling over and scuttering in hot hailstones from the stove brought Winifred back with a screech. She upbraided Persis for a useless scullery maid and threatened Forbes with a skillet. She was enjoying herself tremendously. She ordered Persis to set the table in the breakfast-room, but refused Forbes permission to help her.

But he slipped away a little later, when she went to rummage the ice-room. He found Persis drifting about in a lake of golden sunshine, distributing delicate chinas and looking like a moving figurine of bisque. There was a pleasant clink of silver as she laid the knives and forks and spoons, and he thought how wonderful she would be in such a little home as he could offer her, how she would grace the quarters at an army post. She smiled on him, and her smile was sunshine. He went at her once more with that rush of desire. She put up her hand to fend him off, and he knocked a cup out of it.

They knelt together to pick up the pieces. He began: "While I'm down here on my knees, I ask you again—" She put her hand to her lips in warning, but he seized the hand. She snatched it away and rose to her feet just as Willie Enslee came in.

Forbes, still on his knees, set busily to work picking up the scattered petals of the china. He felt guilty as a caught burglar, but the unsuspecting Willie paused on the threshold to yawn. Willie was always yawning on the threshold of discovery.

"'Morning! 'Morning!" was his almost swallowed greeting.

"We just broke one of your cups," said Persis, "while we were setting the table."

"So long as you don't break the table, I suppose I'm to be congratulated. Had a fearful time this morning without my man. Had to fill my own tub, put own buttons in, shave self—cut a map of Russia on face. Couldn't get tie tied to save life. Persis, you'll have to help your little Willie with his bib."

So Persis knotted his scarf for him while Forbes grew restive at the sight. Willie was proprietory in his tone, and he clung drowsily to Persis' arm while her hands hovered about his throat. But when the task was done he toddled through the swinging-door to see what wreck had been made of the kitchen.

"You see!" said Persis, reproachfully, putting down the silver very slowly. "You nearly got caught."

"But what of it?" Forbes broke out. "I love you. I'm not ashamed of my love or of you. I want you to be my wife."

The boyish manly sincerity of this convinced her and filled her eyes with a morning haze.

"You do? Really?" She moved on to the next place. He followed her.

"Of course I do. Will you?"

She continued slowly circling the table, with side trips to the sideboard, and he followed with a great ado of helping her. The two were making a slower job of it than either would have required alone.

"It's rather fun being proposed to while one is setting the table," Persis murmured. "We're getting terribly domestic already."

"You'd be so beautiful domesticated," Forbes urged.

"But so somebody else thinks — and we're on his grounds." And since it was characteristic of Persis to express a virtue in a sporting term, she shook her head. "We're not playing strictly according to ·Hoyle. It's not quite cricket."

"I know it," said Forbes. "And I—I dare you to come outside—off the place."

"All right. I will, the first chance I get."

"The first chance you get to what?" said Mrs. Neff, who appeared as suddenly as Cinderella's witch. And she looked a trifle witchy this morning without the rejuvenating spells of her maid. "I couldn't help overhearing, but my eyes aren't open. I didn't see anything."

Persis surprised Forbes and Mrs. Neff by her frankness.

"I was saying I would take a long walk with Mr. Forbes the first chance I get."

"Good work!" said Mrs. Neff, quite earnestly. "I was

telling him what a love of a couple you two would make."

Persis turned on her in amazement. "You were telling Mr. Forbes that?"

"Yes, I was. When a woman gets as old as I feel of mornings, she has the right to be a matchmaker. You two go on and work out your own salvation and I'll keep Willie off the scent. If I could prevent Alice from marrying Stowe Webb, and you from marrying Willie, I'd retire on my laurels. I dote on conspiracies. That's where Alice gets her knack for plots."

This to her daughter, who sauntered in just in time to receive the facer and gasp:

"Why, mother, what do you mean?"

"Oh, I can smell a mouse even if I can't trap it right away. I know you telephone him and write him and all that. I used to when I was your age. Only, I fooled my mother and married the man I wanted to. If I'd married the one she wanted me to, I'd be one of the richest women on earth instead of a starving twice-widow with a pack of children to drive to market."

"Isn't she the most appalling mother a poor child ever had?" Alice gasped. "Sometimes I think I ought to take her over my knee and spank her."

Forbes and Persis paid little heed to the usual duel of these two women. They were thinking of the complexity of outside interference in their own program of quiet communion.

Persis' mind was full of reproof for Mrs. Neff; but she was silenced by the presence of Alice, and Ten Eyck's appearance, and the irruption of Winifred with a great tray of egg-gold and bacon-bronze.

It was an informal gathering at that breakfast-table. Important articles of toilet had been forgotten, and there were no maids or men to repair the omissions. But too great correctness would have been an anachronism at Winifred's table. Everybody had gone to bed early and tired, and had slept longer and better than usual. Doing without was a new game to these people, and they made a picnic-ground of the breakfast-room.

Even Willie tried to romp with his guests, but he lacked the genius for hilarity, and his jokes consisted principally of repeating exactly what somebody else had just said, then laughing as hard as he could.

He told Persis that he wanted to show her the farm, and the new fountain in the sunken gardens, and he told her in such a way that the others felt themselves cordially invited not to go along. But they were used to tactlessness from Willie, and they merely winked mutually.

Willie seemed to feel the winks in the air, and to realize that he had not done exactly the perfect thing, so he reverted to his favorite witticism: "You take Mrs. Neff, Mr. Forbes " (he was getting the name right at times now). "You take Mrs. Neff and go where you please. You turtle-doves will find several arbors and summer-houses and lovers' lanes scattered around the place. I'll tell the gardener and his men to keep out of the way. Come along, Persis."

Forbes watched them off with a look of jealousy that did not escape Mrs. Neff. She put a kindly hand on his arm.

"After all, he owns the place; he's the host—a poor thing, but our host. She'd rather be with you, and you'd rather be with her; but you'll have to wait. You'll probably get plenty of each other soon enough."

Winifred detailed Alice and Ten Eyck to wash the breakfast dishes. The turn of the others would come later. Persis and Mrs. Neff were to make the beds.

"Winifred was born to be a poor man's wife," said Mrs. Neff, as she led Forbes across the lawn. "She dotes on cooking and pot-walloping and mending, and she had to be born with a mint of money, and the only man that ever cared for her is Bob Fielding, who will hardly let her lift her teacup to her lips, for fear she'll overwork herself.

"Now Persis is as dainty as a cat, and as hard to boss. And she has a fatal attraction for men who can't afford to keep her. Willie's the only suitor she ever had that has more money than she could spend. And I think she likes him less than anything on earth except work."

Forbes was tempted to confess to Mrs. Neff what he had divulged to Ten Eyck, but he postponed the miserable business. It was an uncongenial company for proclaiming one's poverty.

The surroundings were as tempting as Naboth's vineyard was to Ahab. He understood why men grow unscrupulous in the hunt for great wealth.

Mrs. Neff led Forbes about the place, which she knew well. But the beauties were only torments to him. Below the climbing marble stairway to the temple there was a broken stairway winding down the hill. It meandered like the dry bed of a stream, between brick walls, bordered with flowers, with now and then a resting-place, or some quaint niche where a little statue smiled or a fountain trilled and tinkled.

At two stages of the descent there were circular levels with ornate shelters and aristocratic plants. From the lowest shelf there was only a path dropping down the long hill to a distant wall; beyond this a ragged woods like a mob of poor shut out from a rich man's place.

"That wall is the end of the Enslee estate," said Mrs. Neff.

"There is an end to it, then?" said Forbes, more bitterly than he intended.

"There's an end to everything, my boy," Mrs. Neff brooded, with a far-off bitterness of her own—"an end to wealth and love and—everything."

"Who owns that place off there, I wonder?" said Forbes.

"Nobody in particular," said Mrs. Neff. "Some old cantankerous absentee that won't sell. Do you want to buy it to be near Mrs. Enslee? Willie has offered him all sorts of money, but he won't let go. You might have better luck."

Forbes again ignored the assumption that he was wealthy, and said:

"There are things, then, that even the Enslee money can't buy?"

"Many things," said Mrs. Neff. "Persis' love, for one, and Willie's own happiness, and a foot more of height and a certain charm, and—but aren't we stupid and cynical this beautiful morning?"

"Are we?" Forbes smiled.

"We are, and I have a right to be," said Mrs. Neff. "But you haven't. You are not white-haired, nor old, nor a woman."

"Are those the only causes for unhappiness?"

"They are three of the worst, and the most incurable."

But Forbes was too young in his own anxieties to give much importance to her ancient plaints, though she was not too old to understand his. He was glancing upward now and then to the little temple. It was visible from here, though the two figures in it were small and blurred with light.

Forbes was sure that Enslee was proposing to Persis, for he gesticulated, pointed at the landscape and the house. He was evidently commending these to Persis, laying them at her feet, begging her to become at once the châtelaine of this splendor.

Forbes wanted to abandon Mrs. Neff and fly to the rescue of Persis. He wanted to break in on that proposal, prove to her how much better he loved her than Enslee did, how much greater happiness she could have with him than with Enslee. But he made no move in that direction. It was one of those simple things that almost nobody can find the courage to do. He loitered with Mrs. Neff, hating himself for a skulker.

He could not know that he pleaded well enough at a distance. His absence wrought for him against Willie

Enslee's presence. Willie was indeed commending his estate to Persis, urging her to marry him at once and settle here for the summer, except what time they might spend abroad or on the yacht, or his other palace at Newport.

But while he pleaded Persis was searching Enslee's landscape for Forbes. The view had been entrancing from the temple with Forbes at her side. Now she felt that it was not after all so satisfying. The very fact that Willie praised it brought up suspicion. She would prefer to choose another landscape, one better suited to her and Forbes, not a second-hand landscape built along some other person's lines.

It would be a joy for Forbes and her to pick out a hundred acres or more—not too far from New York; perhaps among the hunting and poloing colonies on Long Island. While they were building they could cruise.

But perhaps Forbes could not afford a yacht. She must not run him into extravagances. Well, after all, the suites *de luxe* on some of the ocean liners were not so bad, with their own dining-saloons attached. By omitting the yacht they could have a stunning town house. Mrs. Jimmie Chives wanted to sell her place for a song, and nearly every room in it was imported bodily from some European castle or mansion. With a few changes it could be made quite a habitable shack.

And so, while Willie pleaded in his nagging way, her own imagination was attorney for Forbes. Only it was imagining a Forbes that did not exist, a fairly rich and decently leisurely Forbes. Down below, looking up to her with such eyes as lovers in hell cast on their beloveds in heaven, was the real Forbes, poor, hard-worked, with no financial prospects beyond a minute increase of wage by slow promotion. And he had only a few days more of leisure before he resumed the livery of the nation.

CHAPTER XXXI

LUNCHEON was breakfast again with a few additions. Winifred had lost the hang of the range, and what successes she had were ruined by her inability to corral the herd on time. The soup was salted beyond the sanction of even the most amiable palate. The chickens were guaranteed not to be resurrections from a cold-storage tomb; but they would have been the better for a little longer hanging and a little shorter cooking. The vegetables had not been salted at all, nor warmed quite through.

"The average is perfect," was Ten Eyck's verdict.

"And the salad's fine, Winifred," said Mrs. Neff, in a desperate effort to console the despondent cook, who retreated to the kitchen and cried a little more salt into the soup.

Ten Eyck rubbed his sagging waistcoat and groaned:

"This is the emptiest empty house-party I ever went to."

"It would have been a noble institution in Lent," Persis sighed.

"You would come," Willie snapped.

"Thank heaven," Alice purred, "I have a five-pound box of chocolates in my room."

Mrs. Neff glared at her. "He'd better save his money. Or has he an account at Maillard's? You can't live on candy, you know."

"It's quite as nourishing as the Congressional Record," said Alice.

"Deuce all!" cried Ten Eyck. "But family matters

aside, we've got to do something about food. I've survived the fireless and foodless cooking at breakfast and luncheon, but the dinnerless dinner would finish me. Winifred can afford to bant, I can't. I'm going to give a party. We'll all dine over at the Port of Missing Men and have dinner on me; that will get us through until to-morrow at least."

This was agreed upon with enthusiasm. Winifred was tactfully proffered a vote of thanks and a vacation. There remained only the afternoon to kill. Persis thought to steal a few minutes with Forbes, and they struck out for the sunken gardens, but Willie came panting after them and constituted himself their guide.

He was like one of those pests that can rob the Pitti Palace of interest and make the Vatican an old barn. He led them through the gardens, the greenhouses, the stables, and the kennels. Here a little sea of beagles flowed and frothed round Persis' feet. They were a relic of the days before the hunting fever left Westchester for Long Island. They were mad for exercise, and so were the horses in the stables.

"We must take these poor nags out for a run," said Persis, looking at Forbes, who accepted with his eyes.

"All right, we will. To-morrow morning," said Willie; and Forbes resigned with a look.

Unable to shake off Willie, Persis pleaded the need for a little sleep and retreated to her room. Forbes wandered about, puzzled at the appalling loneliness he could feel in so beautiful a place with so many people around and only one missing.

Eventually, however, the sun, which had begun the day with such ecstasy for him, began to approach the top of the western hill, and the caravan set out for the Port of Missing Men, which proved to be a little cottage of an inn set upon the edge of a small mountain and surveying a vast panorama.

On the piazza the crowd dined well, and returned

through the great park to the homeward roads, for when they reached the Enslee bridge it was like coming home. The wings of the motor had made it possible to run twenty-five miles to dinner and twenty-five miles back in almost negligible time; but the exultant speed of the journey and the multitude of sights that had fled past fatigued the mind like a long voyage, and it was once more a subdued company that gathered before the living-room fireplace.

Silence fell upon them all, and they sat once more staring into the flames, each finding there the glittering castles of desire.

Prout came in with more logs of wood and tiptoed out, shaking his head in stupefaction at this latest game of these amazing people.

At some vaguely later hour Persis rose and went into the adjoining music-room. Forbes longed to follow, but feared to move. She strummed a few inexpert chords on the piano. Then she went to the victrola and searched among the black disks. A little later she called out:

"Everything in this house is last year's. There's not a turkey-trot on the place, or a tango."

A little later she spoke again, "Here's a bit of ancient history." She cranked up the machine, set the needle to the disk, and "The Beautiful Blue Danube" came twanging forth from a scarred record that riddled the melody with curious spatterings.

The once world-victorious rhapsody had almost a dirge-like tameness now; but it brought Willie to his feet, and he began to circle the room with Persis. She drooped over his inferior shoulders like a wilted flower.

Ten Eyck scooped Alice off the floor and danced in double time. Forbes bowed to Winifred, but she waved him away with a heavy hand. Mrs. Neff beckoned him. "I'd rather be second choice than a wallflower. That music takes me back a thousand years."

She glided with an old-time dignity. Forbes tried to

keep his eyes from Persis and heed Mrs. Neff's reminis-
cences.

"Waltzes, waltzes!" she wailed. "How much they
meant once to me. There are no dances like the old
dances."

"There never were," said Forbes. "I reckon that
twenty years from now old folks will be shaking their
heads and telling how sweet and dignified the turkey-
trot was compared with the epileptic crawl and the
hydrophobia skedaddle they'll be doing then."

"I reckon so," said Mrs. Neff. "I can just remember
when the polka was considered immoral."

Other waltzes were played, but Willie's appetite for
them was quenched after the first. He sank into a chair
by the living-room table and took up a story in an old
magazine.

Persis waltzed with Forbes more often than with the
others; but Willie never knew. In fact, it was not long
before his head grew heavier and heavier, and finally,
with his chin in his necktie, he slept.

The dancing, the copious wine, and the sudden warmth
of the weather soon led to the opening of doors. From
the music-room one stepped out into a kind of cloister
opening on the lawn.

Eventually Persis set a two-step record whirling on the
machine. Forbes asked her to dance with him. As they
were passing one of the doors a little gust of summer-
night air blew upon them so appealingly that Forbes
swung Persis across the sill and stepped out into the
cloister, where the moonlight streamed like a distant
searchlight.

The music followed them, but muffled, by the pat of
their feet along the tiled floor. To silence this noise
Forbes danced across the margin of stone out upon the
smooth, short, silent grass. Persis made no resistance,
and he danced always a little deeper into the lawn, a
little farther from the house. He danced her round the

inky plumes of a cluster of cedars. These shut out the lights from the door. The music was quite lost here, and Persis hummed the tune herself; seemed to croon it into his very heart.

The music must have stopped in the house long before they knew it, and some one must have put on a disk in whose hard-rubber surface was embedded the voice of Sembrich singing a waltz-song of Chopin's.

This angelic melody floated on the air as if it came from nowhere and everywhere, and Forbes and Persis fell into the swift rhythm of it. They must needs dance furiously fast to keep up; but the music brought with it some of its own resistless energy.

Out here in this moon-world they seemed to be utterly aloof from the earth. They seemed to whirl like twin stars in a cosmic dance to the music of the spheres, the song the stars sing together. The Milky Way was but moonlit dew on the lawn of the sky. And they darkled between the planets in a divine rhythm on a vast orbit, until at last a breathlessness of soul and body compelled Persis to end the occult rite.

The moonlight fell about her in a magic veil, and Forbes could not let her go. He caught her closer to him. But before his lips could brush her cheek, she broke his clasp and said:

"We must get back."

"Oh, please!" he implored.

"The others will wonder."

"What of it?"

"We can't afford to set them talking."

"We can't afford to waste a night like this in a stuffy room."

"There will be other moonlight nights."

"How do you know? We can't be sure."

"The moon is pretty regular in its habits."

"But we may not be alive. It may rain to-morrow. And the day after I must be getting back to my post."

"Really? Oh, that is too bad!" There was such deep regret in her words that he took courage to say:

"If we could only walk together a long, long distance! Doesn't the moon seem to—to command you to march?"

"Yes; but—but my slippers are all wet with the dew."

"You could change them."

"And what would the others say?"

"Must they know?"

"How could they help knowing?"

"If you told them all good night and went to your room and changed your slippers, and came out later, and I met you—"

It was a very elaborate conspiracy for him, and she gasped:

"Do you think I'm quite mad?"

"I know I am, or it seems that I'll go mad unless I can be with you in this wonderful light."

"It is wonderful, but—even if I were crazy enough to do as you say you would spoil it all—you wouldn't be good."

"Oh yes, I would. I promise."

"Solemnly?"

"I solemnly promise that I will not annoy you. I will not presume to—to kiss you unless you ask me to."

"That ought to be safe enough," she laughed. "Well, I'll think it over. And now we really must get back. Alice and Murray are at the door looking this way.

They returned slowly to the cloister, discussing the beauty of the night and the brilliance of the moon. Persis told on herself; confessed that she had been foolish enough to dance on the grass, and her shoes and stockings were drenched.

Willie, who was partially awake, supplied the necessary excuse for absence. He demanded that she change at once and not risk pneumonia.

"If I'm sent to my room I won't come back," said Persis, and yawned convincingly. This set up a contagion of yawns. Everybody was instantly smitten with sleepiness. There was no necessity to keep awake, and they were all easy victims of the demands of long-deferred sleep.

There was some flurry over the nightcap drinks, and a leisurely exit of all except Persis, who left immediately. When the rest went up to their rooms Forbes went to his.

He waited with frantic impatience for the light to go out in Ten Eyck's room. It was nearly midnight when Forbes felt it safe to venture out into the hall and tiptoe down the stairs. He had just arrived there when Persis stole down and met him. There was no light except a shaft of moonshine weirdly recolored by a stained-glass window. They did not venture even a whisper. He took her arm and groped with his free hand through a black tunnel to a blacker door, which opened stealthily and admitted a flood of moonlight.

Persis was dressed warmly, and she had put on high boots and a short, thick mackinaw jacket. But she shivered with the midnight chill and with a kind of ecstatic terror.

Forbes had planned his route. He would avoid the ascending stairway to the temple of Enslee's worship, and lead her to the sunken gardens, which he had longed to explore with her at his side.

They did not wade out into the mid-sea of the lawn. He remembered Persis' dictum that behind the blinds there are always eyes. Like snickering truants they skirted the balustrade, the shadowy privet hedge, the masses of juniper and bay and box, till they reached the point where the winding stairway dropped down between its high brick walls.

The shadows were doubly dense here, and Persis hung back, but Forbes laughed at her for a poltroon, and she refused to take the dare. He was so afraid that she might fall that he finally suggested:

"If you are afraid of stumbling here, I—I'm not forgetting my promise; but I just wanted to say that I—I don't mind holding on to you, if you want to ask me to."

She declined with whispered thanks. Down, down the walk drifted. At length they heard a murmur—the mysteriously musical noise of a fountain. They rounded a few more curves and came upon a niched Cupid riding a dolphin, from whose mouth an arc of water poured with a sound of chuckling laughter. The green patina that covered the bronze was uncannily beautiful in the moonlight, and the water was molten silver.

They stood and watched it like children for a long while. Then Forbes urged Persis along to the lowest of the circular levels.

There he led her to a bench and dropped down beside her. They both looked off into the huge caldron of the hills, filled with moonlight as with a mist.

The ragged woods in the distance were superb now in blue velvet. Everything was ennobled—rewritten in poetry. Everything plain and simple and ugly took on splendor and mystic significance. Every object, every group of objects, became personal and seemed to be striving to say something.

Persis and Forbes sat worshiping like Parsees of the moon, in awesome silence, till Forbes could no longer hush the clamor in his heart.

"Miss Cabot," he said, "I promised not to annoy you. Would it annoy you if I told you that—that I love you with all my heart and soul and being?"

"How could you love me?" she answered, softly, hoping to be contradicted. "You've known me only a few days."

"There are some people we live with for years and never like nor understand; others we know and love the moment our eyes meet."

"And did you love me the moment our eyes met?"

"Long before that. I loved the back of your hat and one shoulder."

"Do you tell everybody you meet the same thing? It's rather a stale question to ask a man, but you do seem rather impulsive on so short an acquaintance."

"Short acquaintance? We've seen each other more than most people see of each other in six months. I know you and I know myself, and I know that I shall never be happy unless I can be trying to make you happy."

"I am very happy just now," she murmured.

"But we can't sit here forever, and we can't even be together for more than a day or two. I want you for my own. I don't want to see you only—only on—Mr. Enslee's property."

"Which reminds me," Persis said, with a tone of dispelled romance, "that we are still on Mr. Enslee's property, and it doesn't seem fair to him."

"Then let's leave Mr. Enslee's property."

"How? In an airship?"

"See that wall down there. That is one of the boundary lines. If we were over that I could tell you some things that I've got to tell you."

"It's an awfully long way."

"Not so long as you think."

"No, no; it's easy to descend to Avernus, or whatever it was; but to get back! I'd never have the strength for that."

"It's not far. Let's walk to keep warm. You are cold, aren't you?"

"Frozen, that's all. Well, come along, I'll go part way with you."

They set out upon the little path. There were no trees to shelter them now from the moon, and its light seemed to beat upon the hillside like waves. The moon that draws the sea along in tides could not but have its influence on these two atoms, and on the blood that sped through their tiny veins. The moon filled them with the love of love.

Constantly pausing to turn back, but finding it easier to drift on down than begin the upward climb, Persis went on and on, arm in arm with Forbes. By and by they reached the boundary wall. He helped her to set one knee upon it and mount awkwardly. He clambered up and sat down at her side. Their backs were toward the Enslee demesne, their feet in the unknown.

And there, without delay, Forbes told her that she must be his wife, told her that he loved her as woman had never been loved before.

His hands fought to caress her, his lips tingled to be again at her cheek, but he kept his promise.

Yet the influence of the promise was potent on her, too. She knew that he was in an anguish of temptation, and she glowed with his struggle. The moon and the width of the world, the silent night-cry of the world in the lonely dark, and the yearning light filled her with a need of love. She regretted the promise, she wished that he would break it, and her absolution waited ready for his deed.

But his sense of honor prevailed upon his hands, though he could not keep silent about his heartache.

"Couldn't you possibly love me, Miss Cabot? Couldn't you possibly?" he pleaded; and she whispered, with a sad sweetness:

"I could—all too easily, Mr. Forbes, but I am afraid to love. I thought I never should love anybody really. And now that I know I might, it is so terrible an awakening that I—I'm afraid of it."

"Don't be afraid," he implored. "Love me. Let yourself love me."

"I'm afraid, Mr. Forbes."

"Then if you're afraid to love, it's because you don't, because you—can't."

This hurt her pride. Her heart was so swollen with this new power that it would not be denied either by herself or him.

"Yes, I could! Oh, I could! But I mustn't—I mustn't let myself love you—not now—not so soon."

"Then I must wait," he sighed, and said no more. And she sat in a silence, though there was a great noise of heartbeats in her breast and in her temples and ears.

She began to shiver with the night and with her excitement. She wanted to say that they must start back; but her tongue stumbled thickly against her chattering teeth. The world was bitter cold—so far from him. In his arms would be warmth and comfort as at a fireplace. She was lonely, unendurably lonely and wistful.

And he sat at her side in an equal ague of distance and need.

Finally he took his eyes from the moon and bent his gaze on her. He saw how her shoulders quaked.

"You're cold, you poor, sweet child—you're cold. I'm dying to take you in my arms, but I promised—I promised."

She was afraid to surrender, and afraid to defy the will of the night. The chill shook her with violence again and again till she felt the world rocking, the stone wall wavering. Then she leaned toward him and whispered:

"Kiss me!"

He could hardly believe that he heard, but he caught her to him and sought her lips with his. Immediately she was afraid again. Again she hid the preciousness of her mouth from him, writhed and struggled and twisted her face, hid it in his breast. But now he fought her with gentle ruthlessness, took her cold cheeks in his cold hands, and, holding her face up to the moonlight, kissed her eyes, and her dew-besprent hair and her cheeks, and pressed the first great kiss on her lips. They fled from him no more.

Only a moment she lingered in Elysium, and then she sighed:

"We must go back—we must! I hate to, but there's to-morrow—and the people! What wouldn't they think if they saw us?"

He knew that they would not think the beautiful and

holy thoughts that filled his heart and hers, so he consented to climb back from this lowly heaven to the Upper Purgatory.

Her strength was gone, and he had little of his own; but somehow he helped her up. Again and again they paused to rest, and every time he tried to tell her that he was poor, and at each pause found her lips so sweet that he could not speak of so mean a thing as money and the meaner lack of it.

And behind her aching brows there were wild decisions made and unmade to tell him that she had no right to his love until she had released herself from her pledge to Enslee. But at each pause she, too, put off the harsh truth. It was sacrilege to intrude the name of Enslee into this divine communion.

They could not harm the perfection of that bliss by any other confessions than their love.

And this is one of the pitifulest things in this world, that people lie mutely lest they spoil a beautiful truth; they put off till to-morrow what would mar to-night; they spare some heart-pain; they pay some virtue too exclusive court, and lo, they find afterward that they have brought about only corruption and confusion and damnation.

So Persis and Forbes climbed slowly the winding stairway, and their mood was one of hallowed reverence for God and His beautiful world. They paused to wish even the little bronze Cupid well, and his dolphin and the stream of living water; the moon had deserted it now, but still it chuckled. Forbes and Persis skirted the balustrade with a guilty rapture, avoiding the almost daylight of the moon-swept lawn. They opened the door with the innocent stealth of good fairies.

They mounted the stairway with their arms about each other's bodies, and in the hall above they kissed and whispered, "Good night! Good night! Good night!" and tiptoed in opposite directions.

WHAT WILL PEOPLE SAY?

At their remote doors they paused to throw kisses into the black dark toward each other's invisible presences.

Forbes turned the knob of his door with fierce caution, and waited to hear Persis close hers. There was a faint thud and a little click like a final kiss. He tiptoed across his sill, and was just closing his door after him when he heard somewhere in the hall the soft thud of another door, the click of another lock. His heart leaped as if a fist had seized it suddenly. Some one else had been in the hall. In the deep black there was no telling whose door it was. But some one else had been in the hall.

CHAPTER XXXII

LIEUTENANT FORBES had known what it was to bivouac in the black of night in Mindanao, surrounded by wild men native to the trees and as stealthy as the dark, and armed with blow-guns, carved, painted, sometimes studded with gems, but emitting poisonous darts. He had stood then trying to peer them out in the gloom, knowing they were there and unable to descry them.

So he stood now gripping his door-knob lest it turn in his hand and betray him. He realized that he and Persis had lingered in a social ambush. They were in no peril of life, but the unknown spy might let loose upon them an envenomed dart from the silent, the sometimes jeweled blow-gun of gossip.

Forbes' eyes fought in vain against a dark that was like a black bandage. He felt sure that it was not Ten Eyck's door that had thudded so slyly shut. But he could not even guess whether it were the door of Enslee or of one of the women.

He waited and waited, hoping that a light would be made, but there was no glimmer along any sill. Even Persis was evidently undressing in the dark, or in the moonlight that must be pouring into her room.

Forbes visioned her there chilled and tired, her sleepy hands fumbling at the sepals of her clothing till she stripped them off and stood glimmering in the blue a moment before she slipped into that creamy nothing he had seen her wear at the window. And then he visioned her with chattering teeth and shivering hands immersing her lonely beauty in the sheets, snow-white, snow-cold, like a nymph returning to her brook in winter-time. He felt immensely sorry that she should be cold and alone.

He wondered if she prayed at her bedside, and thought of her as a nun in one long, white line of beauty, from her brow bent down, to the palms of her little bare feet upturned on the floor. He hoped that she would not pray too long lest she catch cold. And this seemed a kind of sacrilegious thought, like individual communion cups.

All these things he thought as he waited, gripping the door-knob and listening fiercely for a sign of the eavesdropper. And lest she should have been too cold to pray, he prayed for her, that calumny might not be the reward of her innocent love, the sweet surrender she had made of her discretion and her good repute into his keeping.

Yet he feared for her. He doubted that the secret observer would think her free of guile. He did not fear for himself. The man would be regarded at worst as a successful adventurer, but the woman despised for an easy victim or a willing accomplice.

Forbes reproached himself for bringing this blight on Persis. It was he that had dragged her protesting from the house, persuaded her to steal forth, led her into the distance, and kept her while the respectable hours slipped by.

The only atonement he could make was to proclaim as speedily as possible that their love was honest and that they carried the franchise of betrothal. To-morrow he must make sure of her. He closed his door with the utmost caution, and got out of his clothes and into his bed with all possible silence. He was exhausted with the long day of love's anxieties and triumph, and the new anxiety he had stumbled into. He had yet to tell her how far from rich he was. He had yet to persuade her to leave this golden world of hers for the parsimony he offered.

Perhaps her courage or her love would flinch from the sacrifice.. Then he could not protect her from the un-

known sneerer. Indeed, if the unknown listener were
Enslee, Forbes would not stand as the protector of Persis
at all, but as a ruthless tempter of another man's love.
If it were Ten Eyck, he would have ground for reviling
Forbes as one whom he regretted sponsoring, a wolf
admitted into the fold in sheep's clothing. Or if it were
one of the women—everybody knows what mercy females
have for one another.

In the chaos of his perplexities he fell asleep, and did
not waken till the whir of the telephone on his wall
called him from his slumber. Winifred's voice gruffly
informed him that his breakfast was waiting for him.

When, as little later as he could manage, he joined the
group already at the table, he tried to read in the "Good
morning" of each some telltale hint. Mrs. Neff's A.M.
languor might mask a reproach. Alice's casual glance
might mean aversion. Ten Eyck's reproving frown might
be a comment on his tardiness or a rebuke for his bad
faith. Winifred's curt manner might be merely her way
of play-acting a surly cook, and it might represent disgust.

Willie Enslee smiled—smiled! Was it a crafty sneer,
or was it simply his stinted hospitality? If Enslee knew
that he was clandestine with. Enslee's sweetheart, how
could Enslee smile? He must eliminate Enslee, at least,
from his suspicion.

Persis alone greeted him with heartiness; her blessed
and blessing eyes were like kisses on the brow. But
Persis did not know that they had been watched.
She had closed her door first. How was he to tell her?
how put her on her guard?

Forbes ate his breakfast in the mixed humor of a detective and a suspect. He studied the others, and they
seemed to study him or to avoid him. He could not
settle upon even a theory.

After the breakfast he sought an opportunity for a
secret word with Persis. She was told off to the bed-

making squad. She was even to do his room! He caught her at the foot of the stairs. She warned him with a gesture, and he broke the news to her without preparation:

"Last night when we were saying good night some one else was in the hall."

Her lips parted in a gasp of terror, and her eyes whitened. "How do you know?" she whispered.

"I heard her—or him."

"Who was it?"

"I don't know. I can't even guess," he mumbled.

"Do you think it could have been— All right, Mr. Forbes, I'll be careful of your razor-blades."

This last aloud for the benefit of Mrs. Neff, who came by and spoke with icy severity—was it ironical?

"Chambermaids are not allowed to flirt with customers in this hotel." She went on up; and Persis followed helplessly, leaving Forbes distraught.

Later he saw her at his windows beating his pillows. The intimate implication thrilled him, and he threw her a kiss while pretending to take his cigar from his lips, and she retreated into the embrasure to answer it with a secret waft from her own mouth.

Forbes had hoped to be invited to ride with Persis, and had put on a pair of civilian riding-breeches and his army puttees. But he was ignored in the program for the day, announced by Enslee, who decreed that he and Persis would ride over to the Sleepy Hollow Country Club, by the quietest roads they could find, while the rest were to motor across. They would all have luncheon together and return in the same way. "If that horse of mine doesn't break both of our fool necks," he added.

"What about Persis and her horse's neck?" Ten Eyck asked, speaking Forbes' own uneasy thought.

"Oh, Persis can ride anything," Willie said. "She's a born centaurette, while a horse and I are like oil and water—only oil always stays on top, and I don't."

But Forbes did not feel so sure of Persis as Willie did.

He ventured to say as much when she appeared, but she laughed at him:

"Horses are not among my afraids. I've ridden since I graduated from the back of a Great Dane to a Shetland pony. I've got rubber bones; when I fall off I bounce back."

He could make no further protest, and hung about in the futile discomfort of an old woman. There was no reassurance for him in the behavior of the horses, which two stablemen brought up the hill with a difficulty that led Ten Eyck to comment:

"Are those men leading horses, Willie, or flying kites?"

There was a slight break in Willie's laugh as he said: "My horse had better behave or I'll let him find his way home alone. I wish I had a parachute."

Persis was wearing the bowler hat and the coat and breeches and boots Forbes had seen her in that morning in Central Park. He knew how well she rode in the bridle-path, but he feared for her in the motor-swept roads. He told her so, but she laughed again.

She set her foot in the stirrup, flung her leg across the saddle, and warned the groom away. While Willie got one foot in the stirrup and went hopping hither and yon in pursuit of it with the other, Persis was getting acquainted with her own mount, humoring him in his school-boy hilarity, and sharply repressing any malicious mischief.

The moment Willie was aboard the two horses whirled and charged down the winding road in a mad gallopade. And Forbes' heart galloped in his breast as he wondered if he should ever see her alive again. He had felt this same fear for her that first day on the Avenue, when her motor shot forward so wildly. He was always feeling afraid for her.

CHAPTER XXXIII

THE motor passengers were in no haste to be gone, and they loitered, watching the mad riders on their breakneck descent, now hidden, now revealed again by a swerve of the road, a jut of hillside, or a group of trees.

Forbes was sure at every vanishing that they would never come into view. But they always did, and getting their horses in hand at last, finished the hill with sobriety, trotted across the granite bridge, and turned to wave good-by.

They were as small as dolls on toys where they jogged along the distant high-road. A tiny motor-cycle, whose thumping flight was faintly audible even at such a distance, whizzed round a curve and almost cut the horses' feet from under them. The animals lifted their hoofs well out of danger, but they came to earth again out of the cloud of dust, and Forbes dared to resume the business of breathing.

He saw that Enslee was a well-schooled rider who annoyed his horse a good deal, yet ruled him somehow. But Persis was perfect to the saddle, part of the horse, as fearless and as expert in her smart gear as any cowgirl of the plains.

Forbes watched her till the last curve blotted her from his sight, and yearned after her like a child left behind from a picnic. He looked at his own riding-costume ruefully, and said that he would better change. But the others would not wait for him. Mrs. Neff urged:

"They're very becoming. Keep 'em on. You've got good legs, and you make Willie look like a wishbone."

Enslee had sent his own driver and his own car to take them to the club, and with an unusual thoughtfulness had ordered the robe-rack filled with lilacs. And so they rode behind a screen of purple beauty, and breathed in a spicy air filtered through flowers.

Forbes continued his search for a clue to last night's eavesdropper in the manner of his fellow-passengers. They were all in high spirits, which might be in any one's case either ghoulish glee or innocence. As a matter of fact, Mrs. Neff's enthusiasm was owing to her knowledge that Senator Tait was at the Country Club; but she did not tell Forbes lest her daughter hear. Alice was rapturous in the knowledge that Stowe Webb had arranged before she left New York to be at the club against just such an opportunity as this; but she did not explain to Forbes lest her mother hear. Winifred was buoyant because Ten Eyck had promised her a few sets of tennis, and she saw herself already whole ounces leaner. And Ten Eyck was cheerful because the world usually amused Ten Eyck when the weather was fit. And to-day, as old Gower put it, "The weder was merie and faire ynough."

Merry and fair enough for any wight, and the scenery wonderful. After a few swift miles of country whose old walls, well-groomed meadows, and shapely forests gave a look of England, the land rose higher and higher, till the car swung out at last on a height commanding a river in the utmost contrast with England's stream. As Ten Eyck put it, "The Thames and the Hudson are as much alike as a pearl necklace and an anchor-chain." The water came down between its hills in tremendous calm, and the Palisades opposite were no longer sheer cliffs, but a congress of ponderous masses like reclining gods along a banquet board.

The homes responded, of necessity, to the scene. In place of the ballroom levels and exquisite parks along the reaches of the Thames, with its flat punts and its houseboats moored in shady niches, these lawns sloped and rolled in massive sweeps, fronting a mighty stream.

Forbes' heart could not rise to the bigness of the scene; it was too much tossed between the hope that the next turn might reveal Persis, spick and span on a glossy horse, and the fear that some of these countless whizzing, hooting motors might frighten the beast into panic and hurl her under the swarming wheels.

Ten Eyck seemed to note the anxiety that kept his eyes shuttling this way and that, for he remarked, as if quite casually:

"Small chance of meeting Persis and Willie here. They said they'd try to keep off the busiest roads, and Willie has probably got himself lost somewhere in the twists and turns of Sleepy Hollow. Sleepy Hollow is just where Willie belongs, all right; he is the most headless headless horseman that ever threw a pumpkin. I'll bet he turns up late to luncheon and makes a spectacular entrance on the back of his neck."

Ten Eyck was as nearly right as a prophet is required to be.

The car reached its destination without encountering Persis or Willie. More majestic than the usual country club, that of Sleepy Hollow was approached by a stately entrance gate. The road wound between broad lawns, where children played among tropical thickets of veteran rhododendrons tall as trees, and studded with flowers as big and brilliant as Chinese lanterns. The club-house was a pile of creamy brick, tall and spacious as a hotel. The servants were in livery, some of them already in summer white, with dark collars and lapels—"to distinguish them from the members," said Ten Eyck.

Ten Eyck and Winifred offered Forbes a racquet in their tennis game, but he preferred to be alone with his loneliness. He accepted Ten Eyck's suggestion, however, that he might care to go round the links, and Ten Eyck procured him a bag of clubs and a caddy, promising him ample time for at least nine holes before Persis could arrive.

Mrs. Neff, meanwhile, had vanished with Alice. She had learned that Senator Tait was on the golf-course, and had dragged Alice forth. Mrs. Neff loathed walking, but to-day she announced a determination to reform. Alice went along with double reluctance. She lost her chance to get word to Stowe Webb, who did not know she was coming, and she feared she might find him on the links in some spot exposed to her mother's far-sweeping vision.

Forbes, left to his own devices, and feeling like a dolt for golfing in horse costume, dawdled about marveling at the luxury of the club and the splendor of the views that met the eye everywhere within or without its walls. At length he reached the golf-grounds squired by a lean little caddy, who might almost have crawled into the bag of sticks and passed for one of them.

With the usual luck of beginners and re-beginners at a game, Forbes did his best work at the start. His first drive from the first tee drew such a white arc across the sky that even the caddy was moved to an exclamation of applause, hitched his sack on his shoulder, and set off in search of the ball with vicarious pride.

The ball waited for Forbes in a position so good as to be almost suspicious. It was an ideal brassy lie; but Forbes, thinking now of his form, just missed it with surprising nicety, and sent gouts of turf flying. According to the rules, he was to replace them; and, according to custom, he affected not to see them. His score mounted rapidly while he mauled the air and the grass around the ball, and when he finally got away he had lost his temper and the respect of the caddie irretrievably.

As he worked his way up a steep ridge green and vast as the back of a tidal wave he saw at the top of the height a bunker thrusting out into the sky like the comb on the top of a Spanish woman's head. He paused for his approach, to let two women clear the way. He recognized Mrs. Neff and Alice, but they did not see him. Mrs. Neff seemed to be in a mood of displeasure. There was vexation in her very heels.

Thinking the pathway clear, Forbes mumbled "Fore," and, picking the ball up neatly in his iron, sent it over the edge of the bunker with a hurdler's economy of gap. And just as it escaped the top a head arose, followed by a pair of shoulders.

Forbes shrieked an *ex post facto* "Fore!" but it was drowned in the snort of pain and rage from the man, whose left shoulder-blade stopped the ball.

As Forbes ran forward with abject apologies a glaring face peered over the bunker and roared out:

"Damn it, man! Where do you think you— Why, it's you! Harvey, my boy!"

"Senator Tait!" Forbes cried, darting for one corner of the bunker as Senator Tait dashed for the other. They paused, turned back, and made for the opposite ends, stopped short foolishly in the middle, and laughingly clasped hands over the ledge.

"I'll come round," said Forbes; and the Senator met him, put his arms about him, and hugged him with a fatherly roughness. After he had told Forbes how much he had grown and how fine he was, and Forbes had exclaimed how young the Senator looked, the Senator hugged him again.

"I can't believe that you are yourself. The first time I saw you was in your father's arms; you were about half an hour old, and your father said you were very handsome. I couldn't see it at the time, but you've improved. I wish he could see you now. I was with him, you know, when his horse fell with him and—"

"Yes, I know," Forbes murmured. "You were his best friend—our best friend."

"It's a shame that we've lost sight of each other. We mustn't any more. Life's too short to waste in not seeing people we love. I must say, though, I'm rather hurt at your not looking me up before. Mrs. Neff has just **told** me you've been in town nearly a week."

"I—I've been very busy," Forbes stammered.

"So I hear, you young scoundrel!" Tait growled, jovially. "You're at the heartbreaking, heartaching age, and no time to spend on old duffers like me when young beauties are drooping on every bough. But what's this Mrs. Neff tells me about your being rich? I hadn't heard it. I hadn't expected it, either, for your father was a better fox-hunter than a financier. What did you do—invent some new explosive—or a new gun?"

Forbes smiled bitterly and explained the foolish mistake, too foolish to correct at first, and later embarrassing.

The Senator stared at him a moment searchingly with a tender inquisition, then said:

"Unless you're golf-hungry, let's send the caddies back and have a talk."

"By all means," Forbes agreed; and even as he cast his glance about in search of his caddy he looked farther to see if Persis were not visible somewhere from this Pisgah height. He was fond of the old man, but he loved the young woman.

15

CHAPTER XXXIV

FORBES' caddy was standing by the ball, and came in with it, cannily claimed his pay and tip for the full course, and hurried back with the Senator's caddy to pick up other fares. They took both the golf-bags with them to put away.

Tait and Forbes strolled aside from the traffic of the golf-course and found a quiet seat in the shade.

"And now tell me," the Senator said; "but first have a cigar?"

He took out a portly wallet stuffed with brown backs, the famous cigars made expressly for him in Havana. Forbes accepted one and sniffed its bouquet.

"It's a shame to waste these in the open air," he said, and sprung a cigar-lighter he carried, holding the flame to Tait, who waived it with a sigh:

"Doctor's orders."

"Then I won't."

"Go on; I carry them for my friends. I love to see others enjoy what I can't. Well, I will smoke just one to celebrate the prodigal's return." And he took a cigar from the case as tenderly as if it were forbidden ambrosia. As Forbes made a light again, he asked:

"What's this about doctor's orders? You're the kind of picture that goes with the testimonials—after taking."

"I'm a hollow sham, my boy; bad heart, bad liver, fat and sluggish, ordered to Carlsbad, but I hate to go. May have to," he puffed. "Did you see my daughter Mildred at the club-house?"

"No, I don't think so. I don't suppose I'd know her. She was a little tike in short skirts when I saw her last."

226

"She's a big woman now—regular old maid—fanatic on charities—fine mind—great heart. Thinks too much about the poor and the downtrodden to be very cheerful company; but somebody ought to look after 'em, I suppose. She's one of those hotheads that are trying to make the world over. Sounds hopeless, but they do get a lot done. She thinks poverty is no more necessary than slavery was. And she says the same of the oldest profession in the world.

"Good Lord, Harvey, what that child knows! Her mother to her dying day never heard of half the things that young spinster discusses, and has never had a flirtation so far as I know. Her conversation is really what has turned my hair white. Things that used to be kept for the medical books or smoking-room conversation she tosses off glibly, earnestly, and—to me! And spends my money, too, on scientific rescue work among women who—whew! And to think her mother and I didn't dare to tell her things! Now she tells 'em to me! She knows more about the seamy side than I do. But she's wonderful, Harvey. I'm afraid of her, but I do admire and love her. Women like her make these mad tango-trotters look pretty cheap."

Forbes resented the unintended criticism on the wonderful soul the tango mania had enabled him to meet and know so well so soon. He murmured something formulaic about his eagerness to see Mildred, and then he added, with a little hint of raillery:

"You congratulated me on my wealth. Am I to congratulate you the same way for your success with little Miss Neff?"

The Senator stared at him. "My success with little Miss Neff? What do you mean? Who's little Miss Neff? Alice?"

"Yes."

"The girl that was just here with her mother?"

"Yes."

"What success should I have with her?"

Forbes was confused, and tried to back out, but Tait would know, and Forbes at last explained: "Alice says that her mother is trying to marry her off to you."

Tait's eyes popped, and his mouth gaped stupidly, then he swore with sonority, and blurted out: "Do you mean that that old haridan of a Cornelia Neff has gone mad enough to— Why, Alice is younger than Mildred! I thought of her as a little tot. I tweaked her cheek and told her how sweet she was, and never dreamed she'd grown up yet. So that's why Cornelia has been so hospitable to me. I had a kind of sneaking fear that she wanted to add me to her own regiment of husbands. But it's her daughter, eh? Well, I'll be double— Is Alice in on the game, too?"

"Oh no; Alice is crazy to marry Stowe Webb."

"Poor old Jim Webb's boy, eh?" Forbes nodded. "Well, why doesn't she?"

"He has no money."

"Oh, she's one of those."

"He hasn't even a job."

The Senator puffed like an unmuffled cut-out, and he frowned like a pirate, then he began to chuckle in the manner of a pirate ordering the plank put over the side.

"He hasn't a job, eh? Well, I'll get him one. I'll pay that old lady in her own coin. Make a fool out of me, will she? Well, we'll see what an old politician can do to countermine an old lady."

"Speaking of politics," said Forbes, "the papers are full of the possibility of your being an ambassador somewhere. Is there anything in it?"

"Well, my old friend the President has written me a few letters and whispered it in my ear, but I don't want to go. I'm too old. I like my own country and my own slippers. Foreign languages and foreign cooking and all that would play the devil with me. I don't want to go."

228

WHAT WILL PEOPLE SAY?

Forbes laughed at the spectacle of a big, rich man pouting like a reluctant child against having a sweetmeat forced on him.

"Then why are you going?" he grinned.

"How did you know I was?"

"Because you said you didn't want to. We only say, 'I don't want to,' when we're just about to."

Tait looked at him in surprise. Forbes was not the type from whom one expects epigrams and generalizations. That was among his chief attractions. Tait laughed sheepishly.

"Well, I'll tell you, Harvey. There's just one reason— I'm worried about Mildred. She's getting in too deep with her crusades and causes. She's done enough. She mustn't lose her own life as a woman—a wife—a mother. I'm old-fashioned enough to believe that that's a woman's first business, as a man's first business is to build a home and keep it. Afterward all the charity and uplift they can do is legitimate and worthy. But first pay your debts, I say, before you make donations. Now I can't pry Mildred loose from her clubs and committees. No marrying young man will go near her. There's no encouragement to the pink nonsense of love in an atmosphere of tenement-house needs, tuberculosis exhibits, and the harrowing statistics of white slavery.

"I got an idea that if I went abroad as an ambassador she'd have to go along to take care of me and run the social end of the embassy. She'd have to dress up and give dinners, and go places and dance and meet cheerful people, and—well, who knows? Anyway, my last business on this earth is leaving my only child provided for, and I'm worried because—because—well, I'm too fat around the heart, and my neck is too thick, and the doctor tells me to be ready. You understand?

"My father went that way. He had to be very careful of his health, and one day, when he was about to go out in the rain, my mother told him he must wear his rubbers.

229

He bent over to pull on an overshoe, and—he just went
on over and sprawled out on the rug—dead."

He stared off into space, and seemed not to be a venerable old man any more, but a lonely orphan with the
sad eyes of boyhood in the presence of death.

Forbes knew what it means for a man to think of the
death of his first great man, his father; and his hand
wrung the Senator's. Tait looked up, smiled sadly, and
returned the pressure with his big, soft fingers.

"I wish I had a son to leave her with, Harvey; then I'd
feel better, but my only boy—well, he married the wrong
woman, and she drove him to the dogs, deceived him and
tormented him, and—finally he had to make her divorce
him. And he loved her in spite of it—he was ashamed of
his love; but he couldn't kill it; she couldn't kill it; drink
couldn't kill it. But the two of them killed him. Oh,
Lord, Harvey, it's a cruel world, and we're so helpless! I
could have done so much for my boy; but I couldn't
help him in the one way he needed help. I couldn't make
the woman over.

"Don't repeat his mistake, Harvey. Don't let a pretty
face and a fascinating body blind you to a bad, selfish
heart. Don't let yourself love the wrong woman. You
can do a good deal with your heart if you hold a tight rein
on it and keep it on the right road. There are fine enough
women on the straight road, just as beautiful, just as
passionate with the right man. If only—"

He paused, looked at Harvey, who was looking everywhere but at the Senator. He was searching the landscape for Persis, and he was as restless among his own
thoughts as the young usually are when the old are com-
menting on the helplessness of life. The young know so
much better. It is the young who have theories of the
universe and who expect to carry out their hopes; it is
the old scientists who are bewildered and who merely
observe and accept.

But Tait did not notice Forbes' inattention. Rummaging among the confusions of his own griefs, he had come upon a bright hope. What if Forbes should be the man to win Mildred away from her avocations back to the main business of love? He was such a youth as even Mildred could hardly ignore or despise. He had little money, but Tait had more than enough for the two, and he had made many a poor man rich.

He smiled. He felt like apologizing to Mrs. Neff for stealing a hint from her. Why should not old men engage in the pleasant chess-game of match-making, too? What better task could he undertake than making this beloved son of his old comrade the husband of his own beloved daughter?

The idea was so exhilarating that it almost leaped from his heart. But he was politician enough to realize that such a plan would be frustrated in advance by premature publication. This was a benevolent conspiracy that must be kept dark.

He studied Forbes with admiring affection. His heart went out to him as to a son, or, better yet, a son-in-law. He put a hand on Forbes' shoulder to claim him just as Forbes started with a sudden elation, just as a light broke forth in his eyes.

Tait followed the line of Forbes' gaze and made out a man and a woman on horseback turning in at the gate marked "Exit Only." That was like Willie Enslee. If any gate could excite his interest as an entrance it would be one marked "Exit Only." Tait could not see who it was; he hastily got out his distance-glasses and put them on. But a glowing wall of rhododendrons and cedars concealed the riders by the time his great tortoise-shell spectacles hobgoblined his eyes.

Forbes spoke. "Sha'n't we stroll back to the club-house? I'm expected there for luncheon."

"By all means," said Tait. "And I want you to meet Mildred again."

"I'd love to," said Forbes, absently. He said nothing

more, but strode on so rapidly down the steep slope that Tait had to take his arm for support and to hold him back.

"You're visiting at the Enslees', Mrs. Neff tells me," the old man panted.

"Yes."

"Excuse my fatherly familiarity, but how can you afford to gad with those wild asses?"

"I can't."

"What's her name?" Tait laughed.

"I may be able to tell you later, and I may not."

"Well, my boy, I don't know who she is, but I bet she isn't worth it—not if she trails with the Enslee pack."

"Oh, but she is beautiful—she is wonderful."

"You must be hit damned hard."

"Am."

And then, not heeding the connotation, he exclaimed, as Persis emerged from the eclipsing shrubbery:

"There's only one woman can ride like that."

Tait stared again, and now he made her out. Instantly, with the exultance one feels over a secret some one else lets slip, he cried: "Oho, my boy, that's the woman who keeps you here! Mrs. Neff hinted at it, but I wouldn't believe it till I had it from you." His gloating sank again to fatherly solicitude as he pleaded earnestly: "For God's sake, boy, don't love her! Of all women don't love Persis Cabot! She's the most heartless of them all."

Forbes was tempted to ask him how he could accept a reputation as a proof of character, but he was still calm enough to pay Tait's white hair the homage of silence. Tait, feeling the import of his silence, grew uneasy, and demanded:

"Harvey, it's not possible that you love her—actually love her?"

"Is it possible not to?"

"But you've not known her long."

"No, but I've known her well. Do you know her?"

"Yes, and I knew her mother. Once I thought I loved her mother. But I had less money—when I proposed to her than I have now—Heaven be praised!"

"Heaven be praised?"

"Yes, for she might have married me. Harvey, a certain part of the society here is like a big aquarium. The people are all fish—the men goldfish, the women catfish. Their blood is cold—Lord, how cold! Just look at their eyes! Hard eyes, hard hearts. They despise sincerity; they laugh at honest emotion."

"But Persis has soft eyes," Forbes broke in, "and a warm heart."

"Has she?" Tait sighed, feeling that the siren had already sung Forbes' wits away. "Well, maybe, in the moonlight. But she'll soon freeze. Now, if she had been born poor—"

"But, Senator, the rich can't all be bad," Forbes complained.

"The rich are no worse than anybody else as a class," said Tait. "My father and mother were rich, and they were as good and sweet and simple as any poor people that ever lived. They were like Romeo and Juliet. The Montagues and Capulets were both rich. But if young Mr. Montague had been poor we might have had a different story. Or, if you had only gone into finance."

"It's too late for me to dream of money. I'm a soldier."

"And it's too late for you to dream of Persis Cabot, not merely because she's wealthy. One class is as good as another; it's the set that counts. And she gallops with the rich runaways. Their life is one long stampede. There are rich women who toil like slaves for the poor, who lead lives of earnestness and purity, who respond to every appeal, and make organized charity possible. But there are others, rich and poor, that never think of anybody but themselves, never have real pity except for themselves, never toil or fret except for their own amusement. And those people gravitate together into colonies and cliques. Don't run with that pack, Harvey."

He was not the first man of eld that had warned youth against beauty. Nor was he the last that shall fail to be heeded. He tried another tack.

"I understand that Willie Enslee expects to marry her."

"She doesn't expect to marry him."

"How do you know?"

"Oh, I have my reasons for believing that she doesn't love him."

"Nobody ever accused her of that, but—well, does she think what Mrs. Neff thinks—that you have money?"

Forbes did not answer except with a blush. The Senator spared him any pressure on that point. He said, simply:

"Enslee has a lot of money—more than her father has. In fact, her father is in a very bad plight."

"How do you know?"

"I am about six bank directors, Harvey, and a few other things. Her father is about to be forced into involuntary bankruptcy; her father's pet railroad may go into receiver's hands to-day or to-morrow."

"Poor Persis!" Forbes groaned. "Poor Persis!"

There was such anguish in his tone that the Senator gripped his arm hard and murmured:

"Do you care so much for her?"

Forbes stopped short and stared into the old man's eyes. "A man like me loves once, and loves hard. If I lost her, my life wouldn't be worth the snap of my finger." And he added in a raucous voice, "Or the click of a trigger."

The Senator leaned heavily on him and closed his eyes in a wince of pain. He had heard his own dead son speak just that way.

When he opened his eyes he saw that Forbes was smiling glowingly.

WHAT WILL PEOPLE SAY?

"Look at her, Senator! She's so beautiful! I can't let Enslee have her! Look at him! He's as afraid of his horse as his horse is ashamed of him. What's he up to now? Rein him in, you fool! He'd drive a hobbyhorse into hysterics. And now he's sent Persis' horse in the air! What's the matter with him? Why doesn't he—"

But the fault was not Enslee's, nor was he so bad a rider as an expert like Forbes might think. As the event proved, even Persis could not control her mount in the face of what was happening unseen by Forbes. A chauffeur, relying on the fact that he was on the exit road, was driving a big red six at high speed along the curves. He had not seen Enslee and Persis till he was almost into them. He swung aside so sharply that he almost capsized, and ran into something sharp enough to rip open a shoe.

This was just one too many automobiles for the horses Persis and Enslee rode. They had been curbed and scolded and kept in hand all morning; but to have a dragon leap at them from the cedar-trees was too much. They went frantic, dancing erect, and threshing the air with their fore hoofs. And then the tire exploded like a cannon, and they went mad. They feared nothing but what was behind them; nothing could hurt them but their terror.

They crashed through cedars and rhododendrons, and plunged across the lawn to the clear space of the golf-links. Forbes saw the demon look in the white eyes of Persis' horse. He had seen mustangs in that humor shake off their tormentors and tear them wolfishly with their fangs.

"He's got the bit in his teeth!" he groaned. "He'll kill her! My God, he'll kill her! She can't hold him! I've got to get him somehow."

He had a fierce impulse to meet the horse, leap at him, catch him by the bridle and the nose and smother him

235

to a standstill. But Tait had seen a policeman killed trying to stop a horse so, and he flung his arms about Forbes.

"No, you won't!" he gasped. "You can't stop him! I won't let you risk your life—not for that woman."

"Let me go! Let me go!" Forbes pleaded, unwilling to use his strength against the old man. But Tait clung to him, seized him anew as Forbes wrenched his hand loose; fell to his knees, but still held fast and was dragged along, moaning:

"My boy, I love you like a son. You sha'n't risk your life—not for her!"

Then suddenly his clutch relaxed; his fingers opened; he rolled forward on his face, his white hair fluttering in the grass.

And Forbes, hardly knowing that he was released, felt himself free, and ran with all his might to intercept the plunging monster, who came snorting his rage, flinging his huge barrel this way and that, and shaking the white saliva from his mouth.

CHAPTER XXXV

PERSIS met equine wrath with female rage. The fiercer the horse plunged the harder she beat him with the crop, the more bloodthirstily she stabbed his sides with her keen-spurred heels. Her hair flung looser and looser, and at length set free her hat, and then shook out its own tortoise-shell moorings and flew to the winds. She sawed at the horse's head, stabbed him with the spurs, railed at him with shrill voice, and fought him as a Valkyr might have fought her charger panic-stricken at the noise of battle.

Even the old man, who lay on the ground clutching at his heart, could not but feel a thrill at the wild beauty of the girl; her long hair flowed and writhed smokily, her face was the more commandingly beautiful for the very merciless hate that fired it; her girlish body in her boyish costume was strangely alive. Her thighs gripped the horse's sides visibly like arches of steel. All this beauty Forbes saw also, and more, for he saw with the eyes of idolatry; and yet more again, for his beloved was in mortal danger. He ran in a frenzy of fear and determination. As he and the horses met on their converging paths Persis shrieked to him: "Keep away! Keep away!"

None the less he leaped for the bridle with both hands flung out. But she would not let him endanger himself. She threw all the power of both her arms and her weight on the farther bridle, dragging the horse's head aside till he swerved out of Forbes' reach.

Forbes sprawled on the turf; but at least he had not

237

been struck by the hoofs or knees of the horse. And then the horse came down in turn, thrown out of his stride and with his head brought round so sharply that he came down on his shoulder and almost broke his neck.

Persis went through the air like a pinwheel, and those who witnessed the affair gave up her and the horse for dead. But she clung to the bridle, and got up on all fours. For once Persis was awkward. She and Forbes met and stared like quadrupeds, and the horse rolled over on his belly and stared too.

What had almost been a tragedy was turned to a farce by coincidence. If all the corpses in the last act of Hamlet should rise and stare at one another—as they do when the curtain is down—audiences might roar as the golfers and the club servants and members roared at this spectacle.

Willie, meanwhile, had vanished over the hill like the headless horseman Ten Eyck had likened him to.

After the first automatic recovery Persis was overtaken by a wave of terror she had had no time to feel. She turned ashen about the mouth, and a queasy feeling sickened her. Her elbows gave way, and she sank to the ground.

Senator Tait came up with difficulty, forgetting that he had been, perhaps, nearer death on that green battlefield than any other of the fallen. He heard Forbes wailing, as he gathered Persis into his arms and strengthened his own weak knees:

"Persis, my darling, my angel, speak to me! Are you dead?"

Persis opened her eyes with a flash. She began to realize that she had been very conspicuous. "Of course I'm not dead. But what's worse, my hair's down. I must be a sight! And my breeches are torn. Oh, Lord, why wasn't I killed romantically? Turn your backs at once."

The two men stared all the more, but she released herself from Forbes' arms, rose to her feet with some twinges of evident pain, and put up her hair with what few hairpins remained of her store, and borrowed a pin from the Senator's lapel to mend a rip that let one exquisite knee escape to view. A caddy came running up with her hat, and she thanked him.

"Come along," she said; "I feel as if I were on the stage of the Metropolitan Opera House."

The horse got clumsily to his feet, all the battle knocked out of him, and followed weakly till she handed him over to a groom.

Eager to escape the stares that met her and the sympathy and felicitations that greeted her, she walked so rapidly that the Senator dropped back. She found herself alone with Forbes, and she murmured:

"You were wonderful to try to save me as you did."

"As I didn't," he groaned. "You wouldn't let me."

"No, I don't want you ever to risk anything for me, Harvey. But I'm just as grateful—and more than that. If there weren't so many people looking on do you know what I'd say?"

"What?"

"Kiss me." The words came so unexpectedly that he forgot their subjunctive mode. He took them to be in the imperative, and came near obeying. He checked himself in time, and said:

"How soon shall I be able to call you mine before all the world?"

"Do you wish that?"

"Madly! It is my one great wish."

She breathed deeply and caressed him with a delicious smile, and murmured:

"It is mine, too."

And then Ten Eyck and Winifred and Mrs. Neff and Alice, and others of her acquaintance, crowded round, summoned by the flying rumor of the incident. At length some one exclaimed:

"But where's Willie?"

"Good Lord," Persis gasped, "I forgot all about him."

Some one else who had been on the links described Willie's disappearance over the brow of the hill. He had been still attached to the horse when last heard from. But his prospects were reported to be poor.

By the time Persis had reached the club-house and had undergone the ministrations of a maid, who was also a seamstress, Willie came limping up on the terrace, where Persis was seated with the others.

"Oh, there you are, my dear," Willie drawled. "And not a bit hurt, not a hair turned, so far as I can make out, eh? And here I've been worrying myself sick over you—simply sick."

"Well, I'll go out and break a few bones if it would make you feel any easier," Persis answered. "But what happened to you? Where's your horse?"

"Well, I'll tell you. It was like this. You see, that beast I was on went galumphing up the hill playing the deuce with putting-greens, until he came to that big bunker at the top, you know—you know the one I mean—at the top there—the big bunker?"

"Yes, I know."

"Well, he refused it."

"What did you do?"

"I took it alone."

"Where's your horse?"

"I don't know. I hope to God he breaks a leg or rips himself open on barbed wire or something."

There was a vindictive ferocity in his voice that surprised Forbes.

The luncheon, which Ten Eyck had commanded, was announced just then, and they all adjourned to the dining-room. Forbes resented Enslee's habit of "my-dear"-ing Persis, but took solace from the thought that he should soon confound his rival with the news of his own triumph.

Suddenly, in his joy at being near to Persis, he remembered that he had neglected Senator Tait, after promising to meet his daughter. He did not venture to leave his own table; but as soon as the luncheon was eaten, and while Winifred and Mrs. Neff and Persis sneaked off somewhere for their after-coffee cigarettes, he sought out Tait and found him with a tall and self-reliant girl whom he introduced as Mildred.

Forbes made the usual remarks one makes to a little girl one meets again as a grown woman. She had indeed changed from the shy and leggy little minx to this robust, ample-bosomed bachelor girl with the sorrows of the world on her shoulders and pity and courage warring in her resolute eyes.

Recalling what the Senator had said of her appalling lore, Forbes was at some loss for words. He said, at last, the obvious thing, waving his hand toward the great park and the panorama of river and headland spread out beyond:

"Wonderful, isn't it?"

But Mildred, instead of an equally commonplace answer, sighed: "I suppose it is, but I—somehow I can't take much pleasure in beautiful things like these. I keep thinking how the poor kiddies and their worn-out mothers in the tenements would love to see it—and never will. And when I think how much money it costs to build and keep up this place I can't help saying to myself: 'How many loaves of bread this would buy for hungry waifs! how many pairs of shoes! how many lives it could save!' I see this big lawn all overrun with little newsboys and factory-girls and sick men and women."

Senator Tait shrugged his shoulders and smiled at Forbes.

"Isn't she hopeless?"

"She's very splendid," Forbes said, with admiration and also a little awe. The father felt this in Forbes' manner, and it strengthened his resolution to rescue his daughter from her rescue work.

Mildred had not yet learned the exact point where nobility becomes offensive because it is too consistent and too insistent. She had not yet learned that charity, like art, must conceal itself, and that grandeur of soul unchecked by tact provokes only resentment.

But she was young and radiant with unfocused love, and she had seen too much wretchedness. The people whose miseries she relieved did not resent her, but adored her. She was tactful enough with them.

Forbes was ashamed of himself for feeling a little chilled by Mildred's irrepressible enthusiasm for sorrow. He blamed himself, not her. But when Persis returned he thanked heaven for beauty untroubled by any deeper concerns than its own loveliness, and for a heart that inspired desire for itself rather than pity for the submerged myriads.

He bade the Senator and his daughter as cordial a good-by as he could, and promised to meet the Senator as soon as possible in town. Then he forgot them both, for when Enslee's automobile swept up to the club-house door, Enslee's two horses were also brought up, and he imagined Persis riding away again on that dangerous beast with that dangerous escort.

Enslee stared at the horses in disgust. "There are those brutes of mine, and not a bit hurt, either—worse luck. I'll have 'em both sold to somebody who'll work 'em hard and beat 'em harder."

"You'll do nothing of the sort," said Persis. "If you don't want them I'll take them."

"And get your neck broken, eh?" Enslee snarled. "Oh no, you won't. Look at that beast! I'll have his throat cut for him."

There was something in his voice like the edge of a knife, and it made Forbes' blood run cold. Enslee had unsuspected streaks of viciousness. But Persis was used to this quality of his nature, and it did not alarm her. When he said, "Hop into the car, Persis; I'll send a groom over for the nags," Persis shook her head, and answered:

WHAT WILL PEOPLE SAY?

"I propose to show my horse who is master. He can't spill me all over the landscape and get away with it. You ride home in the car, and I'll go back as I came."

"And a pretty fool you'll make of me," Enslee wrangled. "Besides, I haven't ridden much lately; I'm saddle-sore."

"I've been riding every morning in the Park," Persis insisted. "I'll lead your horse back, unless—" She hesitated and looked at Forbes, who leaped at the cue.

"I'd be glad to ride him, if you don't object, Mr. Enslee."

Enslee stared at Forbes, saw nothing ulterior in his eyes, and yielded with a bad grace.

"Oh, all right. Go ahead. Only don't sue me for damages if you get pitched under an auto."

"I won't," Forbes laughed, elated beyond belief by the unimaginable luck of riding at Persis' stirrup for miles and miles.

And so they mounted. Persis' horse was humbled beyond struggle; but Enslee's big black had lately tossed his rider over his head. He tested the seat of his new visitor. Forbes was a West-Pointer, a cavalryman, and the horse had not made more than one pirouette before he understood that he was bestridden by one whom it was best to obey.

Willie tried at first to keep the motor back with the horses, but Persis ordered him to go about his business, and turned off the hard track to a soft road.

And now at last they were free, Forbes and Persis, cantering along a plushy road, a lovers' lane that mounted up and up till they paused at the height to give the horses breath.

Back of them the Hudson spread its august flood between mountainous walls. Before them the road dipped into the deep forest seas of Sleepy Hollow.

CHAPTER XXXVI

"IS it possible that we're actually alone?" Forbes gloated, turning in his saddle to take her in in her brisk, youthful beauty.

"I shouldn't exactly call it alone up here on the mantelpiece of the world in broad daylight," Persis smiled. "But it's nice, isn't it?"

"Wonderful, to be riding with you!"

"I'm immensely happy," she said. "Even the horses know the difference. This morning they hated each other. They wouldn't trot in rhythm or alongside, and they fought like snapping-turtles. Now look at them nuzzle and flirt. Ouch! that's my game knee you're colliding with. It would be better if I rode side-saddle. There were advantages in old-fashioned ways. You ride splendidly, don't you?"

"Do I?" he said. "As you told me the first time I met you, I'm glad you like me."

"I more than that, now."

"More than like me?"

"Umm-humm!"

"Love me?"

"Umm-humm!"

"If I could only brush away all of these houses and people and take you in my arms! If this were only a Sahara or Mojave!"

"I doubt if there's a desert where nobody is peeking. They used to tell me that God was looking when no one else was."

"Well, He would understand."

"Maybe He would see too much. But the human beings don't understand. And they're everywhere. Oh, Lord, I'm so sick of other people's eyes and ears. All my life I've had them on me—servants', nurses', maids', waiters', grooms', footmen's! Sometimes I think I'd love to live on a desert island. Couldn't you buy me a desert island somewhere—a thoroughly equipped desert island with hot and cold water and automatic cooking?"

"I'll see if there's one in the market."

"It would be a fine addition to the same old town and country house and yacht. Had you thought where you will have your—our country place?"

"Er—no, I hadn't."

"Shall you have to be at your post much? Are the office-hours very strict?"

"Pretty strict. We'd have to live on Governor's Island, you know."

"Really? In one of those little houses?" He nodded. "I saw them there once when they gave a lawn fête. I never dreamed I'd live in one of them. They aren't very commodious, are they?"

"That depends."

"Nichette—she's my maid—would make an awful row, and my chauffeur—I suppose we could keep him? He expects to marry Nichette."

"Does he?"

"If they can stop fighting long enough to get married. Does a garage go with the house we should occupy there?"

"I doubt it."

"No garage!" she exclaimed. "How should we manage? It's rather awkward getting to the Island, too, as I remember—a ferry or something. I don't suppose you could arrange to live up-town and do your army work by telephone on rainy days?"

"I'm afraid not."

His heart was thumping. She grew more exquisite as she grew more fairy-like in her visions. He could not tell her the truth—not yet—not, at least, till they had passed through the woods ahead, where there was a promise of opportunity for at least a moment's embrace, at least one hasty kiss.

They jogged on in silence awhile, she pondering like a solemn child, he longing to give her the toys she kept imagining. They drew into the thicket, shady and soft with a breeze that wandered about murmuring "Woo! woo!" and leaves that whispered "Kiss! kiss!" and a deep forest voice that mumbled "Love!"

No one was visible ahead. He turned and stared back. They were shut in by a projecting hill that seemed to close after them like a door. He leaned sidewise with arm outstretched to enfold her waist. But with a quick lift of her hand and a scratch of the spur she carried her horse aside and ahead.

"You mustn't!" she warned. "Really!"

"But no one can see us."

"So we thought in the dark hall. And there was some one there. Do you know who it was?"

"I haven't been able to find out."

"I have!" She spoke triumphantly.

"Who was it, in Heaven's name?"

"Who would be your last guess?"

"Enslee."

"Why?"

"Because he smiled; because he let me ride with you."

"That shows how much a man's reasoning power is worth. That was just who it was."

"Why do you think so?"

"I know so. He told me."

Forbes was dazed; he marveled aloud: "And yet he smiled? He let me ride with you?"

She laughed. "Willie is such an idiot! He knew it was you; but he never dreamed that the woman was me. He thought the woman was Mrs. Neff or Winifred. That's why he smiled at you."

Forbes chuckled a moment, then flushed, as Persis went on:

"He could only hear our whispers, you know, and you can't distinguish whispers. He thought it was a great joke. He laughed his head off. And I laughed too. It was delicious. It came near being serious, though. What do you suppose? He heard the door open below and thought it was a burglar. He had a revolver and a flashlight. The flash wouldn't work—thank the Lord! So he was going to shoot first and then call, 'Who's there!' That would have been nice, wouldn't it? Then he heard our—our kisses. He didn't shoot. He kept quiet, smothering his snickers. He could only judge by the closing of the door who was who. He recognized your door, and he got mine mixed. But you're not laughing."

"It doesn't seem very funny to me," Forbes admitted. "My love for you is no joke. I don't enjoy sneaking about in dark halls and having you mistaken for some other woman."

She stared at him, and her mischief turned to a deep tenderness. She rode closer and put her free hand on his bridle-hand. "How right you are! That's the way I want you to feel, the way I want you to love me." And then she laughed again. "What do you suppose Willie told me? To-night he's going to wait till you sneak out with your lady bird, and then he's going to lock the door and make you beg for admission. That 'll be nice, eh?"

"That means I can't be with you to-night."

"It seems so."

"And you won't let me kiss you now?"

"But we couldn't go spooning about in the daylight, could we? Not even if we were an old married couple, could we?"

"I suppose not. But when—when are we going to be an old married couple?"

"Whenever you say," she said, with a shy down-look. "We'd have to announce our engagement, I suppose, and then it would take a long time to get my clothes made."

"Would it?"

"Yes. I haven't a thing. I'm in perfect rags. And besides, a bride ought to begin new. Isn't it thrilling to be talking of such things! Am I blushing as red as I feel?"

"You're like a rose on fire."

"I feel deliciously a ninny. Can you get away from your hateful army for a good long honeymoon, do you suppose?"

"I don't know. Where would you like to go?"

"The Riviera isn't bad. A trip around the world would be pleasant."

"Wouldn't it!" he groaned. "But I'm afraid I couldn't."

"I suppose the country would be afraid to let you get so far away, with all this talk about trouble with the Mexicans. Oh, well, it doesn't matter so long as we are together, does it?"

"Do you feel that way?" he asked, hungrily.

"Terribly. I love you—I love you hideously much. Watch out! Will you never learn that somebody's always looking?—a whole picnic this time."

They were nearing Pocantico Lake. In a thicket on its shores a wagon-load of villagers had finished its basket-lunch and scattered in a rather dreary effort at inexpensive happiness.

Among the trees the wagon waited pitifully to take them back from their dingy cheer to their dull homes. It was rendered only the more pitiful by a strip of red-white-and-blue bunting. A coat of paint would have become it better.

While the horses cropped the grass soberly a pack of substantial wives cleared away such part of the débris of the banquet as was not scattered about the ground.

As Forbes and Persis rounded the turn that disclosed

the revelers a homely couple evidently in search of a less populous nook severed a highly unromantic-looking clasp. It was hard to see how either took much pleasure from the other. The man was in his shirt-sleeves, with his hat askew; the girl, shapeless and freckled, in a shapeless freckled dress. They squinted their eyes against the sun, gaped at the tailor-made couple on the varnished horses, and stumbled in the roadside gully to let them pass.

"Isn't it ghastly?" Persis whispered. "They were trying to spoon—just as we were. And we both broke up both of us. It makes love rather a silly, shabby spectacle, doesn't it?"

"I don't think so," Forbes said. "I should say that instead of their making love shabby, love covered them with a little glory."

"That's a much prettier way to put it. But shabby people—oh Lord! Look at that family, dear! If that's wedded bliss, give me chloroform."

It was a doleful exhibit on the edge of the woods: a fat, paunchy, sweaty man was taking his picnic in carrying a squally, messy baby. Alongside him a bunchy woman with stringy hair waddled in anserine stupidity, hanging to her husband's suspenders.

"You can't tell which of them's going to have the next one," Persis commented, before she caught herself. "Forgive me, I didn't realize how it would sound."

Forbes laughed sheepishly. "It was what I was thinking, too."

As they rode on she shuddered. "What an odious thing to be like that! Suppose you lost your job in the army and we got very poor, and I had to take in washing, and we had a lot of children; should we be like that, do you think?—should we?"

"You could never be anything that was not beautiful!" Forbes exclaimed, partly because he believed it to be unquestionable truth and partly to quell her ferocious repugnance for anything that was ugly and tawdry.

"Perhaps that awful man told that awful woman the same thing," she groaned, "and believed it! Come on; let's run away from it." She lifted her horse to a gallop and fled so fast that Forbes, for all the authority and help he gave his horse, could not overtake her, since hers was the better mount. As he followed, lumbering and scolding his black beast, he felt that she was indeed too fleet, too elusive for him ever to capture and keep.

But at length she relented, and reined in till he came abeam. Then she urged her horse on again, and they galloped in the mad swoop of a cavalry charge with boots griding together. She forgot her wounded knee, and he forgot his doubts of her.

There were narrow escapes, unexpected swerves round loitering wagons or deliberate wayfarers. Once she rode up a shelving bank to give him room to avoid a mangy canine landlord so earnestly attempting to evict a family of tenants from his left ear that he paid no heed to the risk of his own life or hers.

"If we ride fast on levels, we can take more time later," she said; "then they won't wonder at our being so late."

She was always thinking of what other people would think. He wished that she would forget the eternal audience, the unbroken spectators, now and then. And yet it was intelligent. It was wise. Only he loved her more when she was uttering those childish plans of hers for a life in which the funds were to be taken from a fairy purse automatically replenished as fast as it was depleted.

Yet he feared both of the women she was: the cautious and forethoughtful who might in all wisdom refuse his penury, and the spoiled demander who might resent it.

They trotted now into a park-like domain with roads branching out on either side. At the edge of each of them stood a sign-board warning against trespass and signed with the resounding name of the richest man on earth.

"THERE'S THAT OTHER ME DOWN IN THE POOL, WATCHING THIS ME"

"They say he's worth a hundred or two hundred million dollars," Persis called across to Forbes.

"That ought to be enough," said Forbes. "It's more than we shall have." And he smiled at the comparison. Persis sighed:

"If he could lend us just one million for a few years we could make good use of it."

"I might ask him," said Forbes. "I'll send a boy over for it to-night."

He said it lightly, yet there was a sardonic bitterness in his smile. He understood for the moment why the established poor become so eager to take away from men who were once poor the wealth they have somehow amassed.

It seemed to Forbes that he would never reach the limit of this man's acres. But at last he escaped from the oppression of some one's else success. They cantered through a little village, and crossed rusty railroad-tracks into another ocean of sparsely settled country. It amazed Forbes to find so much wilderness so close to so vast a metropolis. There were long stretches where the woods on either side had a look of the primeval. He felt a longing to explore some of these leafy jungles. He told her his whim, and it was hers.

By and by they came to a grass-matted road that lost itself in ferns and undergrowth. Forbes looked at Persis. Her eyes consented. He laid his bridle-hand on the left side of his horse's mane and shifted his weight a trifle. And his horse shouldered hers into the jungle. Heads bent low, the horses mounted with cautious hoofs till the ferns were brushing their saddle-girths. The prattle of a brook somewhere lured them farther, and they pressed on into a fog of leaves and crackling boughs and flowers. Birds cried warnings and shot through the branches, bearing news of the invasion. Others in sentimental oblivion did not budge, but sat still and went on sawing the air with silver phrases shrilly sweet.

Suddenly the brook was visible, rushing here and there through the woods and making noises that were rapture just to hear. And with that music of water and woods, and that multitudinous beauty about them, they gazed only into each other's eyes, inclined together, and locked arms and breasts and lips in close embrace. They clung together till the soulless horses, nibbling here and there, sundered them.

And then they slid from the saddles and, slipping the bridles to their elbows, walked on with arms about each other's bodies and eyes so mutually engaged that they stumbled like blind folk. At last she sank to the ground at the edge of the brook, and he, instead of helping her up, dropped down at her side.

He took her into his arms again and kissed her and laughed at her.

"I reckon you'll warn me now that the horses are looking."

"No," she said; "but one of them is standing on one of my coat-tails."

So he rose and led the horses to a tree a few paces off and tied them there. When he came back he found her swinging her little boots over a still pool in an alcove of the brook. Its quiet surface mirrored her feet from beneath quaintly. "We're at the antipodes already," he laughed. She put out her hand beggingly.

"It's secluded enough for a smoke. Can you give me a cigarette? I forgot mine." He had nothing but a cigar, and she ventured a puff or two of that, then gave it back and sighed, "I wish we were married and all."

"Why?"

"I'd take off my boots and dip my poor aching feet in that water."

"Why don't you?"

"In the first place, I don't know you well enough to go barefoot before you. In the second, somebody would be sure to come along."

"Not here," he urged.

"Well, then, there's that other Me down in the pool watching this Me, and saying, 'Don't make a fool of yourself, honey.'"

"There are two Persises, then?"

"At least a hundred. But there's one down there. Look, you can see her yourself!"

She knelt above the water-glass, and he bent over to gaze. He saw her looking up at him, and his own image looking up close to hers. They smiled and made faces like children. And when he rubbed his cheek against hers the images imitated the foolishness.

"See, they're mocking us," she said. A little breeze wrinkled the mirror, and she cried: "They're frowning! They want us to be sensible! Come along! They'll be missing us at home."

"At home?" he echoed, reprovingly.

"At Willie's, I mean," she corrected. And then she put his hands away and spoke earnestly. "It came mighty near being home to me. I have a confession to make. I ought to have made it before. I have been amazed at myself for not telling you, for taking your love when I had no right to."

He stared at her in terror, and she smiled with pride at his fear and babbled on almost incoherently.

"Don't be afraid—though I'm glad you are. But I hope you won't despise me. But I couldn't seem to help myself. You're really to blame for being so terribly overwhelming. You see, I—I—I've told you how often Willie Enslee proposed to me, and—well, one day—that very day you saw me in my old hat—the first time, you know—well, I had just had a talk with my father, and the poor old boy was all cut up about his—his money matters. He's too nice and sweet to be much of a financier, you know, and—well, I was scared to death, and I thought the world was coming to an end, and I'd better—better get aboard the ark, you know—and I hadn't met

you then, you know, and Willie proposed again, and I—I
accepted him."

"You promised to be his wife!" Forbes whispered,
chokingly.

"Yes," she answered. "I—you see, I didn't know you.
I didn't dream I should ever meet anybody who would—
would thrill me—that's the only word—as you did, as
you do. I didn't imagine that I should ever love as other
people do—insanely, madly, dishonorably—anythingly to
be with the one I loved. And I didn't dare give up Willie
till I was sure I loved you, and when I was sure I loved you,
I—it seemed so hateful even to mention his name. It
would have been like—like this."

With her heel she pushed a rock into the water, and it
thumped and splashed and curdled the little pool.

"That's the effect his name would have had on our
moonlight, and I couldn't tell you then. Will you forgive me, or do you think I'm a hopeless rotter and a
sneak?"

He smiled at her mixed vocabulary, and gathered her
into his arms. "My love! My Persis! But you'll tell
him now, won't you?"

"Oh, now, yes!" she cried, ecstatic as a comforted child.
"You are glorious to forgive me so easily, and not be
nasty and lecture-y. And see the pool; it's all smooth and
clear again."

He looked, and held back the confession he was about
to make in his turn. The mention of his poverty would
be pushing another rock into the pool. And he wondered
if the mirror would clear after that. He could forgive her
her betrothal to Enslee because that was of the past; but
the lack of money was not a matter for forgiving and forgetting; it was something to endure. It was asking love
to accept poverty as a concubine or a mother-in-law.

He kept silent on that score, and they murmured their
loves and kissed and laughed with contentedness purling
through their hearts, and the world far away. She glanced

back at the horses blissfully tearing young leaves from high branches.

"We ought to keep those horses as a souvenir of our engagement. It would be a pity to let any one else ride the dear old brutes, wouldn't it?"

"It would, indeed!" he said.

"Let's buy them from Willie. He would sell them for a song."

"That's a fine idea," Forbes answered, with a gulp. He knew how much horses like these were worth—and saddles, bridles, and stables.

"We shouldn't want to ride in a car all the time, should we?" she asked.

"No, indeed," he answered. She was at her fairy plans again, and his heart sickened.

"We mustn't let ourselves get fat. Of all things we must avoid that," she said. "We might have just a little car like Winifred's—to hold only two. I could drive down and get you and bring you home. It would save wear on our limousine—or perhaps we won't get a limousine just yet. If we didn't have a big car it would be a good excuse for not having a lot of people tagging round with us everywhere, wouldn't it? I feel an awful longing for a lot of solitude with just you and me. I suppose we'll have to put up with the United States army. But I want to shake the gang I've been running with—at least for a year or so, till you and I can get acquainted. Will you buy me a little car like Winifred's—a good one? There's no use wasting money on the cheap kind. The good little ones cost as much as the good big ones; but once they're paid for, they don't run up repair bills, and they take you where you're going instead of dying under you half-way there. Will you buy me a little car for just us? You can get a darling for about twenty-five hundred; I was asking Winifred."

He made no answer. She turned and looked at him and saw on his face the look she had seen on her father's that day—the look a man wears when he cannot buy his beloved what she pleads for. Now, as then, Persis felt ashamed rather than resentful, and she hastened to add:

"If you can't afford it, old boy, say so. You mustn't mind me. My father says I'm a terrible asker. Just say No, and I won't mind. Promise me that, dear. I want to be a good economical housewife to you; and I was only thinking that if we had a little car it would save taking the big car out, and that saves tires and gasolene and general upkeep."

He heard Enslee's words, "It's the upkeep that costs," and they mocked him again. He realized that in persuading this girl to choose him instead of Enslee, who had already chosen her, he was not only robbing her of a yacht, a palace, two or three palaces, half a dozen automobiles, servants, and servants of servants, foreign travel and foreign clothes and jewels—he was not only robbing her of such things, but he was asking her to learn a new way of life, a habit of infinite denial, eternal economy, and meager amusement.

Experience and common sense—for he had them in large measure in his ordinary life—seemed to bend down and say: "Let your sea-gull go. She'll die in your cage, or she'll break it apart."

But she was in his arms. She was leaning against him, flicking his boots with her riding-crop, and loving him, contented utterly. Romance elbowed Reason aside and said: "See how happy she is. It isn't money that makes happiness. You're sitting on the edge of a silly little brook in somebody's backwoods, and you're happy as a king and queen on a throne of gold."

Common Sense grinned: "Suppose it should rain? This is all very well for a while, but what of next winter?"

Reason and Romance wrangled in his head while she was babbling something in her elfin economy about, "So we won't have two cars yet, just one, a nice big 1913 six, with my chauffeur to run it. Father pays him fifteen hundred a year, and that's good pay. Don't you let him wheedle you out of a penny more."

Forbes' heart cried aloud within him: "My God! her very chauffeur gets nearly as much as I do!" This was the spark of resentment that gave him his start. He spoke bitterly, almost glad that she was dazed. And he put her away from him that both might be free. And he savagely kicked a rock into the smiling little pool and watched it grow turbid as he poured out his confession.

"Listen, honey; you've got a wrong idea of my situation. I'm to blame for it, I reckon. I've been meaning to speak about it, but I didn't—for just the same reason that kept you quiet about Enslee. I'm not rich, honey. I didn't tell anybody I was rich, but the idea got started from Ten Eyck's fool joke about seeing me coming out of a big bank. I told him the truth, and now I must tell you. You'll hate me, but you've got to know some time. I'm not rich, honey."

"What of it, dear?" she said, creeping toward him. "I love you for yourself. I never thought you were rich like Willie. I gave up all that gladly."

"But I'm what you would call—a pauper, I suppose. I have only my army pay."

"Isn't that enough?"

"Plenty of couples seem to be happy on it, but they're mostly the sons and daughters of army people. You've been brought up so differently. Wild extravagances for our people would be shabby makeshifts to you."

"Don't you think I'd be able to adapt myself?"

"Would you?"

"I should hope so. How much is your army pay, if you don't mind my asking?"

"As first lieutenant I get a little over two thousand."

"Two thousand a week? Why, that's not bad at all. Why did you frighten me?"

He laughed aloud, and she corrected herself.

"Oh, two thousand a month. That's about twenty-five thousand a year. It isn't much, is it? But we could skimp and scrape, and we'd have each other."

She had given him his death-blow unwittingly.

He smiled dismally, and groaned:

"Two thousand a year with forage."

She stared at him in unbelief. "Two thousand a year with forage! We couldn't eat the forage, could we? They give you a pittance like that for being an officer and a gentleman and a hero?"

"The hero business is the worst paid of all. Look at the firemen."

"But, my dear, two thousand a—why, our chef gets more than that, and our chauffeur nearly as much; and my father's secretary—everybody gets more than that."

"Not everybody. The vast majority of people get much less. But that's what I get."

She had been prepared for self-denial, but this was self-obliteration. If he had told her that he had the yellow fever she could hardly have felt sorrier for him, or more appalled at the prospect of their union. She loved him, perhaps, the more for the pity that welled up in her. She denounced the government for a miser.

"We're better paid than other armies," said Forbes. "Officers in foreign armies are supposed to have private fortunes."

"I don't wonder," she gasped. "And you haven't any?" He shook his head. "No relatives?"

"None that aren't poorer than I am."

She put out her hand and caressed his brow. "Poor boy, it's cruel, it's hateful! Willie Enslee with all that money, and you with two thousand a year! And no prospects for more?"

"Well, I hope to be promoted captain very shortly—any day now I should get my commission. That carries with it twenty-four hundred a year."

She sighed. "The little car I wanted would cost more than that. Well, let it go. Walking is healthier. It

would save the chauffeur's wages, too. And my maid—
I don't know what Nichette would say. But—well, let
her go. Let everything go but you."

She clasped her arms round him, and he clutched her
tight; but his embrace was like a farewell. She was infinitely pathetic to him. She had so much sophistication,
and was so innocent of so much. She kissed him tenderly,
but her mood was an elegy.

"That knocks out my wedding plans, too, doesn't it?
It was the dream of all my life, the ambition of all my
girlhood." And she fell to musing aloud. "Many's the
night I've lain awake planning that wedding, and that
divine wedding-gown all of ivory satin—with a train a
mile long, and with point lace like whipped cream all
over it, and the veil floating in a cloud about me. And
I was to have counts and barons and things for ushers,
and the belles of the season for bridesmaids—all very envious of me. And the cathedral was to be one ocean of
flowers and silk ribbons, and—and I was to have at least
an archbishop to marry me. And the presents! Oh,
they were to have been so glorious that everybody that
gave them would be bankrupted for life and hate me; and
there were to be no duplicates. And the bridegroom
was to be so wealthy that all the bridesmaids would
loathe me for winning him. And we were to go away in
a private car to a palace built brand new just for me."

He was so fascinated with watching her soul in debate
with itself that he did not speak. He just held her fast
and listened. She went on:

"It was a silly dream. It's not the ceremony that
counts—it's the long life after. Love's the main thing,
isn't it?"

He lifted her gauntleted hand to his cheek and said
nothing. She was silent a long while. Then she pondered aloud again: "I wonder what sort of a poor man's
wife I'll make. I'm afraid I'll be an awful failure. You
know, we were poor once—yes. My father got squeezed

in a corner, and nearly went bankrupt. Oh, but mother and I had to skimp and scrape! I had to turn my old gowns, give up our box at the opera, sell my saddle-horses. We couldn't go to dinners or receptions because we couldn't return them. We sat at home and received— indignant creditors. Oh, the bills, the bills—my God, the bills!

"At the end of a year father found a man who was unbusinesslike enough to put him on his feet again. It was Willie Enslee, of course. We had money once more; we could hold our heads high, snub those who snubbed us, get even with those who had patronized us, or—ugh! insulted us with their sympathy. Oh, money is a great thing, isn't it? It was like coming out of a cave again into the sunlight. I used to say I would face anything rather than poverty again.

"And think of it, Harvey, when we were at our poorest we were spending thirty or forty thousand a year. And we called it poverty. But you and I—two thousand a year—and forage!

"Why, Harvey, it would take you a year and a half of work to pay for the little car I wanted—if we did without a big car and didn't spend a cent on clothes or theaters or the opera or taxies or the seaside or Europe or enter- taining people or servants' wages, and—and ate only the forage. We couldn't have a chauffeur. I couldn't have my maid. I couldn't have any friends—what should I do? I couldn't have anything! Those two horses I wanted would cost a year of your salary. My dress- maker's bills are four or five times as much, and at that I never have anything to wear. Why, Harvey, it's fright- ful! I never knew what money meant before. I don't see how we could ever manage it. I don't see how."

She put his arms away as if they irked her and ham- pered her breath. She was breathing hard. Merely to imagine a life devoid of everything she had always found about her was like a suffocation. She was understanding

how a fish must feel when it is drawn from the water and
flung to stifle on dry pebbles. She suffered such dismay
as overwhelms a rat in the bell of an air-pump when the
experimenter begins to create a vacuum.

She had seen poverty and its wreckage, and her mind
was filled with pictures, not from the charming homes of
moderate means, but from the slums that she had visited
once and avoided thereafter as a nightmare. She had had
friends who had gone into bankruptcy and slunk off into
obscurity to hide its penalties. One very dear woman,
whose husband lapsed from affluence to mediocrity, had
written a few little notes, calmly taken an overdose of a
headache powder, stretched herself out on her mortgaged
chaise-longue and fallen asleep over an unusually sedative
novel. Persis had received one of the notes.

Good-by, Persis dear. You know the situation, and you at
least will understand. Would it be too much trouble for you
to have a little talk with the undertaker man and have things
as nicely managed as possible? Don't let them treat me too
shabbily, will you? I couldn't rest easily even There. You
understand, don't you?

Persis had understood, and, being in funds at the time,
had seen all conducted with taste and even with a little
splendor.

To every one his or her especial cowardice. Persis, so
brave in so many ways, was afraid of creepy things like
caterpillars and creditors and poverty. They spoiled for
her everything that they touched, flower or ceremony or
future.

She was silent a long while. Forbes longingly set his
arms about her; but she did not respond; her hands were
idly rolling her riding-crop up and down the shin of her
boot, for she was thinking hard.

Forbes felt that he clung to the mere clothes of her soul.
Herself was already gone from him. Yet he loved her so

that he found her not unworthy nor selfish nor craven, but infinitely precious and beautiful, difficult to win and wear.

A great many shining throngs of water went down the brook, making all the conversation there was, before Persis began to flog her boots with her riding-crop. She wanted to groan, but as was her custom in torment, smiled instead; and, having something of tragic solemnity to utter, put it forth with a plucky flippancy:

"Well, old boy, I'm afraid all bets are off."

CHAPTER XXXVII

FORBES had been recruiting strength to tell her that he released her; but she anticipated him by jilting him first—and in sporting terms. He stared at her, but he could not see the tears raining down in her heart. He heard her, but was deaf to the immense regret in the little words she added:

"You're pretty poor, aren't you?"

His very forehead was drenched with red shame at such comment from her. She could see how she had hurt his pride, and she put on the solemnity he expected her to wear.

"Oh, don't misunderstand me, Harvey, I implore you! I love you all the more for being just your glorious self. You've paid me the greatest honor I ever had—or shall have. You asked me to be your wife, and you are willing to divide up your pitiful little income with me. You'd give it all to me. You'd run into debt till you smothered. But it wouldn't work out. Mother was right: 'People can do without love easier than without money.'"

"Not people with hearts like yours," he ventured at last to put in as a feeble objection.

"Oh, I'm afraid of this heart of mine," she answered. "If it had any sense it wouldn't have fallen in love with you—you of all men. I knew you weren't really terribly rich, but I didn't think you were so pitifully, cruelly poor."

The epithet reiterated stung him like a whip in the face. He protested impatiently:

"I'm not really poor. Army officers have many ways of saving expenses. I might not give you princely luxuries, Persis, but I'd make your life happy."

263

His resistance gave her something to fight, and her re-sentment at fate welcomed it.

"Me happy at an army post? With nothing but poker for you and gossip for me? No, thank you!"

She caught a twitch of anger in his brows, and she grew harsher:

"Look here! Would you give up your career for me?"

"A woman can't ask a man to give up his career," he answered; and she retorted with the spirit of her time:

"Then why should she give up hers for him?"

He looked an old-fashioned surprise. "And have you a career?"

"Of course I have. Every woman has; and nowadays a woman has got to look out for herself and her future, or she'll get left at the post."

"And what career have you?" he asked, amazed.

"Marriage. It's the average woman's main business in life, Harvey. If she fails in that she fails in every-thing."

"Then you think the poor have no right to marry?"

"Oh no, I'm not such a fool as that. There are people with simple tastes who can be happy on nothing a year—sweet domestic women who love to manage and cook and sweep and mend and sew. There are lots of unhappy rich women who would be thoroughly contented if they were the wives of laboring-men. But that doesn't happen to be my type. I can't help it. I grow positively sick at the sight of a needle. Even fancy stitching hurts my eyes. And I can't help that. There are lots of poor women who are making their homes hells because they have no money. They'd be angels if they didn't have to economize. Some people, rich and poor, take a sensuous delight in watching a bank account grow, and they get more thrill out of saving a penny than out of getting some-thing more beautiful for it.

"But I'm not one of those. I'm a squanderer by nature. I hate to be denied things. I loathe counting the cost of things. I can't endure to see some one else wearing better things than I've got on. I want to throttle a woman who has a later hat than mine. Oh, I may be a bad one, Harvey, but it isn't my fault. I am what I was born to be. I've got to marry money, Harvey. I've just got to."

He cried out against her self-portrait as a libel. "Oh, Persis, don't tell me that you are mercenary—a woman with a big heart like yours."

"I'm not mercenary exactly; I loathe money as money, but I like nice things. I have to have them. I'm trying to be honest with myself and with you—in time—before it's too late. It's hard; but I didn't arrange the world, did I? I didn't choose my own soul, did I? But I've got to get along with what was given me, haven't I? I tell you I'd ruin your life, Harvey. You'd divorce me in a year."

"Don't talk like that, or you will ruin your own life! There's a big tragedy in store for you, Persis, unless you—"

She was so tortured with disillusion and with the death of her first romance that she grew very hard.

"Well, so long as it isn't the tragedy of being unable to pay my bills and of eating my own cooking I can stand it. I'd rather be unhappy than shabby. But it's growing late; we must get back."

He aided her to her feet, untied the horses, and offered her his hand for a mounting-block. But she said:

"We can walk quicker here than we can ride." Taking her bridle in her arm, she set out swiftly. She seemed once more to be running away from something—a shadow of poverty, no doubt. He felt unspeakably sorry for her. Again he was about to offer her back her heart when an abrupt light broke over her face. She paused, laughed, turned to him.

"What a fool I am! My father set my sister up in business as a British peeress and bought her her husband and settled a whacking dower on her. He can do the same for me and keep the money in this country—and get me a real husband. He could give me enough for us both to live on comfortably."

"I reckon I could hardly accept that arrangement," Forbes said, as gently as he might.

"You see!" she cried out. "You expect me to murder my pride and accept poverty, but you won't accept wealth because you must keep your pride. You couldn't object to my having the money to spend on myself, could you?"

"No, I could hardly object to that," he said.

"Well, then, if everything goes right with my father's plans we'll have love and money and all. It will be wonderful—heaven on earth! Kiss me!"

She put up her lips, and he kissed them and found them bitter-sweet. Then she strode on with a lilting joy, humming a song and putting her horse to his paces to keep up with her. Forbes remembered what Senator Tait had said of her father's impending doom, and her rapture was a heartbreak to him—a final irony.

As they issued from the green cave of the forest and walked down to the State Road to take the saddle, a motor came along. Two men were in it. The driver stopped the car in front of Persis, and the other man lifted his hat. It disclosed a shock of brindle hair and half of one eyebrow gone.

"Can you tell me if this road leads to Briarcliff?" he asked.

"Yes, I think so," Persis answered.

"Thank you, Miss Cabot," he called out, as the car whirred away.

Persis stared after him in amazement. "Now who was that? How did he know my name?"

"By your pictures in the papers," Forbes suggested.

"No," said Persis; "I've met him somewhere. Oh, I know. He's a reporter on the—some paper. Lord, I hope he didn't misconstrue our being here. I didn't like the grin on his face."

CHAPTER XXXVIII

THE reporter's fleering smile and his acidulous "Thank you, Miss Cabot," convinced Persis that the man had, with the sophistication reporters learn too well, put the worst possible interpretation on her forest promenade with Forbes. This was all that it needed to turn her disappointment into dismay, her bewilderment into panic. She had lost rhythm with her life and the world.

She thrust one boot into its stirrup, swung the other across the saddle, and jerked her horse's head impatiently. Her temper threw his motor machinery out of gear, and he found himself with at least two too many feet. He bolted and sidled in a ragged syncopated gait, snorting and flinging his head angrily. She could not get him into meter with himself or her, or with the horse that Forbes brought clattering alongside.

At first she had felt infinitely sorry for Forbes and indignant only at the fate that made him poor. As she rode her fretful horse she began to feel infinitely sorry for herself and indignant at Forbes. He had permitted her to think that he had ample means. He had encouraged her to love him seriously. Her resentment was the fierce resentment people feel when those they love and idealize do not live up to the standards set for them.

Forbes had come into her life like a bull sauntering into a china shop. A moment before his entrance everything was arranged, orderly, exquisite, and formal—a little cold, perhaps, but charmingly definite. Now everything was crashing about her. She must walk warily among the fragments or she would suffer.

Persis was an orderly soul, and had not suspected that she was also a passionate one. She was more like Forbes than either of them understood. For all the deep intensity of his nature, training had made him first the soldier. In battle he was the fiery warrior; but battles were infrequent, and almost all his days had been spent in acquiring and instilling precision, exactness in the manual of arms, rectitude in the lines of drill formations, perfection in uniform and equipment, in the company books and reports—everywhere.

So Persis had acquired from infancy the rituals of household service, the proprieties and their observance, the arrangement of ceremonies, social book-keeping. And now she was discovering what a disorganizer love is, what an anarch among plans, what a smasher of china.

Before the advent of Forbes she had almost given up the expectation of love. Then out of nothing the fates evoked this man. If he had confessed even a pittance of twenty-five thousand a year, that would have meant at worst "love in a cottage"—cottage being an elastic word. Friends of hers owned cottages of palatial dimensions. But two thousand a year—with a prospect of twenty-four hundred a year! She simply could not imagine it.

She tried to mask her anger under an unusually cheerful manner. She spoke with approval of the landscape, chattered vivaciously about everything, and all the while was burning with resentment. It was small wonder that Forbes felt the blight of her wrath when the very horses knew of it. The most determined politeness can never imitate the fine flower and bouquet of genuine enthusiasm. But what could Forbes say to set things right? The one effective speech would have been a declaration of independent means, a smiling disclaimer of poverty: "I was only joking; I am really very rich."

That would have re-established the *entente*. But that was the one thing Forbes could not say. He rode on at Persis' side, a silent and dejected prisoner of circumstances, a spy captured in the enemy's camp in the enemy's uniform.

Eventually they reached the Enslee place—the mountain that was Enslee's, with the stately pleasure dome he had decreed there. The majesty of it belittled Forbes still more. The beauty of it shamed him.

They trotted across the granite bridge and urged the horses to the ascent.

The horses plodded doggedly up and up, and the beauty of every spot as they reached it wore away Persis' anger. It was difficult to feel a bitterness against anybody, even against the fates, when they permitted some aromatic shrub to throw an almost visible veil of perfume about her, and another to dandle before her eyes a smiling throng of blossoms almost audibly singing like clustered cherubim. The mere dapple of shadow and sun-splash was felicity, and the white road that curved among its lawns was voluptuously sinuous, like a tawny Cleopatra on a green divan or one of Titian's high-hipped Venuses.

The gardening was formal, the swards were shaved, the trees seemed to have been whisk-broomed, the shrubs had been curled and scented; but they were beautiful, and only wealth could have collected them or kept them at their best. And above them all loomed the house, a château of stately charm enthroned in beauty.

Forbes saw how good it was, and coveted it. But it was as if Naboth of Jezreel had envied Ahab, the King, his garden. Persis also saw how good it was, and she could possess it all, become the châtelaine of this place.

She spoke her thought aloud:

"It's this sort of thing, Harvey, that I love and need—beautiful things and plenty of them."

"I understand," Forbes groaned.

"If only you could get them for us!"

"If only I could!"

A little farther she checked her horse, whose trunk was heaving like a bellows. It was in a little colonnade of trees with an arched roof of green leaves in more than Gothic confusion. Birds were everywhere, fluting, fighting, and building.

"Listen to them, Harvey," Persis murmured, with a kind of sad joy, as he reined in alongside. "It's their courtship-time, too. And the male bird is the better dressed of the two."

Forbes noted how sweet her throat was as it arched back; and the under surface of her chin, how beautiful. They were no longer his to admire, and bitterness came into his heart. His smile was close to a sneer as he said:

"The males put on their Sunday best and pour out their finest songs, and the lady bird chooses, they say, the one that wears the best clothes."

She gave him a look that was both rebuking and rebuked, and urged her horse along. But a little later her response to beauty filled her again with the contentment of repletion, and she checked her horse by the marble-walled pool, whose surface was broken and circled here and there by gleaming red fish with lacy fins and tails; they were darting and leaping in acrobatic ecstasies.

"They're making love, too, I suppose," Persis said, a trifle anxiously.

And he was still aggrieved enough to answer: "And the fish ladies also select the gentleman with the most gold."

She stared at him a moment, hurt and shamed. Then she flung back at him:

"Then you oughtn't to blame us—us other females for making the wisest choice we can. It must be a law of nature."

"It must be," he sighed, so humbly that she regretted her victory. She would have put out her hand to comfort him, but she saw above them Willie Enslee leaning across the balustrade. She lifted her horse into a jog-trot, and they rode into the court, where a chauffeur waited to take the horses to the stable.

Willie greeted them in his whiniest tone.

"Where on earth were you? We've been home for ages."

"We got off the main road," Persis said, as she climbed the steps, followed by Forbes, "and the horses were tired and—"

"I was awfully anxious. I was about to start out to look for you."

"There was no occasion to be anxious."

"Besides, your father telephoned you."

"My father! Is he back in New York?"

"No; he telephoned from Chicago. He was just leaving on the twenty-hour train. He couldn't wait till you got back."

"What did he have to say?"

"Lots." Willie looked uneasily at Forbes, as if he were in the way.

"I'll be changing for dinner," Forbes said, with uncomfortable haste.

"You'd better be cooking the dinner," Willie said. "Winifred is counting on your soldierly experience to help her out."

So Forbes went to the kitchen to salute and report for duty. As he entered the house he looked back to see Enslee leading Persis toward the marble steps to the little temple where he proposed regularly.

Forbes' heart thudded heavily in his breast. He felt helpless to protest or intervene in any way. Persis was up at auction. He had bidden her in under a misapprehension of the upset price, and she was put back for sale again.

CHAPTER XXXIX

AS she mounted the steps with Willie, Persis felt something of Forbes' regret. She was a slave on the block, and the man she wanted for owner was crowded from the mart.

"What did father have to say?" she asked, in a dull tone already despairing.

"I—I—it wasn't very pleasant."

"Hand it to me."

"He said to break it to you gently."

"Well, speak up, Willie. Break it! For the Lord's sake, break it!"

"Sit down, won't you?" He led her to a bench in the temple. "I hardly know where to begin."

"Begin at the ending."

"Well, you see, your poor governor—"

"Has lost all his money?"

"Well, yes—in a way."

"It's getting to be rather a habit with the poor old boy, isn't it? Is he smashed up badly?"

"Pretty badly."

"The house in town and the country place will have to go?"

"I'm afraid so."

"The cars and the horses—my car, too?"

"Looks like it."

"Then I needn't worry about it's being a last year's model," she laughed. Willie stared at her admiringly.

"Gad, but you're a good loser."

"I try to be; an easy winner, an easy loser. I'm awfully

sorry for father, though. Did you—did you tell him anything?"

"I told him we were engaged."

She shivered and mumbled, "What did he say to that?"

"He seemed immensely relieved. He said, 'God bless her.' His voice was very faint, but I think that's what he said."

"Perhaps he said, 'God help her.'"

"Maybe he did," Willie sighed. "Anyway, we're to meet him in town to-morrow."

He stared at her with hungry eyes, and his little lean fingers crept toward the exquisite hand of hers that lay supine, relaxed, with upturned fingers like the petals of an open rose. He took that flower in his hands timidly. She looked down into his famished eyes and smiled pitifully—perhaps a little for him, certainly for herself.

He overestimated the tenderness in her gaze and squeezed her fingers in his. She winced and drew her hand away.

"I'm awfully sorry I hurt you," he said.

"It was this ring again," she explained, though she had not meant to say the "again."

"My ring? Our ring?" he murmured, with such joy that her sportsmanship compelled a last effort at playing fair.

"Under the circumstances," she said, "I think I'd better return it to you—with thanks for the loan."

"I don't want it back!" he gasped. "I won't have it back."

"You didn't agree to marry a beggar."

"I want to marry you—just you," he pleaded. "The engagement stands."

"You're terribly polite, but I can't—not for charity."

"Charity—bosh!" he stormed. "I can't get along without you. You couldn't get along without a lot of money, Persis. If—if you'll let the engagement stand

I'll put your father on his feet again. I'll—I'll do anything."

"How put him on his feet? I thought he was smashed?"

"He went to Chicago to raise a lot of money. He couldn't. He's coming back to face the music. It's a funeral march unless—unless—well, I could take up his obligations. I don't understand it very well myself, to say nothing of explaining it to you. But I've got a lot of money, and money is what your father's enemies want. He'll be all right if he's tided over the shallow places. So for my sake and your governor's, let me announce the engagement."

"Think what people would say. It looks so hideously mercenary on my part."

"We can prove that we were engaged before this thing threatened. Everybody will have to confess it's a true love match on both sides. Please, please, Persis! pretty please!"

She resigned herself to all the shames she foresaw, and sighed:

"All right, Willie, it will brace Dad up a bit."

"Is he the only one you think of?" Willie pouted. "Haven't you a word of—of love for me?" He wrung her hands in his little claws again, and they set her nerves on edge. She wanted to shriek her detestation of her plight; but she controlled herself enough to keep down her feelings. She could not, however, mimic love where she felt loathing—the best she could do was to mumble:

"We can't very well play a love scene up here before everybody, can we? I may feel more enthusiastic when I've had a bath and a change of costume."

She broke from him and hurried down the steps. He overtook her half-way to plead:

"Let me announce our engagement now—to the people here."

"Not now," she pleaded; "not here!" And she ran on. But he followed chuckling. He had a great dramatic idea.

CHAPTER XL

THAT was an extraordinary dinner. The famished aristocracy hovered about the kitchen porch like waifs, pleading for the privilege of assisting. Ten Eyck wanted to scour the cake-dish or put raisins in something. He and the rest were set to work dusting the palatial dining-hall and bringing forth the best Enslee plate. Willie stood by and warned them to be careful. He was in so triumphant a humor that he felt nearly like breaking something himself.

When at last the board was decked, the candelabra alight, fresh flowers lavished everywhere, and chairs arranged, the guests were ravenous.

"Do we dress for dinner?" said Ten Eyck. Winifred threw a boiled potato at him. It grazed Mrs. Neff, who swore splendidly and was prepared to respond with a mop when disarmed.

It was one of the necessities of the feast that the entire body of guests should be also the corps of waiters. The service would have appalled the shabbiest butler. There were woeful collisions at the deadly swinging doors; wine-glasses that had been made in Bohemia and monogrammed there were splintered. A wonderful soup-tureen of historic associations was juggled and lost. It fell on a venerable rug of every color except spilled soup. The tureen was picked up empty and badly dented.

But nothing could check the riot. There were battles around the serving-tables in the kitchen and the pantry and at the sideboard. Those who got their plates filled rushed to their places like fed dogs dispersing each with its bone.

Winifred was exhausted by her long day's work. She made no pretense of toilet, but followed her viands in and slumped into her chair with sleeves rolled up, knees apart, and the general collapsed look of cooks.

Forbes had taken off his coat for his kitchen work. Winifred would not let him put it on again.

"My butler and footmen eat with their livery on the back of their chairs," she said. "We'll make this a regular banquet in the servants' hall."

The idea pleased everybody but Willie. They had all happened into the servants' dining-rooms during the meals of those weary ministers, so now they sprawled and gobbled and chattered in the best imitation they could improvise.

"Our own people are probably eating at our own tables at home," said Mrs. Neff, "and passing scandal with every plate."

"There's the one thing missing to make this a true servant's soirée," said Ten Eyck—"a lot of down-stairs gossip. I am now Willie's man: 'Whatever do you suppose I turned up this morning whilst I was unpacking the mahster's bag after his trip to Philadelphia—a receipted bill for five-and-twenty dollars for Mr. and Mrs. William Jones, one night's lodging, so 'elp me!'"

Everybody glanced at Willie, but he giggled. "You flatter me."

Alice, with the sophistication that young women have apparently always had except in fiction, put up her hand reprovingly to Ten Eyck.

"No depravity, no depravity! Remember my young mother is present. Now I'm our second man talking to my maid: 'My Missus, for all she's so crool to her darling dorter Aluss, do you knaow the hour she come in lawst night? Nao? Four o'clock this mornin', she did! Strike me if she didn't!'"

Mrs. Neff smiled and retaliated: "Now I'm Alice's Hibernian maid: 'At that the ould shrew had nothin'

on Miss Aluss. Whilst her mother was toorkey-trattin',
wasn't the darlin' child after tahkin' four dollars' worth
of baby-tahk over the telephone to that young bosthoon
of a Stowe Webb.'"

"How on earth did you find out?" said Alice.

Mrs. Neff's answer was further revelation of the domestic secret service: "It's a nice little colleen, Aluss is,
and pays me liberal for smooglin' notes in and out of the
house. And then the ould woman pays me still more
liberal to bring the notes to her first. It's a right careful
mother she is."

Alice stared in horror, and Mrs. Neff tee-hee'd like a
malicious little girl. Winifred came to Alice's rescue with
a cross-fire:

"Now I'm Mrs. Neff's secretary talking to my little
niece's governess."

"Help, help!" cried Mrs. Neff. "No fair, Winifred.
I had to discharge the cat. If you dare, I'll give an
imitation of your laundress talking to—"

"I surrender," said Winifred, hastily.

"Go on," said Ten Eyck. "As Connie Ediss sang,
'It all comes out in the wash.'"

Mrs. Neff put up her hand. "As official duenna of
this family, I think we'd better change the game or put
out the lights."

"That's a fine idea!" said Ten Eyck. "A game of tag
in the dark."

"Not in my dark!" said Willie, sternly, with a calm
incisiveness that surprised everybody and ended the project before it was begun.

Ten Eyck complained: "We came here to be rid of the
spying servants, and we've been more respectable than
ever."

"Crowds are almost always respectable," said Mrs.
Neff, "unless they're drunk."

"Everybody is almost always respectable," said Ten
Eyck. "Even the worst of us only sin for a few minutes

at a time. A murder takes but a moment, and thieves are notorious loafers. This talk of a life of sin is mostly rot, I think. Sin is a spasm, not a life."

"It's the remorse and the atonement that make up the life," said Mrs. Neff.

"Good Lord, how funereal we are," said Persis, "talking about sin and spasms and remorse when the flowers are blooming and the moonlight is pounding on the windows! We ought to be——"

"Washing the dishes," said Winifred, rising. "Come on, the all of youse, clear up this mess and get into the suds. Persis and Mrs. Neff and Alice are the dish-washing squad to-night, and Willie and Murray can wipe them dry."

"We haven't had our smoke yet," protested Mrs. Neff. A respite was granted for this.

Everybody smoked but Alice.

"What's the matter with you, Alice?" said Winifred. "Sore throat?"

Alice shrugged her shoulders and answered, "Ask my awful mother."

Mrs. Neff flicked the ashes off her cigarette. "My father always used to tell my brothers that tobacco wouldn't hurt them if they didn't smoke till they were twenty-one. I think it applies to women also."

"Great heavens!" said Winifred, pretending to put away her cigarette, "I've ruined my life. No wonder I'm wasting away."

"Eighteen is the legal age for women," said Ten Eyck.

Winifred resumed her cigarette with a mock childishness. "Then I can just qualify. I was eighteen last——"

"Last century, my dear?" Mrs. Neff cooed.

"For that you can scrub the pots and pans, darling," Winifred crooned. "And I was going to let you off with the wine-glasses. Another crack like that and I'll have you stoking the range."

"I am a martyr in the cause of truth," Mrs. Neff groaned. "Come on; let's get it over with."

Winifred was a sharp taskmaster, and so bulky that none of the women dared to disobey. Nor the men either. Forbes was for helping Persis and saving her delicate hands, but Winifred would not have him in the pantry at all:

"The little snojer cooked the dinner, and he gets a furlough. If I could trust the rest of you I'd walk with him in the moonlight and let him hold my dainty white mit in his manly clasp."

Forbes was banished, and spent his exile pacing up and down smoking and peering in at the window, where Persis, aproned and wet-armed and with a speck of soot on her nose, buried her jeweled fingers in greasy dish-water, and smoked the while her customary cigarette. She was more fascinating than ever to Forbes, whose mind kept ringing the domestic chimes.

When the kitchen and dining-room chores were done to the satisfaction of Winifred, who demanded as much of her amateur scullions as she would have demanded of her own servants, they were all exhausted. Returning to the living-room, they sprawled in those inelegant attitudes that tired laborers assume. Their minds were jaded with their muscles.

"I never understood before why my servants are so snappy at night," said Mrs. Neff. "If anybody speaks to me I'll cry."

"Pull down your skirts, at least, mother," said Alice.

"They're too far away," sighed Mrs. Neff. "And nobody's interested in my old legs."

Alice, with the fierce decency of the young, rose wearily, bent down, put her mother's ankles together, and covered them with the skirt.

"Isn't it odd," sighed Mrs. Neff, "how we pretend that old people must go along to chaperon the young? It ought to be the other way about."

Alice was too tired to get up. She sank on the floor and laid her head on her mother's knee. And Mrs. Neff put out a thin, white hand upon the girl's soft hair.

"It's a nice little girl, sometimes," she sighed.

"And it would be a nice little mother," said Alice, "if—"

"Don't say it, my child. He's not the man for you at all. I know best. I'm thinking of your happiness." Alice shrugged a skeptical comment.

Her mother went on: "Do you remember how you had all the chocolate creams you wanted—once? You couldn't look at one for a year after. Well, living on love alone is like trying to live on chocolate creams alone. And he couldn't afford even to keep you in chocolate creams."

Alice made no answer. She sat studying her own thoughts.

Forbes felt a sudden kinship with Alice's absent lover and beloved, this Stowe Webb, whose crime was lack of money. He imagined that Persis' mother had told her the same cold things that Alice was hearing now. He began to believe that many daughters must hear such financial talk against love from their mothers. He had heard so many married women scoff at love as a delusion. He wondered if, after all, it were not really man, rather than woman, who is the romantic animal.

"Men," he pondered, "write the great poems and the great romances, paint the great pictures, fight the great fights against nature and ignorance and oppression and poverty. They compose the great music, supply the demand for love songs and love stories, and build the places to love in. Then they lay their wealth and ambition and achievement at the feet of little women, and each little woman selects from those that gather at her feet the one that she thinks will dress her best and house her best and give her the best time."

He had read much in books, written chiefly by gallant gentlemen whose flattery was greater than their accuracy, that woman was a slave, a toy, a plaything, a victim of man's cruelty. Now he began to believe that in the vast bulk of instances the reverse was true. The little women

set their feet on the men's necks and rode upon their
shoulders, and when they were displeased pulled the
men's hair, poked fingers into their eyes, or abandoned
them entirely.

He felt again what he had felt when he studied Fifth
Avenue and its womankind; for every woman's finery
some man pays. Woman was the grasping sex, the exact-
ing, yet extravagant sex. The eternal feminine was the
eternal calculatrix.

He had wondered what these women paid for what they
got from men. He believed now that he had found the
answer. They paid with their bodies, their kisses, the
encircling of arms, the cooing of tender words. In return
for so much money they granted permission to spend
yet more.

He studied Persis; how beautiful she was, how soft and
gracile, how apt to endearments! Yet she held herself
at a price, at a high price, and called it pride, self-protec-
tion. What was it but self-exploitation?

Yet what man ever desired an object less because it
was beyond his means? Persis was certainly no less adorable to Forbes because he could not buy her. He would
have to get along without her. But, having once held her
in his arms while she held him in hers, he would never
cease to desire her. Like the father of a spendthrift child,
he rather felt ashamed of himself for being incompetent
to meet her demands, than contemned her for making them.

After a while of silent meditation Mrs. Neff spoke up,
briskly:

"There's only one thing that would rest me, and that's
a tango. Where are those records we bought this afternoon?"

On the homeward way the motor party had passed a
shop where disks were kept, and had bought up the entire
visible supply of latter-day tunes to replace the dances
of yesteryear. There was general agreement that it was
high time to turkey-trot again.

"I'll run the machine," said Winifred. "Bob Fielding isn't here, and I'll be true to his memory for a dance or two."

"I choose to dance with Major General Forbes," said Mrs. Neff, "unless he's otherwise engaged."

"Before we dance," said Willie, "I have an announcement to make. Ladies and gentlemen, so to speak"—he cleared his throat and ran his fingers round inside his tight collar—"I am about to—er—give birth—er—to an after-dinner speech—my first and only."

"Hear! Hear!"

"Some time ago Miss Persis—er—Cabot, whom you all know, did me the—er—unspeakable honor of consenting to become Mrs. William—er—Enslee. Circumstances rendered it—er—advisable to defer—er—the publication of the glorious—er—news, so to speak. But Miss Cabot has to-night given me—er—permission to announce—"

"I have not!" Persis broke in; but Willie put up his hand.

"Order in the court—er! Anyway, now you know the worst. You behold in me the happiest man on—er—earth."

There was a round of applause, and Ten Eyck proposed "three lusty chahs and a tigress for the—er—bride and—er—groom—er."

Forbes felt as if a shell full of shrapnel had burst at his feet. Military instinct brought his heels together, and he stood as erect as Dreyfus did when they tore the buttons from his tunic and snapped his sword in two before him. He stared at the revel that broke out around Persis and Enslee. In his eyes it had something of the hideousness of savages dancing. It was a torture dance, and he was the man at the stake.

CHAPTER XLI

FORBES tried to smile, but his muscles seemed unable to support his lips. He heard much noise, yet distinguished nothing till he seemed to wake suddenly at finding Willie Enslee smirking up at him.

"You haven't congratulated me, Mr. Ward—er—Forbes."

Forbes seized Enslee's small hand and wrung it, and said in a tone more fitted to condolence:

"I do congratulate you, indeed, and Miss Cabot, I—I congratulate her."

He tried to look at her, but Willie was clinging to his hand and driveling on: "I want to thank you for—er—at least trying to save her when her horse bolted this morning. They told me you were—er—quite splendid, and I take it as a—er—personal favor."

"Don't mention it, please."

"And now let's—er—dance," said Willie. "I will dance with the blushing bride, if you don't mind. Let 'er go, Winifred."

Winifred set off the Victrola, and a blare of nasal cacophony broke from the machine imitating a steamboat whistle; then ensued a negroid music of infinite inappropriateness to Forbes' tragic mood. He saw the woman who loved him, and whom he loved, tagged and claimed by a contemptible pygmy, the accidental inheritor of wealth. He saw his beautiful Persis in the fellow's incompetent arms and her body drooping over him as if he had carried her off in a kind of burlesque rape of the Sabines. The music was not Wagnerian epopee, nor were the words something from Sophokles; it was a romping ditto about

> 'Way down on the lev-ee
> In old Alabam-y,
> There's daddy and mam-my,
> There's Ephraim and Sam-my
> On a moon-light night.

Forbes felt Mrs. Neff's presence in front of him. Her wiry arms clutched him and danced him away. She was chattering reproaches because he had not taken her advice and captured Persis for himself. And her unwitting irony ran on against the words that Alice and Ten Eyck were singing as they danced:

> Watch them shuf-flin' along,
> See them shuf-flin' along.
> Go take your best—gal—real—pal,
> Go down to the lev-ee,
> I said to the lev-ee,
> And join that shuf-flin' throng.
> Hear that mu-sic and song.
> It's simply great—O mate.
> Waitin' on the levee, waitin' for the *Robert E. Lee.*

Forbes felt a ribaldry in the whole situation, an intolerable contumely. He watched Persis darting here and there as Willie urged her. The little whelp could not keep time to the music, and his possession of Persis was as grotesque as the presence of a gargoyle on a cathedral. But cathedrals are thick with gargoyles, and life is full of such pairings.

For the second dance Forbes demanded Persis, and she granted him the privilege with some terror; the look on his face had alarmed her.

The music now celebrated "dancing with the Devil; oh, the little Devil! dancing at the Devil's ball." There was a fiend raging in Forbes' heart, and something infernal in the frenzy with which he whipped Persis this way and that.

"Why didn't you tell me?" he groaned. "Why didn't you warn me? The last I knew was that you and I were to be married. And suddenly that man speaks up and claims you. And you don't deny it. What in God's name does it mean?"

"Not so loud, my love!"

"'My love?'" he quoted. "You can call me that?"

"You're not going to make a scene, are you?" she whispered, trembling in his arms.

"A scene!" he laughed. "Is that your greatest terror in life?"

"One of them."

"You intended to marry him, and you let me kiss you! Were you simply making a fool of me?"

("*At the Devil's ball, at the Devil's ball.*") .

"No, Harvey, no! I love you. It is you that were making a fool of me. I can explain, but I don't think you would understand."

("*I saw the cute Mrs. Devil, so pretty and fat.*")

"When will you explain?"

"The first chance I get."

("*Dressed in a beautiful fireman's hat.*")

"To-night?" .

"I don't dare. Willie is going to stand guard, as he said he would. Seeing you dancing with Mrs. Neff, he was just telling me what a joke it would be to lock you out. He's going to pretend to go to bed. Then he's going to slip down-stairs, lock the front door, and wait till you and Mrs. Neff come back. Isn't it ridiculous?"

("*Dancing with the Devil; oh, the little Devil!*")

"Everything on earth is ridiculous, but nothing is so ridiculous as I am."

"Don't say that, dear."

"'Dear!'" he echoed, bitterly. "When do I see you, I say?"

("*Dancing at the Devil's Ball.*")

"There's no chance."

"Then I'll make one. I'll—I'll come to your room."

"Oh, in Heaven's name, are you mad? Or do you think I am? Mrs. Neff's room adjoins mine. She could hear the softest whisper."

"Then let Willie Enslee lock us out."

She saw that he was in a frenzy. He had the bit in his teeth. He would bolt in a moment. She thought hard and swiftly. Then she said:

"There's just one way. When I was playing chambermaid to-day I wandered about and found the servant's stairway in the service wing. It leads down into the kitchen. We could get from there into the dining-room and the drawing-room. There's a great window there—well cut off from view. I don't think Willie or anybody would see us there. Listen for Willie's door, and when he has gone down into the front hall, slip out and tiptoe down the service stairs to the kitchen and wait for me there. Will you?"

It was a nauseating rôle to play; but he was bent upon making a last appeal to her before they returned to town on the morrow. He whispered his assent to the elaborate deceit, and made a whirlwind of the last measures of the tune, "Dancing with the devil; oh, the little Devil! dancing at the Devil's ball!"

And then he and Persis, dizzy on the swirling floor, reeled to chairs and sat gasping for breath. Mrs. Neff, passing on Willie's arm, urged Forbes to give Alice the next dance, and he obeyed, surrendering Persis to Enslee, who was so elate with triumph that only the braggart pomp of the tango could express him.

Alice was lonely and forlorn, and so much in Forbes' mood that they were unintentional parodies on each other. Forbes remembered his talk with Senator Tait, and, feeling that Alice was desperately in need of comfort, told her the whole conversation. If she resented the discussion of her affairs and her mother's plans, she kept silent; but when he told her that Senator Tait had vowed to help her defeat Mrs. Neff's match-making plot by giving Stowe Webb a position she became a mænad of joy. She italicized every other word, and declared herself insanely grateful. She declared now that she simply idolized the Senator, and had always thought him the most adorable of men in every respect except the quality of husband.

"I'm afraid he won't give Mr. Webb much of a salary to begin with," Forbes said, to moderate her fantastic hopes.

"Oh, I don't care how little it is," Alice panted, "so long as it's enough for us two to live on, if we have to live in a Harlem flat eleven stories high and no elevator!"

She made so startling a contrast with Persis that Forbes regretted thinking her shallow and hysterical. Under her volatile explosiveness was evidently a deep store of loyalty, as under Persis' reposeful manner was a shifty uncertainty, a terror of consequences. "Still waters run deep" was plainly as fallible as any other proverb, for very shallow ponds may lie very calm, and very spluttering geysers may come from far underground.

But it is one thing to approve and quite another to love. Forbes admired Alice, but he loved Persis. He approved Alice as much as he distrusted Persis. But he loved Persis.

CHAPTER XLII

THERE were not many more dances before Willie, in his new capacity of Benedick-to-be, declared for early closing hours, and ordered his guests off to bed, warning them that the next morning the caravan would set out on its return betimes in order that Persis might "break the news to her father as soon as he got back." So Willie phrased it, and flattered himself that it was rather considerate and tactful to put it so.

When good-nights were said, and Forbes had gone to his room, Ten Eyck came in to smoke a night-cap cigar. His words were congratulatory, but his intent was sympathetic.

"You looked a bit cut up, old boy," he said, "when Willie, with his usual tact, exploded the news of his marriage. I hope you weren't hit too hard. I warned you, you know."

"I know," said Forbes; "I promised you I wouldn't take Miss Cabot seriously. I—I admit I was surprised. That's all. And it rather shocks me to think of so—so—of her tying up with a man like Enslee. That's all."

"It's her own choice," said Ten Eyck. "And it's a good choice. She can't bankrupt the Enslee estates, and she'll earn all she squanders. Being the wife of Willie Enslee is not going to be any sinecure, believe me.

"And the sooner she's married to Enslee and beyond your reach, the better for your peace of mind and the efficiency of the U. S. A. Get back on the job, Forbesy. You're too important a man to be wasting yourself even on a siren like Persis. I believe in sirens, and I like to hear 'em sing; but they don't convince me one little minute, and

288

I drop anchor at a safe distance from the reef. Promise me you won't let Persis haunt you. Get yourself a pretty canary and forget the siren, eh what?"

"That's the best of advice," Forbes assented.

He thought that he sounded convinced; but Ten Eyck shook his head and masked a sigh as a yawn.

"Am I as deadly as all that? And papa always told me that the man who gives the best of advice might better have saved his breath for blowing out his candle. Instead of more advice I will now do so. Good night!"

And he closed his door.

Forbes knew that Ten Eyck was right, and told himself so. He told himself that common decency, self-respect, Persis-respect, and respect for the rights of a host and a fiancé forbade him to keep tryst with Persis. And having resolved that the one thing he ought not to do was to sneak down the servants' stairs, he sneaked down the servants' stairs—after he had put out his light, opened his door delicately, and waited till he heard Enslee open his door and tiptoe down to the entrance hall.

As Forbes waited in that least poetic of bowers, the kitchen, he felt like a thief. He had abundant time for pondering what a destroyer of dignity love is. But Persis came at last, and so silently and so vaguely through the moonlight that he could hardly believe her to be more than a phantom.

She gave him a hand, however, that was warm and human, and when he caught her in his arms and she yielded rather than struggle, her body was as real as rose-leaves and lilies, a delight to his embrace; and her cheek such a sweetmeat to his lips that he dismissed all scruples as follies beneath contempt.

When she had extricated herself from his clasp she took his hand and led him through the butler's pantry and its swinging door, across the moonlit dining-room, through a majestic somber portal into a cave of black gloom, which was the salon.

19   289

"Have you a match?" she whispered. "If you haven't I have."

"I have a cigar-lighter," he whispered.

He snapped the little engine, and a small, blue flame threw a sickly light that helped them to find a channel through the islands of chairs and divans and tables, to the lofty hangings masking the windows.

The wee taper gave Forbes a glimpse as well of the place he was in.

This superb chamber had not been opened to the present guests. It was still in its winter garb, the portraits in shrouds, and chairs and tables disguised in winding sheets. There was the hint of a mortuary vault about the place. The walls were of Istrian stone hung with gray tapestries of unhappy lovers. The floor was of marble devoid of rugs—they were rolled up against the walls like mummies. The mantel was a huge carved structure. In this dull light it might have been a funeral monument. Noises seemed to be repeated here with spooky comment, and to Forbes the spirit in the air was ominous.

Persis knew the room well, and remembered it as she had first seen it glowing with color, flooded with sunlight, and crowded with gorgeous people; she did not feel the oppression that weighed on Forbes.

To her it was a clandestine romance—the sort of poetic encounter she had read about in ever so many books. Her heart was beating with terror of discovery and ecstasy of adventure. When she gained the window she reached up and persuaded the hangings back on gently tinkling rings. A well of moonlight was revealed — a broad, padded seat in front of a tall mullioned window. Within the window was a smaller window, and she swung this back.

Into the dreary air of the unvisited room flowed a little brook of perfumed breeze scented with the lilacs it streamed across. It shook with all gentleness the hair about Persis' face and the soft lace around her throat. For now she was not in boyish riding-duds with collar and cravat, but in the exquisite trifle of a silken house gown she had put on for dinner.

She was so beautiful in Forbes' eyes that the very faults he had found in her seemed to enhance her. The absence of utility and reliability and other homely virtues seemed to leave her the unmarred unity of futile, fragile loveliness. But this was the fantasy of the moment only. She had no sooner spoken than she was committed to something more than a vision for the eyes.

She smiled at him, and he gathered her up into his arms once more and gave and took a blindly sweet kiss from her smiling lips.

When he released her from this constraint she sighed luxuriously:

"Well, Harvey, it seems as if all the happiness in the world had to be sneaked, doesn't it?"

Instantly he realized again the dishonesty of their communion.

"Is that your creed?" he groaned.

"It's my experience. Stolen fruit, you know——"

"I hate stolen fruit. I want to have the right to own—you."

"You do—pretty nearly."

"I want everybody to know it. I want you to be my wife. It's not too late, if you love me."

"Oh, there's no question of that, for I do love you. You are—it's funny how hard it is to find new expressions for anything you really mean, isn't it? All I can think of is the same old comic-paper line: you are the only man I ever loved. But—oh, Lord, if you only had a little more money! For I sha'n't have any, Harvey. My father can't give me any. I've just found that out. He can't get enough to save himself. I can get enough for us both if I take Willie.

"It's horrible talk, Harvey, but it's business. It's for your sake as much as mine. If I married you I'd drive you mad. I'd rather have you hate me lovingly, as you do now, than have you hate me loathingly, as you would if I became a millstone round your neck. You'd be faithful and work hard and try to love me, but I'd be simply unendurable.

"My brother—you haven't met him; he's loafing through college—he knows more about sport than he does about books. He's always talking about prizefighters and class. He's always telling about some poor fellow getting knocked senseless because he strayed out of his class. I remember one brilliant welterweight champion who lasted only one round with a broken-down heavyweight. My brother said the welterweight got what was coming to him because he hadn't intelligence enough to stay where he belonged. I'm trying to do that. I'm horribly tempted just to fling everything to the winds and run away with you. I'm starving for your love. My heart says, 'Put love before everything else—'"

"Obey your heart!" Forbes broke in, at last. She shook her head.

"But my brain says, 'Think of the long, long future!' A woman spends so little of her married life with her husband. It's the long days that count, the days she spends with other women, with rivalries, jealousies, with economy, economy, economy. That's what I'm afraid of. Economy would play the devil with me, Harvey. Two thousand a year and forage! I'm afraid of it."

"So you will marry this rich man. And then?"

"Then I shall probably learn to hate him."

"And to love somebody else?"

"I shall never love anybody but you, Harvey. I've never told anybody else my real mind as I have you, for I am trained to conceal—always to conceal."

"But don't conceal from yourself the failure you are going to make of your life. No woman can play false to her heart and prosper. I beg you not to despise my love."

"Despise your love!" she cried. "It's myself I despise. Ah, Harvey, try to understand me."

"I can't! I can only warn you."

"Oh, don't warn me! Don't lecture me! Just love me! Let's not think of the future—it's always full of tragedy. If we married in all our love, we should meet so much unhappiness! The most loving love matches I've known have burned out—ended in divorces and open scandal, or scandal concealed like ostriches for everybody to see and laugh at. Two people fall in love and meet opposition and run away together to a preacher. Then they have nobody to oppose them, so they oppose each other. And by and by they run away from each other and don't meet till they get to a divorce court in some small town to avoid the notoriety."

"And you think that you will escape that by marrying without love?"

"Yes. Because I don't expect love. I sha'n't expect Willie to be a romantic saint, and then hate him for not living up to my specifications."

"But yourself—your body—you will give that to him?"

She closed her eyes and turned ghastly white as she whispered: "I suppose so. That's the usual price a woman pays, isn't it?"

He flung her from him as something unclean, common, cheap.

From the huddle she was in she whispered:

"I understand. I—I don't blame you."

There was a sort of burlesque saintliness about her meekness that nauseated him. He did not realize that she forgave him because his rage seemed a proof of his love. She would have forgiven him with bruised lips if he had struck her in the face.

He loathed himself for his vicious wrath, but he almost loathed her more for compelling it. Yet when she got to her feet and stood clinging to the velvet curtain, and mumbled:

"It was better that this happened before we were married, wasn't it? And now that you are cured of loving me I may go, mayn't I?"

He stared at her; his lips parted to utter words he could not find; he put out his hands, and she went back to his arms. And she cried a little, not forgetting even in her grief to sob stealthily lest some one hear. And he understood that, too, and hated her for her eternal vigilance. Even while he kissed the brackish tears from her cheeks and eyes he hated her for being so beautiful and so wise, so full of passion and so discreet.

She wept but a little while, and then she was quiet, reclining against him in silence and meditating.

And he pondered the mystery of his own behavior. A sense of duty and a sense of honor had always guided his acts hitherto. This woman acted upon him like the drug that doctors use for controlling violent patients and the criminal insane; it leaves the senses all alive but annuls the power of motion.

Here he was, convinced to the very depths of his soul that it was abominable to embrace the betrothed of another, yet he did not take his arms from about her, he did not put her away from him. Instead, he held her fast even when she made to go. And yet he blamed her.

This much at least he accomplished in the long silence: he ceased to blame Persis and accused himself, tried himself before the tribunal of his own soul, and denounced himself as guilty of treason to himself and her and the laws of the world. But he did not put her from him.

And now, having condemned himself, he followed the usual program and forgave himself. He bent down and kissed her forehead and her hair, and tightened his arms about her. She did not answer his kiss. Once more he felt, as in the sunlight by the brook, that he held only the shell of her, while her soul—that other man's soul of her —was gone voyaging.

But now it was in the cold of night, in the dark chill of

a room long closed up like a grave and her body was the only warmth in the room, or in the world for him. It seemed to glow like an ember breathing rosily in ashes.

And now gradually desire grew imperious, the angry, sullen desire of Tristan seeing his Isolde given to another man to wife. He burned with resentment at the ill-treatment accorded him by the fates, who saved his love and her love for this mockery, this money-infected, money-paralyzed romance. His wrath rose in revolt against a world where such a sarcasm was possible. The laws of the world became suspect with the mercy of the world. The pangs of disprized love were so bitter that he began to claim revenge, revenge especially on her.

He clenched his arms about her with a new and different ardor—no longer the sacred fervor of a lover who protects his affianced from himself, but the outlaw that raids and desecrates.

She understood and was afraid and fought against him, but her mutinous love fought for him. And nature, and the moonlight, and the scented breeze purring at the window fought for him. All her beauty clamored to surrender. She was already lost when some last impulse of horror cried out against the irreparable profanation. Even as her arms went round him she murmured:

"Help me! Harvey, help me!"

CHAPTER XLIII

IN the panic of her soul there was just honor enough
awake to raise that prayer, and in the fury of his there
was just honor enough left to answer it. It was the one
irresistible appeal she could have made — the cry of
"Help!" that never falls in vain on the ears of a man
unless he has become a beast—or a god.

Mysteriously the almost stifled cry released from the
dungeon of Forbes' soul all the powers of decency;
they took possession of him anew. His senses and his
muscles obeyed, and he was now so pure-hearted a de-
fender of Persis' integrity that he resisted even the little
moan of almost regret that escaped her tormented soul
when he let her go.

The aftermath of the ordeal was an ague of reaction.
The blood seemed to flow backward into her heart. She
was overwhelmed with the terror one feels for a disaster
narrowly escaped, and with shame for the realization that
the credit was none of hers.

Forbes did not take her in his arms, but contented himself with closing out the breeze that seemed to have turned
colder now, and with wrapping about her quivering
shoulders the heavy velvet of the curtain.

Whatever other flaws she had, Persis was not marred
by self-conceit. Even her nobler motives she tended to
reinterpret from some cynical point of view. When she
was calmer she spoke with that intelligence of hers that
always chilled Forbes' idealizing heart.

"I can't tell you how grateful I am, Harvey, and how
ashamed. I didn't know I was so—so hopelessly like

other people. I didn't know I could forget myself so completely. But I've learned my lesson. I've had my scare. And I must keep away from the edge of the cliff. We mustn't meet alone this way any more, Harvey. I love you too well, and I don't want to go altogether to the bad, do I? It isn't that I'm good; I'd love to be good, but I'm afraid I wasn't meant to be. But I must be sensible. I mustn't be a fool. A woman risks too much, Harvey. It's too hideously unfair. The consequences would be nothing at all to you—and might be utter destruction to me. I told you there were a hundred Persises in me. And now I've seen one of them face to face that I never knew was there. I've got to starve her to death. We mustn't meet alone any more, must we?"

He could not say anything without saying too much. So he simply shook his head and pressed her hand, and, rising, led her from the niche of peril. With his free hand he found his cigar-lighter and snapped it; but it would not flame, and they stumbled through an archipelago of furniture, jostling together, more afraid of contact with each other than of any other danger.

They walked into the wall, but, groping, found at last the door and entered the dining-room again. The moonlight was gone, and the first tide of daybreak was seeping through the windows. There was no rose-color in this dawn. It promised to be a gray day.

They hurried to the kitchen and came back indeed to life in its most material surfaces, a chill, drab light beating upon pots and pans.

They bade each other good night and good-by there; but their embrace was appropriately matter-of-fact, galvanized ware upon cold iron. They tiptoed wearily up the service stairway and into the main corridor above.

Here, too, there was daylight like dirty pond water. Persis went stealthily to the railing of the stairway, and, glancing down, beckoned to Forbes, who moved to her side and peered where she pointed.

He saw that Willie Enslee, exhausted by his vigil, had fallen asleep on a sumptuous divan. The divan would have honored a palace, and Willie's pajamas were of silk, and his bathrobe was of brocaded silk. But after all it was Willie Enslee that was in them. And he slept with his little eyes clenched and his mouth ajar. And a cold cigarette was stuck to his lower lip.

Forbes was impelled to taunt her with a whispered: "There is you husband. Go to him!"

But when he looked at her she was so wan and pitiful that he could not be as pitiless as the wan daylight was. She was making an advance payment on her price; and she was shivering and lonely. So he kissed her icy hands and whispered to her how beautiful she was and a sorrowful "God bless you!" and sneaked back into his room, his bachelor room.

Had he paused as once before to throw her another kiss, he would have found her with her arms stretched out to him pleading for rescue from the vision she had seen and the unspoken taunt she had understood. But he did not look back, and she dared not knock at his door. The click of his lock frightened her, and she fled to her room like a ghost surprised by the morning.

CHAPTER XLIV

WHEN Forbes shut the door upon Persis (and unwittingly shut out her little gesture of appeal to come back, be stronger than she was, and rescue her from herself in spite of herself) he looked from his room upon a world that was just the colorless color of the glass in his window.

There was a menace of rain in the sky, and the dawn was a colorless affair, neither night nor morning. The day woke like a sleeper that has not rested well.

As a mere formality Forbes took off his clothes and lay down. Life was colorless ahead of him. The woman who had fascinated him utterly had utterly disappointed him. She loved Forbes, but not his penury; she would marry Enslee's money, but not Enslee. She wanted success in life—called it her "career"!

Men, he knew, put their careers first, made everything subservient to success, asked their women to kowtow to it. Perhaps women were going to do the same thing. Perhaps they had been all these centuries hunting success and disguising the materialism of their ambition under more romantic words, aided in their deceit by the numberless gallantries of authors. Perhaps Persis was not different from millions of women, except for being frank where the others were hypocrites, more or less intentionally.

This thought softened his heart toward Persis, and he regretted it. He did not want to think softly of Persis any more. It unnerved his resolution, and uncertainty and irresolution were terrific strains on a man of action and precision. If he could renounce Persis with contempt he would be able to close that incident and resume

299

the progress of life. But to find in every beauty of hers something of ugliness, and to find in every cruelty of hers something to respect and something to pity, was the paralysis of decision.

How could he hate her when he loved her so madly, and was so unhappy out of her sight? How was he to endure it that she should marry another man, and how was he to prevent it?

He tossed between sleeping and waking, between condemnation of Persis and acquittal, between resolutions to cut her out of his heart and his life, and resolutions to win her yet. Eventually he heard people stirring about the house, and he rose drearily.

The shower-bath gave forth a lukewarm drizzle that neither stimulated nor soothed him. Outside, rain was falling lazily in a gray air that hid the hills and gardens as if the sky, too, were a curtained shower-bath.

He began to pack his suit-cases. As he was folding one of his coats there dropped from its inside pocket a mesh of beribboned lace. It surprised him by its inappropriateness. He picked it up, and it was the nightcap that had fallen from her tousled hair as she looked from the window into that wonderful dawn of day before yesterday. What a liar that dawn had been! It was illustrious and spendthrift of promises. To-day's dawn was the fulfilment. That was romance, this was truth. The nightcap itself was but a snare, a broken snare.

He flung it angrily back to the floor and went on packing his bachelor things to take back into his bachelor future. The little cap lay huddled—as she had crouched when he flung her out of his arms. She had whispered, "I understand." It seemed also not to reproach him. But it was very beautiful. He could not leave it there for some servant to find. Especially not, as she had prophesied just such a result and he had promised to keep it secret. He picked it up. It was fragrant and pink and silken and lacy—as she was.

He rebuked himself for venting his spite on an inanimate object, a nightcap of all things! Thence he was led to reproach himself for condemning Persis. She, too, was knitted and bow-knotted together with the sole purpose of being exquisite. As well blame the nightcap for not being a helmet as blame Persis for not being a heroine.

He found himself caressing the cap and murmuring to it. He folded it tenderly and slipped it into the suit-case. Then he took it out and put it in the inside pocket of his waistcoat. It seemed to nestle there, and he felt a lurch in his heart, as if Persis had just crept back into it and curled up to sleep. He buttoned them in, Persis and the nightcap, and, closing his suit-cases, carried them down-stairs as one does in a hotel where there are no bell-boys.

He found Willie Enslee staring at him, rubbing his eyes. Willie had wakened only a moment before, had realized the hour with bewilderment, had tried the front door and found it still locked. He was just wondering where Forbes and Mrs. Neff had spent the night when Forbes walked down the stairs and said "Good morning!" but with a queer tone and an odd something in his eyes.

Willie drowsily answered "G'maw!" and stared harder, for Mrs. Neff came down the steps after Forbes. She was sneezing so violently that she had to cling to the banister-rail to keep from sneezing herself into space.

She did not see Willie; but her appearance and her sneeze confirmed his theory. He backed out through a side door and made his way through the kitchen and up the stairway there to his own room. His mind was still fumbling with the riddle of how Forbes and Mrs. Neff got in.

He wondered what he should tell Persis when she asked him what had happened during his night-watch. He had promised her great things from his practical joke. But she never asked him, and he was so greatly relieved that he never broached the subject himself.

Breakfast was served more slipshoddily than before.

Even the novelty of the experience had gone. Henceforward Winifred was converted to the vital importance of servants.

Persis was the last to appear. Mrs. Neff greeted her with:

"Persis, your eyes are all red. Have you been cry-cr-cry-ing-g-gk!" She finished with an almost decapitating sneeze. It gave Persis a hint.

"I caught cold, too," she said. "The change in the weather."

The explanation sufficed to satisfy Mrs. Neff and to convince Forbes that Persis was dangerously apt at concealments.

When the breakfast was eaten the dishes were washed and dried at Winifred's direction. But when it came to what Forbes called "policing the camp," it was unanimously voted to leave that to the gardener and his wife, or to the caretaker on his return.

The three automobiles rolled up through the rain, all shipshape for the storm, with tops hooded and side-curtains buttoned down snugly.

Forbes remembered that other rain with Persis in the taxicab. How much better the opportunity here, with the world shut out from view and two hours' cruise ahead. But he was again consigned to Mrs. Neff's car, and it was Willie Enslee who had Persis and the opportunity. Forbes could not follow even the flutter of her veil. All he could see ahead was the shoulder of Mrs. Neff's chauffeur and the windshield studded and streaked with rain.

There was no landscape to divert the mind, only his imagination of the courtship Willie would be paying to his newly announced fiancée. Forbes pictured the privileges he would exact, and Persis would not deny. And he gnashed his teeth in wrath. In the cave of Mrs. Neff's car Alice had nothing to say. She was thinking too eagerly ahead. Mrs. Neff had nothing to say. She was wondering what Alice was so cheerful about.

And so the car pushed south, with no passing scenery to indicate progress, only the bumps and teeterings, the swerves and slitherings, and the nauseating belches of noise made by the horn. Eventually the wheels ceased to run upon irregular ground and glided on asphalt. This must be New York.

At Seventy-second Street they turned off Broadway and crossed Central Park. At the eastern gate Mrs. Neff's chauffeur checked his car alongside a whale-like mass, from which Willie Enslee's voice was heard shrilly calling through the rain:

"Good-by, Mrs. Neff! Good-by Alice! Good-by Mr. Wa—er—Forbes. Awfully glad you could come. See you again. Go on to Miss Cabot's house." This last to his own driver.

Mrs. Neff and Alice cried in unison: "Good-by! Had lovely time! See you soon!"

And out of space came the disembodied voice of Persis as from a grave: "Good-by, Mrs. Neff! By-by, Alice! Good-by, Mr. Forbes!"

"Good-by, P—Miss Cabot!" he called. Her voice trailed away as if it were her soul going to death, and his voice followed with an ache of despair in it. Mrs. Neff caught the pathos hovering over the cries like overtones sounding above and beyond a tone of music. She said:

"Too bad you let Willie take her away from you; it's not too late yet if you've any ambition."

Forbes smiled dully, and Alice said:

"Mother, you do say the most tactless things!"

"I had set my heart on that love-match," sighed Mrs. Neff.

"Better begin at home," said Alice, with unusual cheer.

Mrs. Neff changed the subject. "We'll get out at our house, if you don't mind, and the man can take you to your hotel."

"That's mighty kind of you," said Forbes. He helped them to alight, promised to call, and re-entered the car.

On his way to the hotel he pondered what Mrs. Neff had said. It cheered him until he realized she was still assuming that he had a respectable income. If she had known the truth she would have thought him as unfit for Persis as she thought Stowe Webb unfit for Alice. She would have approved Persis' theory that such a wedding was impossible.

It is doleful travel that takes one home from an unaccomplished errand—only Forbes was not returning even to his home. His home was as shifty as a Methodist minister's. At present it was a hotel, and after that the army post.

And now those duties which he had dreaded so to resume became in his mind a refuge. He had spent a few wild days pursuing a will-o'-the-wisp of a woman's whim through a moonlit marsh, never sure which turn it would take, sure only that it would not be where he expected it to be.

After such a maddening recreation there was a kind of heaven in the thought of living according to a rigid program. At such an hour a bugle would exclaim and drums would ruffle, and the day's work would begin. At such an hour a roll-call would be due, or a sick-call, or a guard-mount call, or a headquarters call. Certain books were to be inspected and corrected; certain men were to be taught to do certain things exactly so. If there were ever a doubt, the answer was printed in a book, or in an order numbered and dated.

Everything was gloriously impersonal and objective, accurate and material.

Forbes understood the spirit of old convicts who, after cursing their penitentiaries for years, are let out into the world's turmoil, and by and by return, pleading to be let in again.

Only yesterday he had been trying to concoct schemes for postponing the date of his return to duty; now he was resolved to anticipate it.

WHAT WILL PEOPLE SAY?

He paid his bill at the hotel—with further erosion of the bank-account—and took the Subway and the ferry to Governor's Island.

The first sentinel he encountered recognized him for an officer by his shoulders and his carriage; and, halting on his post at just the right distance, faced outward and presented arms with decorative rigidity. As Forbes' hand went to the brim of his derby hat it felt a vizor there, and his heart went up in thanks. And his eyes went to the colors!—the little piece of wrinkling sky in the corner and the red stripes swimming in luxurious curves.

Next Forbes noted a doting smile half hidden by a saluting hand. It was a sergeant who had served with him in the Philippines; the very man Forbes had been shouting to when the bullet passed through his cheek; the very sergeant who had carried him half a mile to a field hospital in a rain of sun that beat upon the head like a thug's sandbag. That was man's work. Forbes returned the salute and shook the hand of the sergeant. As he remembered, he had got the sergeant out of some woman scrape. Why should good soldiers always be so easily defeated by women?

And next he met two officers he had known in West Point and in Cuba and at Manila. The small army of the United States seemed hardly more than a large club.

One of these officers, Major Chatham, dragged Forbes to his home for dinner—as pretty a home as a man could wish, with as pretty a wife and two children. And they had a maid to wait on them—and they kept a little automobile, too, the major being his own chauffeur. They seemed happy. Perhaps it was only manners, but the wife seemed as happy as a lark—or, rather, a canary. And yet Forbes could see how she differed from Persis. And he was glad that he had not brought a sea-gull down there for a mate.

He left, after his first cigar, on a pretext of unpacking. In the late twilight the sea-gulls that swung and tilted and dipped about the bay like little air-yachts did not seem so desirable, after all. He declared himself emancipated and contented. He thrust his head high and bulged his chest and walked soldierly.

And so he prospered till he was alone in his quarters, and the dark closed in and he turned on the light, and set about the establishment of his effects with all the fanatic neatness and order a West Point training could give a man.

He put his coats and overcoats on the hangers, and the trousers in their holders, flat and creased, and set his shoes out in rows, and the boxes of belts and spurs, and the sword-cases, and the various hat-boxes. He took off his civilian coat and waistcoat—and found in the inside pocket that perfumed nightcap.

And then he wanted Persis! He thirsted and hungered for her. He fevered for her. He called himself names, reasoned, laughed, cursed, tried to read, to write; but "Persis! Persis! Persis!" ran among his thoughts like a tune that can neither be seized nor forgotten. He put out the light, flung up the curtain and the window, and a soft breeze moving from the ocean up the bay seemed to pause like a serenader and croon her name. The torch of the Statue of Liberty glowed like a chained star, and it seemed to be that planet which was Persis and which he could not reach.

Only last night she was in his arms, in his power, and so afraid of him that she cried to him for help from her love; and he had given her up—given her back to herself!

He had kept her pure that Enslee might take her intact! His nobility seemed very cheap to him now. He repented his virtue. If he had taken her then he could have kept her for his own. Now that she had escaped she would never risk the danger again. She had told him so. And she could be very wise, very cold, very resolute.

That night was a condensed eternity. The next morning's duties were performed in a kind of somnambulism.

WHAT WILL PEOPLE SAY?

The second day brought his commission as captain. He glanced over it listlessly and tossed it aside.

For years he had fretted for this document, focused his ambitions on it, upbraided a tardy government for withholding it so long. And now that it was here he sneered at the accolade of it. The increase of pay was a mere sarcasm; it brought him no nearer his planet than going to the roof and standing on tiptoe would have done. The commandant congratulated him. His fellow-officers wrung his hand. He was no longer to be called "Mr. Forbes," but "Captain Forbes." He had a title. But what was the good of it? It did not even make him a rival of Enslee, whose only title was "Little Willie."

Now and then the profundity of his gloom was quickened with resolutions to seek Persis, to storm her home and carry her off. Perhaps that was what she was waiting for. He had often read that women love to be overmastered. Then his pride would revolt. It was not his way of courtship.

But at least he would telephone her. Then he remembered the fruitless effort he had made to discover her number—that mystical "private wire." Ten Eyck would know it. He would call up Ten Eyck. With the receiver off the hook and Central asking, "Number, please?" he grew afraid and answered, "Never mind." He dared not invite another of Ten Eyck's fatherly lectures.

Besides, if Persis cared enough for him to grant him an interview she would seek it herself. But perhaps she had called up the hotel and found him gone. Perhaps she was afraid to call up the post and have him summoned. Women do not like to call up men's organizations; it is like visiting them.

No! she had undoubtedly crossed him off her books, as he ought to cross her off his. He ought to write the word "Dropped" under her name, as under that of a soldier who was out of the service.

And so he tossed hope and despair like a mad juggler

who cannot rest. On the third day, when he came from the parade-ground, he was informed that he had been wanted on the telephone. He was to call up such a number. "Yes, sir, it was a lady's voice, sir."

It must be Persis. No, it might be an operator in a hotel. It might be her maid. It might be anybody. It proved to be the telephone-girl in the office of Senator Tait.

In a moment, by the occult influence of the telephone, the unknown woman vanished and Senator Tait's soul was in communication with his. The genial heart seemed to quiver in the air.

"That you, Harvey?"

"Yes. Hello, Senator."

"You sound mighty doleful, my boy. Anything the matter?"

"No, I'm all right."

"Are you sure you're not dead? You disappeared so completely I thought you might be. You sound as if you wished you were."

"Oh no, I'm all right."

"Can't you come up to the house for dinner to-night?"

He realized that this would mean meeting Mildred— and dressing in his evening things. He did not want to put on his evening things. They had danced with Persis last. He did not want to meet any woman. He was in mourning. All this flashed through his mind while he was inventing an excuse of official duty.

"To-morrow night, then?"

"Terribly sorry. I can't get off."

"How about lunch? At the club—to-morrow."

"I'd like that."

"I have something to discuss with you."

"I'll be there! At one?"

"Fine! One o'clock. Metropolitan Club. Do you know where it is?"

"I'll find it."

"Good! Perhaps Mildred can be there."

"Fine!" His voice wavered. He was trapped. He had not guessed that the club would have an annex. The Senator felt the constraint across the wire. It hurt him, but he laughed.

"Cheer up! Maybe she can't come!"

"Oh, I—I hope she can. She's—I'd love to see her, I assure you."

"All right. Don't worry. Good-by."

The Senator was laughing, but there was a wounded pride in his voice. Forbes hung up the telephone, feeling a cad and an ingrate.

CHAPTER XLV

THE next forenoon, having obtained the privilege of absence, Forbes crossed from Governor's Island to Manhattan Island, took the Subway from South Ferry to Fifty-ninth Street, and, entering Central Park, kept along its southernmost path till he reached the Plaza, where he paused a moment to admire Saint - Gaudens' statue of General Sherman, a gilded warrior on a gilded horse squired by a gilded girl—Victory or Peace or something, he was not sure just what.

In his present humor of misogyny he wondered why it was thought to be necessary to put a woman in everything. Of all the campaigns where she was lacking, surely the March to the Sea was among her most conspicuous absences. But he admired the lean warrior with the doffed hat and the splendid stride of the big horse—a very different horse from the Park horses he found, with their tan-clad grooms clustered at the mounting-blocks near by.

Toward this starting-point fat women with looped-up skirts and top-hats and little knock-kneed girls in breeches were hurrying. He smiled with the superiority of a cavalry officer.

Among the living caricatures were a few expert riders. Suddenly Forbes' heart shivered and raced with a feeling that a certain one of them might be Persis. Surely there could not be another back so trim, another grip so firm. But it was his longing that created the resemblance, for as the horse whirled and loped away he caught sight of the woman's profile. It was less like Persis' profile than like the horse's!

But the moment's agitation had gone like an earth-quake through his calmed soul. It shook down the towers of resolution and independence and sickened him with the instability of his poise.

He would have turned back from his engagement, but he had not even the strength for that much action. He crossed the Avenue to where the Metropolitan Club stood four square in its gray and white dignity. As he passed through the carved and colonnaded entrance - court a motor-car deposited two women at the door of the annex.

He feared that one of them might be Mildred; but he was unnecessarily alarmed. Mildred had pleaded official duties. She had shown the same reluctance Forbes had revealed. Perhaps she saw through her father's motives. But the old Senator was willing to wait. He was a born compromiser, a genius at making fusions out of factions.

When Forbes entered the club and asked for Tait, the doorman consulted the roster-board, and, finding a crib-bage peg opposite the Senator's name, sent a page for him. He was not far to fetch, and he was in a humor of Falstaffian heartiness. He came upon Forbes' foggy mood like a morning sun. He was just what Forbes needed.

He clapped his arm across Forbes' shoulder, and, as he registered him in the guest-book, wrote the new word "Captain" large, and pointed to it; then dragged Forbes to the cigar-case and commanded "the biggest cigar there is, one with a solid-gold wrapper." He treated the forlorn victim of a woman's jilt as a notable worthy of notable entertainment. It was the lift that the prodigal son got when he slunk home and was met with a bouquet instead of blame.

He led Forbes into the great central hall, with its white-marble cliffs and its red-velveted double stairway mount-ing like a huge St. Andrew's cross, placed him on a settle where a platoon of men might have sat a-knee, and gave the bell a royal bang. He recommended a special cocktail, and joined Forbes in it in joyous disobedience of his physician's warning.

When the cocktail arrived Forbes gave him the army toast of "How!" and Tait answered "Happy days!" On the way up to the dining-room he led Forbes through the building, pausing before the crimson opulence of the two reading-rooms; the lounging-room, with its windows commanding Fifth Avenue; the card-rooms, deserted battle-fields now; the board-rooms, where committees gathered to settle huge financial destinies, the solemn library walled solid with books.

Forbes wondered at the almost complete absence of other people in the club; but Tait explained that most of the members were hard-working millionaires who lunched down-town "or took their dinner-pails with them," some of them hardly stopping to eat a sandwich from a desk leaf.

On the top floor their luncheon awaited them at a table by the window. As Forbes drew his napkin across his knee he gazed down at the corner of the Park and the lake where white swans drifted like the toy sloops of children. From this height the hills and curving walks looked miniature as a Japanese garden.

When the clam-shells were emptied they were replaced with chicken, a second waiter served rice, and a third curry. It was strangely comforting to be well served with choice food in a beautiful room above a beautiful scene. He felt that in places like this wealth justified itself— wealth the upholsterer, the caterer, the artist, the butler.

Forbes looked down at a shuffling vagrant slouching across the Plaza. He felt sorry for that man, and yet was glad that he was here instead of there. He wished that he himself might belong to this delightful place they called the "Millionaire's Club." He longed for riches, especially as they would mean Persis. He remembered what she had said: "The rich can get anything that the poor have, but the poor can't get what the rich have." The rich Enslee could even get Persis.

He sat musing bitterly, forgetting that he had a host, and unaware that the host was looking at him with sad affection, not resenting his listlessness, but hoping to relieve it. Remembering Forbes' father, Tait knew that he must move warily about that sensitive Forbes pride, as swift to strike an awkward hand as a caged tiger that greets an unwelcome caress with a wound.

Tait hesitated to open his real business. He began obliquely.

"Well, I've just fired the first gun in my war with Mrs. Neff."

"Yes?" said Forbes, drearily.

"Yes," said Tait, positively. "Just before you came young Stowe Webb was here—nice young fellow. I sent for him, and said to him: 'Young man, Miss Alice Neff, whom I believe you know'—he blushed like a house afire—'tells me,' I said, 'that her mother objects to you because you have no money.' He flashed me a look of amazement, and I said: 'If you need money, why don't you make it?' And he said: 'How can I?' 'Why, money is growing on bushes everywhere,' I said, 'just waiting to be picked off; poor men are getting rich every day,' I said; and he said: 'Yes, and rich men are getting poor. My family is one of the bushes, and we've been pretty well picked. My father left me nothing but his blessing, and I can't pawn that,' he said. 'Still, I'm not dead yet,' he said. 'I'll show you all some day.' And I said: 'There must be something in any man that a good girl loves and believes in. And any girl that's worth having is worth working for, and if she really wants you she'll wait for you.' And then I lowered my voice about an octave and growled, 'I wonder if you have the grit to go out in this hard old world and work for that girl and— and earn her?' He said, 'You bet I have!' So I said: 'Well, I know where there's a job you might get; it's small salary and a lot of work at first, and by and by a little more salary and much harder work; and you won't be able to see her often; perhaps not at all for a long while; but eventually, if she'll wait, you'll be able to support her as well as any girl needs to be supported who has love in the bargain. Do you want that job, young man?' I said, glaring at him. And he said: 'Lead me to it!'"

Forbes listened with eagerness and envy. The portrait of Alice, who would wait till her lover worked his way up to a competence, contrasted sharply with Persis, who would not accept the competence Forbes already had. He asked, with an effort at enthusiasm:

"And what is the job?"

"I'm going to make him my secretary, at twelve hundred a year, at first. He won't be worth it, and I'll have to do all my own work for a while; but I'll give him his chance. I won't pamper him. I'll test him out—and her, too. If they can't stand the test they wouldn't last long in the battle of matrimony."

"Your secretary?" said Forbes. "Does he know any law?"

"I'm not going to be a lawyer. I'm going to be a diplomat—in Paris."

"Splendid!" cried Forbes, reaching across to squeeze his hand. "I congratulate the country—and France. I envy you Paris. I've never been there."

"How would you like to go?"

"How should I like to be a major-general?"

Tait opened his lips to say something important, then stammered, and said instead:

"Waiter, give Captain Forbes some more of that curry. It's good here, isn't it?"

"Splendid," said Forbes, who had hardly touched what was on his plate.

Senator Tait shifted uncomfortably, made to speak, pursed his lips, eyed Forbes, and then said, with abrupt irrelevance:

"I was wrong, I see, about old Cabot."

"Were you?" Forbes mumbled, with a sudden flush at the broaching of that dangerous theme.

"Yes, I said that he was to be closed up, forced into involuntary bankruptcy, and all that."

"Wasn't he?" said Forbes, weakly.

"No, he got money and credit and a new start—from the Enslee estates. There is a rumor that his daughter is to marry Willie Enslee. I thought that perhaps you—did you—did you hear anything of it—from Enslee?"

Tait made an elaborate pretense of indifference and showed a violent interest in the leg of a chicken. Forbes turned curry-color with shame as he answered: "Yes, Enslee announced the engagement himself—the very day I saw you last."

His head drooped as if his neck could no longer hold it up. Tait noted his harrowed look and broke out angrily:

"Don't be cut up, my boy, just because she's fool enough to marry a bigger fool than herself."

"Oh, please!" Forbes protested. He could have struck a younger man in Persis' defense, but he could only appeal to so old a man as Tait. Tait, however, persisted:

"You ought to be glad to be revenged so neatly."

Forbes was in desperate case; he laughed bitterly. "Revenge is a little late. My life is ruined. I might as well put an end to it."

The old man stared at the tragic face, the brow corded with veins, the eyes fanatic with despair. He could not believe that so brilliant an officer could kill himself. And yet men did kill themselves—several thousand every year. When Forbes' father was a young man courting the fickle young beauty who was later to become the so steadfast wife and the mother of Forbes, they had quarreled, and Forbes' father had been frantic with grief, had threatened self-destruction. Tait himself had taken the revolver away from him and helped to lift him across the dark waters of jealousy. It startled him to see the father's black despair repeated in the son. He felt that he must repeat the rescue.

Yet, as humanity is constituted, tragedy becomes grotesque when it is repeated. He felt a certain helpless amusement at finding the son just as desperate as the father had been. He had laughed the elder Forbes out of his gloom. He attempted to ridicule the son free of the same obsession. He spoke in a low tone surcharged with an anxiety whose exaggeration was too dolorous to catch.

"You say that you can't stand the loss of Miss Cabot, and you might as well commit suicide?"

"I might as well."

"I'll tell you, Harvey, let's commit suicide together!" Forbes' haggard glance showed that he was not yet awake to the old man's parody of his solemnity.

"Do you mean it?" Forbes asked.

"Yes," Tait murmured; "all good Americans go to Paris when they die—let's go to Paris."

Now Forbes caught the twinkle in his eye. It took him off his guard. It was as if some one had made a funny face at a funeral. A guffaw of laughter escaped him. It shocked him and shamed him, but it shattered his depression.

Tait seized the opportunity of Forbes' disorder and urged his idea:

"I've got to have a military attaché, you know. I could get the billet for you."

"Why select me for the honor? You'll be beset with applications."

"Yes, but I like you, Harvey. You are your father come to life again. I love you—as if you were your father —or my son. I'm old. I need young shoulders to lean on. I've nobody else but you. And you need me. You've had a whack in the solar plexus. You're seeing stars. But you mustn't let 'em count you out. Once you get your breath you'll be as good a man as you ever were. But don't lie down and take the count.

"Besides, I can help you while you're helping me. It's a new world for you, Harvey. Nobody ought to die without seeing France and England—the Old World that's so much newer than ours and so much wiser in so many ways. It's your opportunity. It may mean wonderful things for you. You can't refuse. You won't refuse, will you?"

The very impact of his blows pounded Harvey's cold heart to a glow. The word "opportunity" glinted like a shower of sparks in the night. He smiled in spite of himself. He felt such a leap of new blood in his arteries, such a rush of fresh air into his lungs, that he seemed to waken from a coma. He could not speak, but he thrust his hand across the table and wrung the Senator's fat old fingers till they ached.

CHAPTER XLVI

WILLIE ENSLEE was as little masculine as a man could be without being in the least effeminate. Ten Eyck, whose French was more fluent than exact, called him "*petite*." His head was small and childish, and the more infantile for a great rearward overhang that would have looked better on a yacht. His voice was high and trebling in its sound. His costumes were always of next season or the season after next. Yet, carefully as he dressed, his clothes never dignified him nor he them. Rich as he was, he attracted few parasites.

Now, no one realized Willie Enslee's defects half so thoroughly as did Willie Enslee. But his failings did not amuse him as they did other people; he could not laugh with the world at himself. He knew the world laughed at him, and not without cause, and yet he hated the world for its laughter. He hated everybody he knew almost as much as he hated himself. To this misanthropy there was one exception—Persis. He hated her, too, in a way, for she never concealed her scorn of him, and she ridiculed his foibles before his face; but he found her so beautiful that he loved her while he loathed her, desired while he abhorred.

He found her cold and flippant to his most earnest moods, but he assumed that she was cold and flippant to everybody else. She certainly had that reputation, and he comforted himself with the feeling that, while she may have failed in response to his ardors, it was not because she was in love with anybody else.

So little jealousy he had—or, rather, so slow a jealousy—

318

that the silly theory of Forbes' flirtation with Mrs. Neff sufficed to prevent him from paying the slightest attention to Forbes' conversation with Persis. Lack of jealousy is sometimes a form of conceit. Perhaps it was this feeling that no woman could prefer any other man to an Enslee that led him to ignore the ordinary caution of a lover. Perhaps it was just his idolatry of Persis, his inability to believe her capable of the infamy of duplicity.

But somewhere in his soul there must have been a latent spark of suspicion which might some day burst into a consuming flame, for into his dreams came now and then little glints of uneasiness. He dismissed them as the results of indigestion, but they persisted.

One day, shortly after his return from his Westchester estate, he sat down in the living-room of his town house to read the evening papers. All of them published the announcement of his engagement to Persis, under the general heading of "June brides." There were portraits of Persis in various poses and costumes. Willie saw no picture of himself, and the allusions to him were mainly concerned with "William Enslee, Esq., son of the famous William Enslee."

Willie took so much pride in the fame of his betrothed that he was not jealous even of her monopoly of the newspaper attention. He felt only a great pride in being the future owner of all that beauty.

He lolled on the divan and smoked the cigarettes of prosperity. The divan was so comfortable, and his satisfaction so soothing, that he grew drowsy. His jaw fell open as his eyes fell shut. The newspapers dropped to the floor, and he was asleep.

Into the room, which was now almost ready for the closing of the house and the emigration to Newport or the country, came his mother, a young matron whose aristocratic face and figure were markedly Spanish. Her black hair was fogged with gray at the temples, as if with a careless powder-puff. She pushed back the covering of the mirror over the mantel that she might catch a glimpse of her hair.

She brightened at the vision she saw within, and not without reason, for she had broken many hearts in Cuba and in New York before the elder William Enslee won her and married her. The only result of the union had been that at his death he left a widow who was more attractive than a widow has a right to be, and a son who was less attractive even than is expected of a millionaire's son.

As Mrs. Enslee stared at her image in the looking-glass Willie's heavy breathing caught her ear, and she heard that he was asleep even before she saw him. And then she spoke sharply:

"But you mustn't sleep here. Go to your own room— or the club."

"Let me alone," Willie protested, with querulous anger, still befuddled, and relapsing at once into sleep.

"When I was young parents weren't spoken to like that," said Mrs. Enslee, forgetting how she used to speak to her parents. She paused to muse upon her man-child. She felt sorry for him, but sorrier for herself for having him. As she watched him he began to mumble a gibberish. She bent closer to hear. Then his hand, hanging limply near the floor, began to clench and twitch.

Suddenly from his lips broke a half-strangled gurgle, then a wild shriek of "Persis! Persis!"

His own outcry seemed to waken him. His eyes flew open, and he stared about him as if searching for some one whose absence bewildered him.

His mother peered into his eyes, and he clutched her by the arms, staring at her. Then he mumbled:

"Oh, it's you," and smiled foolishly, and laughed as with a great relief.

"What is it, my boy?" said Mrs. Enslee.

"I must have dropped off to sleep. It was only a dream."

"What was it?" Mrs. Enslee repeated; but he spoke with a sickly cheer:

"That's the one consolation about nightmares, when you wake up—thank God, they're not true!"

"But what did you dream?" Mrs. Enslee demanded till he explained:

"Well, it seemed to be my—er—wedding-day. And I was standing there by Persis—I was—er—fumbling in my pocket for the—er—ring, and feeling like a fool—because she's so much taller than I am—and the preacher said, 'If anybody knows any—er—reason why these two should not be—er—wed, let him speak now, or forever—'"

"Yes, yes," said his audience of one.

"There was—er—silence for a minute. Then a man stood up in the church—I couldn't see his face—but he was tall, and he called out—er, 'I forbid the banns! She loves me. She is only marrying that man for his—er—money!' I turned to Persis and said: 'Is that true?' And she said: 'I don't know the man. I never saw him.' And then, when she said that, he gave her one look and—er—walked out of the church. And the —er—ceremony went on. But Persis shivered all the time—er—just shivered, and when I kissed her her lips were like—er—like ice. Then the music began, and we marched down the aisle—and then—then we—er—er—no, I won't tell you."

"Go on—please go on!" the mother pleaded; but Willie grew embarrassed, and his eyes wandered as he stammered:

"Well—at last—we were in our room—and I—er—she shrank away from me as if I were—er—a toad. And she swore she hated me—and loved the—er—other man. Then I saw everything red—I hated her. I wanted to throttle her—to tear her to pieces. But she ran to the window and fell, all—er—tangled up in the veil and the long train. I tried to save her—but I couldn't. And then — when it was too late — my love for her came back, and I cried, 'Persis! Persis!' and—er—woke up. Mother, do you believe in—er—dreams?"

"No, no, of course not," said Mrs. Enslee, without conviction. "Or else they go by contraries."

"Ugh! How real they are while they last. I can't get over it."

"Well, of course, I'm not superstitious," Mrs. Enslee insinuated; "but, if you are, perhaps—I just say perhaps—it might be a sort of omen that you'd better not marry Persis, after all."

"Not marry Persis!" Willie gasped.

"There are other women on earth," Mrs. Enslee suggested.

"Not for me!"

Mrs. Enslee pondered a moment before she took up the debate again. "But do you think she loves you as much as you'd like to be loved?"

Willie laughed. "Huh! nobody ever loved me like that; nobody ever will."

"Except your mother," said Mrs. Enslee, laying her hand on his hair. Willie hated to have his hair smoothed, and he edged away, laughingly bitterly.

"I'm afraid even you've found me—er—unattractive, mother. I couldn't have been much to be proud of even as a little brat. I never had a chum as a boy. I never had a girl—er—sweetheart. It wasn't that I didn't like other people, but other people can't seem to—er—like me."

He pondered the mystery so tragically that Mrs. Enslee caressed him, and said: "You mustn't say that. *I* adore you."

Willie eyed her with a cynical stare. "Don't be—er—literary, mother. I remember when I was a little boy how lonely I used to get in this big old house. Poor father was so busy heaping up money I hardly knew him by sight. Once he—er—passed me on the street and didn't speak to me! Then at night you used to give big dinners.

I had to eat early and alone up in the—er—nursery. But I used to lie awake for hours, and when the doors opened I could hear laughter. And often there was music. You used to go down to dinner after I had gone to bed."

"But I always stopped in to kiss you good night, didn't I?" the mother urged, in self-defense.

"Sometimes you would forget," Willie sighed. "Then I'd be left there alone with the governess. I didn't want to—er—speak French to a governess. I wanted to—er—talk to my mother. And when you did stop in to kiss me, your lips sometimes used to—er—leave red marks on my cheek."

"Willie!" Mrs. Enslee gasped; but he went on:

"I couldn't put my arms around your neck for fear I'd—er—disarrange your hair, and even that was—er—dyed!"

Mrs. Enslee turned on him in rage. "Willie! How dare you?"

He rounded on her fiercely. "You know it was! You know it was!"

"You little beast!" Mrs. Enslee cried; but Willie laughed maliciously.

"See! See! Now you're showing your—er—real feelings to me."

Mrs. Enslee controlled her pain and her wrath, and implored: "Come, my boy, let's be friends."

"Oh, that's all right, mother," said Willie. "Friends is the word. It's too late for anything else."

"You're in one of your nasty moods, Willie," said Mrs. Enslee, retreating from this hateful situation. "But we were talking of Persis. You must decide about her."

"I have decided."

"You won't marry her, then?"

"Not marry her?" Willie repeated, like a sarcastic echo. "Of course I will. And why not?"

Motives are hard tangles to unravel, especially a mother's toward other women. Perhaps Mrs. Enslee was really afraid of Persis. Perhaps she wanted to assure herself of the future ability to say, "I warned you." Perhaps it was just motherly jealousy of the new proprietress of Willie's time and attention. In answer to Willie's "Why not?" she insinuated: "People might say she is marrying you for your money."

"Well, what of it? What if she is?" Willie stormed. "What else is there to marry me for? My—er—beauty? What does it matter, so I get her? Why do dukes marry —er—chorus-girls—when they can afford 'em? Because they want 'em! That's why, isn't it? What fools they'd be not to take 'em if they want 'em and can get 'em?"

His mother shrugged his troubles from her shoulders and left him to ferment in his own vinegar. But Willie was not happy. He was getting what he asked for, and it was not what he wanted. Perhaps he had never been truly happy in his whole existence. He had been amused at times, but usually then with a cynical delight in somebody's misfortunes or mistakes.

How could he have been thoroughly happy when he had never been truly well? What health he had was a negation, a convalescence; it was at best a not being sick. He was of a fabric that broke down and wore through constantly. He could understand the definition of happiness as "having a splinter in your finger and getting it out."

But the joy that comes from bounding arteries, glowing skin, a galloping heart, a volcanic desire to laugh because the soul is bursting with laughter, or to sing for mere song's sake, or to be an instrument in the symphonic universe when it is playing one of its mighty ensembles —that cosmic happiness was unknown to Willie Enslee.

When he found a rapture he always found something the matter with it; there was a worm in the apple, a slug in the salad, a fly in the ointment, a flaw in the diamond. And so it was with his one big ambition—Persis. He had won his choice of all the world's women. And now his mother was asking if he thought she loved him, and if people would not question her motives. She was already perhapsing and better-notting.

And he was dreaming dreams that somebody else had a priority in her heart. Of course, dreams were follies. According to some superstitions, they went by contraries. But they are as hard to disbelieve as a convincing play. One may not be sure that Josephine was untrue to Napoleon; but he knows that Mrs. Tanqueray II. had a most inconvenient lover, and that her past spoiled her husband's daughter's future.

So Willie, emerging from the playhouse of his nightmare, wondered who it was that was likely to interrupt his wedding with Persis. He suspected everybody except Forbes. Him he canceled at once from the list, because Forbes had met Persis only a week ago, and had never seen her alone, and had, furthermore, devoted himself to Mrs. Neff. He set Forbes down as a fortune-hunter willing to marry a much older woman of moderate means. He doubted if he were important enough for an invitation to the wedding.

He could not decide upon any other man to fit the faceless vision of his nightmare, that shadowy being who stood up in the dream-cathedral and claimed Persis for his own. He was tempted to ask Persis. But he was not tempted long. Naturally she would deny it; but what if she should confess? Then he would have to give her up. And he wanted her more than anything else on earth.

He resolved that the one safe step was to get Persis safely married at once and take her away from all of her acquaintances. Aboard his yacht would be one secure asylum. When they tired of that they could travel Europe, and the moment any old friend appeared he could decamp with her overnight.

He chuckled triumphantly over this plot, and set about its perfection. He rejoiced to be in a position to compel

Persis by way of her father's necessities. The support he had advanced to the "old flub" he could threaten to withdraw unless the wedding were hastened. That would clinch it.

And then he glowed with the imagined scenes of the honeymoon. Persis might not love him as he wished, but he would have her for his own. He would have as much of her as any man could be sure of in possessing a woman. He knew he was not handsome, but he knew handsome men whose homely wives were notoriously false to them. Did he not know of wild romances that had ended in mutual contempt? Did he not know of unpromising beginnings that had ended in happiness? Monogamy was a gamble at best. And at worst he should have Persis for his own for a while.

CHAPTER XLVII

WHEN Willie's mother left him in the aftermath of his nightmare she went to pay her duty call on Persis, to welcome her formally into the family and proffer her the use of the family name.

There was the most gleaming cordiality on the surface of their meeting, but the depths of both streams were a trifle murky. Willie's mother understood now why her own husband's fierce old mother, known as "Medusa" Enslee, had received her with such constraint on a similar occasion. That mother had had to give up part of her name, too, and step back from being queen to being queen-mother, with endless confusion in the newspapers, the invitations, the correspondence, and the gossip.

The present Mrs. Enslee felt now a sympathy for the old woman she had hated. But it crowded out the sympathy she should have felt for Persis, who was suffering what she had suffered as a young-woman-afraid-of-her-mother-in-law.

It was bitter for Willie's mother, still beautiful, feeling herself as young as ever, to realize that henceforth she must be the "the elder," or, worse yet, the "old Mrs. Enslee." Perhaps in a year or two a grandmother! It would be just like Persis to hasten that ghastly day.

At present Persis was not thinking of motherhood. She would have called it quite a ghastly day herself—one to be postponed by every ingenuity and subtlety known to American womanhood. She was thinking of her new name.

"You'll be Mrs. Enslee, and I suppose I'll be Mrs. William Enslee, or Mrs. Little Willie, sha'n't I, mama?

327

Do you want me to call you mama, or shall I stick to Mrs. Enslee?"

"As you like, my dear," said Mrs. Enslee, with a little shudder at being "mama" to a strange woman and a rival. Persis rattled on in ill-managed embarrassment.

"It will be pretty mixy with two Mrs. William Enslees, won't it? Like two in a single bed—pardon me! I'll have to be awfully good or awfully careful, sha'n't I, for fear my letters may fall into your hands? But I'll promise not to give away what I find in yours if you won't tell on me."

Mrs. Enslee was rather pleased than offended at this. At least it credited her with the ability to create scandal.

She was like Mrs. Neff in hating to get too old to be suspected.

She smiled at Persis with Spanish coquetry, and offered her aid in the appalling details of announcing the engagement. It was the new mode to use the telephone for the more intimate friends. For others there were letters, calls, advertisements, luncheons, and dinners in all the exquisite degrees of familiarity.

She and Persis were going into business for a while on a large scale—a business for which Persis was peculiarly fitted and in which she developed an extraordinary energy.

When Persis had returned to New York from the Enslee country place to find her father helpless and dejected, the offer of Willie's aid had acted like a magic elixir. It had meant the payment of old bills, or their enlargement, and the opening of new credits. Dealers whom the mercantile agencies had secretly filled with alarm for the Cabot accounts had been subtly reassured.

In place of letters of pathetic appeal for a little something to meet a pay-roll there came letters announcing private views of new importations. Persis' own father called her his loan-broker, and said that she had earned the usual commission; he ordered her to buy new things.

He complained of the shabbiness of her hats. Why hadn't she bought the lot she had spoken to him about some time ago? She did at once—and more.

Persis was like a child waking from a bad dream to find that it is Christmas morning and that its stockings are cornucopias spilling over with glittering toys.

And what woman lives that does not find more rapture in shopping with a full purse or an elastic charge-account than in any other earthly or spiritual pleasure?

The barbaric love of beads and red feathers and mirrors has never been civilized out of the sex. The male succeeds in love and elsewhere by what he thinks and makes and gives; the female by what she looks and wears and extracts. The shops are her art-museums, her gymnasiums, her paradises, and the privilege of reveling among them is more voluptuous than any other of her sensualities. Shopping takes the place of exploration. That is her Wanderlust.

And so when Willie Enslee arrived at the Cabot house with all his weapons ready to force Persis to an early marriage, he was astounded—he was even dismayed—to find that she offered no resistance, but greeted his proposal with delight. It was like making ready to besiege and storm a castle and being met half-way there by flower-girls instead of troops. Persis was so instant with acceptance that he took credit to himself. He cherished a pitiful delusion that she wanted to marry him—was actually in a hurry to marry him!

But it was because she had seen in the shops the new things for this year's brides. They were absolutely ravishing! Whatever they are in reality or in retrospect, fashions are always ravishing as they dawn on the horizon. Such beauties brighten as they make their entrance and wither as they take their flight.

To prepare herself for a wedding did not mean—to Persis, at least, whatever it may mean to other women—that she must prepare her soul for a mystic union with a

stranger soul. It meant that she must prepare her wardrobe for the inspection of all sorts of critics, from the most casual to the most intimate. It meant not only buying a veil and some orange blossoms and a meekly glorious white dress, but it meant outfitting a private department store. It meant preparing for travel and a prolonged campaign known as a honeymoon, rather than entering shyly into obscurity and domestic bliss. It meant not half so much what the groom should think and see as what to show and what to whisper to the bridesmaids, hysterically envious and ecstatically horrified.

Persis' father had nearly bankrupted himself once before over the wedding of Persis' sister into the British peerage, when she ceased to be the beautiful Miss Cabot and became the Countess of Kelvedon, and had the privilege of being nineteenth in the fifty-seven varieties of precedence among British women.

Mr. Cabot had learned nothing from that investment. He encouraged Persis to extravagances she would never have dared even in her present mood. It was like chirruping and taking the whip to a horse that was already running away.

He sent a long cablegram to Persis' sister, insisting that she come over at once for the wedding and bring the Earl and the eight-year-old Viscount of Selden, the six-year-old Honorable Paul Hadham, and the five-year-old Lady Maude Hadham. Persis received at once a brief reply from the Countess:

"Congratulations old girl snooks says awfully glad to be with you if papa pays the freight we are stony. Elise."

"Snooks" was the Earl of Kelvedon. Sometimes Elise called him "Kelly" for short. Papa cabled the freight— and "freight" was beginning to describe his burdens. But he was in for it; yet he felt that, come what come would, he should henceforward lean comfortably on the Enslee Estates.

Persis kept him signing checks till he was tempted to buy one of those ingenious machines by which one signs twenty at a time.

Persis was running amuck among the shops. She was in a torment of delight—a cat in a cosmos of catnip. The equipment of the humblest bride is a matter of supreme effort. To make a Persis Cabot ready to enter the dynasty of the Enslees was a Xerxic invasion.

The wedding-gown, though it was designed and builded with almost the importance of St. Paul's Cathedral, was the least part of the trousseau. Willie was to take her yachting and motoring and touring—perhaps around the world. They were to be presented at court if the Queen forgave the Countess her latest epigram in time. They were to visit capitals, castles, châteaux, gambling-palaces, golf-links, beaches, spas. Costumes and changes of costumes must be constructed for all these; for each costume there must be a foundation from the skin out. If it had been possible, the skin would have been changed as well. They do their best in that direction—these women with their pallor for a gown of one color and their carmine for a gown of another.

Persis had to have a going-to-the-altar gown, and a going-away gown, and going-to-bed gowns, getting-up gowns, going-motoring costumes, and going-in-swimming suits, dinner-gowns, house-gowns, tea-gowns, informal theater-gowns, opera-gowns, race-track togs, yachting flannels. And these were of numberless schools of architecture from train-gowns to tub frocks and smocks, from lingerie dresses to semi-tailored one-piece and two-piece suits, coats, and coatees, and coat-dresses, and sport-coats, opera wraps, rain slip-ons.

And there were colors to choose from that made the rainbow look like a study in sepia. And there were fabrics of strange names—crêpe, tulle, serge, taffeta, brocade, charmeuse, paillette, jet, batiste, voile—what not?

And there were the underpinnings to all these—the

stockings and garters, the corsets and chiffon corset-covers and combinations, chemi-pantalons and petticoats. And there were the accessories — hats, caps, bonnets, gloves, fans, parasols, veils, jabots, collars, aigrettes, boots, shoes, slippers, powders, paints, cerates, massage-cream—*ad infinitum*. And in every instance there must be a choice.

The complexity of a woman's wardrobe! A man is fitted out in a small haberdashery and a tailoring establishment, a hat shop and a shoe store. For woman they build Vaticans of merchandise in order that she may make an effect on—other women!

Persis had so many dresses to try on that she had two pneumatic images made of her form to stand in her stead. She had the servants' tongues hanging out from running errands. Delivery - wagon drivers and messenger - boys kept the area doorbells ringing early and late.

There was so much mail to send out that she hired two secretaries. Ten Eyck called on her just once, and was used as telephone - boy, package - opener, stenographer, change-purse, box-lifter, memorandum-maker, doorbell-answerer, gift-cataloguer till he was exhausted.

"How does a man ever dare to marry one of you maniacs?" he said. "Marriage isn't a sacrament with you; it's a massacre. They have a money macerator at the mint that destroys old greenbacks. Why don't they get a couple of brides to do the work? A wedding costs as much as a small war."

Persis might have retorted that wars were quite as foolish a waste as fashions, and not half so pretty. A new style in projectiles, the latest fabric of armor plate, the mode in airships—these things, too, come and go, cost fortunes, and are soon mere junk. But Persis' head was too full of other things, and her mouth too full of pins, to make any answer to Ten Eyck.

If Forbes had called he might have seen that Persis was a great general, or at least a great quartermaster, equipping not an army with one uniform, but one poor little frantic body with an army of uniforms. And Forbes would have been glad to take that body without a shift to its back and wrap it in one of his own overcoats and ride away with it. But for Willie she must loot Paris.

Still it was her career. Forbes would not give up his for her; why should she give up hers for him?

If Forbes had been leading his company to war he would have felt sorry for Persis, bitterly sorry to leave her, afraid for her; but he would still have gone, as men have always gone. He would not have been immune to bugles or the gait-quickening thrup of drums. He might have hummed love songs to her, but "Dixie" would still have thrilled him. He would not have neglected his uniform or his tactics. He would not have skulked from a charge or dodged a shell on her account.

That was his trade. This was hers. And Persis was as happy as a man is when he is going into battle. She was happy because she was busy and because she was buying, exercising choice, spurning, pillaging among cities of beautiful things. She dozed standing while skirts were draped; at night she simply fell into bed and was asleep; her maid drew her skirts from her hips and her stockings from her legs as if she were dead. But the next morning she woke without being called, and began the day with new ferocity of attack.

She had not forgotten Forbes. The thought of him hovered about her heart. She paused now and then, with hand on cheek and eyes far away, thinking of him so intently that the saleswoman had to speak twice to her, or the dressmaker to lift her arms into the position he wanted for the try-on.

Sometimes she woke from dreams in which she seemed to feel Forbes' arms about her. As she woke they were withdrawn, as if he fled. She would weep a little and lick the salt from her lips and find her tears very bitter. She would pout at Fate and muse: "Why couldn't it have been

Harvey instead of Willie? Oh, what a pitiful sacrifice I am making of my life!"

But her anger or despair in these humors was not half so intense as her despair at finding that some color could not be matched or that a color chosen in electric light was wrong in the daylight, or her anger because some tradesman failed to keep his word or some caller came to wish her well at a busy time, when true well-wishing would have shown itself in keeping out of the way.

A president could hardly have given more thought to selecting his cabinet than Persis gave to the choice of her bridesmaids, those lieutenants who must stand by in the same uniform like moving caryatides. There was the enormously important subject of their costume to debate. Since the livery that suited one style of beauty was loathsome on another, there was no little politics to play.

Persis invited the four elect to a luncheon at her club, and by having her ideas clear and enforcing them in a delicately adamant tone she managed to close the session in two hours. It was good work, and it was necessary; for the bridesmaids' costumes must be ready in time for the photographs.

She managed the luncheon so well that she finished it ahead of the time she had told her chauffeur to call for her. She left the bridesmaids all talking at once, for she had an appointment with one of her dressmakers. As she came down the steps of the quaintly colonial Colony Club she found no taxi in sight. She would not wait to have one summoned. The brief walk would do her good. She set out briskly down Madison Avenue and turned into Twenty-ninth Street to cross to Fifth Avenue.

This brought her to one of the few churchyards in almost grassless New York—the pleasant green acre of the Church of the Transfiguration, known to theatrical history as "The Little Church Around the Corner," and to the elopement industry as another Gretna Green.

As she approached it a taxicab drew up at the curb,

and Stowe Webb and Alice Neff bounced out, almost bowling Persis over, as usual. Both had a much dressed-up look, and Alice carried a little bouquet.

Persis was in a hurry, but she scented excitement. When the two lovers had apologized for their Juggernautical haste she asked, with the demurest of smiles:

"And what are you children doing in this dark alley?"

"Oh, we're just—just—" Alice stammered.

"Does your mother know you're out?"

"Naturally not," Alice smiled, more cheerfully.

"Mischief's brewing. I've got to know."

"Can you keep a secret?"

"That's my other name—Inviolate."

Alice hesitated, then took a precaution. "Cross your heart and hope to swallow fish-hooks?"

Persis drew an X over her heart, and vowed: "I am full of fish-hooks."

Alice looked up and down the street cautiously, then spoke in a whisper of awesome solemnity: "Well, then, Stowe and I have given mama the slip, and we're going to—to—"

"Get a chocolate-sundae with two spoons!"

Alice bridled with indignation. "Certainly not! We're not children! We are going to run away and be married."

Persis nodded her head gravely. "That was what I was afraid you were going to say. But why this haste?"

"Well, you see, Stowe has just got a job—umm-humm! It's a terribly important post—secretary to Ambassador Tait."

"Ambassador?"

"Yes; the Senator is going to France, and Stowe is to help him out."

The young secretary spoke in, trying not to look as important as he felt: "I simply can't endure the thought of leaving Alice all alone over here. So we're going to get married."

"Fine!" said Persis, with subtlety. "I suppose you get a whopping big salary."

"Indeed he does!" said Alice. "Twelve hundred a year! It's wonderful for a beginning."

Persis suppressed her emotions at the talk of salary. She hated the word; but she exclaimed, "Wonderful!" Then she turned to Stowe to ask: "Does the Senator know you're going to bring a bride along?"

"No; we're going to surprise him."

Persis thought of her appointment. It was vitally important, but she felt a call to duty. She thought it was rather good of her to heed it. She bundled the two young people back into the waiting taxicab in spite of their protests.

"Take us for a little drive, Stowe," she said. "I want a word with you. Tell the man to go down Washington Square way. You're not so likely to meet her mother."

CHAPTER XLVIII

STOWE obeyed reluctantly, and the taxicab groaned on its way. Persis set Stowe on the small flap-seat and turned so that she could skewer him and Alice with one look.

"Now, Alice," she began, "let's be sensible." Alice looked appealingly at Stowe, but Persis objected. "Don't look at him—look at me. First, who's going to support you children when you are married?"

They answered like a chorus: "Why, he is (I am), of course."

"Alice, dear, how much has your mother been allowing you for pin-money—say, five thousand a year?"

"Oh, she claims it's more than that. We had an awful row the first of last month."

Persis looked very innocent and school-girlish as she said: "And Mr. Webb gets twelve hundred?"

"Yes."

"Now, Alice, I'm very backward in mathematics, so you'll have to tell me: if one person cannot live on five thousand a year, do you think two persons will be perfectly comfortable on twelve hundred?"

"Oh, but I'll economize!" Alice protested. "It will be a pleasure to do without things—if I have Stowe."

"Yes," Persis sniffed, "almost anything we're not used to is pleasant for a novelty; but in time I should fancy that even economy would cease to be a luxury. And where in Paris do you plan to live on your twelve hundred?"

"At a hotel, to begin with," Stowe suggested.

22   337

"Oh, you'll eat your cake first, eh? Not a bad idea; you're sure of getting it, then."

"Then we can get such ducks of flats in Auteuil."

"The Harlem of Paris," Persis sneered, then grew more amiable. "A duck of an apartment is all very well, my dear, for those who have wings; but climbing stairs—ugh! Four flights of stairs six times a day—that's twenty-four flights. Seven times twenty-four is—help!"

"One hundred and sixty-eight, I believe," said Stowe, after a mental twist.

"Bravo! You're a regular wizard at mathematics," said Persis. "One hundred and sixty-eight flights of stairs a week, and fifty-two times one hundred and sixty-eight is how much? Quick!"

"You've got me there. I fancy I could do it with a piece of chalk and a blackboard."

"Well, it's a million, I'm sure," Persis summed it. "Think of that! a million flights of stairs the first year of marriage! What love could survive it? And how many rooms is your sky-parlor going to have?"

"Seven and bath."

"On twelve hundred a year?" Persis gasped. "Aren't you going to eat anything?"

"Well, we could manage with two."

"Two rooms!" Persis gasped again. "And your mother's house has thirty! Two rooms? Why, where will the servants sleep?"

"We sha'n't have any servants," Alice averred, stoutly.

And her husband-to-be protested: "No, Alice, I'll never let you soil your pretty hands with work."

Persis pressed the point. "But really, now, what about food?"

"You can do Wonders with a chafing-dish," said Alice.

"And a chafing-dish can do wonders with a stomach," said Persis. "Bread and cheese—that is to say, Welsh rabbits—and kisses as a steady diet?" She shook her head.

Alice made another try. "Well, everybody says you can buy almost everything in cans."

"Including ptomaines. Oh, children, you don't know what's in store for you."

"Of course we shall have hardships," Stowe confessed; "but nothing can be worse than this uncertainty, this separation."

"Oh yes, it can, Stowe!" Persis cried. "There are harder things to bear than the things we lose, and they are the things we can't lose."

"The things we can't lose?" said Stowe; "that means me, I suppose?"

"Oh, Alice, come back to earth," Persis urged, with all her might. "Think how tired you'll get of living in a dark little pigeonhole away up in the air, with no neighbors but working-people. And when your pretty gowns are worn out, and you lose your pretty looks and your pretty figure and your fresh color—for those are expensive luxuries—and when you see that your husband is growing disappointed in you because the harder you work for him the homelier and duller you become—that's a woman's fate, Alice: to alienate a man by the very sacrifices she makes to bind him closer; and when—"

"Oh, don't tell me any more whens," Alice whimpered. "What do I care? I want Stowe. He needs me. We are unhappy away from each other."

Persis shook her head like a sibyl. "Be careful that you don't find yourselves more unhappy together. For some day you'll grow bitter. You'll remember what you gave up. You'll begin to remind him of it—to nag—and nag—oh, the unspeakable vulgarity of it! And then you'll ruin Stowe's career—just as it's beginning. The Senator doesn't want a secretary with a wife. You'll always be in the way. Stowe will have to be leaving you all the time or fretting over you. You'll hamper his usefulness, and check his career, and grind him down to poverty, break his spirit."

"Oh, I don't want to do that!" Alice wept. "I mustn't do that!"

"Then wait—wait!" Persis pleaded. "Marriage is risky enough when there is no worry about money. But when the bills come in at the door love flies out at the window."

Stowe seized Alice's hands with ardor. "Don't listen to her, Alice."

"But I'm frightened now," Alice wailed. "It's for your sake, Stowe. We mustn't—not yet. And now may I please go home where I can cry my eyes out."

Persis in triumph called the address to the chauffeur. Stowe Webb, in the depths of dejection, left the cab and stared after it with eyes of bitter reproach.

Alice's tears were standing out like orient pearls impaled on eyelashes as she said good-by to Persis at her own curb.

"You hate me now," said Persis, "but you'll be very glad this happened some day."

"I don't hate you," said Alice. "I know you're terribly wise; but I—I wish you hadn't come along."

Persis laughed tenderly. "It's only for your happiness, Alice darling. Well, good-by!"

Persis felt that she had done an honest day's work of Samaritan wisdom, and ordered the cab to make haste to her dressmaker. A he-dressmaker it was, who, like a fashionable doctor, found it profitable to behave like a gorilla and abuse his clients. He turned on Persis and stormed up and down his show-room. He threatened to throw out all her costumes. She bore with him as meekly as if she were a ragged seamstress pleading for a job instead of the bride-elect of an Enslee.

When she had thus appeased his wrath he changed his tune to a rhapsody. She was to be the most beautiful bride that ever dragged a train up an aisle, and she should drag the most beautiful train that ever followed a maid to the altar and a wife away.

CHAPTER XLIX

PERSIS was not the only busy person in New York. Willie was kept on the jump preparing his share of the performance. The ushers were to be chosen, and their gifts, and a dinner given to them; and his list of friends to receive announcements and invitations must be made up, and the bride's gift selected, and the itinerary of the honeymoon arranged, his yacht put into commission, and a dinner of farewell to bachelorhood accepted and endured.

He hardly caught a glimpse of Persis all this while, and when he heard her voice on the telephone it was only to receive some new list of chores. He missed the billing and cooing that he knew belonged to these conversations. His heart ached to be assured of Persis' love; but she was incapable of even imitating the amorous note with him. When he pleaded for tendernesses she put him off as best she could by blaming her brusqueness on her overwork, as one who does not wish to sign oneself "Yours faithfully" or "affectionately" or even "truly" writes "Yours hastily."

But Willie's incessant prayer for love harassed her. It was a phase of him that had been unimportant hitherto. And it alarmed her a little. It would have given her greater uneasiness if she had not had so many other matters to worry her, if she had not had so many fascinating excitements to divert her.

Forbes was busy, too. Senator Tait had easily arranged his appointment as military attaché. He had his duties to learn in this capacity. He had to polish up his French and take lessons in conversation and composition, and learn what he could about the French military establishment and procedure. And he had to make ready for a long residence abroad.

To him, too, preoccupation was an opiate for suffering. Ambition and pride were resuming their interrupted sway. So long as he was busy he counted Persis as one of the tragedies of his past, and his love of her as a thing lived down and sealed in the archives of his heart.

But when he had an hour of leisure or of sleeplessness, she came back to him like a ghost with eery beauty and uncanny charm. He found her in nearly every newspaper, too. The announcement of her engagement brought forth a shower of portraits. There were articles about the alliance between the two families of Enslee and Cabot, about the bride's style of beauty, her recipes for beauty, silly accounts of interviews she never gave, beauty secrets she never used, exercises she never took, opinions on matters on which she had never thought. She was caught by camera-bogies on every shopping expedition, at the steeple-chases, at the weddings of other people — everywhere. There were moving pictures of her; pictures of her in her babyhood, her girlhood, in old-fashioned costumes and poses. Women began to copy her hats, her coiffures, her costumes. An alert merchant with a large amount of an unsalable material on hand named it "Persis pink," and women fought for it. It became a household word, or, its substitute nowadays, a newspaper word.

Forbes was dumfounded at the publicity of Persis. He was tempted to believe that she had gone mad and hired a press-agent. But a woman who marries a rich enough man needs no booming to-day. The whisper of her engagement starts the avalanche. She becomes as public as a queen or a politician or a criminal.

The incessant encounter with Persis' beauty in every newspaper, morning and evening and Sunday, and in the illustrated weeklies, kept Forbes' wound open. He could not escape her. It was like being a prisoner at a window

where she was always passing. She smiled at him everywhere, and always with the shadow of the Enslee name
imminent above her.

On the morning of the day he sailed, as he held
his newspaper between his coffee and his cigar, certain
head-lines leaped up and shouted at him from the top of
a column with a roar as of apocalyptic trumpets. He hastened to his room to be alone while he read the chronicle
of what was already past.

MISS PERSIS CABOT
WEDS WM. ENSLEE

HEAD OF THE FAMOUS HOUSE
MARRIED AT ST. THOMAS'S
YESTERDAY AFTERNOON

Reception at Bride's Home

**Earl and Countess of Kelvedon among Distinguished Guests.
Church a Mass of Bloom.**

The marriage of William Enslee, the present head of the great
dynasty of Enslee, and Miss Persis Cabot, the famous beauty,
daughter of an equally distinguished family, was celebrated at
4:30 yesterday afternoon in St. Thomas's Church, Fifty-third
Street and Fifth Avenue. This was the largest and most brilliant wedding of the season.

The chancel of the church was banked with rambler roses and
white daisies, against a background of camellia-trees and towering palms, and the way to the altar was marked with bay and
orange trees. The altar was a mass of bridal roses under an
immense trellis of trailing smilax.

While the guests were arriving a recital was given by an
orchestra, which played several selections at the bride's request,
including the "Evening Star" from "Tannhäuser," the prelude
to "Lohengrin," the gavotte from "Mignon," and Simonetti's
"Madrigale."

The ushers who seated the guests included the bride's brother,
LeGrand Cabot, Murray Ten Eyck, Robert Gammell Fielding,
and Ives Erskine.

The full vested-choir service was used for the ceremony, and

343

Barnby's "O Perfect Love" was played as the processional.
The bride walked down the nave with her father, who gave her
in marriage, being preceded by the ushers, bridesmaids, matron,
maid of honor, and flower-bearers. The bride wore a robe of
heavy white satin, the skirt being draped with long motifs of old
family lace and finished with a square train, which was edged
with clusters of orange blossoms. The bodice was cut low and
square in front, of lace and chiffon, with a deep collar of rose
point lace of square and distinctive cut at the back. Her tulle
veil was arranged about her head in cap effect, held by a coronet
of orange blossoms. Her only ornament was a superb necklace of diamonds, the gift of the bridegroom.

She carried a cluster bouquet of white orchids, an ivory
prayer-book that was also carried by her mother at her wedding,
and a Valenciennes handkerchief.

The Countess of Kelvedon, the bride's sister, was matron of
honor. She wore a costume of soft white charmeuse, with an
overskirt drapery effect of green chiffon, almost as deep in color
as jade-green, and the upper part of her gown was a combination
of satin and white chiffon, with a V opening at the neck. Her
round leghorn hat was encircled with jade-green satin, and topped
at the side with bows of green ribbon and pink roses. Her only
ornament was a solitaire diamond suspended on an invisible
platinum chain, and she carried a bouquet of Mme. Chatenay
roses.

Her two little children were the flower-bearers, the tiny Honorable Paul Hadham and the exquisite little Lady Maude
Hadham.

The four bridesmaids, the Misses Winifred Mather, Emma Gay,
Lois Twombly, and Frances Iselin, also wore gowns that were
a charming combination of white and green. Wide panels of
green chiffon fell from the back of the shoulders to the hem of
the ankle-length skirts of charmeuse, which disclosed white slippers with large rhinestone buckles. The green chiffon crossed
the shoulders in fichu effect, and the elbow-length sleeves were
edged with bands of green. Their leghorn hats of brown straw
were trimmed with green satin and white chiffon, and faced with
black velvet, with upright bows of green at the side. They each
carried bouquets of roses, sweet-peas, and field-daisies, tied with
pink satin streamers, and their ornaments were locket watches,
the gift of the bride.

The ceremony was performed by the rector of the church,
assisted by . . .

Twenty-five hundred invitations were sent out for the wedding. The church was quite full, and the residence of the bride's

parents, where the wedding reception was held, was crowded to its utmost. Mr. and Mrs. Enslee received congratulations in the Cabot drawing-room. A collation was served in the . . .

Some of the wedding-gifts were shown in rooms on the third floor. They were . . .

After the reception Mr. and Mrs. Enslee will leave almost immediately for a honeymoon cruise on Mr. Enslee's yacht. They will tour Europe later.

Among those invited to the wedding were . . .

The paper dropped from Forbes' hand. The irrevocable was accomplished. She was Enslee's, body and soul and name.

CHAPTER L

FORBES had not been invited to Persis' wedding. She had debated the matter feverishly and resolved that it was the lesser slight to leave him out of the twenty-five hundred who received the double-enveloped engravings. There was a certain distinction in being omitted, and she knew that he could not account it an oversight. She had been tempted to write him a letter. She scrawled off a dozen and tore them up in turn. What she had to say could not be put on paper. Besides, it would be hideously indiscreet.

But Forbes was present in her thoughts. He was the chief wedding guest in her soul. He seemed to kneel between her and the groom and try to shoulder him away. This added a last terror to the multitude of her frights—frights ranging in importance from a fear that she might kneel on her veil and pull it askew to nameless terrors of the bridegroom.

There had been a lilt of gaiety in trying on the bridal robe for the rehearsals and the posings before the camera. But when she made her final entrance into the snowy costume it seemed to be entering into the shroud of maidenhood. The journey to the church was like a ride in her hearse, only that the progress through the streets was difficult because of a crowd so dense that mounted policemen could hardly push and trample lane enough for her to reach the awning.

And under the narrow canopy a rabble jostled her and peered into her face, even plucked at her robes, as if she had been a French princess on her way to the guillotine.

346

The rabble inside the church was hardly less insolently inquisitive for being better dressed.

The preliminaries of the march; the whispered instructions and warnings; the corrected blunders; the stupidity of her father, made a child by the shame that sweeps over a father at delivering his girl-child to a man to possess; the sudden grief of her sister, the Countess; Persis' almost overpowering tempest of desire to flee from the church and run to Forbes for refuge—a whirlpool of emotions and memoranda and impressions.

And then the march beginning, the organ blaring, the ushers setting forth, and her sister and the children and the maids of honor; herself clinging to her father's arm, which trembled so that she rather supported him than he her; the arrival at the altar, where Willie was standing, a sick green from church-fright; the waiting priests, the rites, the hush of the throng to hear the answers; the strange piping tone of Willie's voice; the odd sound of her own.

Now she was filled with a realization of the awe of this great deed, a realization so vivid and so new that it seemed to be her first understanding of it. While she was kneeling in the prayer her thoughts were not soaring aloft, but swirling with thoughts of Forbes and memories of his embraces, a sense of his arms clasping her now so that she could hardly breathe, a wondering if his eyes and thoughts were on her, and where her nightcap was, and a swooning recollection of her cry of "Help me, Harvey!" a frightful impulse to leap to her feet and cry again to him to help her—then sick shudders at the blasphemy of such thoughts amid the sacraments at her husband's side— for Willie was already her husband, she wore his ring. He had kissed her. They were standing up again. They were signing something. They were leaving the church. It was over. It was just beginning. She was no longer her own; nor her father's. Her father could not protect her from this man at her side. Nobody could. The police and the judges and the laws were drawn up to keep her his.

Everybody was congratulating her, everybody was smiling, everybody was grinning to think that the marriage was not yet consummated. Back of all the gorgeousness and the glitter and the music and the sacrament waited the hideous profanation, the grossness, the violation of all that was precious and secret and holy.

She had a blurred sense of returning to the carriage and to the house, and of the mob there, the clatter of tongues, the price-mark appraisal of gifts, the swinish greediness about the buffet, the smirking repetition of the same banalities, the lines of drifting hands, the faces that floated up like melons on a stream and spoke and sometimes kissed her. But what did it matter who kissed her now? They were Willie's cheeks and Willie's lips. She was all Willie's, now and for evermore.

Eventually, when she was white-mouthed with fatigue and eager to swoon out of the pandemonium, some one took pity on her, and she was spirited away to her room and her bridal livery taken from her. The weight of the veil and the train had been greater than she knew. The blossoms were lifted from her head, and in their place a little black straw hat with a frill of black tulle was pinned. And in place of her white satin a simple Callot gown of sage-green cloth was fastened about her girlhood the last time.

She looked to be only a smart young woman, but she was now truly in the robe of sacrifice. They whispered about her and called her "Mrs. Enslee" with immemorial mischief; but it was still Persis Cabot that slipped from the house and met Willie, still a bachelor. They hurried into the limousine and sped to that clandestine meeting in the hotel suite where they were to tarry till the morrow. And then the yacht was to take them on a long cruise across an ocean of bliss to the unknown continent beyond the honeymoon.

And now the crowdless silence seemed to ring in her ears. She had heard so much noise and suffered so many stares and vibrated to so many excitements that the abrupt hush left her dizzy as on the edge of an unexpected abyss. It was like one of Beethoven's symphonies, where sound is piled on sound and speed on speed till the storm sweeps toward an intolerable climax, and just as the thunder and the lightning are to come there is instead a complete hush; and then a little oboe voice twanging.

She had been swept and spun in a maelstrom, an eternal crash! crash! crash! Then suddenly she was alone in a room with this little man. She heard the thud of the door like a coffin lid. She heard the lock click; she saw him peering at her with a fox-like slyness. He was whipping off his coat and waistcoat and fumbling at his scarf. And his words were in his whining, oboe voice:

"Well, that's over. And, thank God, I can get out of this damned collar before it chokes me!"

That was his first comment on their solitude! But it was better than the love speeches he tried to make next.

She sank into a chair; but he was wrapping his arms about her. He was trying to say pretty things, and making a complete fiasco. He was kissing her with ownership, and she dared not turn her lips from his, though all her soul was averted.

He was tugging at her hatpins and pulling her hair naggingly. She rose, controlling her impatience, and spoke with a meekness that amazed her:

"Nichette is there. She will—help me."

He grinned peevishly.

"Nichette, eh? I thought we were to be alone—for once? Well, send her away—as soon as you can."

He spoke already with command, and she said, with that sick meekness:

"All right, Willie."

She slunk away and was afraid to meet the eyes of Nichette. And even Nichette wept at her ministrations.

And then she sent Nichette away. At the door Nichette paused to stare through eyes of water, then ran back and clasped Persis and kissed her, and ran out and closed the door.

And Persis waited for her husband. Her thoughts were bitter. She was utterly ashamed. It was not the beautiful shame of a bride whose lover knocks at her door. She was understanding her bargain. She had kept herself for Willie Enslee. She had fought off lovers and love and fled from her own heart that she might be worthy of Willie Enslee and his money! Her body was no longer a shrine. She had rented it to the highest bidder. And the tenant had arrived.

CHAPTER LI

AS Forbes had once surveyed the tide of Fifth Avenue from the upper deck of a motor-bus, so now, from a sky-scraping ship he watched the thronged traffic along the spacious avenue of the Hudson River and the broad plaza of the bay.

Among the tugs, noisy and rowdy as newsboys, the waddling ferry-boats, the barges loaded with refuse or freight-trains, the passenger-boats and excursion-boats, and the merchantmen from many ports, a few yachts picked their way superciliously, their bowsprits like up-turned noses, their trim white flanks like skirts drawn aside.

Among these yachts, though Forbes was unaware of it, was the *Isolde*, known to those who know such things as a ridiculously luxurious craft, a floating residence. Persis had christened the yacht at Willie's request, and he had accepted the name as a good omen, since he said: "I always have a perfect sleep when *Isolde* is under way."

Persis, herself now an Isolde wedded to one man and loving another, passed the famous sky-line which seemed to continue another Palisades, only fantastically carved and honeycombed with windows. When these cliffs of human fashioning were pulled backward, there was a space of dancing water, and then Governor's Island, with its moldy old mouse-trap of a fort.

Never dreaming that Forbes was on the liner that had gone down the bay a few moments before, Persis fastened her binocular on the island and tried to pick him out from among the men whom distance rendered lilliputian.

351

She selected some vague promenader and sent him her blessings. If he ever received them he never knew whence they came.

Forbes was groping toward her in thought like a wireless telegrapher trying to reach another and unable to come to accord. Forbes was entering upon the Atlantic Ocean for the first time, and Persis was embarking on another sea equally new to her, for marriage is a kind of ocean to a woman. Maidens struggle toward it and consecrate themselves to it from far inland; they come forth upon the roaring wonder of its cathedral music; the surf flings white flowers at their feet. They venture farther and encounter the first shocks of the breakers, and thereafter the sea lies vast and monotonous with happiness or grief and their interchange. But the prosperity of the voyage is less from without than from within the boat. Persis was not lucky in the captain she had shipped with.

To-day's Persis on the boat was altogether another woman from yesterday's Persis. The toil and fever of preparation, the bacchantic orgies of purchase, the dressing up, the celebration of the festival—these were the joys of the wedding to her, and she had drained them to the full. They left her exhausted and sated. The anticipation was over, the realization begun.

In some wiser communities the bride and groom separate for a day or two after the ceremony. But Persis had no such breathing-space. Persis was delivered to Willie Enslee in a state of fagged-out nerves, muscles, and brain. To him, however, the weeks of preparation had been a mere annoyance, a postponement, a prelude too long, too ornate. And when at last the prize was his he found the fact almost intolerably beautiful. He possessed Persis Enslee! She had no longer even a name of her own. Miss Cabot had been merged into the Enslee Estates.

One does not expect to-day the childlike innocence that was revealed or pretended by the brides of other years. Nowadays even their mothers "tell them things." And

Willie knew that Persis was neither ignorant nor ingenuous. Her gossip, the scandal she knew, the books and plays she discussed, her sophisticated attitude toward people and life had long ago proved that, whatever she might be, she was not without knowledge. She knew as much as Mildred Tait, and her talk was nearly as free, but always from the cynical, the flippant, or the shocked point of view.

Willie did not expect to initiate an ignoramus into any unheard-of mysteries. He expected at most a certain modest reluctance and confusion. He was dumfounded to be met with icy horror and shuddering recoil. After the first repulse the terror with which she cringed away from his caresses enhanced her the more.

He imputed it to a native purity. He believed—and it was true—that she had come through all the years and temptations and the dangerous environments with her body and her soul somehow protected to this great event. It was a kind of purity. But not what he thought it.

Persis' creed—if she had thought much about it—would have been the creed of many a woman: that love sanctifies all that it inspires; and that unchastity is what Rahel Varnhagen defined it — intercourse without love, whether legalized or not.

If Persis had married the man she loved, the man whose touch was like a flame, she would still have been terrified; but love would have hallowed the conquest, changed fright into ecstasy, and glorified surrender.

Willie's touch had always chilled her clammily. What she saw in his eyes now offended her utterly, filled her with loathing and with panic as before a violation. But after this first rebellion she regained control of her fears and reasoned coldly with herself. When she had said "Yes" to Willie's courtship, and when she had made her affirmations in the church, she had given him her I. O. U. She was not one to repudiate a gambling loss. She forbore resistance, but she could not mimic rapture. Yet rapture was part of the bargain. Soul and flesh could not pay the obligation her mind had so lightly incurred.

And now it was Enslee that recoiled, strangely smitten with an awe, a reverence for her and her integrity. "You are a saint," he murmured, "an angel, and I am a brute. You are too good, too wonderful!"

Persis was startled at being treated with reverence. It was perhaps the first time she had ever been held sacred. She accepted this tribute in lieu of the others, and they left the hotel as they had entered it, still bachelor and maid, though they wore the same name.

But she was alone upon the ocean now, and she feared her husband more than before. She found him somewhat ridiculous in his uniform, with his yachting-cap a trifle top-heavy for his slim skull. Yet he was the owner; his flag and his club pennant were fluttering aloft. And Persis felt sure that he had repented of his mercy and was ashamed of his asceticism.

He ogled her as he paced the unstable deck, and found her more beautiful than ever, clad in a trim white suit and curled up in her chair like a purring kitten, the sun sifting over her through the awning like a golden powder. And he knew that she was his. He paused at her side and mellowed her cheek, pinched the lobe of her ear, and pursed his lips to kiss her red lips. She winced, then frowned, and shook her head.

"Why not?" he demanded.

"The crew is watching," she explained. And he retorted:

"They expect us to be a little silly, don't they? They'll think it stranger if we aren't than if we are, won't they? Even those Scandinavian sailors are human."

And so—for the sake of the Scandinavians—she accepted his caresses.

It was such a sarcastic parody of her own code that she laughed aloud. She was good sport enough to laugh at herself when the joke was on her.

But it was bitter laughter; and it ended on the margin of hysteria. She conquered that—for the sake of the Scandinavians. But she felt altogether forlorn, miserably cheap, fooled.

That bitterness of hers embittered Enslee. He felt that he was being made ridiculous in the sight of man and God and himself. He remembered proverbs about mastership, about women's love of brutality, their fondness for being overpowered.

He grew fiercely petulant, sardonic, ugly. He whined and swore and muttered. And, finally, to that mood she yielded, feeling herself degraded beneath her own contempt.

And now Persis was married and not married. Strange fires were kindled and left to smolder sullenly. Unsuspected desires were stirred to mutiny and not quelled. Latent ferocities of passion were wakened to terrify and torment her. And only now she understood who and what it was she had married. Only now she realized what it meant to marry without love and to marry for keeps. The vision of her future was unspeakably hideous. Her life was already a failure, her career a disaster.

Persis had always loved crowds and the excitement they make. It was only with Forbes that she had found contentment in dual solitude, in hours of quiet converse, or in mute communion. Next best to being with him was being alone, for then she had thoughts of him for company.

Now Forbes was banished from her existence by her own decree. Willie was to be her life-fellow for all her days and nights, while her youth perished loveless.

And now once more she pined for crowds. Solitude with Willie was an alkaline Death Valley without oasis. She grew frantic to be rid of him, or, at least, to mitigate him with other companionships. And he who had been restlessly unhappy without her found that he could not be happy with her, because of the one mad regret that he could not make her love him as he loved her.

Mismated and incompatible in every degree, they glared at each other like sick wretches in the same hospital ward. The next evening as they sat at table in the dining-saloon it came over her that for the rest of her days she must see that unbeautiful face opposite her. She felt an impulse to scream, to run to the railing and leap overboard, to thwart that life-sentence in any possible way. But she kept her frenzy hidden in her breast and said, with all the inconsequence she could assume:

"To-morrow they'll be playing the first international polo game."

Even Willie heard the shiver of longing in the tone. It meant that the honeymoon was already boring her. His heart broke, but all he said was:

"Er—yes—I believe it is to-morrow. Like to go?"

"Oh no," she murmured. "I was just thinking what a splendid sight it will be. Everybody will be there, I suppose."

"Er—yes—I suppose so."

She lighted her third cigarette since the soup, and, rising from the table, drifted to the piano clamped to the walls of the drawing-room. Her mind was far off, and her fingers, left to themselves, stumbled through a disjointed chaos of melodies from nocturnes to tangos and back.

Willie stood it as long as he could, then his torment broke out in a cry more tragic than its words:

"For God's sake play something or quit."

She quit.

She walked to a porthole and stared out at the dark waves shuffling past like stampeding cattle.

He apologized at once. "I'm sorry. I didn't mean it. I apologize."

"Oh, that's all right," she sighed, with doleful graciousness. But when he knelt by her and put his arm around her she slipped from his clasp and went out on the deck. He followed her. But neither of them spoke.

The moon on the sea spread a pathway of dancing white

tiles. She wanted to run away, to step forth on that fantastic pavement and follow it out of the world.

To Forbes, on a distant ship in midocean the same moon was spreading the same path straight to him. He stared into its shifting glamour till his eyes were bewitched. He could see Persis walking on the water in the boudoir cap and the shimmering thing she wore that morning.

They were thinking of each other, longing for each other, and the space between them was widening every moment.

It came over Persis with maddening vividness that she had made a ruin of her happiness. All the wealth was nothing but mockery. Even the hats and the multitudes of dresses were wasted splendor, weapons of conquest to be left in an armory.

The night grew more and more wonderful. The moon was like a white face flung back with unappeased desire. The wind across the waves tugged amorously at her hair and whimpered and caressed her. And she was with Willie Enslee, the unlovable, the hideously uninteresting, the intolerable. She was handcuffed to Willie Enslee for life.

The ache of longing that thrilled the night world thrilled Enslee's heart, too; and he crept close to her, his adoration, his wife, the only soul on earth he deeply loved. He set his cheek against hers and clenched her in his arms fiercely. And immediately he encountered that hopeless antipathy, though all she said was a faintly petulant "Don't, please!"

It struck him in the face like a little fist. He moved aloof from her in abject humiliation and thought hard, took out a cigarette, tapped it on the back of his hand, puffed restlessly, threw the cigarette over the rail, and a moment later took out another. There was no need for words. The air throbbed with Persis' detestation of the voyage. The sailing-master passed. Willie called to him:

"Svendsen!"

"Yes, sir!"

"Put about and make for home."

"I beg pardon, sir."

"You heard!"

"Aye, aye, sir."

The commands were given in the distance, a bell rang remotely in the engine-room, and the stars wheeled across the sky as the yacht came round.

The phosphorescent sea revealed the wake they had plowed in a long straight furrow of white fire, and now there was a sharp curve in the line. And shortly they were paralleling its dimming radiance.

They were bound for home. The mere thought of the word brought a tragic chuckle from Enslee's heart. Home was a word he could not hope to use. Home was a thing he must do without.

CHAPTER LII

PERSIS was sorry for her husband, but just a trifle sorrier for Persis. She solaced herself with the thought that it was partly for Willie's own sake that she consented to go back, since if she stayed out in that solitude with him any longer she would go mad and jump overboard. And he would not like that in the least. A bride in town would be worth two in the ocean. Besides, a suicide on a honeymoon would be sure to cause a fearful scandal. She could imagine the head-lines.

Willie was a darling to yield so easily. It showed her how much he loved her—also how meekly he obeyed her. That is always an important question to settle. Perhaps it is what honeymoons are for—training-stations in which husbands are broken to harness and taught to answer a mere chirrup; it saves the whip.

But the comfort Persis took in finding that her husband was her messenger-boy ended as they came up the bay again. She suddenly realized that for Willie and her to be seen at the polo games, when they had so ostentatiously set out on their honeymoon only two days before, would provoke a landslide of gossip. Everybody on earth would be at the polo games, and she and Willie could not hope to escape attention. They would be ridiculed to death behind their backs and to their faces. Therefore they must not go.

She explained this to Willie, and he shook his head and broke out, peevishly:

"Why the bally hell didn't you think of all this in the first place?"

"In the first place, Willie," said Persis, "you are the man of the family, and supposed to do the thinking. In the second place, I won't be sworn at."

"I wasn't swearing at you, my love. I was just swearing. Well, if you don't want to go to the polo games, where in—where do you want to go—up to the country place?"

Here was a problem. She was sure that she did not want to be alone in a country house with Willie. That would be worse than the yacht. Since she could not endure either to be alone with him or to go among crowds with him, the dilemma was perfect. Already there was another incompatibility established.

She was mad for diversion, and, being herself a polo-player of no small prowess, she was frantic to see the effort of the British team to wrest back the trophy. But a stronger passion still was the determination to evade gossip.

She and Willie, therefore, sneaked from their yacht to their house in town. They astounded the servants, and there was much scurrying and whisking.

They dined together alone, though Persis was eager to be in a restaurant where there was music. She was like a child kept in after school. She flattened her nose against a window-pane and stared out at life. After dinner the prospect of an evening with Willie rendered her desperate. They could at least go to the theater somewhere. Nobody was in town; they would be quite unnoticed. But when nobody is in town the theaters close up. There was nothing they had not seen or had not been warned against. Willie proposed a roof-garden—Hammerstein's.

They went, and beheld a chimpanzee that rode various bicycles, smoked a cigar expertly, and spat with amazing fidelity to the technique of the super-ape; also a British peeress who danced in less clothes than the chimpanzee wore.

Ten Eyck was there. He tried to hide from Persis and

Willie, not because he was ashamed to be seen by them, but because he was afraid that Persis and Willie would not want to be seen by him. He had cherished no illusions for the success of the match on its sentimental side, but he had expected them to see the honeymoon through. He kept out of their sight, but they stumbled on him during the intermission, when the audience crowded into a space at the back of the roof where a patient cow was milked by electricity at an uncowly hour, and where couples rowed boats up and down an almost microscopic lake.

Ten Eyck had not expected Persis and Willie to join this hot and foolish mob. But he felt a hand seize his arm. He turned and looked into Persis' eyes. She welcomed him as a rescuer, but it was Willie that urged him to sit with them. Ten Eyck's hesitation was misconstrued by Persis. She said:

"Perhaps he is—er—not alone."

"Oh yes, I am," Ten Eyck hastened to say. "I'll join you." And he went with them to an upper box. Even Ten Eyck felt a little shy.

Persis and Willie knew what he was thinking, and they were like a pair of youngsters caught spooning. Only their misdemeanor was that they had been caught not spooning. Ten Eyck ventured to speak.

"So the penance is over already? I thought you two doves were still on the ark."

"We are, officially," said Persis.

Ten Eyck wanted to help them out, so he said:

"What's the matter? Did the yacht puncture a tire or lose a shoe or—"

Willie attempted to carry along the idea by saying:

"It was trouble with the sparker." And he did not understand why Persis blushed and Ten Eyck blurted.

They were rescued from this personal confusion by what would have thrown any audience into a panic ten years before and now was greeted almost with apathy:

the appearance of the British peeress in a costume that was hardly more than Eve wore after the eviction. A gauzy shift was all she had on, with a few wisps of chiffon as opaque as cigarette-smoke. Shoulders, arms, and all of both legs were as bare as her face.

No policeman interfered, and not a sermon had been preached against her. Nudity had lost its novelty, and her posturings and curvetings were regarded with as academic a calm as if she were a trick pony or an acrobat. There was much laughter later when a male comedian burlesqued her, with a bosom composed of two toy balloons, one of which escaped, and one of which exploded when he fell on it.

"I think this age will go down in history as the return to nature," Ten Eyck said, struggling for some impersonal topic. "Women in and out of vaudeville have left off more and more of their concealments, till the only way a woman can arouse suspicion now is by keeping something on. And I can't see that we are any worse—or any better. An onion is an onion, no matter how many skins it has on or off. We'll see bathing-suits on Fifth Avenue next season."

He did not know that the next season was to bring a sudden revolution and divert women from disclosure to the covering of their bodies with chaotic fabrics till they resembled dry-goods counters in disarray.

Philosophizing did not interest Willie. He came always back to the individual. By and by he wrestled with silence, and asked:

"Er — whatever became of that — er — soldier you brought up to the farm? Stupid solemn fella—Ward—or Lord—or something?"

"Forbes, you mean?" said Ten Eyck, taking pains not to look at Persis. But he could feel her eager attention in the sudden check of her fan.

"That's it—Forbes. Still at Ellis Island—or is it Ward's?"

"Governor's," said Ten Eyck. "He's been made military attaché at the French Embassy. Sailed for Paris the other day with Senator Tait—and—and Mildred."

Persis' whole body seemed to clench itself like a hand. But Willie, everlastingly oblivious to significant things, driveled on:

"Paris, eh? Racing season's on over there now. How'd you like to run across for the Grand Prix, Persis?"

"Paris is a nice place," said Persis, with a mystic veil about her voice.

And now Ten Eyck looked at her. Their eyes met. His were angry, and hers fell before their prophetic ire. She stammered a little as she said:

"I like London better. We could make the Royal Cup at Ascot if we hurried. My sister could take care of us in the country."

But Ten Eyck slapped his knees impatiently, glared at her, and growled:

"Bluffer! Good night!"

And he was gone without shaking hands.

"What did he mean by bluffer?" said Enslee. "Doesn't he like your sister?"

"Apparently not," said Persis. "And he used to be crazy about her. She threw him overboard for 'Kelly.'"

CHAPTER LIII

WILLIE had arranged for supper at home. As they left the theater and sped through the streets crowded with uncharacteristic mobs Persis thought longingly of the tango-hunts she had indulged in during the past season. But there was no one to dance with her now. And she realized that she would be impossibly conspicuous as a café-hunting bride with a husband who abhorred this whole chapter in the chronicle of diversion.

Alone with Willie in the Enslee palace, which Ten Eyck described as "a sublime junk-shop," Persis was oppressed to melancholia. The air that came in at the windows had a mournful breath. The peculiar aversion for the city, that overtakes New-Yorkers in the late spring seized her and shook her. The mansions neighborly to theirs were boarded up now, with only a caretaker's window alight here and there. There was nobody even to summon by telephone as a rescuing third party to make a crowd out of the appallingly tiresome duet with Willie.

"This town is a cemetery," she exclaimed, as she quenched her eighth cigarette stump. "Opening a house here now is like opening a grave in Woodlawn at midnight. You've got to take me away or leave me in Bloomingdale."

"What about Paris?" Willie suggested.

She remembered Ten Eyck's eyes, and said, "Let's make it London."

"I'll get what I can to-morrow. You wouldn't like to cross in the yacht?" he asked, haughtily. "*Isolde's* all right in the ugliest weather."

She shook her head violently, and yawned and spoke

364

so eloquently of her fatigue that he slunk away to his own room.

The next day he set his secretary to work running down a berth on a steamer. Everything seemed to be gone. People whom the panicky times had reduced from wealth to anxiety were crossing the ocean to places where they could economize without ostentation. The final report was that the only suitable berth was the imperial suite on the new *Imperator*.

"Did you grab it?" said Willie. The secretary shook his head.

"Why the devil didn't you?" Willie snapped.

"They ask five thousand dollars for it."

Even Willie winced at this. "I don't want it for a year," he groaned. "Just one voyage."

"It has a private deck, a drawing-room, two bath-rooms, two servants' rooms—"

The "private deck" decided Willie; but when he told Persis he laid stress on the price he paid; not from any braggart motive, but as a pathetic sort of courtship.

Persis smiled a little. It was something. But when she found the private deck she took pains to invite other passengers she knew to make it their own piazza. Among the passengers were Mrs. Neff and Alice.

After Persis had thwarted Alice's elopement with Stowe Webb the boy had been tempted to go to Mrs. Neff and plead with her to withdraw her ban, seeing that he was now a man of affairs with an assured income. But he imagined what she would say when she asked him the amount of that income; and he imagined her smile. She did not have to ridicule his fortune. The sum itself was so petty that it ridiculed itself.

He and Alice had met clandestinely a few times at the houses of friends, but both were young and both were timid, and their friends were cynical with discouragement. Alice wanted to go to watch him off at the dock, but had

not dared, and only sent him a tear-blotted steamer letter.
And while he was down in his state-room reading it she
was locked in her pink-and-white virginal chamber crying
her blue eyes crimson on her bed. She never spoke of
him to her mother, and Mrs. Neff did not know what had
become of him.

So the two child-lovers pined away. New York became
a deserted village to Alice, and Stowe found the ocean a
congenial waste, for he felt in his breast an Atlantic loneliness. Nor was Paris less sad; its allurements were only
thorns; he felt that he must be true to his little wife-to-
be, and it seemed that even to indulge in the more innocent gaieties would belie his desolation.

Then Mrs. Neff grew just a trifle too shrewd. Noting
that Alice never spoke of Stowe Webb, she made up her
crafty old mind that the two young wretches were meeting secretly. Since nothing happened at all, she all too
cleverly decided that something was about to happen, and
resolved to nip the passion-flower in the bud. She read
Alice a long curtain-lecture on the perfection with which
children obeyed their parents when she was young, then
dilated on the advantages of European travel in broaden-
ing the mind, and drew such a glowing portrait of her own
benevolence in offering Alice the opportunity of going
abroad that the girl began to foresee what was coming,
and what real motive was actuating her mother. By the
time Mrs. Neff arrived at the heartbreaking news that
she was about to drag Alice off to Paris the simple child
was able to dissemble her ecstasy and give a convincing
portrayal of a daughter who would rather go anywhere on
earth than to France. Like Br'er Rabbit, she pleaded
not to be thrown into the briar-patch of all places. So
she was thrown into the briar-patch. Alice was on her
way to Paris.

She took Persis into her confidence, and Persis found
a dreary pleasure in the joke. She even forbore to warn
Alice against the folly of marrying into poverty. She

was not so satisfied with her own triumph as to recommend her example to others.

There was, as there will always be, a certain joy in having the best and the most expensive things of every sort. But there was, as there will always be, a disappointment in getting by merely wishing or commanding; especially as the fairy gift of wishes has always carried a few amendments: "You may have anything you wish for except—" Whereupon the "excepts" become the only things sincerely wishable.

Persis found London at the height of its June festivity. The President of France was visiting the King of England, and there were state banquets and state balls and state everything, mingled with private celebrations that rivaled them in pomp; and a horse-show, and horse-races, regimental polo tournaments; the annual hysterical wholesale celebration of nothing in particular.

Many of Persis' school-girl friends were duchesses, countesses, marchionesses, mere ladies. Lady Crainleigh, whom Persis had once beaten in a potato-race at a country horse-show in Westchester, gave a dance where seven hundred guests were present and where titles were as common as pebbles on a shore. Persis wore her "all-around" diamond crown, and danced with a Russian grand-duke and a prince or two.

The tango and the turkey-trot had spread overseas, and royalties trod on Persis' toes as they bungled the steps like yokels. It was fantastic to hear the trashy tunes of American music-halls resounding through the ballrooms of mansions and palatial hotels.

At the Royal Ascot the Queen sent a duke to fetch Persis to the royal box, and spoke amiably of her sister.

But, however Persis glittered abroad, when the inevitable time came to become mere woman and go to bed, she must always return to the nagging presence of Willie, infatuated the more by the inaccessible distances her soul kept from his.

WHAT WILL PEOPLE SAY?

With his harrowed face, his unwelcome caresses, his unanswerable prayers for a little love, he ceased to be tragic. He became a pest.

Persis was learning wherein wealth, as well as poverty, has its poverties, its nauseas, its petty annoyances, its daily denials, its hair-cloth shirts.

She began to feel that if she had married Forbes and made her own clothes she could not have grown wearier than she grew from putting on and taking off the complicated harnesses devised by intoxicated dressmakers.

Sometimes she declared that she would rather trim one bonnet and wear it the rest of her life than try on any more of the works of the mad hatters of Europe.

And what mockery her splendor was!—for the ulterior purpose of gorgeousness is love. Humanity has stretched its mating season throughout the whole year, but the meaning of bright plumage remains an invitation to courtship, a more or less disguised advertisement: "Behold, I am ready. I am desirable!"

Persis was dressing herself up for yesterday's party. Men courted her still, slyly and disgustingly, but she felt herself insulted by the adventure, degraded by the implications. Whatever other faults she had, Persis was not promiscuous. There was nothing of the female rake in her nature. She was meant to be loved by many and to love one. Her heart had selected its one among the ones; but the hand had married elsewhere. There was great danger for her soul if she did not meet that One. And greater danger if she did.

CHAPTER LIV

PARIS and London were like two rival circuses bidding for the public, beating tom-toms, blowing horns, and sending out band-wagons and parades. While Persis was wearying of the English side-shows, Forbes was tiring of the French. The wounds Persis had inflicted on his heart and his pride were still fresh and bleeding. The fever had not left him. At the thought of her, or the sight of her name frequently in the daily papers, or her portrait in the illustrated papers, the scarlet shame of his defeat still ran across his brow, still the hunger for her gripped him, regret sickened him.

Senator Tait had not enjoyed the progress of his conspiracy. For secretary he had taken Stowe Webb, who moved about like an immature Hamlet with a heart draped in black. For military attaché he had brought Forbes, whose thoughts flew backward to the past instead of scouting ahead. For acting ambassadress he had brought a daughter who, though torn away from her New York charities, found new miseries to engage her everywhere. Even on the ship she had sought distress—in the stokehold, in the steerage and the second cabin. Instead of holding hands in moonlit nooks and funnel-corners, she was taking up purses, sterilizing milk for sick babies, and selling tickets for a benefit concert.

Forbes admired Mildred profoundly, but he preferred his own sorrows to the woes she discovered in other people. Mildred liked Forbes immensely, in a motherly, elder-sisterly, trained-nursish way. But of love between them there was no visible trace.

24   369

Tait grew fonder and fonder of Forbes as a son, but he could not contrive him as a son-in-law. The mating of human hearts, he found, was a task beyond diplomacy or politics. He wondered if he would have more success in promoting affection between America and France, the two republics that made each other possible. He wished that he had never undertaken any of his tasks. He felt old, ill, tired. He had agreed to take over the Embassy on the fifth of July. Hardly more than a week remained of his freedom, and that week was the big week of the year—the *grande semaine*.

He did not know that other dangers lurked in ambush ahead of himself. Mrs. Neff, ignorant of Stowe Webb's office, had come straight to Paris from the *Imperator*, bound to expose Alice again to the Senator's inspection. More dangerous yet was Winifred Mather. Tait had been warned of Mrs. Neff, but not of Winifred.

The heavy times in Wall Street had played havoc with Bob Fielding's means and with his spirits. The gradual jolting down and down of values, and the buying public's desertion of the market left the Stock Exchange like a neglected billiard parlor, where in the absence of customers the professionals played against one another—for points.

Bob Fielding was so big that when he was happy he was a Falstaff, but when he was unhappy he was a whale ashore. Winifred liked him happy. She grew weary of her blue Behemoth and began to think again of Senator Tait. She reasoned that he really needed a wife; it was a handicap to the Embassy to have only an elder daughter to run its social branch, especially such a daughter as Mildred, with her exasperating to-morrow's virtues and her last year's clothes. Winifred felt it her patriotic duty to marry the Embassy over.

She had a widowed sister in Paris, Mrs. Mather Edgecumbe. With her as complotter and under her ægis Winifred attacked Senator Tait in a campaign so skilfully arranged under so many disguises that Tait was left hardly a minute to himself. All his invitations included Forbes and Mildred and young Stowe Webb.

At one of them, a night fête in Mrs. Mather Edgecumbe's house in the Rue de Monceau, with musicians in Persian costume playing in the garden under the illuminated trees, Mrs. Neff and Alice were included unbeknown to Winifred. She was aghast at the tactical mistake, and she was curt enough when Alice, hastening as usual in one direction and looking in another, ran into her.

"Oh, it's you Alice. How are you? I didn't know you were in Paris. Followed the Senator over, I suppose."

"I suppose so," said Alice. "Did you?"

"Where's your mother?"

"She's probably looking for me. I hope she doesn't find me. Have you seen Stowe?"

"Somewhere," said Winifred, with a perceptible thaw. "Does your mother know he's here?"

"If she did, should I be here?" Alice giggled, and laughter bubbled from Winifred, too. It continued with increase as Alice went on: "The Senator and I have come to a perfect understanding. He knows I don't love him, and that I do love Stowe. He gave Stowe his job as a starter to get me with. Yes, he did! My awful mother, of course, is always conspiring to leave the Senator alone with me. Sends us driving and Louvre-ing together. Well, that angel man, the Senator, just waits till mama is safely out of sight, then he notifies Stowe and goes away about his business and leaves us together."

"Oh, then the Senator's devotion for you is all for Stowe's sweet sake?" and there was a rapturous little break in Winifred's voice.

"Of course. Isn't he an angel?"

"He is, indeed!" said Winifred, with a sigh of relief so deep that Alice stared at her in surprise and exclaimed:

"Why, do you really want him?"

Winifred bridled as proudly as she could, but Alice only gasped: "Heavens! here comes that awful mother of mine. Don't give me away!" And she fled from tree to tree.

There was small risk that Winifred would violate the secret left with her, and she greeted Mrs. Neff with an unprecedented smile when she swept into the arbor and found there the last person on earth she would have wished to see.

"Why, it's Winifred Mather!" was her undeniable affirmation. "So you are in Paris!"

"Yes, dear. Did you bring dear Alice to Paris with you?"

"I was just going to ask if you had seen her."

Winifred lied with the glibness of long training:

"No, indeed. But I'd love to. Let's look for her."

And she took Mrs. Neff's sharp elbow in her fat hand, and led her in the wrong direction. A moment later she whirled her away from an alley of roses where Stowe Webb was blundering along in such eager search of Alice that he would have walked into her mother but for Winifred's alertness as a chauffeuse.

"She's here somewhere," Mrs. Neff was saying as her eyes ransacked the glittering crowd. "I snatched her away from America to keep her from the possibility of meeting that young Webb."

"What a very clever idea!" said Winifred, and she began to laugh so helplessly that Mrs. Neff grew suspicious. But having no clue to work on, she changed the subject:

"Persis and Willie are here, I see."

"Are they? I telegraphed the dear girl an invitation, but I was afraid she was stuck in London."

"She came over for the *Prix des Drags* to-morrow."

"How does the poor child look after—after honeymooning with Willie; Heaven help her!—and him!"

"She looks—oh, of course, she's still our dear beautiful Persis, but Willie, of course, is the same dear little damphool. Alice's maid, the Irish one, said Persis looked like her heart was dead in her, the creature. She had it

from his man that Willie and she get along like the
monkey and the parrot. But, of course, one can't listen
to servants."

"No, of course not; though God knows what we'd do
for news without 'em."

As they entered the house Mrs. Neff saw Forbes. He
was in his military full dress, and he was standing alone
in a reverie. He was as solitary in the crowd as if he
were a statue on a battle-field gazing through eyes of
bronze.

"There's our little snojer man," said Winifred.

"So it is," said Mrs. Neff, struggling toward him through
a sort of panic of complexly moving groups. "How is the
dear boy? Paris has swept him off his feet, eh?"

"He's the melancholiest man here—the ghost of the
boulevards."

"It's too bad," said Mrs. Neff. "He was the man for
Persis." She reached his side, took his hand, and laughed
up into his face. He came out of a dream and stared
at her foggily, then answered the warm clench of her
little fingers. She said:

"And what are you staring at so hard?—Mrs. Enslee?"
He started at the name—"Mrs. Enslee?"

"Yes, Persis. You haven't forgotten her so soon?"

"Oh no, of course not. But she isn't here?"

"Oh yes, she is, with her brand-new husband."

"Really," he said, trying to sound casual, though the
warning of her nearness frightened him and put his
heart to its paces.

"I'll never forgive you for not marrying her after you
flirted with her so dreadfully."

"Did I?" he laughed, wretchedly. "And you say she's
in Paris?"

"She's right behind you."

Forbes felt as a man feels when some one says,
"There's a rattlesnake just back of you." He became an
automaton of wax and turned slowly as on a creaking

pivot. Yes, there she was. Persis had just come in with her husband. The news, and the presence of the man at her side, sent a shudder through Forbes. The Enslees had happened upon Ambassador Tait, and Forbes could see that the old man was struggling hard to be decently polite to them.

Persis caught sight of Forbes, and her beautiful brows went up as she smiled. He had an intuition that her look was an appeal for mercy. Then she moved on with Willie, to lay off her cloak.

Tait, glancing about, saw Forbes and came to him at once. Mrs. Neff, seeing him, forgot the study she was making of Forbes' emotions. She demanded of Tait: "Have you seen Alice? I hoped she was with you."

"No, I haven't seen her to-night," he answered guilelessly, forgetting his rôle in his excitement.

"Then I must look for her. Come along, Winifred. I can't run about alone."

Winifred did not want to come along, but Mrs. Neff did not intend to leave the Senator in her clutches. She ran her arm through Winifred's and dragged her away.

Then Tait took Forbes by the arm and spoke with a curious sick thickness: "Let's get out into the air a minute."

Forbes was alarmed by his tone and by the prominence of the veins about his forehead and throat. They walked into the garden filled with soft lantern lights like luminous flowers, the moon over all and the strangely zestful air of Paris like an intoxicant. The orchestra in the garden was just finishing a tune, and the orchestra in the house was just beginning an American tango played with a marked French accent. They found a marble seat in a green niche where it was yet too early for flirts to be found.

"Well, Harvey, she's here—that damned woman—and her toy husband."

Forbes smarted under the hatred the man he loved bore for the woman he loved, and when the Ambassador,

374

trying to be cheerful, spoke hopefully, "But, then, that flame has smoldered out, hasn't it?" Forbes only sighed:

"Oh, I think so—I hope so!"

"What's this? What's this?" Tait gasped. "Are you still at her mercy—*her* mercy?"

Forbes made a gesture of distress: "I don't know! The thought of her has never left me. The sight of her again hurts like the bullet I got in that first brush with the Spanish. And she doesn't look happy. There was a shadow over her."

"There ought to be," Tait grumbled. "She's a cold-blooded, mercenary, calculating—"

"Don't!" Forbes pleaded, but the old man raged on.

"She sold herself to a man she didn't love. She's to blame for—"

"The older I grow," Forbes interposed, "the less I feel that people deserve either blame or praise for being what they are or doing what they do."

"Don't waste your pity on her; she had none for you."

"It's not pity—it's—"

Tait clapped his hand to his left side and choked back a cry of distress. Forbes turned to him with an exclamation of alarm. "You ought to see your doctor."

Tait shook his head: "No, he'd only swear at me for disobeying him. I'm all right—if I can only avoid any excitement. Been going a little too hard. It's that damned dilated heart of mine. The doctor said I ought to be in bed to-night."

"Why did you come here then?"

"Oh, young Webb was afraid that Alice's mother would drag her home if she knew I was not about. But I'm a fool. This life is killing me. I ought to run down to Vichy or Evian for a few days."

"Yes; you mustn't delay any further."

"I'll go if you'll come with me, Harvey. For one thing, it will get you away from that woman."

"Oh, there's no danger from her," said Forbes. "She's married now."

Tait shrugged his shoulders: "That's when a woman is most dangerous. Young girls tied to their mother's apron-strings are risky enough, the Lord knows, but when a woman unhappily married meets an old lover who is still unmarried—humph, the weather doesn't last long as a topic of conversation. You come along with me."

Forbes felt doubly humiliated by his position. "I don't like the idea of running away from a woman."

"You're good enough soldier to know that there are times when it is cowardly not to run away. Do we go to Evian-les-Bains?"

"Yes. To-morrow, if you wish."

"Good! And I want you to promise not to see that woman at all to-night. There are a lot of sharp eyes about, and the gossips can work up a big trade on a very small capital. Will you promise?"

"You are needlessly worried."

"Harvey, I never believed in playing with fire. I haven't asked you many favors. Will you grant me this one?"

Forbes was almost filial in his obedience: "Why, of course I promise not to meet her if I can avoid it."

"Good!" Tait rose to his feet with some difficulty. He was weak and shaken with premonitions. When a man's heart races and misses fire he is filled with dismay. He paused to lay his hands on Forbes' shoulders and plead as if for forgiveness for his solicitude. "Harvey, you may think I'm an old fool, but if you didn't run away from this danger, in after years you might have been sorry that you didn't."

"I understand," said Forbes. "God bless you, I appreciate it. I shall always be grateful for all you've done for me."

"I've done nothing but make a crutch of you, used you to fill the place of my own boy. If only you could—but we won't talk of her. But if anything happens to me—"

"Nothing is going to happen to you."

"I know that, but if anything should, I—I want you to promise to take care of Mildred. She'll have money enough—and so will you. I've fixed that—but—she'll need somebody to—well, we'll talk it over at Evian. Let's go home."

He moved on, leaning heavily on Forbes, but Winifred, seeing him about to escape, pounced on him and led him away in search of an imaginary diplomat.

Forbes, left alone, sank again on the marble bench, a prey to his thoughts. He felt that if he waited in this semi-obscurity he would not be discovered by Persis.

But she was hunting for him. She had eluded Willie, and appeared in the garden just as the Ambassador was being haled away. She paused to wait for Forbes to be alone, and at that moment her husband regained her side; she heard his voice.

CHAPTER LV

"I SAY, Persis, I lost track of you in that ghastly mob. I'm sorry. By the way, wasn't that tall fella in the uniform the same Lieutenant What's-his-name that was honeying around Mrs. Neff?"

Persis was in too fierce a mood to continue that nonsense. She turned on Willie as a she-wolf turns on a terrier at her heels:

"Oh, Lord! Can't I escape you for a moment? Do go somewhere and smoke something. Or if the worst comes to the worst, drink something; but don't stand there making green eyes at me like an ape."

"Green eyes like an ape!" he echoed, stupidly. "Well, I'll be—" Then an unusual vigor of wrath stirred him. "Look here, Persis, I won't have you make fun of me. Everybody else laughs at me, even for winning you. They think you've made a fool of me, and they think you couldn't have married me except for my money. I don't suppose it could be love—nobody ever did love me. But whatever it was that made you marry me, you did marry me, and, by gad, you've got to remember it."

"There's no danger of my forgetting that," Persis snapped, frantic lest Forbes escape her. "Don't be odious! Don't make me hate you."

Willie grew the more fierce. "Well, I'd rather have you hate me than make a fool of me. I won't be laughed at—I won't."

Persis groaned with repugnance: "Oh, you've ceased to be a laughing matter to me, Willie."

Willie was about to reply in kind, but he gave her a

long look and, seeing how beautiful she was, grew more tender. "Everything seems to have ceased to be a laughing matter to you, Persis. What has come over you? Before we were married you were always laughing—at everything, everybody. I used to love to watch you. Even when you guyed me I didn't much mind—because there was fun in it. I used to say I'd give everything I possessed just to have you about, and see the world through your eyes. But from the time we were married you quit laughing. Hang it all, I married you to cheer me up a bit. What in Heaven's name has changed you?"

Before this weakness she relented a little. "Oh, nothing has changed me. Don't worry about me. I'm just a trifle bored with life."

"I've bought you everything you asked for, haven't I?" he asked. "Gad, your dressmaker's bills were enough. But the minute a gown came home you sickened of it. You tired of the theater, of the opera, of dancing. When I took you to the Royal Ascot you yawned as the horses came down the stretch. I bought you three new automobiles, and when we came down from Dieppe to Paris at a million miles an hour the pace scared me cold, but you— you went to sleep."

"It was soothing," she smiled.

"Soothing? Gad! do you want a bally flying-machine?"

"If it could take me to another planet."

Never dreaming how eager she was to be rid of him, he tried to please her in every manner save the one sure method of going away. He grew desperate: "Isn't there anything you want that money can buy?"

"I don't want anything that money can buy," was her dreary confession. Somehow he seemed at last to understand.

"I suppose you're just tired of me," he sighed—"everlasting me. I must be a nuisance to you. Lord knows I am to myself!"

She looked at him with suddenly gentler eyes. In contemning himself he was commending himself. The best approach to a human tribunal, as to a divine, is a humble and a contrite heart. She put out her hand to him, but he did not see it; he set off to find some one to lead him to a Scotch highball. And Persis, now that she was rid of him, was free to glide forward to the marble bench, where she could see Forbes half concealed in a grotto of shadow and a mood of gloom.

The thought of what she was about to do gave her pause. She realized the atrocity of attempting to keep Forbes in mind when she had taken such solemn vows so publicly. She must be kinder to Willie. She tried to dismiss her conscience by telling herself that it would be childish to run away from Forbes. She caught sight of Mrs. Neff hovering about with the recaptured Alice. She dreaded what interpretation Mrs. Neff would put upon her appearance in the environs of Forbes. She remembered with what fierce criticism she had always met the slightest indiscretions of other married women.

A wife's progress must be along a tight wire, and she must walk it exactly. The least step aside attracts attention and invites disaster like the inaccuracy of a Blondel crossing Niagara and carrying a man on his shoulders.

Persis hesitated, breathing hard with enormous excitement over so small a matter. While she hesitated an Italian duke who had been a little too gracious in London approached her like an erect cobra. Her skin crawled at his manner. Yet he had no worse motive than she was dallying with.

Before she could exquisitely make it clear to him that with all due deference she despised him, she saw Senator Tait hurrying toward Forbes, greeting hastily those who stopped him and thredding the increasingly mucilaginous crowd till he reached Forbes' side. Then the two men made their way out beyond the intervening mass.

Persis went back into the house and danced with the

Italian duke what he called "*il trotto alla turca.*" She was so distraite that she never knew how well he made love and how badly he danced.

Later she happened upon the surreptitious Stowe Webb, and learned that Senator Tait and Forbes were leaving Paris in the morning to take the waters somewhere— Vichy, Carlsbad, Marienbad, or Matlock; he was not sure where.

Now Persis regretted her hesitation. She had wasted a precious opportunity to warm her chilled soul with a word from the beloved lips and a look from the eyes and a pressure of the hand that were dearer than any other in the world to her.

She was amazed at her own ability to suffer so much from the loss of so little. She felt an impulse to be alone with her anguish, to huddle over the hearth where the ashes could at least remind her of how warm and cozy she once had been.

She sent for Willie, and he came with a slight elevation of manner which showed that he had found some one to arrange him at least one Scotch-and-soda.

He was demonstrative in the car and very affectionate in the elevator at the Hôtel Meurice, where they were stopping. This did not endear him to Persis.

His man exchanged a glance with her maid as they peeled off their wraps. When man and maid had been sent to bed Willie came shuffling into Persis' dressing-room where she sat staring at her doleful beauty in the mirror. He saw how listless she was, and was awkwardly eager to cheer her up. He could not have depressed her more than by trying to cheer her up. Even he realized his failure eventually and yawned sonorously:

"We're married, and I suppose we've got to stay married—for a while, at least. But I hate to see you unhappy. It's an awful slam on me to have you so blue before the honeymoon is really begun."

"Don't worry any more, Willie," she said, gently.

"I suppose I'm just like a child on Christmas afternoon. I always used to get blue after I'd looked over all the presents and broken most of my toys—and grown tired of the others—and eaten too much candy. And I thought, 'So this is the Christmas I've waited for the whole year long! It doesn't amount to much. I've had all that money can buy—and—and I'm too tired to sleep.'"

"I used to feel like that, too," he said. "And I remember that I usually turned back to some cheap old toy; usually it was a little lead soldier—my first love."

"First love!" she murmured.

He tried to shake off gloom as a wet spaniel shakes off water.

"Oh, I say, Persis, buck up! Don't feel like this. "You're so beautiful; you're simply ripping to-night." He laid his hand on her bare arm. She started at his touch and before she realized it gasped, "Please don't paw me."

He stared at her, aghast: "Do you hate me as much as that?"

"Oh, I don't hate you, Willie! It's myself I hate," Persis cried. "You mustn't mind me; I'm just a little blue and lonely."

He laughed gruesomely. "Bride and groom together on honeymoon, and both terribly lonely! Gad! I wonder if other married couples come to feel this way when the honeymoon turns to green cheese. And do they just bluff it through? It reminds me of that chap in Hogarth's *Mariage à la Mode*, where the wife is yawning and the husband is sunk back in his chair in a dismal stupor. Only he was drunk—I think I'll get drunk."

He stumbled out to find his usual nepenthe. When he came back her door was locked.

CHAPTER LVI

PERSIS sat in grim communion with her image for hours. She faintly heard her husband's tapping on her door, and calling through it at intervals in thicker and thicker speech. But it was like a far-off rumor from a street. She was in session with herself.

She took her boudoir cap from her hair, and sat in the cascade of it peering through as from a cavern, and smoking always. She was smoking much too much, but she felt a companionship in tobacco. As she held the cap in her hand she thought of Forbes; and the remembrance was so joyous that she vowed to brave the world to get back to him.

But she pondered what the world would say of her, how it had dealt with the others that had openly defied it, and she was afraid. Then she vowed that she would take her love secretly and cleverly. She would hunt for Forbes till she met him and regained him.

Then she pictured how he would look at her when he understood. She imagined him starting back from her as from something abhorrent. She threw a cigarette-stub at her face in the mirror and gasped: "Pagh!" She could endure anything better than such cheapening of herself in Forbes' eyes. And after a while she began to think of her self-respect. She had only herself. She must keep that self precious.

Worn out at last with her silent war, she bent her head on her crossed hands and fell asleep among the fripperies of her dressing-table. · These temptations in the wilderness come to people in various places. This tired butterfly fought with evil and won the duel in a boudoir in a fashion‑able hotel in Paris.

Hours later she woke in broad daylight and crept to bed with tingling arms and aching forehead. She did not wake again till noon. Nichette had tiptoed about her like a sentinel and had kept Willie at a distance. He discharged her a dozen times, but she simply shrugged and sniffed and answered him in French too rapid for him to follow or reply to.

When at last Persis sat up with her coffee and crescents on her knees, Nichette read to her the news in the French columns of the Paris *Herald*. She learned that Ambassa‑dor-elect Tait and his entourage had gone to Evian-les-Bains.

Willie came in with new plans for Persis' diversion. He suggested a visit to Switzerland and Lake Geneva. She would have liked to go to the mountains. There was something heroic in them. But Evian was closely adjacent to Switzerland. She nobly suggested Norway and Sweden. The thought of fjords and midnight suns and things was also heroic.

In the meanwhile she must make haste to dress for the *Prix des Drags*, and she took some interest in the choice of a gown sufficiently striking to insure success in the fierce rivalry of that great costume race.

Everybody said that the world had not seen such undressing in public since the Grecian revival at the time of the Directoire. Persis was not the least astounding figure there. She felt that, after a deed of such sacrifice as she had achieved in forswearing love, she had earned an extra license in her draperies. Willie raised a tempest about her gown, but she felt that she had done enough for him. She was suffering that morning-after sullenness which follows unusual indulgences in virtue as well as other excesses.

Life once more was a tango. She shifted from costume to costume like a dressmaker's model. She went the rounds of *thés dansants*, and musicales, and embassies, town houses, hotels, and châteaux, watering-places, and mountains, lakes, and seas. But she kept away from Switzerland till she read that Ambassador Tait was at his desk in Paris; and then she avoided Paris and went to Trouville.

And so the days totaled into weeks, and the weeks became a month, two, three, six. She fled from boredom to boredom. She skimmed the cream of life and whipped it, and it turned sour. Though her abiding-places were all oases and her tents were of silk, she led only a Bedouin existence. After all, she and Willie were but tramps— velvet-clad hoboes. Variety became monotony, luxury an oppression, contentment a will-o'-the-wisp.

She went to America and found that loveless contentment was not among the Yankee inventions. She went back to Europe, and it was not among the Parisian devices. There was everything for sale on the Rue de la Paix except peace. She had not come to Paris purposely to find Harvey Forbes, but she had sickened of being good, and she had grown nauseated with denying her heart. If fate willed that their communion should be renewed she would no longer tamper with destiny.

She wondered if time had cured Forbes' love. She wondered if he cared for some one else—Mildred Tait, for instance, or some Parisian witch. At the mere thought her heart beat like the wings of a wounded bird, and she knew that she loved him and always would love him.

Half a year of Willie's tempers and whinings, his indigestions and colds, and his diminishing patience with her whims, his growing habit of complaining of her extravagances, his quarrels with their servants, with every waiter, every messenger-boy, and hotel-keeper, had worn out even her courtesy. They quarreled shamelessly in private, and with less and less caution in public.

And now she was beginning to feel that she earned all she got, and was paying usury on her money, and being badly treated in the bargain. She was arriving at that sick frame of mind that makes cashiers and statesmen and married people unfaithful to their trusts.

This was her humor when she met Forbes again. She had tried in various ways to gain invitations to affairs of the Embassy. But Tait wasted no diplomacy on cutting out the Enslees. He was the more brutal about this since he felt that he was guarding his daughter's welfare.

Mildred had made herself dear to the more earnest elements of Paris. She had grown somewhat less of a joke to the more frivolous. The entertainments at the Embassy were not quite so Puritanical now, and her costumes had amazingly improved since her father had put her under the direct control of a tyrannical dressmaker of world-wide fame.

Whether she were growing to be merely a habit with Forbes or not, they were more and more together. They fought bitterly on the question of war, which she considered an unmitigated horror and he believed to be the loftiest form of tragedy. But the whetting of mind on mind was producing sparks, and Tait hoped that some day one of them would set their two hearts on fire.

He was preparing for that day by making Forbes less poor. His post kept him from taking advantage of the financial secrets he stumbled on. But when he put Mildred in the hands of a dressmaker he gave the financial destinies of Forbes to a retired capitalist, who juggled Forbes' five hundred dollars into a thousand in a pair of weeks; and that thousand into three. Then he encouraged Forbes to borrow, indorsed his notes and speculated with the proceeds pyramidally. He was enjoying it as a form of chess. At the end of half a year Forbes was talking as much of the Bourse and Argentines as he was of projectiles and trajectories.

Having assured Forbes of enough money in bank to give him a salubrious self-confidence, Tait dropped hints of a certain clause in his will and sat back to watch the result. He was counting on receiving as his Christmas gift the news that Forbes and Mildred were to be married, and he was polishing up a joke about giving them inside rates on the consular fees for that complicated ceremony.

And then the Enslees came to Paris in an unusual snow-storm, and winter set in about the old man's overworked, undermined heart. He did his best to keep Persis and Forbes apart; but when were the old ever vigilant enough to thwart the young?

CHAPTER LVII

ONE day Mrs. Mather Edgecumbe found the Enslees shivering like a pair of waifs in a restaurant famous for its cuisine and infamous for its heating arrangements. She asked them if they were coming to the *thé dansant* she was giving at her home that afternoon. They had forgotten all about it, and Persis pleaded an engagement with her doctor. Mrs. Edgecumbe was "so sorry. There would be hardly any Americans there, then, except the old faithful Ambassador and Captain Forbes."

Persis' heart warmed instantly, but she said she was afraid that she had some other engagement booked; in any case, they might drop in for a minute. She shivered with exultance and blamed it on the chill.

When five o'clock came round Persis carelessly remembered the half-promise to Mrs. Mather Edgecumbe. Willie was out of humor. Persis angelically urged him to stay in his room and nurse his cold. Her unusual thought for his welfare startled him. It delighted him. He decided to stay by her and get more of the tenderness she was lavishing to-day. She could not shake him loose.

The *thé dansant* was a failure in Mrs. Mather Edgecumbe's mind, and in her sister Winifred's heart, for the storm kept most of the Parisians away, and the Ambassador sent word by Forbes that he would be tardy if he came at all. He pleaded motives of state. But he sent Forbes with his apologies.

Forbes, having been on a visit in his official capacity, was again in uniform. His eyes and cheeks were aglow from the cold, and Persis watched him with adoration as he came nearer and nearer.

WHAT WILL PEOPLE SAY?

He did not see her, even when he paused to talk to Mrs. Edgecumbe, so close to Persis that she could have touched him. And when she could not endure the delay any longer, she thrust her hand beneath his eyes, and murmured: "Captain Forbes doesn't remember me, but I met him in New York ages ago."

Her voice, suddenly leaping out of the grave of memory, terrified him. He whirled so quickly that his sword caught in her gown. He knelt to disengage it, and there was laughter over the confusion, and then Mrs. Edgecumbe was called away by a new-comer, and they were left together.

Persis beamed upon the complete disarray of all his faculties, and spoke with affected raillery, though her own mind was in a seethe.

"At last we meet again! And how magnificent we are in our gorgeous uniform! It's only the second time I've seen you in it. And I believe we are no longer plain Mr. Forbes—but Captain! Captain Harvey Forbes, U. S. A.! And they say we are rich now. What a pity I didn't wait a little!"

Forbes was hurt at her flippancy. He smiled dismally, and she purred on: "I assure you your title and your wealth are vastly becoming; almost as becoming as all these buttons and epaulettes and things." She walked around him, looking him over like an inspecting officer. "Um-m! How very nice! Magnificent!"

"Oh, I beg of you—" Forbes protested, tortured with chagrin.

But she went on, "And a sword, too!" She ventured even to pull the blade a little way from its scabbard. He would have killed a man for doing that, and he almost wanted to kill Persis as she tantalized him with a strange mixture of ridicule and idolatry. "I've no doubt the boulevards are strewn with the broken hearts of Frenchwomen. Who could resist you? I'm sure my own heart isn't anywhere near healed. It was very cruel of you, Harvey, to throw me over and run away after you had stolen my poor young affections."

Forbes was distraught; he groaned, "I see you've not forgotten how to make fun of me."

But Persis went on in mock petulance: "It wasn't at all nice of you to cast me off just because I married Willie."

This gave Forbes a chance to return her ridicule and he asked, "By the way, how is your excellent husband?"

"You can see for yourself. There he is, still unable to learn the tango and trying to teach it to a fat Marquise."

Forbes attempted that most uncivil of tones to a woman, the ironical: "I hear that you and Mr. Enslee are the most devoted of couples."

"Oh, it's a silly custom that married people should pretend to be congenial during their honeymoon," Persis said. "Thank heaven, my initiation is almost over."

Forbes was genuinely horrified at such dealing with a subject so sacred as marriage; he forsook irony for his usual forthright utterance:

"Surely your—your husband doesn't neglect you?"

There was a touch of quick anxiety in Forbes' tone that showed how deeply he still cherished her.

"Neglect me?" Persis quoted. "If he only would! Willie does tag after me even more than I could wish; but he is growing restless. I can usually escape him by staying at home. He's doing the music-halls very thoroughly. If I can only suggest some very shocking *revue* I am assured of an evening alone. He is going to one over on Montmartre to-morrow night. I shall be quite deserted. We are stopping at the Hotel Meurice."

There was so dire a meaning in her hint and so much danger in playing again with the fire whose scar he still bore that Forbes ceased fencing and slashed: "Why do you torment me? You refused my love once."

"Never your love, my dear boy," said Persis, with

abrupt seriousness. "I never refused your love—only your hand. I always encouraged your love."

"But I was poor," Forbes sneered.

"Yes, you were poor," Persis said, taking his own word and turning it against him, "and I knew less than I do now." She walked away to a niche beside a statue where they could talk without being overheard, but, being visible, were chaperoned by the crowd. She sank upon a settle of gold and old rose and motioned him to her side. Then, while her face and her fan proclaimed that their conversation was of the idlest, her voice was deep with elegy:

"Harvey, try to be just. If you had been rich—oh! if you had been rich!—then, as you are now, Harvey, then I could have believed that such a thing as a love-match is feasible."

"But I was poor!" Forbes reiterated, with a knell-like persistence.

"That was Fate's fault, not mine," said Persis, in all solemnity. "But haven't I been honest with you? You declared that you loved me; I confessed that I loved you."

"Was it honest, then, not to give me your heart?"

"My whole heart has always been yours for the asking—and still is."

Forbes recoiled with a sudden: "What are you saying? You have a husband now!"

"What does that prove?" was Persis' grim reply. "I don't owe him anything in the inside of my heart. He didn't buy that, thank God! Before the world, I owe him everything, and I should be the first to abhor any open indiscretion, for my ten commandments are condensed to two: 'Don't be indiscreet!' and 'Beware of what people will say!' What more could a husband ask?"

Forbes tossed his hands in despair. He gave her up. She and her creed were beyond his understanding. "A fine code, that!"

"It is the morality of half the world, Harvey, rich or

poor, city or country," Persis declared. "The crime consists in being found out."

"Do you realize what you are saying?" Forbes demanded, eager to shield her from her own blasphemies. But she ran on unheedingly.

"Even I have a heart; and why should I play the hypocrite before you of all men? Before Willie Enslee? Yes; he is my husband. Before the gossipy world? Yes; it is the one duty I feel I owe that man. Ours was no marriage for love."

"But it was a marriage," Forbes urged, stoutly, and rose to escape.

"Yes, but after all, what is a marriage?" Persis demanded, like a Pilate asking, "What is truth?" She rose to her feet, but paused as ardor swept her headlong. "Do you think it possible for any woman to live her life out without a lover? She may cherish the memory of a dead man or a faithless man; or throw her affection away on a fool or a rake; she may keep it a secret almost from herself, but never, never, never believe that any woman can exist without some man to pay worship to."

Forbes could only attempt a weak sarcasm, "Is it impossible that a woman should love her husband?"

In a daze he fell back to his seat, forgetful that he left her standing; but she was too much engrossed with her great problem to heed this; she went on, earnestly:

"Any woman may love her husband for a little while; or in rare case for a lifetime, especially if he beats her or is a drunkard." Then her unwonted oratory on abstract subjects palled on her. She came back to the concrete instance with an abrupt, "But Harvey, Harvey, why should we be wasting time talking about love?" She bent over him, but he did not even look up at her. He shook his head helplessly.

"I wasn't bred in your world. I can't understand a thing you have said."

His aloofness of manner gave Persis a sense of loneliness,

and she wailed to him as from afar, though she sank down close to him. "But can't you understand how fate has made a fool of me? I married for wealth and to cut a wide swath. Well, I have the wealth. I can cut the swath. But I've found that my ambition isn't enough, any more than your soldier ambitions were enough. Harvey, I'm lonely, terribly lonely. My heart is empty; it is like an old deserted house, and a ghost haunts it, and the ghost is—I don't have to tell you who the ghost is?"

"And you know," Forbes echoed, "what ghost haunts me."

Persis was melted by his kinship with her suffering. She leaned so close to him that her very perfume appealed to him as the perfume wherewith one flower calls to another in the noontime of desire. And she said: "Harvey, I'm going to tell you a terrible secret that I've hardly dared to tell myself: I—I crossed the ocean to find you!"

He was suffocated with longing for her, and horror of her. He gasped, "My God! on your honeymoon!"

Everywhere in that day there seemed to be a band somewhere playing a turkey-trot. There was such a band here, and such music was to be expected; but there was something whimsical about the fact that the tune this band struck up now was a rag-time version of "Mendelssohn's Wedding March."

Persis was so eager to be in Forbes' arms again, and the dance was so ample an excuse, that she smiled into his mask of horror. "We haven't danced for .ever so long."

A wanton whoop of the violins swept away all such solemn things as honor, decency, duty. He rose and caught her in his embrace. It was the same girlish body, irresistibly warm and lithe. They swung and sidled and hopped with utter cynicism. The only remnant of his horror was a foolish, bewildered, muttered: "How could you?"

"Come to Paris?" she asked.

"Yes."

"Because I felt you still loved me as I still love you, and because I thought you were—perhaps—afraid."

"Afraid, eh?" He laughed, his professional soldier's pride on fire. "Well, I don't think you will find me a coward."

And he tightened his arm about her like a vise and spun her so dizzily that, though she was rejoiced by his brutality, the discretion that was her decalogue spoiled her rapture. She felt again that swoon of fear, and made him lead her back to their niche.

She did not know that Ambassador Tait had come in and had watched the vortex, was watching now with terror the look on Forbes' face and her answering smile. He could not hear their words—he did not need to. He knew what their import would be. The burlesque of the wedding music was the final touch of sarcasm.

Persis, ignorant of his espionage, sighed, "Oh, it is wonderful to be together again!"

"Wonderful," Forbes panted. "But it is in a crowd, and you are married."

"That does not mean that I am never to see you alone, does it?" she asked, anxiously and challengingly.

Forbes was still wise enough and well enough aware of his own passion to say, "But discovery and scandal would be the only result."

"Not if we were very discreet," Persis pleaded, thinking of those lonely months.

"But your husband?"

Persis uttered that ugly old truth, "If we can evade gossip abroad, we shall be safe enough at home."

And as if in object-lesson, Willie Enslee joggled up that very moment. He showed the influence of mild tippling on a limited capacity, and, coming forward, shook hands foolishly and forcibly with Captain Forbes. "How d'ye do—Mr. Ward," he drawled.

"Captain Forbes, dear," Persis corrected.

"That's right. I always was an ass about names, Mr. Ward. I haven't seen you for years and years, have we? Have you met my wife? Oh, of course you have."

Forbes was revolted. There was something loathsome about the little farce. Enslee reminded him of the clown in "I Pagliacci," and Persis, like another Nedda, was determined to finish the scene. Tucking her fan under her thigh, she said with innocent voice, "Oh, Willie, I've lost my fan somewhere; would you mind looking for it?"

Obediently Enslee turned and wandered about, scanning the floor carefully and chortling idiotically, "Fan, fan, who's got the fan?" And so he floated harmlessly and blindly out of the cloud that was thickening around his household.

Persis laughed. "You see what an ideal husband Willie is?" But Forbes, who had a strong stomach for warfare with its mangled enemies and shattered comrades, shuddered at this tame domestic horror. He blurted out:

"It is all the more shameful to deceive a fool."

"Oh, now you're becoming scrupulous again!" said Persis, who thought pride of little moment in the face of the victory she had set her heart on.

But now she was confronted by an adversary of more weight and acumen than Willie, a man whose trade was diplomacy and politics. Ambassador Tait came forward. He was a little pale and weak, and he felt his heart laboring in his breast, but he had at least one more good fight in him, and when he found Forbes plainly enmeshed, though struggling, in Persis' gossamer web, the old man resolved to make the fight at whatever cost.

After a moment of hesitation he came briskly forward with a blunt: "Pardon me a moment, Mrs. Enslee, I have an important communication for the Captain. These state secrets you know." And he led Forbes to an adjoining room, the library, where he said in a low tone, "Har-

395

vey, my boy, I've cooked up an imaginary errand to get you away from her."

But Forbes tossed his head at this aspersion on his ability to take care of himself. He answered, "I'm not afraid."

Tait's eyes grew very sad, though his lips smiled when he said: "Well, I'm afraid for you. You're not responsible when you're in her magnetic circle." Then, seeing that Persis had resolutely followed them into the room, he raised his voice for Persis' benefit: "You'll find the papers on my desk. Read them carefully and sign them if they're all right. They must be mailed this evening." Then he deliberately pushed the reluctant and faltering captain from the room, hardly leaving him time to say, "You'll excuse me, Mrs. Enslee?"

Persis understood it all and answered with thinly veiled pique, "I'll have to." But she would not surrender him so easily. She called after Forbes, "I'll expect you back as soon as you have signed those—alleged papers."

The Ambassador was jolted. He could think of nothing to say. He watched Forbes go, then started to follow; noted that Persis was alone, and remembered the laws of courtesy enough to ask:

"May I send you an ice—or your husband?"

"An ice—or my husband?" Persis was forced to smile at such a collocation. "Neither, please. Sit down, Ambassador."

Tait had not expected this. With a hesitating "Er—ah! Thank you!" he seated himself as far as possible from her on a leather divan. Immediately she rose, crossed the room, and sat next to him. There was no escaping her now, and Tait felt like calling for help.

Persis forsook all the modulations of diplomacy and cut straight to the point. "Ambassador Tait, why don't you like me?"

"Why, I—I admire you immensely," he gasped, amazed.

"Oh, drop diplomacy; I'm not the President of France!"
Persis said, with a whit of vexation. When a woman
answers a compliment with anger she means business.
Persis repeated: "I said, why don't you like me?"

"But—I—I—" Tait fumbled for a word; then, somewhat angered by his discomfort, met a woman's directness
with a man's bluntness. "Well, why should I?"

Persis parried his rudeness with a return to gentle
measures; she beamed. "I'm very nice! I was good to
my mother. I'm good to my husband."

"But are you?"

"I'm as good a wife as he deserves. You've seen
him?"

Tait smiled in spite of himself, for he was one of Willie's
numberless non-admirers. Now Persis, seeing him smiling, returned to open attack:

"Last summer you took Captain Forbes to Evian-les-
Bains to get him away from me. Didn't you?"

Tait was off his guard; he stammered: "Certainly not—
that is—well, how did you find it out?"

Persis shrugged her shoulders and smiled. "My
mother took me to England when I was very young to
get me away from a beautiful butcher's boy. She succeeded; she was a woman. You won't; you're a man."

"Help, help!" Tait gasped, in a parody of fear that had
a groundwork of reality.

"You love Captain Forbes, don't you?" Persis lunged
at his heart again; and he answered, solemnly:

"Yes, I do, as if he were my own son."

"Why don't you want me to see him?"

"Why do you want to see him? You're married."

"But they don't keep women in harems nowadays.
Paris is very dull this winter. Don't take Captain Forbes
away again."

"As I remember, you gave him marching orders once
yourself. You mustn't mind if he goes of his own accord
now."

"But he won't go of his own accord if you don't make him. Why do you? You're not afraid of me?"

"Oh, but I am."

Persis laughed with a kind of pride. "Really! You flatter me! But why?"

Tait twisted his big, soft hands together and stared at her a long while before he could speak. "This is very embarrassing, Mrs. Enslee; but since you are so frank, let me ask you one question. Will you answer it frankly?"

"That depends upon the question." Persis chuckled, never dreaming of its nature. When it came it was:

"Are you in love with Captain Forbes?"

She laughed evasively now. "What a remarkable question!"

The old lawyer repeated the demand:

"Are you in love with Captain Forbes?"

"I think he is very nice," she dodged. "But what has that to do with our friendship?"

"Everything," Tait answered, with tightened lips. "Mrs. Enslee, your father and I rowed together in the same college crew, and Harvey's father was my best friend. May I speak freely to you?"

She responded immediately to the almost affection of his tone. "I wish you would."

"What little success in life I have had," Tait began, with the somewhat formal speech of an orator, "has been due to my habit of foreseeing dangerous combinations and preventing them, or running away from them. The most dangerous combination on earth is a woman, a man, and another man. No married woman has a right to the—I believe you said 'friendship,' of a man who cares for her as Harvey cares for you."

She extracted from his warning only the hidden sweet. "And he does care for me still!"

"But you've married another man."

"Of course," she answered. "But do you think that

I can find Mr. Enslee so fascinating that I must give up all my friends?"

"Friends!" Tait exclaimed, with bitterness. "In my day, Mrs. Enslee, I have seen some of the proudest families in New York dragged into the mire of public shame by tragedies that began as innocent experiments in friendship. Don't risk it, Mrs. Enslee. You are on dangerous ground."

She mused aloud. "And you think he loves me still?"

Tait tossed his mane in despair. "Good Lord! That's all my words have meant to you? Well, since we are talking so bluntly, you'll perhaps permit me to say that I know you are not happily married. Everybody knew you never would be happy with Willie Enslee."

"I thought I'd be as happy with him as with anybody-else," she answered, meekly; "but since you assume that I am not happy, why deny me the friendship of a man whose society I am fond of? Don't you think that everybody has the right to be happy?"

"Indeed I don't!"

"Doesn't the Constitution, or the Declaration of Independence, or something guarantee everybody the right to life, liberty, and the pursuit of—"

"Yes, the pursuit!" Tait cried. "But the Constitution doesn't guarantee that anybody will get happiness, and there are laws that take away life, take away liberty, take away even the right to the pursuit of happiness."

She was on unfamiliar ground among constitutions. She was more at home in emotion. "Let's not get into a legal debate. All I know is that Harvey used to love me, and I loved him too much to marry him, because he was poor, and because I was bred to reckless extravagance. Besides, I had ambitions. I didn't know then what a vanity they were. But now—well, I don't pretend to be a saint, but I have a heart—a kind of heart. I love only one man on earth. You know that he still loves me. Don't rob us of the happiness we can find in each other's society—the innocent happiness."

A gesture of unbelief escaped the Ambassador. "How long could such love remain innocent—when it begins by being unlawful?"

"But I love him," she insisted, "and he loves me with all his heart. Some day, I presume"—the coming sorrow cast its shadow over her already—"some day, no doubt, he'll find somebody he loves more, and he'll marry her. He can have anybody now; but when he came to me he was poor; he needed money. But I also needed money! Things have changed; money has come to him, as it always comes, too late. But that's no reason for robbing me of my chance for a little while of happiness. And you mustn't—oh, you mustn't rob him of the happiness I could give him!"

Tait was always afraid of himself when his tenderness was appealed to, for he knew from experience that such an appeal if harkened a moment too long, would smother all judgment, all resistance. He felt his heart yearning toward Persis' world-old cry, "Happiness! happiness! a little happiness!" He tried to be harsh.

"But, my good woman—my dear girl—you had your chance; you made your choice. You must pay the price. We can't all have the love we want. I can't. You can't."

Persis laid her hand on his arm. "But why? Why?"

And Tait, after a weak temptation, girded himself for the eternal battle with unholy happiness, and answered with Mosaic simplicity:

"Because it is against the law."

"But you know," Persis returned, unabashed, "you were once a lawyer—you know that the laws in the books are only made for those who haven't the skill to bend them without breaking them."

"Such a love as yours is against the great unwritten laws of society."

Persis would not be crushed with precepts. She sneered: "Society! Is anybody on the square? Why shouldn't we be happy in our own way?"

Tait hesitated, then answered coldly: "There are ten thousand reasons, Mrs. Enslee. I'll give you the one that will appeal to you most strongly: 'You're bound to get found out.'"

"Don't you think I have any discretion? Do you think I am a fool?"

"The first sign of being a fool is trying to play double with the world. Some day—let me warn you—some day you will find yourself so tangled up in your own cleverness that you will be delivered, bound hand and foot, to the shame—yes, the shame of a horrible exposure."

She blenched at this facer. "Don't speak to me as though I were a criminal!"

He struck out again. "Then don't become one. You have no right to love Captain Forbes, nor he to love you. It is a simple question of duty."

"Duty?" she raged. "I want happiness. I'm like a hungry woman standing before a window filled with bread. Your duty says, Stay there and starve. But it isn't duty that lets people starve. It's being afraid."

Tait put off all restraint of courtesy. "Oh, I understand your creed. It's the creed of your set. You're not afraid of any risk. You fear nothing but self-sacrifice. Your greatest horror is being bored. But you'll find that there is a worse boredom than you suffer now—the ennui of exile, of ostracism. The very set that practises your theory is the most merciless to those that get found out. It's like a pack of wolves on the chase. The one that falls or is wounded is torn to pieces by the rest, and then they rush on again. I mean to save Harvey from that pack at any cost."

She had no refuge but a prayer. "I implore you not to break my heart."

Tait donned in manner the black cap of a judge. "Such hearts as yours ought to be broken, Mrs. Enslee, for the health of the world. I understand you. I don't blame you. I don't blame your mother in her grave. It was her breeding, as it is yours and that of your pack. You are the people who bring wealth into disrepute. The noise of your revels drowns the quiet charities of the rich who are also good and busy with noble works. I'm afraid of you all. But I don't blame you. I don't blame the criminals, the thieves, madmen; but I fear them. And in all mercy I would mercilessly put them out of the way of doing harm to the peace of the world."

Persis saw that for once appeal could not melt. She said, with resignation: "Then you are my sworn enemy?"

"No," Tait protested, "I would be your friend as far as I safely can. But I love Harvey as a son. I would save him from the fire of perdition, beautiful as it is, bright as it is. And you are the fire."

"And so you will fight me?" Persis faltered.

"To the death!" the old jurist cried, as he got heavily to his feet; "though it breaks Harvey's heart—and your heart—and mine." He staggered weakly and jolted against the divan.

CHAPTER LVIII

PERSIS, forgetting that he was her enemy, leaped to his aid with instinctive womanliness. "You are ill; let me get you something."

Tait straightened himself with an effort, saying: "I'm all right now, thank you. I mustn't let myself get excited, that's all." He was touched by her sudden charity in his behalf. He gazed at her sadly, and, taking her hand, spoke venerably as a father. He was too sad for her sake to be sad for his own. "I'm sorry for you, little woman. You've a big, warm heart; but this is a cold, hard world, and you mustn't try to break its laws. They are based on the scandals and the tragedies of thousands of years, millions on millions of foolish lovers. The world is old, my child, and it is stronger than any of us. And it can punish without mercy. Don't risk it."

An almost unknown earnestness stirred Persis. "You're right, of course. I suppose I must give up all hope of happiness. It's my punishment. I'll take my medicine like a little man."

"That's splendid!" Tait cried. "Live square—in the open. Respect the conventionalities; they're the world's code of morals. If you really love Harvey, let him go his way."

"I'll prove to you that I do love him!" she said, laughing nervously. "I'll give him up. He used to think I was heartless and mercenary. He shall go on thinking so. It's awfully hard, but it is the one way I can help him, isn't it?"

The old man squeezed her slim hand in both of his.

"It's the one way. God bless you! And you won't see him again?"

"No," she said, with all the vigor of her soul. Then she caught a glimpse of Forbes. He had returned hurriedly. He was looking for her. She amended her promise: "Except to tell him good-by. I've got to tell him good-by—and make him think I was only—only fooling him, haven't I?"

The old man's triumph collapsed again. But he could not demand everything. He nodded and left her as Forbes appeared at the door. With the mocking laughter of fiends, the band brayed another tango. It was faint in the distance, but it was a satanic comment. Persis made haste to get her business done.

"Well, Harvey, good-by. I'm off to Capri to-morrow."

"But I thought—" he stammered. "You're not going to leave just as we meet again? I thought—"

"You never could take a joke, could you, Harvey?"

"But you said—"

"I'm sorry, Harvey. But I'm married now."

She was turning his own weapons on him. He was befuddled with her whims. He repeated, "You told me you loved me, that you were unhappy."

"You ought to have known I was only fooling you. I'm Mrs. Enslee now. And whom God hath joined—"

He was beside himself with rage. She had wheedled him out of his honor, and now she mocked him where she had left him. He sneered:

"God didn't join you and Enslee. God's voice doesn't speak every time a hired preacher reaches out for a wedding fee! It was the devil that joined you, and God keeps you asunder. God joined you with me. He meant us for each other. But you hadn't the courage to face a little poverty. You wanted prestige and position, and you bought them with the love that belonged to me. You haven't the courage now to deny that you are unhappy, that you love me still."

She trembled before the storm of his wrath. "But I don't—I don't love you any more. I am happy."

"You can't look me in the eyes, Persis, and repeat that lie."

She tried vainly to meet his glare. She mumbled weakly, "Why, I'm happy—enough."

"Do you love me still?" he demanded.

"N-no! Of course not!"

He wanted to strike her, primevally, for a coward, a liar, a female cad. He controlled himself and groaned: "Well, that makes everything simpler. Good-by."

She seized his arm and threw off the disguise. "Harvey, Harvey, I can't stand it. I can't endure the thought of it. I can't live without your love. I don't care what happens. I never did love anybody else but you. I never shall."

His love came back in a wild wave. He seized her blindly, and she hid blindly in his arms, sobbing: "I am so unhappy, so unutterably lonely! You must love me, Harvey, for I love you. I love you."

They were as oblivious of their peril as Tristan and Isolde in the spell of the love philter. Only the old Ambassador, who had hovered near to shield their farewell, saw them. The vision was like a thunderbolt. To hear of a scandal, to be convinced of it is as nothing to seeing it. That comes like an exposure, an indecency, a slap in the face. The Ambassador was furious with disgust. He stormed into the room: "Can I believe my eyes? Are you both lost to common sense? Is this your discretion, Mrs. Enslee? Do you realize where you are?"

Persis toppled out of Forbes' relaxed embrace, and spoke from a daze: "No—I forgot—I must be out of my mind."

Forbes came to her defense: "You mustn't blame her. It was my fault."

"No, it was mine," Persis insisted. "But I couldn't help it."

Tait was filled with contempt. "What if it had been any of the guests that had found you two maniacs as I did. What if I had been Enslee!"

Persis was as amazed as he was. She muttered, "I know—I know—but I can't stand everything."

Tait tried to patch up his broken plan. "Harvey, you've disappointed me bitterly. But I give you one more chance to retrieve yourself. Promise me never to see Mrs. Enslee again."

Forbes shook his head.

Tait could hardly believe his senses. "My God! Must the deep friendship of two men always be at the mercy of the first woman that comes along? Harvey, Harvey, I beg you to give this woman up!"

"I can't."

Tait's voice glittered with anger. "You've got to! I command you to! You can't commit this infamy and remain with me!"

Forbes set his jaw hard. "I resign."

Tait snapped: "I accept."

Persis was frantic at this outcome of her passion. "No, no! Oh, don't! I'd rather die than be the cause of a breach between you two." She clutched Tait's arm. "Don't listen to him!"

Forbes seized her other hand. "I'll not give you up again. You belong to me."

"You are wrecking my trust in humanity," Tait groaned; then his wrath blazed again. "But I'll break up this intrigue at any cost, even if I have to tell Enslee."

Persis stared at him in a panic. "You couldn't do that."

Tait had made one step to the door. He hung irresolute before the loathsome office of the tattle-tale. "What in the name of God is a man to do? If I tell your husband I am a contemptible cad. If I don't tell him I am your accomplice." He pondered deeply, and chose between the evils. "Well, I'd rather have you two think me a cad than to be a criminal and a coward." He took another step to the door.

Persis clung to his sleeve. "Oh, I implore you!"

He shook her loose. "I am going to tell your husband what I saw."

And then the man most deeply concerned appeared in the doorway. Willie Enslee stumbled at the sill and spoke with a blur: "Pershish, itsh time we were dresshing for d-dinner."

Tait looked at him in disgust, then at Persis and Forbes, who stood cowering with suspense. The old man shivered in an agony of decision. "Mr. Enslee, I must tell you—"

He clapped his hand to his heart, and strangled at the words: "I must tell you—I must tell you—good night!"

He could not force his tongue to the task. The fierce effort broke him. He wavered. A sudden languor invaded him. His muscles turned to sand. He crumbled in a heap.

Forbes ran to him, and with all difficulty heaved the limp huge frame into a chair that Persis pushed forward. He straightened the arms that flopped like a scarecrow's, and steadied the great leonine head that rolled drunkenly on the immense shoulders. And he spoke to Enslee as if he were a servant.

"Run for a doctor—quick—you fool!"

Willie staggered away, almost sobered with fright. Persis stood wringing her hands. Through her brain ran the music of the tango they were playing:

> At the devil's ball, at the devil's ball,
> Dancing with the devil—oh, the little devil!
> Dancing at the devil's ball.

She ran to the door like a fury and shrieked: "Stop that music! For God's sake, stop that music!"

The music ended in shreds of discord. The dancers paused in puppet attitudes, then turned like a huddle of curious cattle and drifted toward the door. Persis returned to Forbes' side, and, bending close, heard the old man speaking thickly as his hands fluttered feebly about Forbes' arm.

"Harvey—I'm so—sor-ry for you—and for her. Take care of—my poor—ch-child, won't you?"

"Yes, yes!" Forbes whispered.

"And—and Harvey—I wanted to—to die in A-mer-America. Take me b-back and bury me—at home, won't you?"

"Yes, yes!"

The soft hands glided along Forbes' arm in a fumbling caress.

"Th-thass—a goo' boy. You've been a—a—a—a son to me. Har-har-vey. Goo'-b-b— Good-by!"

Forbes bent down and pressed his lips to the old man's forehead.

Liveried servants with wan faces glided through the crowd, and, lifting the chair, struggled from the room with its great burden, the old head wagging, the lips laboring at the messages they could not accomplish.

Forbes followed the chair as if it were already the coffin of his ideal among men. Persis waited in a trance, shaken now and then with sudden onsets of ague, but otherwise motionless, her whole soul pensive. Willie hung about her, whining:

"I say, old girl, let's be getting home—I feel all creepy. Awfully unfortunate, wasn't it? Let's be getting home. Rotten luck for the Ambassador. Nice old boy, too. Let's be getting home."

Persis did not answer. By and by Willie went in search of his coat and her furs. The other guests dispersed. Outside there was a muffled hubbub of chasseurs calling carriages and cars, of horns squawking, of doors slammed.

Winifred could be heard sobbing in the room where the musicians were putting up their violins and slinking out. Mrs. Mather Edgecumbe was audible in the stillness telephoning the alarm to the Embassy.

Persis stood fixed, still staring where Forbes had gone. Suddenly her face lighted up. Forbes wandered back all bewildered. She forced her hand on him, and he took it idly. It was some time before he could speak that ultimate word "Dead!"

Persis wrung his hand and sighed:

"Poor old fellow! I'm sorry he hated me so bitterly. He said he'd fight against my happiness till he died, and now—"

Forbes did not hear her. He was thinking only of the foster-father he had lost. He mumbled, with dark dejection:

"I'm alone now—alone!"

But Persis' face was overswept with a shaft of light. Glancing over her shoulder, and seeing that no one was near their door, she moved closer to Forbes, laid her other hand on his, and spoke with all meekness and with a questioning appeal.

"Not alone, Harvey? I'm here."

He opened his clenched eyes a little and met her upward gaze. He closed his eyes again against her. She waited. Only a moment, and then with a sudden frenzy he gripped her in a mad embrace and smote her lips with his. She closed her eyes in ecstasy.

Immediately he started back from her in horror, groaning: "What am I thinking? And he's just dead!"

"He's dead, but I live!" She meant only to soothe him, but through her low voice an exultance broke like a bugle of triumph, and she whispered again: "I live! I live!"

So the eyes of Jael must have widened when she had driven the nail through the temples of Sisera.

In her victory she remembered discretion and glided aside from Forbes just before Willie entered the room with a servant carrying Persis' furs.

"Come along, Persis," Willie complained; "we can't stay here all night."

"I'm quite ready," she answered, with bridal gentleness.

Then, "Good-by, Captain Forbes; so glad to have seen you again. Good-by."

She offered her hand formally, and he took it formally, dumbly. As it slipped warmly, reluctantly from his grasp it was replaced by the clammy, bony fingers of Willie, who was doing his best in the gentle art of consolation:

"Awfully sorry, old chap. These things have got to happen, though, haven't they? Don't take it too hard, and if you get too blue come round and let us try to cheer you up a bit. We're at the Meurice."

"Thank you," said Forbes. He bowed and did not raise his eyes for fear of what might be smoldering in the eyes of Persis.

CHAPTER LIX

IN the exceeding industry of the days following the death of Ambassador Tait, Captain Forbes found no chance to see Mrs. Enslee. Their meeting would have been perilous. The Ambassador had received his death-stroke in their presence.

Physicians, police, reporters, all demanded minute descriptions of the event, and from the first Forbes blurred the account so that Persis should not be drawn into it. He emphasized the strenuous diplomatic labors of the last week and the final afternoon. He italicized the presence of Mr. Enslee at the moment of death, which came, he said, without immediate explanation. He described how the Ambassador's father had died—just died while pulling on his overshoes.

He lied about the last words of the Ambassador in spirit at least, for it was sadly incomplete truth to say that the Ambassador, after discussing trivial matters, had said, "Mr. Enslee, I must tell you good night," and fallen to the floor.

Yet the account was not questioned. Enslee was too befuddled to know or, when the shock sobered him, to remember. Persis could be trusted to keep silent. In fact, she retired from view "prostrated with the shock." It was explained that the Ambassador had been a classmate of her father's, an old friend of the family's.

The story was telegraphed and cabled about the world. As usual, every newspaper published a minutely circumstantial account with a pretendedly *verbatim* statement of the last words, and, as usual, the accounts were as discrepant mutually as they were commonly remote from the truth.

The idea that the Ambassador's death might be concerned with an intrigue between Mrs. Enslee and Captain Forbes occurred perhaps only to one mind on earth, and that the too-sophisticated brain of a reporter in New York, a brindle-haired man with half of one eyebrow gone. He could not confirm his suspicion even enough for publication, so he hid it in the cellar of his soul, alongside the memory of seeing Persis Cabot walk out of a lonely forest with a man he afterward learned to be Forbes.

When this reporter—Hallard, his name was—was comfortably drunk he would discuss New York society's rotten state of morals, usually with a horrified barkeeper, forgetting his own morals and that of his class and of the other classes low and middle that he knew well enough. He would add: "There's lovely li'l lady growin' a peach of a scan'al—um-m, a pippin!—swee' li'l dynamite bomb. Story's going to break some day, and I'm lovely li'l feller's goin' to break it."

But he would not tell the name. He was holding that in trust for whatever newspaper should be employing his fanatic loyalty at the time of the break. And he was waiting, listening, following.

Persis had been soft-hearted enough to feel the pity of the Ambassador's death. She had wept a little for her stricken enemy, and she suffered some acute stabs of repentance as the instrument of his assassination. But regret was mingled with the lilt of victory and successful evasion—even with blasphemous prayers of gratitude to the Lord for saving her from exposure in the matter. She had fallen on her knees to pour out this thanksgiving, and piously or impiously promised her Lord not to be indiscreet again.

One's god is apt to be one's ideal servant magnified.

As the daughters of joy in old Florence used to keep a votive Mary in their rooms and pray to it for success in their offices, so Persis whispered to her heaven words of praise and gratitude for aid in escaping the consequences of her mad whim to nestle in Forbes' arms.

She went to the Ambassador's funeral, partly as a tribute of awesome esteem, partly as good sportsmanship toward a beaten adversary, and chiefly because it would have been conspicuous to stay away when almost every other American in Paris was sure to be there. She compelled Willie to go along, an unwilling and unwitting chaperon.

She saw Forbes in the church, but at a distance, and noted with a gush of pity how haggard and lonely he seemed. She hoped that not all of his grief was for his dead friend. She longed to go to him with comfort, but she ventured only a nod from afar and one of her slow, sweet, tender smiles.

Forbes had been kept intensely active at the Embassy, where the Consul took over the interrupted duties of the Ambassador's office, but left to Forbes the personal details of the funeral ceremony, the closing up of the house, and the arrangements for getting Mildred back to New York. The Ambassador's body was to be taken home to America on board a war-ship proffered by the French Republic.

For three days Forbes was too grimly busy and too grief-stricken to feel more than a longing to see Persis; an impossible desire without impulse to achieve it.

Mildred was, for once, demanding help instead of giving it. The loss of her father was a devastation in her soul. She clung to Forbes as to a brother. Had Persis seen her in his arms she might have felt a jealousy; but not if she could have seen Forbes' heart. That was filled only with a sense of shame. He felt that in denying Mildred his love he had robbed the old man of his last great wish. At times he reproached himself with the very murder of his best friend, the murder of a great statesman, the noble father of a noble woman. And the motive of the assassination was his obstinate devotion to another man's wife!

People have a genius for remorse as for other emotions, and Forbes was of those who can mercilessly indict their own souls. Storms of self-condemnation were succeeded by storms of longing. About him hovered the tantalizing beckoning vision of Persis. He was mad to see her. He kept alternately vowing that he would not go near her and wondering when he should.

At first he dared not make an effort to see her, because he feared to involve her and because he had not a moment he could call his own. He was burdened with tasks of every sort, and in and out of his office he was beset with correspondents like sparrows demanding crumbs of news to cable to America. He had no leisure of his own except the black hours when he sank into his bed.

He would trudge to his room so exhausted, so drowsy, that he could hardly get his clothes off. The moment he lay down he was the prey to a swarm of black emotions that swooped about him like bats in a cave, swooped and shot and chittered, swept him with their vile wings and fastened their claws in his hair. He reproached himself with every wickedness and worthlessness from hideous ingratitude to murder and adultery that dared not take what it lusted for.

Sleepless nights and restless days wore him out until the funeral, an affair of great pomp and enormous impressiveness. When he saw Persis in the church her beauty was overwhelming in the black costume she wore under the shadow of a black hat.

Somehow, after the funeral ceremony, the prayers, and the long ritual, with which the church formally restored the soul to the heaven from which it emigrated and the body to the earth of which it was made, there came a great relief to Forbes—the restful word "Finis."

That night he dined with Mildred. She, too, felt the

relaxation of a burden removed. She almost collapsed into sleep at the table, and her maid supported her to her room. She had wept herself out.

Forbes envied her nothing but her fluency in weeping. He carried about with him the ache of the tears a man feels but cannot release, the unshed tears that scratch the eyes like blown grit. He longed to be a boy again and cry his heart out as he had cried when his father was brought home dead. He longed to weep stormily as he had wept when the boy he was had been denied some luxury he greatly desired—honey, or a staying home from school, or some wild animal for a pet.

The thought of Persis came to him now with the charm of all three—honey, truancy to duty, and danger. He lifted the telephone from the rack to ask her permission to call. He put it down again, his heart beating as if he had touched a snake. He went out into the air.

It was a typical, sharp, wet winter night in Paris, the chill going with a peculiar directness straight to the marrow of the bones and freezing the body from within outward. Forbes had buffeted blizzards and the still, grim, icy airs of Dakota when the mercury seemed to crowd into the bulb of the thermometer to keep warm. But he wondered if he had ever been so cold in his life as he was now, when the thermometer had not reached even the zero of the French centigrade.

Paris was not Paris. The sidewalks were not peopled with tables, and the restaurants were deserted within. There were few people abroad, for the audiences were at this hour in the theaters and the home-keepers were at home. Nobody loitered in the streets but a few miserables, and they were wretchedly cold.

Forbes was so desperately lonely that he resolved to call upon Persis, even if he had to talk to her husband. He walked to the Meurice, but dared not turn in; he went on by. Later he was back again. Three times his courage—or his cowardice—failed him. The last time he stopped short as if he heard a sudden "Halt!"

Willie Enslee was just stepping into a car with two other men, violently American and manifestly bent on finding in Paris what Paris manufactures for American visitors.

Willie paused and cast his eyes along the street idly while he waited for the other two to precede him. Forbes stepped behind a shelter till Willie vanished.

Forbes, the brave, the upright, found himself dodging to escape Willie's fishy eyes, found himself chuckling over Willie's blindness. Then he cursed himself for a reptile. He turned away from the hotel and started back to his apartment, groaning to himself, "The woman doesn't live that can make a sneak of me."

CHAPTER LX

WHEN he had gone a few hundred paces he whirled about and hurried back to the hotel; asked for Monsieur *et* Madame Enslee; sent up his card; wished he had it back; received a summons to come up; cursed the slowness of the Parisian *ascenseur;* wished it would fall and kill him; moved toward Persis' door as to his execution; and was ushered in by Nichette, who was cloaked and bonneted for an evening out. She left him a moment, then came back and rattled off a string of French, from which he gleaned that he was *voulez-vous'd* to seat himself and attend a little moment. Then Nichette left him and hastened to the corner of the street, where a little waiting *piou-piou* shivered in his uniform.

The hostility Forbes read in Nichette's look was merely her impatience at being kept a few moments longer from her sergeant after having been detained an hour by a quarrel of the Enslees — a quarrel ending in a defiant announcement from Willie that he was going to see the wickedest show he could find in Paris, and from Persis an hilarious "*Bonne chance!* I hope you find somebody to take you off my hands for a while!"

This had horrified Willie as a sacrilege, and he had regretted his vow. But in the court of the hotel he found two Americans who had typically arrived in Paris, and bibulously prepared for a night of social investigation without having taken the trouble to learn a word of French, the distinction of coins, or the system of cab fares and tips. They welcomed Enslee as a life-saver, embraced him, and bade him confirm their worst suspicions of Paris.

27   417

This Forbes did not know, and he misinterpreted Nichette's brusquerie. His own thoughts were brusque. He loathed himself, and hated Persis and blamed her as if she had cast down a net from her window and dragged him to her feet.

He paced the lavishly furnished reception-room of the suite and resolved to escape before it was too late. The thought of the cold loneliness of the streets, of the town, of the world, held him back. He was unutterably forlorn. He sank into a chair and clenched his hands together.

Then he heard Persis' voice. It came through the glistening portières masking the doors to the room adjoining, a kind of living-room. Music and welcome and all of Persis' beauty were in the little hospitable words:

"Come in here, Harvey, won't you? I can't budge, and I'm all by myself."

Wondering where she was and how he should find her, he pushed through the curtains timidly, as timidly as Joseph entering Potiphar's wife's boudoir.

He found Persis cuddled up on a chaise longue of gold and satin. She was almost lost in a jumble of parcels and toys and knickknacks. She had been writing addresses, and the fingers she gave into his were smudged with ink.

She sat like a sultana, with her feet curled under her. She wore a light confection of a house-gown of some astonishingly attractive hue, with plentiful display of white lace and arms and bosom and a good deal of stocking. She wore a boudoir-cap fetchingly awry.

Forbes put her hand up to his lips and laughed as he kissed the smudge of ink. It was the first laugh he had known for days. It was like the first chuckle of rain after a drought. It brought moisture to his eyes.

He clung to her hand. It was now a rescuing hand put out to lift him from the dry well of gloom. He dropped to his knee, and without any coquetry she put her arms around him and huddled him close. His hot cheek knew the ineffable comfort of her silken shoulder; his brow felt her lips upon them. He was at home.

All the strength that had sustained him, all his ideas of duty and honor, were blown away like the down of a dandelion puff by the mere breath of her lips. And now the tears his eyes had refused broke from them in flood. He wept because he was happy and because he had found contentment and refuge. He wept as great heroes and fierce warriors used to weep before tears went out of fashion for men and began to fall into disuse even among women.

Persis mothered him, wondering at his childishness. She did not weep with him. She smiled. She laughed the low, thorough laughter of the victorious Delilah getting her Samson back. She loved him though she betrayed him. She loved the triumph of her beauty, the victory of her soft bosom, over all the hateful inconveniences of law and justice and piety.

By and by he was smiling, too, with shame at his humanity and his return to boyhood, and with the revel of her companionship. She humiliated him deliciously by drying his wet eyelids with her fragrant tiny handkerchief and by the silly baby talk she lavished on him. But it was the only comfortable shame he had felt in the past black days.

And now they were indeed acquainted with each other. She had seen him weep. When a woman has gained that advantage over a man, what dignity has he left? She can make a face at him, and all his pride becomes a laughing-stock.

At length, to avoid the reefs of more important talk, he asked her how she came to be alone, and what all the bundles were for. She explained that she had been shopping betimes for Christmas presents and had been making the things ready for the morrow's American mail; Willie had mutinied and gone vaudevilling: his man had taken the English maid of a neighbor in the hotel to a dance at the Red Mill; and Nichette had refused to miss her soldier's evening out.

Persis made Forbes help her with the remaining packages, and they laughed like youngsters over the knots she tied, and the blots she made, and the things she had bought for all the people she had to buy things for—her father, her mother-in-law, her sister, her sister's children, and an army of servants. When finally the last address was inscribed she felt that she had done enough duty for a month, and voted herself a vacation—also a cigarette. She told Forbes where Willie's cigars were kept, but he made a punctilio of not smoking them, though he had none of his own and would not order any from the hotel.

They talked small talk and love talk; they laughed and cooed. They were congenial to the infinitesimal degree. The world outside was dank and cheerless. They shut it away with great curtains. They forgot that there was any curse upon their rapture. They shut out all their obligations as things clammy and odious.

Nature had selected them for each other. Nature mated them and wooed for them, and did not know or did not care what other plans they had made, what contracts or pledges had been assumed. The true damnation was in the earlier crime: that solemn marriage in the church before the world. The wickedness was begun at the altar: the violation of duty, the breach of the seventh "Thou shalt not." It was there that Persis' feet took hold on hell.

Yet the world had made a jubilee of that occasion. People had put on their best clothes and were proud to be asked to assist. Rather, they should have hidden their eyes from the abomination; they should have resented the request to play accomplice to that indecency. Instead, they celebrated the crime with flowers, and music, and with surplices in a church.

There would be resentment enough, but belated, when

the consequences of that impious sacrifice were reaped, when nature demanded restitution and scoffed at the mortgage. If this night's rite were ever heard of it would be cried out against, the celebrants would be shunned, banished.

None of this is to say that faith should not be kept, however rashly pledged, or that people should make a virtue of refusing to pay the debts they run and repudiating the laws that shelter them.

Persis' earlier crime did not justify or cancel the latter, but added another to it. She had entered with open eyes into her compact with Enslee; she auctioned herself off; he was the highest bidder, and she knocked herself down. She was in honor bound to stay sold. But the very readiness to commit that infamy, the yielding to that temptation, was instruction for the next. Easy bind, easy break.

Her only safety was in keeping away from Forbes. That was the Ambassador's wisdom. He feared the very proximity of Persis and Forbes. He foresaw that, while nature would hold cheap the laws of mankind, mankind would not accept nature as an excuse for lawlessness.

In spite of him Persis and Forbes were reunited. The withes that marriage had bound about her were as nothing to the great changes it had made in her soul. It had taken away the enormous power that exists in maidenhood, with its self-awe and its fierce defense of integrity. That instinct of self-preciousness that had made Persis hide her lips from Forbes' kisses on a far-off day was annulled, for her lips had been Willie Enslee's for more than half a year. Her body had been his toy. He had schooled her to maturity, made a woman of the girl.

And now in the presence of the bridegroom selected by nature and love what protection had she? She had no harem walls to inclose her, no guardians to keep the suitor away or to threaten exposure. She had lost the fawn-like girlishness that would take flight; there was no nun-spirit within her now to cry "Help me!"

What remorse there was was the man's. He blamed himself for overpowering where he was overpowered and decoyed. With the traditional mistake of the man he accused himself of a ruthless conquest when he was really the prey of ancient guile and wile. And this again is not to blame Persis. She was herself the mere puppet of world-old impulses along the wires of sense. She was a victim, too. But her remorse was hardly remorse at all, rather amazement or dismay. It was Forbes that condemned himself for dishonor.

Man is the maker of laws, the upholder of laws, the punisher of those who violate the majesty of the law.

But law for law's sake has little or no meaning for woman. She has her own codes and reads them within. The complex tissue of her loves and hates is her attorney, always plaintiff or defendant, not often referee. She has her glories, and perhaps they are greater than any of man's; but the creation of laws and constitutions and codes is not one of them. She is timid, she is brave, she is merciful, she is ruthless. She may reproach herself for indiscretion, for folly, for misplaced trust, for misguided emotion; but did any woman ever honestly reproach herself for a breach of honor as honor? A disloyalty to religion, yes; to faith, yes; to love, oh yes; but to honor?

Persis was dumfounded at the completeness of her success by surrender and at its rashness. She was afraid that Forbes might despise her; but she felt also the barbaric primeval perfection of the triumph of nature. She had achieved her destiny. She had been female to the male of her choice. She would fight the consequences; she would deny the fact, but she felt that she could never regret it.

Immediately having made conquest of Forbes, she began to own him. She began to resent his other obligations, his other codes; her jealousy began to function.

She implored him to postpone his return to America;

to follow the Ambassador's body on a later steamer; not to go, at least, on the steamer Mildred took—anything to escape the breaking of the rose-chains wherewith she withed him. But his almost filial love for his benefactor overcame even his passion. Nothing could move him from that last foothold on self-respect.

The triumph of love wound up in a war, a downright quarrel, with all the brutality of a married couple. And that came to an abrupt end with the tinkle of a clock sounding the hour. Both of them blenched. It was as if rats fighting heard the bell of the cat.

"You must hurry," she gasped, "Willie is long past due."

Forbes needed no urging. He fled so precipitately that he hardly paused for a farewell kiss. They had time for no future plans. He sneaked along the corridors of the hotel. He feared to summon the elevator lest Willie step out of it. He went down by the stairways. From the entresol he studied the lobby of the hotel to make sure of not meeting Enslee. A detective might have suspected him for a thief had not his manner been the immemorial stealth of clandestine lovers? Love had belittled him thus in one evening.

Little Willie Enslee could have put him to flight, have struck him without resistance, have shot him down without provoking an answering shot.

So Forbes had coerced and terrified soldiers of his who were far superior to him in bulk and brawn. They saw his shoulder-straps and respected them, took a pride in being humble before them. Back of them was the whole power and dignity of the nation.

Willie Enslee wore the shoulder-straps of the husband. He wore that authority, and back of it was arrayed the decency and the safety of human society.

CHAPTER LXI

FORBES took the steamer he had planned to take, though he had such battles with his recalcitrant heart that he did not feel safe till the tender at Cherbourg put away from the ship and left him no opportunity of return.

Equally disconsolate was young Stowe Webb, who had lost his post with his chief, and who was in a panic of uncertainty. But Mildred, on her first day of calm, reverted to habit and began to take thought of the welfare of others. She asked Stowe of his plans, and, learning of his hopelessness, immediately begged him to act as her own secretary—"at an increase of salary because of the extra trouble she would give him."

The reaction from despair to this paradise was so great that young Webb found it hard to maintain the appropriate solemnity. He fired off a wireless to the friend who received his messages for Alice, and when he heard it crackling from the mast it was like a volley of festival sky-rockets.

He told Forbes of his new-found hope and how poor it was at best, and Forbes envied him his very deferment; there was something so clean and beautiful about a young lover trying to earn enough to earn the girl that waits for him. Young Webb was building a home, and Forbes was destroying one.

The arrival in New York brought a new mountain of tasks for Forbes. Mildred had adopted him as an elder brother; she gave him power of attorney in the endless interviews with the lawyers, executors, directors, and the officials in the Department of State.

Forbes soon learned what the Ambassador's hints as to his will had meant. A recent codicil bequeathed to him almost as much as Tait's dead son was to have had.

It seemed to Forbes as if Satan had laid the wealth of Ormus and of Ind at his feet and knelt there grinning over the hoard. There was a further sardonic bitterness in the legacy, since he knew that it had been given him so that he might feel able to make Mildred his wife without sacrifice of his pride.

The thought came to him that he could square himself with the dead and with the living by carrying out this implied, if not inscribed, condition of the deed of gift.

Mildred was a splendid soul. She was not Aphrodite like Persis, but Minerva was beautiful, too. Mildred was far nobler than Persis, who was not noble at all. She would be a magnificent wife. She would make their home a bee-hive of lofty purposes amid serene delights. A union with Mildred would be wonderful. It would crown life.

And he felt that Mildred would not oppose it. He resolved again and again to ask her; but he simply could not tell her that he loved her as a wife ought to be loved. He and Mildred had become so dear to each other as brother and sister that no other affection seemed possible. To marry her would mean not only an infidelity to Persis, but a more cruel infidelity to Mildred.

Unable to fulfil the condition of the legacy, he tried to refuse it. The executors asked him why; his evasions led them to suspect his sanity. Mildred would ask him why? What could he tell her?

He consulted Ten Eyck, but could tell him only that he could not give Mildred the love that was needed to sanctify the marriage. Ten Eyck probably understood more than he admitted. He lifted one eyebrow and lowered the other, as if his mind were divided between two comments. He said:

"I see why you can't go to nice old Mildred and say, 'Dear girl, I wouldn't marry you for a hundred thousand dollars.' That would be an awful black eye to hand a charming lady. But I can't say that your motives of love appeal to me, Forbesy. You sound like the heroine of an old-fashioned novel refusing to marry a rich man because she loves old Dr. A. Nother.

"But whatever you do, Forbesy, don't refuse the money. In times like these, when bank presidents are robbing their children's savings-banks for carfare, don't spurn any real money, or you'll cause several persons to die of apoplexy, and strong men will lead you to the paddedest cell in the house of foolishness.

"Take the money and build an Old Ladies' Home with it; but don't make a solemn jackass of yourself right out in public."

Forbes took the money, promising himself that he would scatter it in beautiful deeds of charity.

But he didn't.

One never does.

In the first place, money in large quantities has singular adhesive and cohesive properties. In the second place, when the news of his wealth was published he received such serial avalanches of begging letters of every sort, noble and ignoble, that he was dismayed. He showed a stack of them to Ten Eyck, who said:

"You could give away your fortune in a week, and make about as much of a show as if you drove a sprinkling-cart along the main street of hell. All millionaires grow callous; if they don't, they cease to be millionaires."

Forbes answered a few of the appeals with cheques, and planned to file the others alphabetically for future reference. But he never got round to filing them.

This was not the only sarcasm of his wealth. He had returned to his duties as a line captain and was restored to Governor's Island. But here again there was discomfort. His fellow-officers envied him his luck, but despised him for not profiting by it. And it did seem peculiarly grotesque that a man of his important means should be trudging about on a drill-ground giving orders to stupid privates and taking orders from stupid superiors. His very men seemed to think he was a ludicrous fanatic. He felt that he must leave the service.

He poured out his woes to Ten Eyck again, who advised caution. "Don't jump out of the frying-pan, Forbes, till you've tested the fire with your big toe. You might be even unhappier out of the army than in it. Ask for a long leave of absence—say, six months, and see how you like it. Then you can resign or go back."

"They won't give me six months' leave without a good reason," Forbes demurred, though he was fascinated by the idea.

"A lot of money is a good reason for nearly anything. Anybody will give a rich man what he asks for," Ten Eyck insisted. "Take some of the high boys out in your car, and blow them off to a gorgeous evening, and promise them some more of the same. Then pop the question."

Forbes made the attempt, and it succeeded with surprising ease; he was granted six months' leave of absence without pay "for special research and experiment."

His research was into the comforts of wealth, and his experiment was the effect of life without labor or ambition.

Forbes had a car now. He had not intended to get one, but after dodging salesmen for weeks one of them lay in ambush for him and carried him off for a ride—a demonstration in disguise. He was so captivated by the 1915 model and the enlarged powers it gave him that he capitulated and bought. He learned to be his own chauffeur; but this was so inconvenient at times that he was soon hiring a charioteer. And, of course, he never skimmed the earth or sped through beauties of landscape that he did not wish for Persis at his side. He had a better car than Enslee's now. He could buy Persis the costly, cozy little runabout she wanted; he could hire her father's chauffeur and Nichette. He could buy her great quantities of clothes, and he had leisure for her entertainment. But he had not her, nor the right to buy things for her.

Away from her he found that time was softening his remorse without hardening his heart against her. His wealth was mockery, his leisure was mockery. His mind was hardly more than a music-box eternally purling one little tune: "Persis—Persis—Persis!"

And then Persis came back, as if his longing had pulsed across the sea. She had no difficulty in persuading Willie to return to New York. He felt positively footsore from travel.

As they came up the Bay on a home-bound liner her heart was beating as if she were entering a dark room full of ghosts. As Governor's Island was reached she studied it again with a marine-glass.

She thought of the little homes of the officers' wives, the little garage-less quarters where there must be so much content. She wished to God that she were living in one of those little homes there.

If she had married Forbes she would never have caused the Ambassador's death; she would not have given herself to Willie Enslee. She could not have had more unhappiness, more loneliness and vain regrets. She would have dwelt in Forbes' arms; she would have been his all day long and all the long nights. All this past and horrible year would have been a true honeymoon. Love would have been wealth enough.

As she had told Alice Neff, "Almost anything that we are not used to is a luxury." She had learned the corollary, that almost any luxury becomes a poverty as soon as one is used to it. She was all too familiar with splendor. She hungered for a life of little comforts. The word "cozy" grew magically beautiful.

She had not been long ashore before she learned the

new status of Forbes. It was Mrs. Neff who told her, taunting her with having jumped into the marital noose with Willie too soon.

She had not been long ashore before she met Forbes. And once more it was Willie who brought her into his presence.

Forbes was now a member of several of the more important clubs. Willie met him at one of them, and asked him to join a crowd he was inviting up to the country place.

Forbes' heart began to knock at his breast at the thought of being with Persis again in the Enslee Eden. A remnant of honesty led him to decline the invitation on the ground of another engagement, but Willie insisted.

"You had such a rotten time there last spring," he said. "I want to make up. There won't be any lilacs yet; but there'll be servants—and something to eat."

Forbes flung off his scruples, and promised to "motor up." The phrase sounded odd in his ears, for he remembered the poverty of his first visit, when he went as a passenger in Mrs. Neff's car.

When he spoke of his car Enslee said: "By the way, if you're motoring up you might bring Mrs. Neff and Alice. The old lady's old car has got the sciatica or something."

So Forbes brought Mrs. Neff along, and Alice. Mrs. Neff had much to say of his wealth. And now that she knew Persis to be out of the running, she had evidently entered Alice for the Forbes stakes. Forbes could feel the idea in the air, and he was exceedingly embarrassed.

He was embarrassed more by his arrival at the country home. The great hill was as bleak as the granite bridge. The trees were shaggy with snow. The house was part of the winter, as white as an igloo. The statues were oddly distorted with icicles and snow; they looked very cold —especially the Cupid in the temple—a windy and forlorn white kiosk where a naked child suffered exile. It struck him as pitifully appropriate to the Enslee menage that Love should be left out in the cold.

Persis received him now in her quality of owner and housewife, with a flock of servants everywhere. He found her in the living-room, surrounded by guests, chattering and lounging and sprawling. He had not seen her since he left her that night in Paris.

She gave him her hand and a few commonplace words, but their eyes embraced and their lips were tremulous with unspoken messages and ungiven kisses.

Her manner warned him, and her apparent neglect of him gave him the cue of his behavior. But there were brief collisions when it was possible to murmur a word or two before one of the numerous other guests drifted up and ruined the tête-à-tête. He pleaded ruthlessly for a meeting; she pleaded for discretion above all things. She reminded him of the great difference between the condition of their former visit and the present. With only a few about them before, they had narrowly escaped discovery; what chance had they now?

As the dinner-hour approached, and the others went up to dress, Forbes lingered, and Persis sat with him a moment in the embrasure of that drawing-room window where they had once held rendezvous. The mystery was gone from it, and the poetry. But they seized each other in one swift embrace of arms and lips. Even this was broken just in time to escape the sight of the butler, who entered to ask a question as to the wines for the dinner.

Persis gave her orders with an impatience that could hardly have escaped the man's notice. She felt a little extra effort at impassivity in his manner, and was sure that he suspected her of more than a hospitable interest in Forbes. She could not resent an unexpressed intuition, but she felt humbled and shamed and afraid.

When the butler was gone she repeated her warning to Forbes, but he took her in his arms again. Her mind told her that she must not go on risking, go on registering faint impressions in the minds of servants and of guests; but her heart would not defer entirely to her intelligence.

Forbes was taciturn at the dinner. Mrs. Neff could not provoke him to vivacity. She noted that his gaze returned constantly to Persis, and that when her look came down the board to him it softened strangely.

After dinner little cliques were formed about the billiard and the pool tables, the card-tables, and a few danced the everlasting tango with some new variation. Forbes and Persis danced together, and many eyes noted the perfect rapport of their mood, the solemn joy they took in the welded union.

"How well they dance!" was the spoken comment; but the thought was, "How congenial they seem!"

Shortly after nine there was an excitement. On the hill opposite a building was on fire. The guests crowded and jostled at the windows. Somebody proposed that they all go to the scene of the blaze. The irresistible fascination of a burning building at night was inducement enough. Motors were telephoned for from the distant garage, and there was a scramble for wraps. Forbes' car was not brought up, and he was invited into Enslee's. He climbed in, but clambered out again to get an extra wrap for Mrs. Neff. A maid had already run for it, and by the time he returned the cars had all gone.

He stood regretting boyishly the loss of the opportunity to go to a fire. He watched for a few moments from the steps, and then turned back into the house. He found Persis at the drawing-room window. She had declined to go. He joined her. Out on the white edge of the lawn they could see the servants in a little mob staring at the pyrotechnics of an upward rain of sparks.

"I'll put out the light. We can see better," he said.

"No, no!" she protested; but he had already found and turned the switch. They were in a cavern of darkness, with one window dimly reddened. He found his way back to her. She urged him to turn the light on again, but he refused. She moved to turn it on herself, but he held her fast, and compelled her back to the deep embrasure, and drew the curtains behind them.

She could count the servants on the lawn outside. They were all there. She felt that it was safe to be alone with Forbes, at least till one of the domestics should detach himself from the group and move across the snowy sheet of white.

They watched in silence awhile the leaping red geyser of the flames. It grew and expanded till it formed a huge ember-mottled orchid with vast petals trembling in the wind.

On the far-off roads they could see the long shafts of motor-lights wavering like antennæ. From all the homes of the region the neighbors were hastening to the spectacle, huge night moths drawn by the flaring lamp.

For a long, blissful while the flame-flower bloomed against the black sky. At last it wilted and failed and shriveled. Then the servants turned back to the house. Persis fled from Forbes' arms to her own room, where Nichette found her, apparently established the past hour.

Forbes waited at another window, and when at last the motors came puffing back the home-comers were too benumbed with cold and too eager for warming drinks to know or care whether Forbes had been with them or not. Any one who might have missed him would have supposed him to be in one of the other cars.

The next day some of the guests rode over to see the ruins. Forbes and Persis went along. To their amazement, what had seemed, while flaming, to be a miracle of enchantments, a palace afire, proved in the daylight to have been a miserable shack whose hollow shams and rotten timbers the flames had mercilessly exposed to public contempt, stark, charred, cold, obscene.

"It was so beautiful while it burned," said Persis. "I can't believe it's the same. It was like a wild rose in the night; but in the daylight it's hideous, it's revolting.

Look at the fraud in the building of the house—the rotten timbers, the ghastly furniture in the back rooms!"

Forbes was about to say that their passion had something akin to this. But as he raised his eyes to hers he saw that she had the same thought.

She shivered and said, "Let's get away from the place."

CHAPTER LXII

NEVER, it seems, has human ingenuity been able to devise a scheme of guardianship that human ingenuity could not thwart. Seeing that seraglio walls, and yashmaks, and eunuchs, and bow-strings, and scarlet letters, and pillories, and divorce courts, and gossips have failed to scare fidelity into the disloyal, perhaps the modern honor system is as good as any. But the honor system is not infallible; and not all the spies of Mrs. Grundy can coerce from without those who are not coerced from within their own hearts.

For those who are willing to devote themselves to deceit and make an industry of other people's property, opportunities have always been infernally provided. Persis and Forbes did not find it difficult to be alone. Solitudes seemed to be created suddenly in crowds, chances to escape and to creep back undetected seemed to be brandished in their faces. The unabated plague of the tango explained their presence at all sorts of hours at all sorts of places. There were morning classes in new steps; between the courses of luncheon at numerous restaurants in and out of town there were dances, and these were prolonged till tea, and after that till dinner, and on until whatever hour of closing the individual cabareteer had arranged with the police. The private hostesses seemed to vie with the restaurateurs.

The dancing frenzy had shown no signs of passing. It had developed into a revolution that swept the world. Dancers who were yesterday unknown, to-day were wealthy. A dancer and his wife had grown to such di-

mensions of fame that influential people rented them a
house on Fifth Avenue, where lessons could be given at
all hours.   A girl who had danced in a restaurant became
a national figure and hired a hall.   The clergy and the
editors fought in vain; the Kaiser and the Pope were un-
heeded; all the nations danced; even the Japanese caught
the contagion.   New steps abounded, became so complex
that it was not easy to change partners.   The turkey-trot
was laughably obsolete.   Everything and everybody was
influenced by the tango in one of its countless forms.   It
had already made itself an epoch in human history.

Willie Enslee was one of the stubborn minority that
refused to dance or go to dances.   After a number of
vain assertions of an authority he could not enforce he
ceased to concern himself with Persis' whereabouts; she
ceased to announce her program in advance or to report
it afterward.

The motor-car was another immense enlargement of
liberty—and license; it was so easy to outstrip pursuit
and outwit espionage.   In two hours one could vanish
into the wilderness and return without evidence of escape.   At distant road-houses and motor-caravansaries
the twang of tango music troubled the country mid-
nights.

And so the intrigue of Captain Forbes and Mrs. Enslee prospered and established itself as the habit of their
lives; their souls adapted themselves to it.   Precautions
against discovery became second nature, like precautions
against disease and accident.   They were bound together
in a kind of secret wedlock, what Tibullus called the
furtivi foedera lecti.

Persis, like another Guenevere, justified herself to herself by the feeling that she was true to one Launcelot;
she flirted with no one else; she kept Willie's home in
order as best she could; she paid him the tribute of outward devotion and public respect.   Above all, she justified herself by her success.   So far as she could see, not

435

a human being suspected her love for Forbes, not a breath of scandal had been stirred.

And all the while gossip was busy with them; evidence accumulated against them grain by grain, as sand-dunes are formed into walls. Everybody spoke of the intrigue to everybody but those most concerned. Nobody warned Persis or rebuked Persis or tattled to Willie. A few fearless persons talked to Persis' father, but he could not believe, or, believing, could not touch so repulsive a topic in his few meetings with his daughter. How could a father accuse his little girl of outrages against a commandment he had been afraid even to mention to her. Several women broached the theme with Willie's mother, who had been suspicious on her own account. She answered the gossips with fervent denials and with vigorous defense of Persis; but she vowed to herself that she would descend upon her daughter-in-law with vengeance. Yet, before Persis' eyes she could only dissemble; then she would resolve to warn her son, but she feared the terrific possibilities of lighting such a fuse. Willie was like herself in so many ways, and half of her blood was from the Spanish aristocracy through an international marriage.

Eventually people began to say that somebody must tell Willie, and some day somebody might. Some day he might stumble upon some tryst, or open a letter, or overhear a gossip's careless word.

Ten Eyck heard plenteous scandal, and he was heartbroken. Even his cynicism could not stomach the intrigue. But even his affection could not bring him to protest.

He had intervened once before in such a scandal; but the husband had forgiven his wife because of her beauty and her gaiety, and both of them had thereafter been his bitterest enemies, because he knew and had said too much. Friends who had merely gossiped behind their backs were reinstated to complete favor.

Everybody felt that Persis and Forbes, in their mad

gallop across another man's boundary line, were riding for a fall. But everybody was fascinated by the breathlessness of the gallopade, the escapes from disaster. Nobody cut Persis, omitted her from a list of invitations, or treated her otherwise than as a valued and charming ornament to the world. Nobody would desert her so long as she kept the saddle, held her head up, and remained attractive.

But should she fall and be dragged in the dirt, then the panic would come; then the majesty of public morals would assert itself, and her friends would flee from her as if she appeared among them chalk-faced and scaly-handed with leprosy.

Meanwhile the poison of their Judas life was wearing upon their own souls. Forbes was growing restive to be at work again upon his career. To be the messenger-boy of a woman's summons grew increasingly irksome. He dreaded an official cognizance of his new career as home-wrecker, and his innate decency was more and more rebellious against the outrages he committed incessantly against his self-respect, his creeds, his codes, his position.

And, last of all, a strange new horror assailed the basking luxury of Persis. It dawned upon her that in spite of all her precautions nature was about to make the use of her that all this rapture was for. Her physician confirmed her dread, and congratulated her—and her husband! She dared not ask his aid in foiling her destiny. She dared not ask anybody's aid. Her life of pleasure-hunting had made a coward of her.

And so at length remorse found a lodging even in her voluptuous life. She understood the fearful responsibility she had assumed to a future soul. And she groveled in abject self-derision to think that even she could not be sure of her child's legitimacy. So helpless a vessel for nature's chemistry she was that she was not permitted to know even that! And she could not so much as be sure whether she even wished it to be love's child or the law's.

The treachery to her own child was so hideous that she would have killed herself had she not dreaded to add murder to suicide. She longed to pour out her woes to Forbes, but she could not bring herself to confess her degradation. He only knew that somehow all the rapture was gone from their union. It had lost even that compensation.

The thought came to Forbes that there was but one way to make their life livable—to make it frank and public. Persis must enter the divorce court, and as soon as possible after marry him. That sort of solution for such intrigues had been much practised of late. It had become so fashionable that protest was losing its vigor.

He opened the subject to Persis. She shrank from it with revulsion. She could not tell him her secret even then; but it was a mighty argument to herself against such a step. She gave other reasons cogent enough in her opinion.

"Anything but divorce, Harvey. I'd rather die than go through it. Willie couldn't do the polite thing. He is a Catholic, you know, and his mother's Spanish blood boils at the divorce habit."

"Then if he won't give it, you can take it, anyway."

"But suppose he should fight. Suppose he should set detectives going back over our trail or bribe the servants. Look at this morning's papers—the ghastly head-lines about Mrs. Tom Corliss—her photographs! Did you read the testimony of the maid at that big hotel? Suppose Willie should get hold of that bellboy who was so insolent to us—the one we didn't dare rebuke and had to tip so heavily. Did you read Mrs. Tom's love letters yesterday? Only one paper dared to print them all. Mrs. Neff said everybody bought it specially. Mrs. Neff laughed till she cried.

"Wouldn't you rather die than go through with it? And, my God, how they would tear me to pieces! The poor people and the middle-class people push through the divorce court in droves—eighty divorces were granted in two hours the other day, Murray Ten Eyck was telling me, and only one paper mentioned it—in a paragraph! But if Mrs. Tom Corliss gets the front page, what wouldn't they give to Mrs. Willie Enslee?"

Forbes said no more. Somehow he was reminded of the time when he was dancing with Persis, and the rose light was suddenly changed to green. There was a charnel odor in the air.

CHAPTER LXIII

THE following afternoon Persis came home from a tango-tea, where she had expected to meet Forbes. Through some misunderstanding he had failed to appear. This left her plans in a decided tangle. He was probably trying to find her by telephone. He would doubtless call up the house. Things were in a mess there, too. An ancient romance in the servants' quarters had resulted in a wedding between the second man and one of the chambermaids. Nichette had been chosen as a bridesmaid and had begged off for the afternoon, as had all of the others that could be spared.

Nichette had long ago been taken into their confidence as a necessary go-between. Persis trembled lest a message from Forbes should fall into inexperienced hands.

To complicate matters Willie had resolved to go to the opera that night and to be on time. He had read an editorial somewhere ridiculing the horseshoe of box-holders for their indifference to overtures and first acts. Willie naturally selected this one evening for his rebuke to the editor. Dinner was to be served an hour earlier than usual.

Harrowed by the multiplex difficulties surrounding an intrigue, Persis was kept waiting at the door a long time in the cold. She was about to rend the tardy footman to pieces when the door was opened by Crofts, the superannuated butler, an heirloom from Enslee's father.

Crofts had long ago reached the age when he was too venerable to wear the Enslee livery. He was an ideal gentleman, respected and loved by all the family and its

440

friends. But as an officer of the household he was deaf, decrepit, and almost useless. Yet he was too much of an institution to discharge, and he simply would not retire.

He was permitted to lag superfluous as a sort of butler *emeritus*. At large dinners he hovered about in the offing correcting and directing with a marvelous tact and an infallible memory for the encyclopedic lore of nice service. For a guest to be recognized by his watery old eyes and named by his thin lips was in itself a distinction.

To-day he was blissfully happy. The young upstart servants had flocked to the wedding, and he was called to the helm. When Persis saw him at the door her heart melted, but it also sank.

"Did anybody call?" she asked, and asked several times in *crescendo*.

"Only Mrs. Enslee, ma'am," he whispered, in his dry, cackling, deaf man's voice.

Persis cast her eyes up in despair and hastened to pay her devoirs to her mother-in-law. The elder Mrs. Enslee was looking radiantly beautiful in her white hair and her black eyes and the assisted red of her Spanish lips, with her cascade of furs falling about her.

She smiled at Persis sadly. Her daughter-in-law was beautiful undeniably. What a pity that she was not also good! But she kept back her reproaches, and said in the most delicate of accents, with her tendency to an exquisite lisp:

"Don't worry, my dear. It's only a duty call."

"Won't you stop to dinner?" Persis urged. "We're only going to have a bite. We're dining early and hurrying away to the opera. Willie is determined to hear the overture and the first act. I dote on 'Carmen,' but I've never been in time for the first of it."

"'Carmen!'" Mrs. Enslee sniffed. "That old slander on my race—as if Spanish women were all faithless!"

"But if it's Carmen for Spain," Persis said, "it's Camille

for France, and Becky Sharp for England, and—who for America?"

"Hester Prynne, perhaps."

"Oh yes," laughed Persis. "Even the Puritans had their scandals; but she was a grass-widow, and the town was so dull, and the preacher so handsome. Can you blame her?"

"Cynical Persis!" Mrs. Enslee sighed. "Well, I shall be late."

"I wish you'd stay," Persis lied, graciously. "You're a picture. And everybody says you are flirting dreadfully with old General Branscomb."

"I hope you don't believe all you hear."

"Only the worst."

"Then you're on the safe side. But remember, my dear, other people can apply the same rule. I'm not the only one who has been suspected of flirting with an army officer." The doorbell had punctuated their chatter several times. It rang again. "Now, who's that? Expecting anybody?"

"No, and I've got to fling into my opera-gown."

"What are you wearing to-night?"

The rhapsody of description was interrupted by the incursion of Willie. He wore his overcoat and top hat into the room, and his key-chain dangled. He was in one of his most fretful moods. He vouchsafed his mother a casual "Oh, hello, *madre mia*," then turned to Persis.

"What the devil has happened to the servants? Nobody to answer the bell. Had to let myself in. Deuced nuisance unbuttoning coat, getting keys out, finding right one. What are we coming to? I'll fire that Dobbs."

"You forget, dear, he is getting married this afternoon."

"We all ought to have gone," said Mrs. Enslee; but Willie has no sense of obligation to his employees.

He ignored the suggestion and raged on, "Well, Dobbs isn't our only servant, is he?"

"No," Persis explained; "but, you see, he's marrying the housekeeper's daughter, and the butler is best man, and the maids are bridesmaids—"

"Romance everywhere," Willie sneered, as he laid off his things and threw them on a chair, "except up-stairs. I suppose that's why my man was so surly when I told him he'd have to stay and dress me. He'll probably cut my throat while he shaves me. I wish he would."

"That's cheerful!" said Persis. "What brings you home from the club so early? It's such an unusual honor."

"I heard something I didn't like—gossip."

"Tell us what you heard," Mrs. Enslee asked, hungrily.

"I prefer not to retail club gossip in my home," said Willie.

"Oh, aren't we punctilious?" Persis railed; and Willie answered, curtly:

"One of us ought to be."

Persis was jarred a trifle, but her only comment was: "Why is it that when men are feeling ugly they always come home early?"

Willie threw her a look of wrath and turned to his distressed mother. "Won't you stop to dinner?"

"Not when there's so much war-paint visible, thanks!"

"But hang it all—" Willie began, and checked himself, for Crofts shuffled through the room. Willie rounded on him. "Oh, somebody at last, eh? Why the deuce was no one at the door? I had to let myself in."

Crofts cupped his hand behind his ear, and crackled, "Beg pardon, sir?"

"I had to let myself in, I say."

"Very sorry, sir, but owing to Dobbs' wedding and your early dinner, sir, the servants have a great deal to do."

"But I rang and rang!" Willie stormed, and repeated, wrathfully, "I rang and rang!"

"Very sorry, indeed, sir," Crofts pleaded. "My hearing isn't as good as it was when I entered your father's service."

"Well, I won't have my house turned into a—an infirmary."

Crofts heard that and withered. "Your father never complained of me, sir."

"You heard better then and jumped quicker," Willie shouted.

The old man, at bay, answered with unintended irony: "I meant no offense, sir, by growing old."

"Oh, get out!" Willie snapped.

Crofts bowed and turned on Persis a pitiful look. She gave him a glance of sympathy, then pointed to Enslee's coat and hat. Crofts took them, and, touching the back of his hand to his eyes and swallowing hard, shuffled away.

Willie's mother rebuked him. "You've broken his poor old heart."

And Persis was more severe. "You ought to be ashamed of yourself."

Willie retorted, more sharply: "Oh, we all ought to be, ashamed of ourselves—for something or other. Crofts isn't the only man on earth with a broken heart."

As Persis stared in wonderment at his unusual mood Crofts came back. "You are wanted on the telephone, ma'am. The gentleman wouldn't give his name."

Persis flinched at this, and stammered, "You'll excuse me?"

Mrs. Enslee answered with a sudden frigidity, "Of course, but I'll not wait. Good-by."

"Good-by!" said Persis, uneasily, and left the room. The moment she was gone Mrs. Enslee put her hand on Willie's arm and spoke in some confusion.

"Willie, I—it's very hard for me to say it. But I think you allow Persis too much liberty."

Willie snorted. "Gad! a lot of good it does an American husband to try to manage his wife!"

"I know, and Persis is very headstrong," Mrs. Enslee

faltered; "but—well, if anything happens, remember I tried to—"

"Enjoying the luxury of an 'I told you so' already, eh?" Willie sneered. "What's up?"

"Oh, nothing—nothing definite—but I—I'm just a little uneasy. It can't hurt to keep your eyes open, can it?"

She had said this much at last. Willie took it solemnly. "What could hurt a man worse than to have to watch his wife?"

"Well, if that's the way you feel, just forget what I've said. I'm a foolish old woman. Good-by!"

Willie let her make her way out unattended. He stood musing till Persis came back, then he wakened with a start, and demanded, "Who was it telephoned you?"

The question took Persis by surprise. "No one that would interest you."

"Are you sure?"

"Since when this sudden concern in my affairs?"

"Aren't your affairs mine?" he pleaded; but she was curt:

"Indeed they're not. I don't nag you with questions."

He answered this with a sorrowful humility. "Sometimes I wish you would take a little more interest."

"You're in a funny mood," she said, more gently.

"It's not very funny to me," he groaned.

"You'll feel better after dinner. Run along and let Brooks dress you."

"What about you?"

"I had my hair done while I was out. I've got to wait for Nichette to get back. I—I'll come up as soon as I— as soon as I write a letter or two."

"All right," he sighed, and went out obediently, but paused to stare at her with a curious craftiness.

CHAPTER LXIV

PERSIS awaited his departure impatiently, tapping her foot with restlessness. She fell into reverie of indefinite duration. The bell rang. She gave a start of joy. Crofts went by on his way to the door. She checked him. "I'm expecting Captain Forbes." He got the name on the third iteration. "If it is he, show him in here." He nodded and set out again. She called after him, "If it is any one else I'm not at home."

She ran to a mirror, preened herself expectantly, and waited with a look of joy. Crofts returned with a card. Persis took it, and asked, "You told her I was out?"

Crofts was alarmed at once. "No, ma'am, I said you were at home."

"But I said I was out to every one except—"

Crofts was in despair at his blunder. "Oh, I'm so sorry! I'm afraid I'm too old and deaf to—"

She relented and patted his hard shoulder-blade. "There, there! don't worry, we'll get through the day somehow. Show Mrs. Neff in; but nobody else except Captain Forbes."

Crofts smiled like a forgiven child, and returned with Mrs. Neff, who bustled in crying, "Ah, my dear, such luck to find you at home."

"So sweet of you to come," said Persis. She was in no mood for Mrs. Neff. She determined to be rid of her. She explained about the early dinner and begged to be excused lest Willie murder her for being late. Persis rang for Crofts, kissed Mrs. Neff a grateful good-by, and fled. As Crofts opened the door to let Mrs. Neff out he let

446

Winifred Mather in. Crofts protested feebly that Persis was not at home, but Winifred came in anyway.

Winifred was just returned from Paris, foiled in her campaign for the late Ambassador, and determined to regain her control over Bob Fielding. She had not seen Mrs. Neff, and she had much to say. Ignoring the helpless Crofts, they drifted back to the drawing-room to swap scandals from the opposite shores of the ocean. In this fascinating barter they forgot the flight of time, forgot even the place they were in, for they fell to discussing Persis and her affair with Forbes.

Winifred had heard of it even in Paris.

"But what does Willie think of it?" she asked; "if he can think?"

"In any intrigue, my dear," Mrs. Neff pronounced, "the last three persons to learn what all the world knows are the husband and the two intriguers."

"I saw Bob Fielding yesterday," said Winifred. "He told me about it on the dock. He's furious at Persis. He said somebody ought to tell Willie."

"He's right, my dear," said Mrs. Neff; "but who wants to do that sort of job? It's like street-cleaning—very necessary and sanitary, but we don't care to do it ourselves, and we don't admire the people who do. Crooked things have a way of arranging themselves in this naughty world. Leave Persis alone. Some day some little accident she couldn't foresee—the mistake of a messenger-boy or a postman or somebody—and bang! out comes the whole scandal. Persis is clever, but she's juggling with dynamite."

It was only the last thirteen words that Persis overheard as she came down to the drawing-room, never dreaming that Mrs. Neff had not gone or that Winifred had come. Her slippers were soft, and her gown made no frou-frou. The voices of the women, softened to a ghoulish stealth, reached her with uncanny clearness.

She paused, struck to stone. Her heart pummeled

447

her till her throat throbbed visibly. She wanted to fall down and die. She wanted to run from the house and from the town. Instead, she shook off every primitive impulse, and, tossing her head in defiance of fate, marched into the room with all the gracious majesty of a young queen going to her coronation. Her costume completed the picture: she was robed for the opera, and she wore her all-around crown of diamonds. She stared incredulously at Winifred, and cried with ardent hospitality:

"Winifred, it's you! I didn't know you were in town!"

And Winifred, assured by her manner that she had not overheard, hastened to embrace her, exclaiming: "Persis, darling! I haven't seen you for a thousand years."

And they kissed each other.

"You see, I haven't gone yet," Mrs. Neff apologized. "Winifred and I fell to talking—about you, of course."

"Say it to my face," said Persis.

Winifred lied angelically. "Cornelia was telling me how famously you and Willie get along. You're so congenial."

Persis recognized the intended obloquy, and beamed in answer: "Willie is a duck of a husband. Why don't you try marriage?"

This was so straight a lunge that Winifred slid in a sly *riposte:*

"Do you ever see that li'l snojer man of yours any more?"

"Li'l snojer man? Have I one?" said Persis, white-mouthed with fear at the directness of the attack, and at the simultaneous tingle of the door-bell. She tried to check Crofts, calling to him as he moved to the door. But he did not hear.

Mrs. Neff was enjoying the rare treat of seeing Persis discomfited, ill at ease. She joined the onset.

"She means Captain Forbes."

"Yes—that's the one," Winifred smiled. "See him often?"

"Oh, once in a long while," Persis confessed. "Why?"

"I just wondered. He used to be so devoted to you."

"Oh, that was ages ago," Persis laughed. And then Crofts came in with his little salver. Persis regarded it with as much dread as if it bore the head of John the Baptist instead of a tiny white card.

Crofts was so proud of remembering his instructions that he murmured, with a senile smile: "You told me you were at home to him, ma'am."

Persis read the name, and it danced before her eyes, fantastically. In the phrase of the prize-fighters, "they had her going." It was all so simple and foolish, yet so naggingly annoying, that she was utterly nonplussed. She stood a moment snapping the card in her fingers. Then she had a mad inspiration. She smiled stupidly between Mrs. Neff and Winifred and said:

"It's my—my lawyer. I—I'll go to the door and see him."

"But I asked him to come up!" Crofts protested in a doddering collapse, and vanished like a ghost at cockcrow.

Forbes appeared at the door. He saw Persis, and there was no mistaking the love in his eyes. Then he saw Winifred and Mrs. Neff, and there was no mistaking his confusion, though he tried to put on a smile of delight at the sight of them.

Mrs. Neff grinned with rapturous malice, and bewildered Forbes utterly by asking three ironical questions and not staying for an answer:

"Changed your profession, Captain Forbes? A lawyer now? Specialty divorces?"

Then she nodded to Winifred, and they made their way out, ignoring Persis' outstretched hand.

CHAPTER LXV

FORBES stared after the two women in complete perplexity. He turned to Persis to ask stupidly: "What did they mean, Persis?"

Persis had lost almost every whit of self-control. She had an insane desire to scream, to hide somewhere and go into hysterics. She sank into a chair and mumbled:

"They know everything."

"Good God, it's not possible! Was it because I came in as I did?"

"Yes, but it wasn't your fault. It was mine and Crofts'."

He made to take her in his arms, but she warned him where he was with a gesture. He sank into a chair, groaning:

"I'd rather cut off my right hand than bring suspicion on you, Persis."

Staring idly ahead of her, Persis maundered in a hollow voice, "And they refused my hand!" The lash of this remembered insult brought her to her feet with a snarl. "They refused my hand! Oh, it's all over now. A war extra couldn't spread the scandal faster than those two women. But I suppose it had to come some day. And we thought we were so discreet!"

She laughed bitterly, for the luxury of self-contempt was alkali upon her tongue. But Forbes could only sigh, "How you must hate me!"

"How much I love you!" she whispered. Even in her panic she had no reproach for the author of her defeat; and as she paced the floor she touched his cheek with a passing caress.

She walked to the window idly and stared out into the street. She fell back with a gasp. "Oh, they saw me!— they saw me!"

"Who?—who saw you?"

"Alice Neff and Stowe Webb just drove up. They waved to me. They're coming here. Good Lord of heaven, at such a time!"

The door-bell rang in confirmation, and Crofts shuffled down the hall. He glanced timidly at Persis, and she nodded her head.

"You can't see them now," Forbes protested; "tell the man not to let them in."

"It wouldn't do any good. Besides, they saw me. Now of all times I must keep up a bold front. Wait in the library, Harvey. I'll get rid of them as soon as I can." He was hardly gone before Alice came running, crying, "Oh, here you are," and seizing the hand that Persis thrust at her absent-mindedly. Stowe Webb seized her other hand and clung to it as Alice rattled on: "We had the narrowest escape! Just as our taxi drew up to your door my awful mother and Winifred drove away — without seeing us!"

"And do you poor children still have to meet in secret, too?" Persis asked with a dreary sympathy.

"Indeed we have to," Webb replied, "and always shall. Her mother won't let me in the house! And I am doing a little better now—two thousand a year. But Alice's mother still calls me a pauper. Our only hope is a runaway marriage. But Alice always remembers what you told her. I wish you could advise her differently now, for we are hopelessly unhappy. We couldn't be more miserable even if we were married."

Alice corroborated this theory. "It's simply terrible the trials we are put to now. But you made it so vivid to me—the other side of it—the sordidness, the poverty, the stairs, the bills; how I should grow plain, and begin to nag; how I should ruin Stowe's career. Oh, why do we women always seem to be getting in the way of the careers of the men we love! Why can't we help them?"

"We can, Alice, we can!" Persis averred, with a sudden energy. "If we begin the right way, if our love is the right sort, if we don't wait too long. Marry him, Alice."

"But you said," Alice reminded her, "that I should miss all the comforts that make life worth while." And Persis answered with a solemnity that was unwonted in her:

"If you don't marry the one you love you miss everything that makes life worth while. If you don't sacrifice everything that love asks, why, love robs you of all your delight in the things you have kept. Your mother will forgive you, Alice. But what if she doesn't? It is better to lack the forgiveness of some one else—of every one else!—than to feel that you can never, never forgive yourself. That is the most horrible thing in life, not to forgive yourself."

"But you talk so differently now!" Alice interposed; and Persis explained it dismally enough:

"I know more now than I did then."

Alice went into her arms, eager to be coerced and decided for: "And you really think it is my duty to go?"

"A woman's first duty is to her love," Persis cried. "Go, marry the boy, Alice, and be true to him—oh, be true to him!—always! whatever—whoever—comes into your life. Love and fidelity!—what a marriage they make!"

Young Webb bent and kissed her hand, saying: "You must be a very good woman to give such noble advice. And Willie Enslee must be a mighty good husband. Come along, Alice, remember your promise!"

He started to drag her out, but Alice hung back and demanded, "Give us your blessing first."

"My blessing? My blessing?" And Persis' amazement was hardly greater than a curious shock of rapture over the unheard-of prayer.

"Yes, for you are so good!" Alice insisted. And Persis, in half-hysterical emotion, waved her shivering hands over them and murmured:

"God be with you forever!"

When they had gone and Forbes came back to her she was mumbling in a strange delight: "I don't believe any one ever before called me good. It has a rather pleasant sound." She was half laughing, half crying. "I've done some good in the world at last."

"I don't believe I ever truly loved you till now," Forbes said. He had played eavesdropper to her counsel, and it had endeared her to him magically. He took her in his arms and she kissed him, and there was a moment of peaceful oblivion. Then the habit of stealth resumed control of Persis. She began anew to hear footsteps everywhere and to imagine eyes gazing from all sides.

"You mustn't stay a minute longer," she whispered. "Willie is at home. You telephoned you had something awfully important to tell me."

"Yes. You've got to help me make the most important decision of my life."

"Can't it wait?"

"No. I must decide to-day. My leave of absence has been withdrawn, and I've been ordered back to my cavalry regiment at once."

So disaster followed disaster.

"Isn't there any way out of it?" she asked, weakly.

"I tried to get the order recalled, but there is some influence against me at Washington."

"Some woman! I know! It's Willie's mother. She has General Branscombe under her thumb."

"But that would mean that she suspected us!"

"A woman always suspects the worst. And she's always right. Well, what are we to do?"

"That is for you to decide, Persis," Forbes said. "I have two letters here, two requests." He produced two formidable official envelopes. "I have influence enough to get either of them granted."

"What are they?" she asked, terrified by the documents.

"This is an acknowledgment of the order and a statement that I take the train to-morrow for New Mexico."

"New Mexico!" Persis gasped. "I shouldn't see you again for a long, long while."

"Never."

"Then I choose that you send the other letter, of course," she spoke almost gaily. "What is it?"

"My resignation from the service."

"Your resignation?" she gasped. "Why should you resign?"

"To avoid court-martial for the crime of stealing another man's wife. Either you go away with me where your husband can't follow, or I go away where you can't follow."

"You don't mean to force a choice like that on me?" she protested. He nodded grimly.

But her frantic soul was incapable of decision; it fled from the effort. The memory of her humiliation before Mrs. Neff and Winifred swept back over her with intolerable shame; she began to stride along the floor again, gnashing her teeth in rage:

"What can I do to silence those women? Harvey, you must help me. Think up some neat lie that will look like the truth."

He was so tired of deception that he groaned aloud. She whirled on him in raucous fury: "Do you suppose I'm going to give in to a couple of frumps like those two? Do you think I'll let an old hen and an old maid down me?—now! Well, hardly! I'm no quitter, Harvey. I never was a quitter, was I? But what can I do? No story would convince them. I must stop their mouths—that's it. Everybody's got a scandal somewhere. What do I know about them? What have I heard?" She beat her head to stir her memory. "If I can't find out something I must make it up."

Forbes glared at her incredulously. "Persis! Are you lost to all decency?"

"You ought to know," she retorted. "But what of that? I'm desperate. I'm fighting for life."

"Oh, my God, Persis, what have we come to?" he moaned. "Is this the result of our love?"

"Yes, this is it!" she laughed. "This is what comes of having a heart. I see now why a love like ours is against all the laws, written and unwritten. It's the wisdom of the ages, Harvey." His very neck rebelled against the galling yoke of their intrigue. He groaned:

"We can't go on with the situation any more. We are getting degraded—driven to lies, and now you suggest blackmail. What next? We must pull up short and sharp, Persis. You must decide this minute: either to go away with me or to stay here without me."

"You've got to stay here and help me fight."

"I tell you I won't fight such a battle. It isn't fighting; it's cowardice, it's treachery. Decide now, once for all. Give me up or free yourself from Enslee and become my wife. You advised Alice to run away; you can't go back on your own advice."

"Oh, but the elopement of a young unmarried couple is a pretty romance; ours would be a hideous scandal."

"But we're all smothered in scandal now. Everybody is talking about us—everybody. The only way to make our love right is to come out before the world and proclaim it."

"And even now, when I should be thinking of you, all I can think of is what they'll be saying of me to-morrow."

"If we do the best we can what difference does it make what people say? Persis, I'd rather die than endure another hour of this underhand life. But I can't give you up. I can't leave you here to the mercy of these people and the evil influences around you. I offer you happiness. We shall be together always. You can't refuse."

"You're right, of course. I've got to decide. I'm

afraid to be alone. I'll go with you. Give me just one moment to get my cloak. I—I can't very well go like this, though, can I—in an opera-gown and tiara? I must change to a traveling-suit. And Willie expects me to go to the opera."

The little things, the little briery things of life were holding her fast, tripping her headlong desires. She grew more irresolute with delay. "It's a terrible step, and it means the end of me. Everybody will cut me dead on the street. My own father will never speak to me again. The newspapers will be full of it. They'll only remember the scandal when they see us. It will follow us everywhere, and come between us and turn even you against me."

Then she shivered and sank into a chair helpless.

"I can't go, Harvey, I just can't go. I'm afraid of what people will say."

That was the acid phrase that turned his love to hate, his adoration to disgust. He broke the vials of his wrath upon her head.

"What will people say?" he sneered. "Is that all you can think of? Why, that has become your religion, Persis. You can stand the lying—the sneaking—the treachery—can't you? You've courage enough for the crimes, but when it comes to consequences, you're a coward, eh? But I'm not afraid of the consequences. I'm afraid of the crimes. I'm not afraid of the gossips, but of giving them cause. I offered you protection, devotion. I wanted to rescue our honor. But you—what do you care for me—for love—for honor? You care only for yourself and for what people will say—well, you'll soon know. But I won't help you to ruin your life. I won't let you ruin mine. I'm sorry I ever saw you. Before God, I'll never see you again!"

He turned to go. A cry of anguish broke from her. She rushed in pursuit of him, flung her arms about him, sobbing: "No, no, I won't let you! You've no right to leave me. I've given up everything for you. I've been everything to you. You can't leave me! Don't, don't, don't!"

He was too deeply embittered to have mercy. Her panic only angered him the more. He ripped her hands from his shoulders, jeering at her: "Agh, you're faithless to your duty to your husband, faithless to your love of me, faithless to everybody — everything."

"Don't say that, Harvey," she pleaded, brokenly. "Take that back."

"You've killed my trust," he raged. "You've killed my love. I hate the sight of you."

She put her hand over his cruel mouth to silence it. "Don't let me hear that from you — pity me, pity me!"

He tried to break her intolerable clasp, but she fought back to him. Abruptly she ceased to resist. She just stared past him. Startled, he looked where she stared. She whispered:

"Some one is behind that curtain—listening!"

The curtain trembled, and she gasped again: "Look!"

A shudder of uneasiness shook him, but he muttered: "It's only a draught from somewhere."

"Perhaps it is," she answered, weakly. "I feel all cold." And then she stared again and whispered: "No! See! There's a hand there in the curtain!"

And Forbes could descry the muffled outlines of fingers clutching the heavy fabric. He hesitated a moment, then he moved forward.

She put out her arm and stayed him, and spoke with abrupt self-possession. "No, it is my place." Then she called, hoarsely: "Crofts, is that you? Crofts!" There was no answer, but the talons seemed to grip the shivering arras tighter. She called again: "Nichette! Dobbs! Who's there?"

There was no answer.

"It's none of the servants," she whispered. Then, after a pause of tremulous hesitation, she strode to the curtain and hurled it back with a clash of rings. It disclosed Willie Enslee cowering in ambush. He held a silver-handled revolver in his hand.

CHAPTER LXVI

A LITTLE groan of dismay broke from Persis' lips as she rushed between Forbes and the danger, interposing her body to protect his. Forbes seized her and thrust her away and leaped toward Enslee.

But Enslee darted aside and, running behind a great carved table, covered Forbes with the revolver, and cried, in a quivering voice, "Don't you move or I'll fire!"

Forbes smiled grimly at the plight, and spoke with the calm of the doomed. "All right, if you want to. It's your privilege. But I wouldn't if I were you. In the first place, I'm sure you'd miss; you don't hold your revolver like a marksman."

"The first shot might miss," Enslee admitted; "but there are five others."

"You'd never pull the trigger a second time," said Forbes, icily. "And there's not one chance in a thousand of that toy stopping me. I've got two bullets in me now —from real guns. And I'm not dead yet. If you should wing me, though, I'm afraid you'd never shoot a second time, for I'd have you by the wrist and by the throat— and I'd strangle you to death before I realized what I was doing."

Enslee quaked with terror, less of Forbes than of his own fatal opportunities and his own weapon; Forbes began to edge imperceptibly closer and closer as he reasoned with the wretch, who, having lost the momentum of his frenzy, was a prey to reason.

"After all, what good would it do to shed a lot of blood?" Forbes urged, gently, as to a child. "It would only publish your disgrace. Besides, people don't indulge in pistol-play any more. It's out of style, man. That ought to appeal to you, if nothing else will. And then it's so unjust. Why kill a man because your wife preferred him to you? It's a free country, isn't it? What does a man want with a wife who doesn't want him? The days of slavery are over, aren't they? If she doesn't love you enough to—" There was such a pitiful sag of Enslee's head at this stab that Forbes spared him more, and went on soothingly: "Better let this whole affair just drop. I was going away. She wouldn't go with me. She didn't love me enough, either. She preferred to stay with you. I'll never see her again. I promise that."

He put his right hand out appealingly. "Come, let's make the best of it and cheat the gossips."

One quick motion and he had struck Enslee's wrist aside and down, and clamped it to the table with his left hand. It was hardly necessary to press his thumb between Enslee's knuckles to force his inert fingers open. Forbes picked up the revolver, pressed the catch to the safety, and dropped it into his pocket. Then he breathed a deep sigh, less of relief than regret, and turned to go. He almost stumbled over the body of Persis. She had swooned to the floor when he thrust her off, and had lain unnoticed while the males fought through their feud on her account.

Forbes stared down at her. Shame and anger had so burned him out that he had no love left for her and no mercy. She seemed an utter stranger to him. He did not even stoop and lift her to a chair. He shook his head, smiled bitterly, and went out.

Enslee hung across the table in a stupor of imbecility. The noise of the outer door, as Forbes closed it, shocked him back to life. He peered about the room and understood. He dropped into a chair and hid his face in his hands.

By and by Persis gradually returned to consciousness.

She rose to her elbow in a daze, striving to collect her senses. With a sudden start she recalled everything, got to her knees, and hobbled with all awkwardness toward Enslee, whispering, haggardly: "Have you killed him? Where is he?"

"Gone!"

"Gone! No, no! No, no!" She raised herself to her feet to set out in pursuit of him, but just as she reached the door she was confronted by Crofts, who bowed once and walked away.

Persis' training and her heart fought a duel in her quivering frame. Then she gained her self-control, turned to Willie, and murmured:

"Dinner."

The marvelously inappropriate word sent through him a shudder of nausea.

Persis appealed to his other self. "Must we take the servants into our confidence?"

"I think you may trust my breeding," he answered, frigidly. He stalked woodenly to the door, held back the curtain, and bowed with mechanical gallantry.

"Thank you!" she sighed. She wavered a moment and clutched at her throat. Then she flung her head high in that thoroughbred way of hers and walked steadily from the room.

And Willie followed in excellent form.

CHAPTER LXVII

IN the famous Enslee dining-room, where brilliant companies had gathered for a generation, giving and taking distinctions, and where Persis in her brief reign had mustered cohorts of pleasure that outgleamed them all, only two chairs were drawn up to the table; and that was contracted to its smallest circle. All the other chairs were aligned along the white marble walls with a solemn look as of envious, uninvited ghosts sitting with hands on knees and brooding. The walls were broken with dark columns like giant servants, and between them hung tapestries as big as sails. The tapestries told in a woven serial the story of "Tristram and La Beale Isoud."

Only three servants waited now: Roake and Chedsey—in the somber Enslee livery, whispering together as they straightened a rose stem or balanced a group of silver—and Crofts, eternally bent in an attitude of deference, standing near the door—the great golden portal ripped from the Spanish castle of one of the senior Mrs. Enslee's ancestors.

For all their listening the servants had been unable to learn the details of the immediate wrangle, though they knew that war was in the air.

Crofts had kept them at their tasks and at a distance, and Crofts either had not heard or would not have told if one of them had presumed to ask him.

He had lived through so many family tragedies that he rather celebrated in his heart a day of good spirits than remarked a period of stress. And of all times, he felt, a good servant shows his quality best when the atmosphere is sultry with quarrel and a precarious truce is declared in the dining-room. To Crofts that was a temple for peace and perfect ceremony. There flourished the genius for self-effacement and the invisible, inaudible provision of whatever might be needed, that made service a high art, a priesthood.

Crofts, in his plain black, slightly obsolete evening dress, looking rather like a poor relation than a servant, had been in his day an aristocrat among servants. To-night he was old and alarmed. He had seen, when he announced the dinner, that he broke in upon some unusually desperate conflict, and his old heart fluttered with terror. He had heard so much gossip at the servants' table, such ribald comment and interchange of eavesdroppings, that he wondered what new stain threatened the old glory of Enslee.

He loved the new Mrs. Enslee. All the servants did— as much as they disliked Mr. Enslee. But they all felt that she was as dangerous in the house as a panther would have been in a wicker cage. And they all gossiped with other people's servants. And one of the maids, on her evenings off, was meeting a very attentive gentleman with brindle hair and half an eyebrow. She didn't know his business, but he was generous; he took her to tango-places, and he loved to hear her talk about her employers.

Suddenly Crofts lifted his head and threw Roake and Chedsey a glance of warning; they came to attention, each behind a chair, watching with narrow eyes where Persis slowly descended, as into a gorgeous dungeon, the three velveted steps leading down through the red-velvet-curtained golden portal.

First they saw Persis' slipper, a golden slipper on a slim, gold-silk stocking. Next the gleaming shaft of her white-satin skirt, with its wrinkles flashing and folding round her knees; and then a rose-colored mist with glints of gold spangles; a few flowers fastened at her waist; the double loop of a long rope of pearls; then her wide, white bosom, with half the breasts revealed in the deep V between. And next her shoulders; her long throat, passionate and bare save for one coil of pearl-rope; and then her high-held, resolute chin; her grim, red lips; her tense nostrils; her downcast eyelids; her brows; and, finally, the crown of diamonds sparkling in her hair.

Her velvet-muffled footsteps grew faintly audible as her heels advanced with a soft tick-tock across the black-and-white chessboard of the marble floor. There was such a hush in the room that even her soft, short train made a whispering sound as it followed reluctantly after her.

Then Enslee's glistening black shoes appeared on the steps; his short legs; the black-rimmed bay of white waistcoat and shirt, and tie, and the high, choking collar, where his fat little head rested like a ball on a gate-post.

In the rich gloaming of the big room the table waited, a little altar alight and very beautiful with its lace and glass and silver and its candles gleaming upon strewn roses.

Overhead the massive chandeliers hung dark from an ornate ceiling powdered with dull Roman gold. It was illuminated now only by the fretful glow of the fire slumbering beneath the carved mantel ravished from a bishop's palace in Spain.

In such a scene the audience of three servants awaited the performance of the polite comedy by the farceur and farceuse, who would pretend to leave their personal tragedies in the wings. The actors made their entrance with a processional formality, faced each other, and were about to be seated in the chairs the men had drawn back a little.

But the dignity vanished when the male buffoon, glancing at the array before him, broke out with a sharp whine:

"Where's my cocktail?"

There was such a twang of temper in his voice that Crofts heard at once, and made a quick effort at placation.

"Very sorry, sir, but, the other servants being away, I was not able to learn just how you had it mixed, sir."

"Just my luck!" Enslee snarled. "When I need a bracer most I can't have one." He shook his head so impatiently that Persis foresaw calamity and hastened to intervene.

"Let me make it for you, dear."

Enslee threw her an ugly glance, and wanted to refuse, but could find no reason to give except the truth: that he hated to accept any more of her ministrations. And truth was the one thing that must be kept from these menials at all cost. So he said:

"Mighty nice of you."

Persis went to the vast sideboard, and, while Crofts fussed about her, handing her the shaker, the ice, and bottle after bottle, she prepared the cup as if it were a mystic philter of love. She poured each ingredient into one of the glasses, and held it up to the light to make sure of the measure; then she emptied its contents into the shaker and filled it again from another bottle; and so when the square, squat flagon of gin, the longnecks of Italian and of French vermouth, and the flask of bitters, had contributed each its quota, she pondered aloud:

"That's all, isn't it?"

Willie, who had strolled to the sideboard in a kind of loathing fascination, spoke up:

"Here, barkeeper, you're forgetting the absinthe."

"Oh yes," she said, recalling his particular among the numberless formulas—"six drops of absinthe and twelve drops of lemon."

Crofts passed her the àbsinthe, and, finding a lemon, sliced it across and handed it to her on a plate. She held it over the shaker and, squeezing, counted the drops.

"Nine, ten, eleven, twelve—oh, there went the thirteenth! That's a bad omen." She was so overwrought that a little genuine fear troubled her. Enslee felt it, too, but would frighten the bogie with indifference:

"Hang the omen, so long as the cocktail's not bad."

Persis nodded with a difficult smile, and, setting the top on the shaker, said:

"Now, Crofts."

The old man was so slow and so feeble with his agitation that she snatched the shaker from his hand and shook it herself, the ice clacking merrily. Then she lifted off the top and poured the cold amber through the strainer into the two glasses and dried her chilled hands on a napkin.

Willie was too eager for the stimulus to go back to the table and take the cocktail there. He lifted his glass.

"We'll take it standing at the bar." And he reached for an imaginary foot-rail, as he had seen the vaudeville comedians do. Persis laughed, and he laughed, but sorrily. Still another idea occurred to him in his determination to enact domestic bliss.

"And now what's the toast? To the absent one?"

The ghastly patness of this unnerved him, but Persis came to the rescue with, "Toasts are out of date." And Willie, setting the glass to his lips, guzzled it in that chewing way they had never been able to correct in him since his infancy. Persis stood a moment with a far-off look of fierce regret in her eyes, then drained her glass swiftly and dabbed her rouged lips with her handkerchief.

Crofts held out a little tray, and Willie set his glass down so hard that the stem cracked. He gave Crofts the blame in a sullen look, then went back to the table and sat in the chair that Roake pushed under him.

He was up again instantly with another complaint. Willie was by nature one of the tribe of waiter-worriers. In his present tension he was doubly irascible.

"Where the devil is my cushion?" he barked. "You know I can't carve without my cushion."

The cushion was whisked under him instantly.

He stabbed at his canapé of caviar with his fork as if

466

he hated it, ate but a morsel of it, and turned aside in his chair. Persis, watching him with anxious eyes, gave Crofts a command in a glance, and the plates were removed and replaced with oysters, the men bringing everything to the table, but Crofts alone serving their Majesties.

Crofts was senile and slow, and unusually aspen with anxiety and the rebukes he had had. His deliberation was maddening to Enslee. The old-fashioned deference of Crofts' manner was only further irritation.

Persis' own heart was wretched enough with its load of shame; she was hard put to it to sit and smile at the husband who had caught her in the arms of her paramour and heard him casting her off. But she had that social understanding of the actor's creed that the show must go on to the last curtain, no matter what had preceded it, or what might happen between the acts, or what might follow. She was certain of only one thing, that she and Willie must sit out this dinner somehow.

The entr'actes in the solemn mummery were the spaces between the courses while the servants left the room for a few moments to bring on the next thing.

When the caviar had been nibbled and rejected, the oysters set down and refused without being tasted, the two men went into the pantry for the soup-tureen and the hot plates. The swinging door oscillated with little puffs of air like sneers, and a breath ran around the tapestries hung on the walls. Ripples went through them in shudders, and, as the wrinkles traveled, averted faces seemed to turn and glance quickly at the Enslees, then turn away again.

With all the surreption possible Crofts and his lieutenants brought in the silver urn and the ladle and the plates, and set them down on the serving-table behind the screen of Spanish leather with its glowing landscape and its gilded sky.

But Enslee's raw nerves shrieked at the soft thud of

plate on tray, the infinitesimal click of ladle on tureen, the very endeavor not to make a sound. He fidgeted, bit his knuckles, wrung his hands out like damp cloths, played a tattoo on the arm of his chair, and passed his hand wildly across his eyes. At length he whirled, and shouted:

"In God's name, less noise! Less noise!"

Crofts turned to bow and made a trifle more noise. And when he took the plate from Roake's tray and set it before Enslee his hand trembled perilously. It was Enslee's favorite soup, a luscious *purée Mongole*. He lifted one spoonful now to his lips and put it away with disgust. His ignominy was so vile that it sickened his stomach. He had been told that his wife was unfaithful to him; he had found it true; he had wrought himself to a frenzy of revenge upon the destroyer of his home; but the lover, instead of leaping from the window like the typical man of guilt, had taken the husband's weapon from him, denounced the wife, and left the wrecked home in triumph.

Enslee had endured all these disgraces; why should he add one more? Why should he play a part before his own menials? Why should he care what they thought? None the less, as mutinous soldiers keep the line automatically, so a lifetime of paying devotion to the ordinances of etiquette held him to the mark now.

Seeing that Persis had not even made a pretense of lifting her spoon to her lips, he nodded to Crofts, "Take it away."

The failure of a dinner was a catastrophe to Crofts, and he forgot his wonted reticence enough to ask:

"Isn't it good, sir? Sha'n't I tell the chef to—"

His solicitude brought him only a reproof:

"Crofts, if you speak again I'll have the other servants serve the dinner. Take it away, I said."

Hurt and frightened, Crofts hurried the soup and its apparatus off. As he slipped out with his aides the

468

swinging door went "Phew!" and the tapestried figures glanced and whispered together.

As soon as he was alone with his wife, Enslee's voice rose querulously:

"If Dobbs ever leaves us in the lurch again I'll fire him for keeps. This old fool gets on my nerves. Everything is going wrong here. The whole house is falling to rack and ruin. Ought at least to have decent servants —if I can't have a decent wife!"

Persis smiled patiently at this, but as with lips bruised from a blow.

"I trust, Willie, that you won't forget yourself. All these doors have ears, you know."

"You bet they have!" he snapped. "And eyes, too. Are you crazy enough to think that lowering our voices will conceal the truth from any one? Don't you realize that those hounds out there know everything that goes on in this house? Don't you understand that your good name and my honor were gossiped away down‐stairs long before my dishonor became public property?"

Persis felt a panic in her own heart at his manner. Still she tried suasion. "I implore you to postpone this. At any moment Crofts will be back."

"Crofts, eh?" Willie shouted. "Crofts! Crofts will be back! Why, do you imagine for a moment that even that deaf old relic is ignorant of this intrigue you have carried on? Don't you know that every servant of ours that has left the house for weeks has carried through the area-gate a bundle of news and innuendo and suspicion and keyhole information, to be scattered broadcast in every servants' hall in town?"

And then he heard Crofts at the door, and in spite of him habit throttled him; he pulled down the comic mask he had pushed back from his dour face. He ransacked his brain for something humorous to serve as a libretto, and he was reminded of a story he had laughed at heartily before he learned that his own household was a theme for laughter.

He began to giggle uncannily, gruesomely. Persis looked at him, wondering if he had gone mad and begun to gibber. But while Crofts and the others served deviled crabs in their grotesque shells he began to explain his elation, overacting sadly:

"I heard the best story to-day about Mrs. Tom Corliss."

Forgetfully Persis, from her own glass house, protested: "Oh, don't tell me anything about that woman!"

Enslee sneered. "Oh, you're always so easily shocked —such a prude, so conventional!"

Persis understood and blanched. "Go on, I'll stand it."

Enslee began to snicker again, taking some support in his shame from another man's disgrace.

"Well, you know old plutocrat Crane?"

"Not old Deacon Crane," Persis gasped, "that passes the plate at church?"

Willie nodded.

"What can he have to do with any story about Mrs. Tom?"

Enslee he-he'd. "That's the fun of it. Mrs. Tom, it seems—one day when Tom was off to the races—entertained the dear Deacon at a little dinner—served à deux. The Deacon used to give her tips on the market and back them himself for her, and she—well, he was talking about the present‑day craze for dancing with bare feet, et cetera; and she vowed that she wasn't ashamed of her feet either; and so she made the Deacon play Mendelssohn's Spring Song on the pianola, and—"

He looked up to find that Chedsey, while pretending to be very busy at the sideboard, wore a smile that extended almost into the ear he perked round for the gossip. Willie choked on his own laughter, and roared:

"Chedsey, leave the room, and don't come back!"

Chedsey slunk away, and Roake became a statue of gravity. Crofts had not heard at all. Willie finished his story without mirth.

"Anyway, Tom Corliss came in unexpectedly just then, and—well, when the Deacon finally got home his wife met him in the hall; he told her he had been sandbagged by a footpad; and she believed him!"

Willie found Tom Corliss' shame so piquant that he began to relish his food. Crofts, a little encouraged, nodded to Roake and led him out for the next dish.

Persis took small comfort from other people's sordid scandals. They seemed to have no relation to the pure and high tragedy that had ended the romance of her own love. Seeing that they were alone again, she expressed her dislike before she realized its inconsistency.

"And where did you pick up all this garbage?"

Enslee was outraged at this ingratitude for his hard work. "Oh, it shocks you, eh? So beautiful a veneer of refinement and so thin!"

"Where did you hear it?" Persis persisted, lighting herself a cigarette to give her restless hands employment; and Willie answered:

"Mrs. Corliss' second man told it to Mrs. Neff's kitchen maid, and she to Mrs. Neff's maid, and she to Mrs. Neff; and Mrs. Neff to Jimmie Chives, and he to me—at the Club."

"At the Club?"

"Where I heard of your behavior."

"You heard of me at the Club?" Persis gasped.

"Yes, that crowning disgrace was reserved for me. Big Bob Fielding took me to one side and said: 'Willie, everybody in town knows something that you ought to be the first to know—and seem to be the last. I hate to tell you, but somebody ought to,' he said. And I said 'What's all that?' And he said: 'Your wife and Captain Forbes are a damned sight better friends,' he said, 'than the law allows,' he said."

The room swam, and Persis clung to her chair to keep from toppling out of it.

"So that's what he said. And what did you say?"

"I didn't believe him—then. I was too big a fool to believe him; but he opened my eyes, and I came home to see what was going on. And I saw!"

Persis was on fire with a woman's anxiety to know if any champion had defended her name. She demanded again:

"What did you say to Bob Fielding?"

And Enslee answered with a helpless, mincing burlesque of dignity:

"I told him he was a cad, and I didn't want him ever to speak to me again."

"And you didn't strike him?"

Enslee cast up his eyes at the thought of attacking the famous center-rush; then he lowered his eyes before her blazing contempt. She demanded again, incredulously: "You didn't strike him?"

Enslee dropped his face into his two palms and wept, the tears leaking through his fingers. Persis felt outlawed even from chivalry. She gagged at the thought: "Agh! The humiliation!"

Enslee lifted his head again, his wet eyes flashing. "Humiliation?" he screeched, in a frenzy of self-pity. "Do you talk of humiliation? What about me? My father and mother brought me into the world with a small frame and a poor constitution. They left me money as a compensation. And what did my money do for me? It bought me a woman—who despised me—who dishonored me before the world. And I'm too weak to take revenge. I'm helpless in my disgrace, helpless!"

He sobbed like a lonely girl, his eyes hid in the crook of his left arm, his elbow on the table, his little hand clenching and unclenching. His tears brought tears to Persis. It was the first time she had ever felt sorry for Willie; had ever realized that a weak man does not select his weaknesses, though he must endure their consequences. She had often justified herself by the plea that she had not chosen her own soul, but must get along with it. That defense was her husband's, too.

The swinging door thudded softly, and Willie raised himself in his chair, but he could not quell the buffets of his sobs, and he dared not put his handkerchief to his eyes. And so Crofts, bending close to remove the crab-shells, noted the grief-crumpled face and the drench of tears; his mind went back to the time when Willie Enslee was a child and wept in a high chair in his nursery. Before he could suppress it the old man had let slip the query:

"Why, Master Willie, you're not crying?"

Willie, with splendid presence of mind, answered:

"Nonsense, you old fool, it's that deviled crab. There was so much cayenne pepper in it, it w-went to my eyes."

Crofts was desolated.

"Oh, I am sorry, sir. The chef shall hear of it, sir. And the roast now—shall I carve it, or will you?"

Willie looked drearily across at Persis. "Do you want any roast?"

She frowned with aversion. "I couldn't touch it."

And Willie shook his head to Crofts. "We'll skip the roast. What follows that? Be quick about it!"

Crofts lowered his voice, as if a game-warden might be listening, for it was after the season had closed. "There is a pheasant, sir—sent down from your own run, sir. It is braised, *financière*. I'm sure you'll like it. You may have to wait a little, seeing as you didn't eat the roast; but it's worth waiting for, sir."

The old man was pleading both for the honor of his menu and for the welfare of his master. Willie nodded curtly, and the roast, that had ridden in so royally on its silver palanquin with its retinue of cutlery and its hot plates, was removed in disgrace.

Once more husband and wife were abandoned to themselves. But now Persis looked with new eyes at the heap of misery collapsed in the opposite chair. All these years Willie had tried to win her love with gifts, with splendors, with caresses, prayers, compliments, and with weak experiments in tyranny. And he had failed dismally. Finally his failure and his shame had crushed him into abjection.

And now her heart went out to him with a melting tenderness. But now she was unworthy to approach him. Now it was she that must plead:

"I'm awfully sorry for you, Willie. You haven't had a fair deal. I never realized what a rotter I've been till now. But if you'll let me, I'll try again; I'll try hard, really, honestly, Willie. The only man I ever seemed to care for has taken himself out of my life. He hates me as you hate me. I haven't much of anything to live for now except to try to square things with you. I'll do better by you. I'll be on the level with you after this. Honestly I will. We'll find happiness yet."

"Happiness!"

Even at this belated hour the world's ambition was so dear to him that he was wrung with longing.

"It might have been possible if I hadn't found you out. I was a fool to trust you so blindly, but I was a happy fool. I didn't know how happy I was till I learned how unhappy I can be. Oh, Persis, how could you—how could you? You seemed so clean and so cold and so proud, and you've let that man make as big a fool of you as you've made of me."

She took her lashings meekly, hoping thereby to achieve some atonement. "I know, I know," she confessed. "But we can keep other people from knowing. We don't have to tell all the world, do we?"

Again the vision of stalking gossip enraged him. "The world—ha! It always knows everything before the husband suspects anything. I've said that about so many other fools I've known. Now it's my turn. Here we sit at dinner in this ruined home as if everything were all right. Think of it! After what I saw and heard I'm sitting here trying to persuade a pack of flunkeys that you have been a good wife to me!"

"It's hideous, I know, Willie. I'll go away to-morrow. You can divorce me if you want to. I won't resist. It will be horrible to drag your name through the yellow papers. But I won't resist—unless you think you might let our life run along as before until gossip has starved to death? We'll be no worse than the rest, Willie. Every family has its skeleton in the closet. The worst gossips have the worst skeletons. Let's fight it out together, Willie, won't you? Please!"

She stretched one importunate hand across the table to him, but he stared at her with glazed eyes. "And go on like this the rest of our lives? Sitting at table like this every day, facing each other and knowing what we know? Knowing what other people know of us? Keep up the ghastly pretense till we grow old?"

She drew back her rejected hand with a sigh, but pleaded on: "It's not very pretty, that's true; but let's be good sports and play the game. We tried marriage without love, for you knew I didn't really love you, Willie. You knew it and complained of it. But you married me. I tried to do what was right. I ran away from him in France, and I tried to love you and unlove him. But you can't turn your heart like a wheel, you know. We've married and failed. But nearly everybody else has failed one way or another, Willie. Nobody gets what he wants out of life. Let's play the game through. You said to me once—do you remember?—you said, 'Gad, Persis, but you're a good loser.' And I've lost a little, too, Willie. I've had a pretty hard day of it, too. Let's be good losers, Willie; let's try it again, won't you? Won't you, please?"

She sat with hands clasped, and thrust them out to him and prayed to him as if he were an ugly little idol. But contrition did not seem to render her more attractive in his eyes. It hardened his heart against her.

"When I look at you I can only think what you've been

to that man; where you've gone, what you've done. You sit there half naked now, ready to go to the opera, to expose your body before the mob—my body—my wife's body. You show it in public—and you dance it in public with anybody—with him! The first time you saw him you were dressed like that, and you danced with him that loathsome tango. You taught him how. And he has taught you how to be his wife—not mine.

"You've set everybody laughing at me. They're all saying I was a blind, infatuated fool before. Now you want them to fasten that filthy word 'complacent' on me. You want me to overlook what you have done and what you've brought me to. I'm just to say: 'Well, Persis, you've had your lover and your fling, and you're tired of each other, so come home and welcome, and don't worry over what's past. It's a mere trifle not worth discussing. What's the Seventh Commandment between friends?'"

She was trying to silence him, but he had not heeded the return of Crofts till the pheasant was placed before him in all its garnishment, and the plates and the carving-fork and the small game-knife. He was ashamed, not of what he had said of her, but of his own excitement.

"Is the knife sharp?" he asked, for lack of other topic.

"Oh yes, sir," said Crofts. "I steeled it myself."

Willie began anew, groping in his tormented brain for something to dispel the silence. The result was a dazed query:

"By the way, my dear, what's the opera to-night?"

"Carmen," she said."

He brightened. "Oh, of course. That's the opera where the fellow kills the girl who betrays him, isn't it?"

"Yes."

"With a knife like this, eh?" And with a fierce absent-mindedness he made a quick slash in the air. The knife was small and curved a little, and it fitted his hand like a dagger. He chuckled enviously. "Ah, he was the wise boy, that Don José. He knew how to treat faithless women. He knew how to talk to 'em. A knife in the back—that's all they can understand."

Crofts was too anxiously trying to avoid spilling a drop of the wine he was pouring to heed the warning gestures of Persis. She felt that the breaking-point of Willie's self-control had been reached. She must dismiss the audience. She spoke hastily:

"Willie, my dear—my dear! Won't you send for some champagne—or sherry. I hate this red wine, and, besides, we've skipped the roast."

"Oh yes," Willie agreed, with abrupt calm. "Crofts, down in the—er—wine-cellar in the farthest end—you'll find laid away by itself one bottle of—er—L'Âme de Rheims—one bottle, the last of its ancient and—er—honorable name. Bring that here."

As Crofts stumbled out on his long journey, Willie commented, ominously:

"It's a good time to say good-by to that vintage!"

His roving eyes discovered Roake standing aloof. Willie snapped his fingers and yelped at him:

"Get out! And stay out!"

Roake withdrew in haste, and Enslee muttered:

"I'm sick of seeing so many people standing around, staring, smirking, listening, thinking about me. I wish I were on a desert island."

He sat forward to the pheasant, set the fork into it, and paused with the knife motionless. Suddenly there were beads of sweat on his forehead, and he was panting hard; then he groaned:

"My God, he took my revolver away from me!"

His eyelids seemed to squeeze his eyes in anguish. When he opened them they were bloodshot and so fierce that they seemed to be crossed. He laughed.

"I was too weak to kill your soldier. But I think I'm just about strong enough to pay you up. Carmen got her reward with a knife, and you're no better than she was."

WHAT WILL PEOPLE SAY?

He looked at the knife; it was beautifully sharp, and it inspired a desire to use it. As a man seeing a gun wants to fire it at something, he felt the call to employ this implement. He pushed back his chair, rose, and groped his way round the table toward her, all crouched and prowling.

CHAPTER LXVIII

PERSIS watched him come, and did not move. It was unbelievable that disaster should fall to such as her from such as him in such a way. He was evidently only playing a part to frighten her.

She blew a puff of smoke from her cigarette and fanned it away with leisure, and smiled.

"You'd look well, now, wouldn't you, if one of the servants came in?"

She laughed at the picture.

"You're laughing at me again!" he groaned. "You're always laughing at me. But you won't feel so funny with this knife in you."

She saw now that he was not fooling. But she despised him for his effort to prove his bravery by a cowardice, and she eyed him with a marble calm worthy of a nobler cause and a better reward.

"Sit down, Willie, and don't threaten me. You don't frighten me at all. But you may alarm some of the servants and give them more of that gossip you have harped on so much."

Her obstinate pluck bewildered him, but he lowered his voice as he commented to some imaginary spectator: "My God! she has no higher thought than that! Even now when death stares her in the face!" Then he had a fanatic's mercy for her. "Why aren't you saying your prayers, you fool?"

She answered him with all the authority she could command:

"Put down that knife! Put it down, I say! You know

I could save myself from any danger by raising my voice. And you know I'd rather die than bring the servants in on such a scene."

"A scene!" he shrieked. "A scene! Why, woman, I'm going to kill you. Don't you understand anything? You've only got a minute more to live. Say your prayers! Damn you! say your prayers!"

There was an insanity in his look that frightened her at last. She tried persuasion now, and her voice was soft and caressing.

"Gently, Willie; gently now, I beg you. You're not yourself, you know. You must control yourself. Please! —as a favor to me."

It was the wrong word. It maddened him, and he snarled: "As a favor to you? You dare ask favors of me? Go ask 'em of the man you've given favors to! The man? The men!"

And this was sacrilege to her one love. Her lip curled in angry contempt, and she turned from him in loathing, muttering:

"You dirty little beast!"

It was his muscles rather than his mind that did it. While his mind was recoiling from the insult his arm had struck out, and the knife had slid deep in the snow of her half-averted left breast; through the petal of a rose, and the satin gown, and the deep white flesh beneath it, and on into the wall of her struggling heart.

The blow and her effort to escape flung her backward, but the heavy chair held her. Before she could remember a wild scream broke from her lips.

As Enslee fell back his hand withdrew the knife. It came out all red. He gaped at it and shuddered, and it fell with a little clatter on the marble floor, flinging a few crimson drops on the black-and-white.

The noise startled him, and he retreated from her, clinging to the edge of the table. He felt queasy, and pushed back till he felt his chair and dropped into it — still

HER OBSTINATE PLUCK BEWILDERED HIM

staring at her and wondering, and she wondering at him.

It seemed a long time before her cry brought any response. Chedsey was in the cellar with Crofts and heard no sound, but Roake was in the pantry. He paused a moment, not trusting his ears, then he pushed the door open slightly and peered through. Other servants came crowding into the pantry whispering and jostling. He motioned them back.

His master and mistress were in their places. Mrs. Enslee looked pale and was lying back in her chair. He slipped through the door and spoke timidly:

"Beg pardon, ma'am; but did you call?"

Persis, at the sound of the door, finding her fan still in her hand, had instantly spread it across her wound. And her first impulse was to deny.

"No," she answered; then quickly: "Yes, I—I am ill—a little—suddenly. Telephone for Doctor—Doctor—the nearest doctor. You'd better run."

He turned to obey, but paused to ask:

"Isn't there anything I can do first, ma'am?"

"No, go! Go!" she fluttered.

"Sha'n't I send some one else while I am gone, ma'am?"

"No, no; keep them all away, all of them, till I ring."

Roake, with a face like ashes, still waited, staring.

"But, ma'am, you are hurt! You are bleeding!"

"Nonsense!" she stormed. "I spilled some claret on my fan. The doctor! Will you never go?" And he ran out through the jumble of servants, ordering them back to their stations.

And then Nichette came stumbling through the golden portal. She had heard the cry above, and had understood the pain and terror in it, and had run pell-mell down the great stairs, her hand whistling on the marble balustrade.

She paused now, clinging to one of the red curtains, and stammering:

WHAT WILL PEOPLE SAY?

"*Madame, Madame! qu'y a-t-il? qu'avez-vous?*"

Persis turned her head dolefully toward the face so wild with anxiety for her sake, and murmured, with a smile of affection and a tender form of speech:

"*C'est toi, Nichette? Ce n'est rien, mais—mais—*" A shiver ran through her. "*Je sentis des frissons. Va faire mon lit. Je me vais coucher.*"

Nichette came forward unconvinced or to help her, but she motioned her off with a frantic hand, crying impatiently, "*Dépêche-toi! veux-tu te dépêcher!*"

And Nichette, mutinously obedient, ran away, leaving Persis shivering indeed with a chill.

And now husband and wife were alone once more. And Willie could only stare and murmur, vacuously:

"What have I done? What have I done?"

"You've killed me, that's all," she answered, with a curious amusement. "It was such a funny thing for you to do, so old-fashioned."

There is a strange fact about wounds in the heart. If they are not so deep that they flood the lungs and smother out life they inspire a wild desire to talk, a fluttering garrulity.

So Persis, now, with that madly stitching shuttle in her breast, and that red seepage from her side, had unnumbered things to say. She chattered desperately, disjointedly:

"Oh, I suppose it had to come. It's what I get for trying to run things my own way. And now the tango-shop's closed up. But it's so funny that you should be the one to—and with a knife! You didn't mar my face, anyway. I thank you for that much. I'd hate to have my face hidden at the funeral. I should hate to make an ugly cor—"

Her lips refused the awful word as a thing unclean, abominable. Her body and all the voluptuous company of her senses felt panic-stricken at the thought of dissolution. She moaned and struggled with her chair.

"No, no, not that! What have I to do with death? I'm not ready to die. I'm not ready to die."

Willie got up and ran to her left side, but shrank back from what was there, and moved cautiously round on the slippery floor, crying: "You're too beautiful to die, too beautiful! You'll not die! The doctors will save you!"

"They must come very soon, then," Persis said, "for I'm bleeding—oh, so fast." She looked down along her side and complained: "See, my gown is quite ruined. And it was such a pretty gown. I'm afraid of my blood. How it gushes! Will it never stop? And it hurts! Willie, it hurts!"

In a long writhe of pain she gathered the table-cloth about her left side as if to stanch its flow. There was a rattle of falling glasses and a chink of tumbled silver as she moaned: "Oh, what shall I do? What shall I do?" And she turned her head this way and that, panting as one pursued, bewildered, utterly at a loss. "Oh, what shall I do? I don't want to die. It's an awful thing to die—just now of all times, with no chance to make good the wrong I've done."

"You can't die; I won't let you die. You're too beautiful to die," Willie protested, and then turned to pleading: "I didn't mean to. I didn't mean to strike you, Persis, at all. It was just my hand. It wasn't me that stabbed you, Persis. I couldn't hurt you, Persis."

"Oh, that's all right, Willie. I understand. I understand things better now, with so few minutes more to live. It is you that must forgive me. I haven't been a good wife to you, Willie. And he—he, of all men!—said I wasn't worth fighting for! Faithless to you—faithless to him! But oh, God knows, most faithless to myself. And now I must die for it."

"You are too beautiful to die! I won't let you die! You can't die!"

"But I must, boy. Don't hate me too much. I didn't

mean to harm you. Some day—long after—you'll forgive me, won't you?"

"Oh, if you only won't die I'll forgive you anything."

"That's awfully nice of you, Willie," she said, with almost a smile. "I wonder if God will be as polite? They
—they usually pray for dying people, don't they? I'm
afraid they'll never get a doctor in time, to say nothing
of a preacher. So you'd better pray for me, Willie."

The idea was so ridiculously tragic that she laughed;
but he would not so far surrender her as to pray. He
sobbed:

"You've got to live! I don't know a single prayer.
You mustn't die, I tell you. You've got to live!" And
he wept his little heart out as he knelt at her side, and,
clinging to her hand, mumbled it with kisses.

She wept, too; moaned, and dreaded the black Beyond,
which she must voyage prayerless. Still she must talk.
From her silence came a frail, thin voice like a far-
off cry.

"It's growing very dark, Willie—very dark! And I'm
drifting, I wonder where? Can you hear my voice away
off there? Better throw me a kiss, and wish me *bon
voyage!* for this—is the last—of Persis. Poor Persis!"

Something of old habit reminded her of the gossip that
would break into storm at her death. This spurred her
heart to strive again. She clutched at the table and at
Willie's arm and shoulder, and held herself erect as with
claws, while she babbled:

"Willie, Willie, I've just thought. They'll try you for
—for murder. The newspapers—the newspapers! Oh,
my poor father! And they'll put you in jail! That
mustn't happen to you—not to one of your family!—not
through me!—no—no, it just mustn't! You must run—
run—run!"

Enslee shivered at the future, and would have fled if
he could have found the strength to rise from his knees.

And then the swinging door puffed softly, sardonically,

and on the tapestries Tristram and Isoud looked at each other and then at her and shook their heads in pity.

Crofts, who had neither heard nor been told, came in with that eminent champagne in a dingy and ancient bottle.

He went behind the screen to untwist the wires and rub away the spider-webs. Then he came forward toward Willie's place to pour the first few drops there, according to the rite, before he filled Persis' glass. He had eased out the cork, and the soul of the wine was frothing forth into the swathing cloth when he blinked at the empty chair; then his eyes went across to Persis. He stared at her in mute amazement. She stared at him. She beckoned.

He put the bottle on the table and shuffled toward her.

She motioned him nearer with a limp and tremulous hand, and he bent down to hear her tiny voice.

"Crofts, come closer—listen to me—do you hear?" He nodded. "Perfectly?" He nodded, wringing his dry old hands.

"Well," she began, "I must tell you—and you must remember. Mr. Enslee and I had a—a little quarrel—and I—I lost my temper—you know—and seized the knife and—and stabbed myself."

The old man did nothing unbecoming to his caste, but he stood doddering and longed to die in place of that beautiful youth. She beckoned him nearer again, and spoke in a strangled voice: "Remember, I did it—myself! Re-mem—"

Her head fell forward, her exquisite chin rested in her bosom. Her body collapsed upon itself, and only the arms of the chair and the table kept it from rolling out on the floor.

But as if even this last ugliness of attitude were intolerable to her, she fought against the chair and the table, and pushed and slid backward till her head was erect. And she was whispering courage to herself, hoarsely:

"Come—come—Persis!"

She seemed to be trying to die like a thoroughbred, a good loser.

And then her head rolled back in the billows of her hair, with the jeweled crown pointing downward and her eyes staring upward. Her wan, pouting, parted lips and the long arch of her perfect throat were themselves a prayer for mercy, offering up beauty as its own undoing and its own excuse.

She was dead.

THE AFTERMATH

THE AFTERMATH

I

WE cannot live to ourselves alone, nor die so. If a man or a dog crawl off to perish in a wilderness, immediately death sets in motion a great activity. On the ground ants muster, flies drum and pound; in the earth worms make haste upward. On the empty sky a speck appears, wings gather, buzzards are overhead. In the bushes eyes peer, paws are lifted and set down with caution; coyotes, hyenas arrive. A city of scavengery is founded and begins to flourish.

Persis had said, "This is the last of Persis." As if there were ever the last of anybody or anything.

Of Persis it was almost the beginning. People were to hear of her now who had never known of her existence. She who had never done anything ambitious or earnest in any large sense was to become the cause of world-wide debate. The newspapers she dreaded so much were to give her head-lines above panics, wars, and empires.

When Persis screamed at the horror and the shame of being knifed, and Roake appeared, and she told him that she was ill, he believed her. He dispersed the servants. They knew, as servants always know, that a quarrel had been raging; but family quarrels were the staple of their lives, and they suspected nothing unusual.

Persis had told Roake to call the nearest physician. The telephone is the confusion of distance; it mixes near and far hopelessly. So Roake called the family physician, Dr. Thill; caught him dressing for the opera. He promised to "be right over."

Then Roake went back to give Mrs. Enslee this word. He found the woeful spectacle of Persis no longer able to hide her wound, no longer thinking of appearances. Enslee was on his knees sobbing. Crofts, too good a servant to express his emotions noisily, had not fallen to the floor or sunk into a chair; he had turned a little aside and stood waiting the next command; only, rubbing his hands together a little harder than usual, while the tears poured across his eyelids.

Roake tiptoed to him and put his hand on his arm, and whispered, "Mr. Crofts."

Crofts put his finger to his quivering lips and, beckoning his underling aside, whispered to him: "No word of this to the rest of the house, mind you. We'd best carry Mrs. Enslee to her room. Then we must help the master to his."

They took Persis' chair by the arms dreadfully; but Crofts could not lift his share of the weight. It was necessary to call Chedsey, and to explain things a little to him and to pledge him to silence for the honor of the house. He sickened of his burden and nearly fainted in the little elevator as they crowded into it with their hideously beautiful freight.

Nichette had the bed ready, and Enslee's man was helping her. Also two other chambermaids had gathered to talk of the scream that had shot through the house. Nichette banished the men while she took what care she could of what remained of Persis—so different an office now from what it had always been to Nichette.

Crofts told Roake to see to things below, and Roake and Chedsey went down to the dining-room. Here there were tasks that were not pleasant. They stared at the ruined graces of the table, the spilled wine and the red-stained flowers, the glasses shattered and fallen, as if an orgy had preceded there. The cook was told that the rest of the dinner would not be served. The laundress was called from her supper to take away the red table-cloth and the napkin. The housekeeper must know that Roake and Chedsey were not to be charged with the breakage. The kitchen-maid was sent to scrub the marble, and on her knees she must follow the crimson trail to the door of the elevator, and wash that, too.

Before the doctor arrived a dozen people had been told that the mistress of the household had killed herself. It was easy to warn them that loyalty to the family imposed absolute silence. But what money or what threat or plea could ever bribe a loose tongue to keep a secret for somebody else?

Then Dr. Thill came in his motor. He left his huge fur coat on the hall floor, and, dashing up-stairs, flung off his evening coat and his white waistcoat, and rolled back his cuffs. He wrought upon the exquisite bare flesh of Persis and upon the stopped clock of her heart with all his science; yet he could not make her anything but a cadaver.

As he toiled he asked questions. Crofts and Nichette told him what they knew, or thought they knew. Willie was supported in and questioned. Remorse and fright made him pitiable. Still there remained a fox-like intelligence. He told the doctor what Persis had told Crofts, but he was so full of contradictions and confusion that Dr. Thill quickly suspected the truth. He was enraged and revolted. The cruelty of the murder was bad enough; but the wantonness of destroying so perfect a machine, as he found Persis to be, was more wicked in his eyes.

Still, he was a typical family doctor. People who were dead were outside his province. His clients were the living, and his business to keep them alive and well. He had foiled death-bed revenges, aborted scandals that threatened ruin to the young; risked his life and his liberty for his patients. His trade was fighting the ravages of sin and error; saving people, not destroying them. He felt no call to deliver an Enslee to the electric chair.

He put Willie to bed, jammed bromides into him, and forbade him to talk or to see any one. He telephoned Persis' father and Willie's mother to come at once. He told them as delicately as he could. It was like breaking a thunderbolt gently. Persis' father was stricken frantic. He could not believe that his beautiful, his wonderful girl was dead. He ran to her bedside, lifted her in his arms as if she were again his little child, called to her, wept horribly over her, imagined the truth, and vowed every revenge.

After the first tempests had worn him out he began to feel that it would not comfort her to add scandal to her fate. He loathed the very name of Enslee; but he had profited by it; he was still involved with it financially; it was his daughter's final name. He joined the conspiracy to bury the truth in Persis' grave. To say that she had killed herself was an appeal for mercy; to proclaim that her indignant husband had executed her for her crimes was a damning epitaph. He solaced himself with the thought that it would be her wish.

Mrs. Enslee was first and last Willie's mother. Her thought was of him; her heart was his advocate alone. She committed herself utterly to his defense.

Dr. Thill was ready to give a certificate that Persis had died of heart-failure. Even the story of suicide would attract the noisy attention of the journals. He left the matter in abeyance for the moment. The needful thing was a few hours of saving peace and silence. He would be glad even to postpone the news from the next morning's to the next evening's papers.

But little things thwart great schemes.

II

ONE of the Enslee housemaids, who had been flirting with the brindle-haired reporter Hallard, remembered in the midst of the panic that he was to take her that night to a moving-picture theater. He would be loitering in the area now. She ran out bareheaded to explain that she could not keep her engagement. When he asked why, she told him falteringly that there had been a death in the family. She apologized for permitting such an affair to interfere with her promised evening out, but he gasped:

"A death in the Enslee family! Gosh, I've spent so many dismal hours on death-watches that it's great to have you slip me a nice little ready-made death like this. Whose was it? Who died?"

The maid felt that she had a clue now to Mr. Hallard's profession: from his cheerful reception of such news he must be an undertaker. She explained that it was Mrs. Willie Enslee who was dead.

"My God! the young one?" he cried, afire with the news possibilities.

"Yes; she killed herself."

This was almost too good to be true. Hallard grew greedy as a miser.

"Does anybody else know of this? Have any reporters called at the house?"

"Nobody; only the doctor."

Hallard looked at his watch. He had time to build up a big story, which was good; but there was time enough for the other papers also to arrive on the ground, which was bad.

"Why did she kill herself?"

"Nobody knows. She had a terrible quar'l with Mr. Enslee, though."

"What about?"

"Nobody could find out."

Hallard thought hard. The name of Forbes occurred to him, for he remembered the time he had seen Forbes with Persis.

"Did Captain Forbes call to-day?"

The maid stared. "Ain't you a wonder! How did you know?"

"Did they quarrel about him?"

"Nobody knows they did, but all of us feels sure they did."

Hallard bade his inamorata good night with genuine affection. She had been worth while.

He went to the door of the house and reached it just as Persis' father arrived in his car and was helped up the steps. Hallard tried to push in with him, but was thrust out. He sent his card in, and it was returned to him.

Dr. Thill threw up his hands in despair at the card. Reporters seemed to be as ubiquitous as microbes. But he realized that it was now necessary to make a formal announcement to the papers. He wrote out for Hallard a statement, and had the housekeeper telephone it to a press bureau, that "Mrs. William Enslee, during a period of mental aberration, committed suicide at her home at seven-thirty o'clock, in the presence of her husband. Mr. Enslee is prostrated with the shock." It was a simple announcement.

Meanwhile Hallard, rebuffed at the front door and at the tradesman's entrance, and rebuffed by telephone when he called up from a booth in the nearest drug-store, was trembling with the opportunities almost within his reach. His was the ecstasy of the writer of tragedies who exults in every new horror that he can inflict on his characters.

Only, the Hallards are dealing in real lives, and not feigned.

Hallard's scent for news quickened at the thought of Forbes. Easily enough he learned the name of Forbes' hotel. He hurried there and sent up his card, with a penciled note: "Would appreciate expert opinion regard to probable fate Philippine Islands in case of war with Japan."

III

THE card found Forbes not yet recovered from the hurricane of passion that had swept through his heart. He was dumfounded at what he had done and said; at his ruthless cruelty, his revulsions from love to hate and back again; at the supreme insolence of his treatment of the husband he had wronged.

He found Enslee's little silver-handled revolver in his pocket and tossed it on the table. He felt that he ought to turn it against himself in self-execution. It was too weak an instrument for such a business. He got out his own big army revolver. But he was not of the type that is capable of suicide, any more than Persis was.

He began to pack his things for his return to hard service away from the frivolities of the city. The sight of his uniforms made him the soldier once more. He grew homesick for the brisk salute of his soldiers, the gruff and wholesome joviality of fellow-officers, the noble reality of his chosen career.

And then he came across her boudoir cap again. It bewitched him. It was so utterly unmilitary, so far from usefulness or importance, all pliant and fragrant and adorably foolish. He put it back in its nest in the pocket next his heart. And his heart quickened its pace.

With that quickening came by reflex a sense of terror. What had become of Persis? He had left her to the mercies of Enslee. It occurred to Forbes that if a man had dealt with him as he had dealt with Enslee he would be so maddened that he would run amuck and slay the first thing he met, and first of all the woman who had dragged him into such shame below shame.

WHAT WILL PEOPLE SAY?

What if Enslee had attacked Persis? Beaten her, or torn her face with his nails, or hurled her out into the street? Forbes felt that he must go to her rescue. The impulse lasted only long enough to be ludicrous. What right had he in that household? What harm could Enslee wreak upon Persis to equal the wrongs that Forbes had done her? He blamed himself for everything, and, blaming himself, absolved Persis, forgave her, loved her again.

In this seethe of moods the card of Hallard arrived with a request for his expert military opinion on a subject that had been one of his hobbies in the days when military ambition was the major theme of his life. It renewed his hope. It was like the feel of something solid underfoot to a spent swimmer in cross-currents.

He welcomed Hallard with cordiality, apologized for the disorder of the room, expressed an opinion that he had met Hallard somewhere before. Hallard said he thought not. As he stated his plans for a Sunday special, a "symposium" of views on Philippine fortification, he picked up the silver-handled revolver on the table and laughed:

"Is this lady-like weapon the latest government issue?"

Forbes did not laugh; he flushed as he shook his head. A wild thought came to Hallard. Forbes might have been present at Mrs. Enslee's death. He might have killed her himself with her own revolver. It was a wild theory; but he had known so much of murder, and had come upon such fantastic crimes, that nothing seemed impossible to him.

With pretended carelessness he broke the silver revolver open and glanced at the cylinder. Every chamber was full but one. Had a shot been fired from it, or had one chamber been left unloaded for the hammer to rest on?

Hallard put down the weapon and talked yellow journalism of the Philippine problem. A little later he said, quite casually:

"Too bad about Mrs. Enslee, wasn't it, Captain?"

The startled look of Forbes confounded his theories.

"What is too bad about Mrs. Enslee?"

"Her sudden death, I mean."

"Her death!" Forbes cried, the world rocking with sudden earthquake. "Her death! Not Persis! Persis isn't dead?"

"Why, yes; didn't you know?"

"My God! My God! how did she die? She was well, perfectly well at—at—this afternoon when I—tell me, man, man, what do you mean?"

Hallard was readjusting his case. He spoke very gently.

"I'm mighty sorry to have told you without warning. I thought, of course, you knew. You were a great friend of the family, weren't you, Captain?"

Forbes whitened at this, but his grief was keener than his shame.

"Tell me, how did she die?"

"The story we get is that she killed herself—stabbed herself!"

Forbes gripped his head in his arms and bowed to the thunderbolts crashing about him. At length his distorted face appeared again and he demanded:

"Who was with her when she killed herself?"

"Her husband."

"Then it's a lie. She never—she wouldn't—he killed her! And it's my fault for leaving her with him. I ought to have known better. I was tempted to go back to her. I shouldn't have left her there with that—that—and now she's dead! He butchered her! I'll kill him for it. I will! He wasn't man enough to fight me—he—did you say you were a reporter?"

"Well, I'm a special writer."

Forbes' words began to roar back through his memory. He began to hear them as they would fall on a stranger's ear. Even in his frenzy he realized the danger of his madness. Talking to a reporter was like crying his thoughts aloud in Madison Square Garden. Grief, discretion, remorse, revenge, assailed him from all sides at once.

He seized Hallard by the shoulder and raged at him.

"Look here! This Philippine idea was just a trick, wasn't it, to startle me and make me forget myself? You fooled me, but you can't get away with it."

He saw his big Colt's revolver in his trunk-tray, and he thundered:

"I ought to shoot you for this, and I will unless you swear that you will never print a word of what I've said, never breathe a word of it to a soul. Promise, or by—"

Hallard smiled and raised his half-eyebrow.

"You're a little excited, Captain, aren't you? You're kind of forgetting that shooting a reporter would be about the poorest way of escaping publicity ever imagined. People would naturally ask what it was you were so anxious to conceal, eh?"

Forbes turned away helpless.

Hallard anticipated his next desperate idea. "I'm much obliged to you, Captain, for not offering me a ten-dollar bill or a new suit of clothes. They usually begin with that. But it rarely works, Captain. We're a shiftless lot, some of us, but we've got our ideas of duty, too."

"Duty to what?" Forbes sneered. "Duty to act as grave-robbers and expose the sorrows of the world to the laughter of the public? To drag families down to ruin?"

"Duty to throw the light into dark places, Captain; duty to make it hard to conceal things the public ought to know; duty to keep digging up the truth and throwing it into the air."

"Truth!" Forbes raged. "What have you got to do with the truth? Would you know it if you saw it? Would you use it if you had it?"

"You bet I would," Hallard said. "If you'll tell me the exact truth, as far as you know it, about the suicide— or murder, as you call it—of one of the most beautiful members of one of the most prominent families—I'll publish it."

"In your own way, yes."

"In your own words, Captain. I write shorthand. Just dictate to me the whole story of your acquaintance with Mrs. Enslee and your reasons for believing that her husband killed her; and I'll not change a word. You can read it, and sign it, and take affidavit that it's the truth, so help you—"

Forbes dropped into a chair, discredited, his bluff called. All the lofty motives and compulsions of chivalry took on an ugly look. Sir Launcelot was an adulterer and a welcher.

The hideously altered face of things shattered him so that Hallard felt merciful.

"I'm sorry, Captain; but you see how it is. You see why reporters get a little hard, why our mouths sag. We don't publish the truth oftener because people won't tell it to us. The truth isn't the pure white lady in a nice clean well that the painters represent her: the truth is a kind of a worm-eaten turnip that comes out of the ground with a lot of dirt on it. We don't print all we find out by a long shot. If we did this old town would make for the woods, and the people in the woods would run to cover in town. I'd be glad to drop this affair right here; but, don't you see, I can't. The Enslees are too big to overlook. There'll be an army of reporters on the job, with their little flashlights poking everywhere. The police will fall in line later. There'll be editorials on the wickedness of society. Society—if there is such a thing —isn't any wickeder than anybody else. The middle classes are rotten, and the lower classes are putrid. But society makes what old Horace Greeley called 'mighty interesting reading.'

"The name of Enslee is going to be a household word, because when an Enslee sins it's like sinning in the grandstand. I saw something like this coming a year ago. I thought it might simmer down; but it's broken bigger than I ever dreamed. You're in for it, Captain. The Great American People is going to rise on the bleachers and holler for blood. It will forget all about you the minute something else happens. Take your medicine, Captain. It will be somebody else's turn soon, for most of us are doing the tango on a thin crust of ashes over a crater. But it's the face-cards that the two-spots like to read about. The minute somebody else that's prominent pops through we'll let you alone. But you're in for it, Captain—'way in. Better crawl under my umbrella and give me the story."

He meant it well, but it was impossible for Forbes to accept his philosophy or his counsel. To Forbes he was a slimy reptile with a hellish mission. Forbes told him so, denied all that he had said, defied him, and turned him out. And now he had leisure to understand the full meaning of it all. First, his grief for Persis broke his heart open. He mourned her as a sweetheart, a betrothed, a wife; mourned her with an intolerable aching and rending and longing, and with an utter remorse because of his last words to her. When she was afraid and distraught he had heaped condemnation on her! And who was he to reproach her? Had he not pursued her, overwhelmed her, made and kept her his? And then to discard and desert her, knock aside her pleading hands and leave her in the clutch of the maniac who had threatened them both! He had taken Enslee's revolver away—as if that were the only weapon in the world!

Never had Persis seemed so beautiful to Forbes as he remembered her now, cowering under his wrath, pleading for pity, rushing to protect him even then, and falling in a white swoon at his feet, as if already dead. And even then he had spat on her and left her!

IV

THE next morning's papers, without exception, gave the death of Mrs. Enslee "under mysterious circumstances" the doubtful honor of the front page, right-hand column. In some of them the account bridged several columns. The head-lines ranged from calm statements to blatant balderdash.

To Forbes, who had not slept all night and had sent down for the papers soon after daybreak, the stories were inconceivably cruel, ghoulish, fiendishly ingenious. The fact that Persis' wedding had been celebrated only a year before was emphasized in every account. She was called a "bride" in most of them, and her "honeymoon" was used dramatically in others. The importance of her family and of Enslee's was exaggerated beyond reason. Her portrait was published even in papers that rarely used illustrations.

Her beauty pleaded from every frame of head-lines till it seemed as if her face had been clamped in a pillory, and that the newspapers were pelting her without mercy or decency.

There was no way of protecting her, no way of punishing the anonymous rabble, no way of crying to the mob how lovable she had been and how impossible it was that she should have taken her own life. Forbes was understanding now how much worse a scandal it implied to say that she had been murdered. A woman might kill herself for any number of reasons, most of them pathetic; but a woman whom her husband puts to death can hardly escape calumny. Her lover was silenced by the reasons that silenced her father.

Forbes had not heard, or had forgotten, what paper Hallard represented. He soon recognized his touch. One paper, and one only, implied that Persis' death might not have been a suicide, but a murder. One paper alone referred to her "interest in a certain well-known army officer who had recently come into a large fortune and was much seen with her."

When he read this Forbes turned as scarlet as if he had been bound hand and foot and struck in the mouth.

Only one morning paper implied that Persis had strayed into the primrose path of dalliance. Not one evening paper failed to emphasize this theory. The editors of these sheets, appearing at their office before dawn, issued their first "afternoon" editions at 8 A. M., and had their "night" editions ready by noon. They all made use of Hallard's material and tried to supplement it.

Before Forbes had finished his breakfast he was visited by the first reporter, and refused to see him. Within the next half-hour a dozen reporters were clustered in the hotel lobby. They lay in wait for him below like a vigilance committee zealous for his lynching.

Forbes felt like a trapped desperado. He dared not venture out into that lurking inquisition. He dared not call upon any of his friends for help, lest they be tarred with the brush that was blackening his name. He had planned to take a morning train to his Western post. He was afraid to go to it now. He was afraid to arrive at the garrison, knowing that the scandal would have preceded him on the wires.

He decided that he must resign from the army before he was dismissed the service for bringing disgrace upon the uniform. There were officers enough whose irregularities were overlooked, but they had kept from the public prints. Forbes had not only sinned, but had been found out.

He felt like a mortgager who sees himself foreclosed and sold up. He had lost Persis, and he was about to lose his career. He wrote out his resignation, addressed the envelope, sealed it, bent his head down in his arms above it, and gave himself up to despair. His loneliness was almost more than he could endure.

By and by a letter was brought to his room. He had refused to answer the telephone, and he ignored the knocks of the hall boys. This letter was pushed under the door. It was from Ten Eyck:

DEAR HARVEY,—Just a line to tell you that my heart aches for you and with you. The thought of Persis dead is almost unthinkable, nearly unbearable to me. What it must be to you I dread to imagine.

I always remember the old Persian philosopher's motto when he was tempted to enjoy joy too much or grieve too much over grief: "This, too, will pass away."

You are too big a man to let this or anything break you down. Bend to it, but don't break.

It occurs to me that you may need a little time to recuperate, where you can't read the papers or hear them bawled under your window.

On Long Island I have a little shack on a sandbar on the edge of the ocean. How would you like to run down there for a few days? You can do your own cooking. If you wish I'll go along; but if you'd rather be by yourself I won't go. I think you'd better be by yourself and think it all out.

I enclose a time-table with the best trains marked.

Take a closed taxi to the station, and you'll not be noticed. If I can do anything, command me.

Affectionately yours,

MURRAY TEN EYCK.

Not a reproach. Not an "I told you so." Not a minimizing of the tragedy. Just a life-preserver thrown to a man in deep waters.

Forbes wrote:

God love you for this. I'll never forget. I'll prove **my** gratitude by sparing you the ordeal of **my** company.

WHAT WILL PEOPLE SAY?

He packed a suit-case, bribed a porter and an elevator man, and escaped from the hotel by one of the service elevators and the trade entrance. He swore to Heaven that this should be the last time he would sneak or cower. He reached his destination without remark, and found it congenially dreary.

There was a furious storm that night. Wind and rain flogged his cabin, and the sea cannonaded the beach. But the shack survived, and the beach was still there in the morning. There was only the wreckage of a little schooner cast ashore.

At first Forbes railed against the heartlessness of the sea. But gradually he came to understand that the ocean is not heartless; it simply obeys its own compulsions, and the wrecks it makes are those that should not have been out upon the waters or those that got in the way of the laws. That was what Forbes had done.

As he strolled the sands or sat and watched the endless procession of waves, waves, waves, hurling themselves upon the shore to their own destruction, in his thoughts memories came up one after another, like waves: memories of beautiful hours that seemed to have no meaning beyond their own brief charm; visions of Persis in a thousand attitudes of enchantment, in costume after costume. He saw her at the theater, lithe, exposed, incandescent; he clasped her in the tango; he clenched her hand at the opera; he saw her riding her cross-saddle in her boyish togs; he clasped her in the taxi-cab in the rain; he walked with her in moonlight and in the auroral rose; he galloped alongside her, strode with her in the woods; he held her in his arms while they watched the building burning gorgeously at night; he saw her in all the lawless intimacies of their secret life—careless, childish ecstasies and wild throes of rapture.

Then he remembered what she had told him of Ambassador Tait's warning: "The world is old, my child, but it is stronger than any of us. And it can punish without mercy."

He was tasting now the mercy of the world, and Persis, lying in cold white state, as he imagined her, was the visible slain sacrifice on the altar. They had indeed sinned. She had chosen wealth instead of love, and then had tried to steal love, too. The simple fact was that they had been wicked. They had duped and sneaked and feasted on stolen sweets. Their punishment was just. Many others had sinned more viciously and prospered in their sin or repented comfortably and suffered nothing. But they were not to be envied altogether.

Somehow to his man's heart it brought a strange kind of comfort to feel that this ruination was not a wanton cruelty, but a penalty exacted. It made the world less lonely; it replaced chaos with law and order. Perhaps other souls would take warning from their fate; perhaps other guilty couples would be frightened back to duty; perhaps somebody tempted by the scarlet allurements of passion would be helped toward contentment with the gray security and homely peace of fidelity.

The world was in a tempest against him. The waves had cast up his beautiful fellow-voyager on the sands. If only their shipwreck might keep somebody else from putting out to sea in pleasure craft unseaworthy and unlicensed!

V

HAD Forbes read the papers he would have known that the storm had not subsided yet. The wealth of Enslee could not bribe the least mercy; it was rather a stimulus to the press.

At the height of the tempest the funeral of Persis was held. Almost nobody attended it, and the few that did were rather drawn by curiosity than respect. Those who knew Persis well were afraid to be seen in the company even of her body. They were busy denying their earlier intimacy or telling how they had foreseen this disaster. She went in lonely state to join the silent throng in the cemetery, and she knew no more of the storm that raged about her than the world knew of the one high achievement of her soul. She was like some little brilliant bird of paradise flung to the ground by a lightning stroke. The storm roared on, the ferocity of the newspaper attacks increased with every extra. The fact that a theory was hinted in an early edition was taken as proof enough for a positive statement in a later. Finally there were demands for the arrest of the husband.

The district-attorney was busy, however, on an Augean task—the cleaning out of the police stable. He delayed or forbore to take up the Enslee matter. He was accordingly attacked as a toady to the rich. This stung him to an investigation.

And at last the police entered into the affair. Enslee was sent for and cross-questioned by commissioners. He was at bay, and he revealed unexpected gifts of evasion. Willie's lawyers stood by him. They were high-priced men, and they earned whatever he paid them. They succeeded in fighting off an indictment.

But even now Hallard and his cronies would not let him rest above ground or Persis beneath. Conflicting bits of Enslee's testimony were published in parallel columns, and his explanation that Persis, in her final rage, had seized the knife from his hand and stabbed herself was declared impossible and unconvincing. Her dying statement, as sworn to by Crofts, stood, however, as the one strong shelter over Enslee's head.

The skeptics insisted that Crofts, being deaf, had heard wrong or been bribed to perjury. None of them dreamed that Persis could have devised that snow-white lie as her atonement to the man she had betrayed. Hallard was obsessed with an idea that if Persis' body were exhumed it would be shown that she could not have dealt the fatal wound with her own hand. He had once organized a campaign against a decision of the court sentencing a valet to the penitentiary, and kept it up until the prison gates were opened and the man gained an opportunity to tell his story anew. He was found guilty again and sent back to his cell; but the despotic power of the press was demonstrated. If Hallard could open the penitentiary, why not the grave in which a *corpus delicti* had been hastily hidden?

With every weapon in the vast armory of newspaper-dom Hallard waged his battle. The political ambition of the district-attorney finally yielded to the coercion. An order was obtained from the court commanding the officials of the cemetery to unseal the tomb where Persis' body had been stored until the great monument Enslee had commissioned could be made ready to weigh her down irretrievably.

Forbes, having regained his courage in his absence in the wilderness, was seized with a mad desire to gaze upon his beloved's face once more and to whisper to her a prayer that she forgive him for abandoning her in her desolation and her peril. Ten Eyck used every plea to dissuade him; but, failing, determined to go with him.

Permission to be present at the exhumation was secured with little difficulty, and the two men joined the group of court officials and the six experts who were to decide from examination whether or not Persis could have inflicted the fatal wound upon herself.

VI

AND so Persis came back again to the world in a mockery of resurrection, back again from the sodden earth to the light of day that had blessed her beauty and not known her sin.

Forbes waited her reappearance in a frenzy of anxiety. It was to him a kind of holy tryst that he must keep at any cost.

Slowly the casket was raised; one by one the screws in the coffin-lid were removed, and at last the board was removed from over the white, white face. Some impulse of protection led Ten Eyck to thrust Forbes back until he himself had taken the first look. He gazed and groaned at the havoc death had wrought in all that beauty. When Forbes pressed forward, Ten Eyck whirled and clapped his hands over Forbes' eyes and dragged him aside, whispering huskily:

"Don't look! In God's name keep the memory of her as she was."

Forbes suffered himself to be led aside. He and Ten Eyck waited at a distance while the tests were made. The knife was closed in the icy fingers, and the exquisite arms moved here and there. Over the cold and silent body the experts wrangled. And the upshot of the desecration was that they could not agree; three of the jurors declared that Persis could not have reached so far around to set the knife in her side; and three that she could have done it, whether she did or not.

Persis, wherever she was, kept her secret. And Willie, abiding the decision in a stupor of terror, thanked God and her for their silence.

WHAT WILL PEOPLE SAY?

The newspapers had much to say of this last phase of the Enslee mystery. They summed up again all the old scandals, and then they, too, went silent. Their readers grew weary of the juggle of facts and falsehoods. The mishaps of other lovers furnished them with unfailing supply of the old mistakes that are the eternal news. Forbes, who had withheld his resignation from the army at Ten Eyck's bidding, was received back into his place, shorn of his ambitions, his youth, and his pride.

Often and often when he is alone he takes from its hiding shelter a little nightcap of ribbons and laces and shakes his head with vain regret.

He thinks of Persis always as she was that morning when the filmy cap fell from her lawless curls. He cannot but feel that there was something elect in her, something divinely beautiful, however thwarted for this world.

But then he loved her, he could forgive her anything. If God loved her, could he not do as much?

When the skies are clouded he remembers her wise little saying, "Behind the blinds there are always eyes." He wonders if there are eyes behind the clouds and beyond the sun. And if there are, and if they are the seeing eyes of perfect understanding, What do those people say?

THE END

MYRTLE REED'S NOVELS

LAVENDER AND OLD LACE.

A charming story of a quaint corner of New England where bygone romance finds a modern parallel.   The story centers round the coming of love to the young people on the staff of a newspaper—and it is one of the prettiest, sweetest and quaintest of old fashioned love stories, * * * a rare book, exquisite in spirit and conception, full of delicate fancy, of tenderness, of delightful humor and spontaniety.

A SPINNER IN THE SUN.

Miss Myrtle Reed may always be depended upon to write a story in which poetry, charm, tenderness and humor are combined into a clever and entertaining book.   Her characters are delightful and she always displays a quaint humor of expression and a quiet feeling of pathos which give a touch of active realism to all her writings.   In "A Spinner in the Sun" she tells an old-fashioned love story, of a veiled lady who lives in solitude and whose features her neighbors have never seen.   There is a mystery at the heart of the book that throws over it the glamour of romance.

THE MASTER'S VIOLIN,

A love story in a musical atmosphere.   A picturesque, old German virtuoso is the reverent possessor of a genuine "Cremona."   He consents to take for his pupil a handsome youth who proves to have an aptitude for technique, but not the soul of an artist.   The youth has led the happy, careless life of a modern, well-to-do young American and he cannot, with his meagre past, express the love, the passion and the tragedies of life and all its happy phases as can the master who has lived life in all its fulness.   But a girl comes into his life—a beautiful bit of human driftwood that his aunt had taken into her heart and home, and through his passionate love for her, he learns the lessons that life has to give—and his soul awakes.

Founded on a fact that all artists realize.

STORIES OF RARE CHARM BY
GENE STRATTON-PORTER

LADDIE.

Illustrated by Herman Pfeifer.

This is a bright, cheery tale with the scenes laid in Indiana. The story is told by Little Sister, the youngest member of a large family, but it is concerned not so much with childish doings as with the love affairs of older members of the family. Chief among them is that of Laddie, the older brother whom Little Sister adores, and the Princess, an English girl who has come to live in the neighborhood and about whose family there hangs a mystery. There is a wedding midway in the book and a double wedding at the close.

THE HARVESTER.   Illustrated by W. L. Jacobs.

"The Harvester," David Langston, is a man of the woods and fields, who draws his living from the prodigal hand of Mother Nature herself. If the book had nothing in it but the splendid figure of this man it would be notable. But when the Girl comes to his "Medicine Woods," and the Harvester's whole being realizes that this is the highest point of life which has come to him—there begins a romance of the rarest idyllic quality.

FRECKLES,   Decorations by E. Stetson Crawford.

Freckles is a nameless waif when the tale opens, but the way in which he takes hold of life; the nature friendships he forms in the great Limberlost Swamp; the manner in which everyone who meets him succumbs to the charm of his engaging personality; and his love-story with "The Angel" are full of real sentiment.

A GIRL OF THE LIMBERLOST.

Illustrated by Wladyslaw T. Brenda.

The story of a girl of the Michigan woods; a buoyant, lovable type of the self-reliant American. Her philosophy is one of love and kindness towards all things; her hope is never dimmed. And by the sheer beauty of her soul, and the purity of her vision, she wins from barren and unpromising surroundings those rewards of high courage.

AT THE FOOT OF THE RAINBOW.

Illustrations in colors by Oliver Kemp.

The scene of this charming love story is laid in Central Indiana. The story is one of devoted friendship, and tender self-sacrificing love. The novel is brimful of the most beautiful word painting of nature, and its pathos and tender sentiment will endear it to all.

GROSSET & DUNLAP,   PUBLISHERS,   NEW YORK

Lightning Source UK Ltd.
Milton Keynes UK
UKOW07f0053240816

281370UK00011B/280/P